CHRONIC
SORROW

D0861151

The Series in Death, Dying, and Bereavement
Consulting Editor
Robert A. Neimeyer

Davies—Shadows in the Sun: The Experiences of Sibling Bereavement in Childhood
Harvey—Perspectives on Loss: A Sourcebook
Klass—The Spiritual Lives of Bereaved Parents
Leenaars—Lives and Deaths: Selections from the Works of Edwin S. Shneidman
Martin, Doka—Men Don't Cry . . . Women Do: Transcending Gender Stereotypes of Grief
Nord—Multiple AIDS-Related Loss: A Handbook for Understanding and Surviving a Perpetual Fall
Rosenblatt—Parent Grief: Narratives of Loss and Relationship
Werth—Contemporary Perspectives on Rational Suicide

FORMERLY THE **SERIES IN DEATH EDUCATION, AGING, AND HEALTH CARE**
HANNELORE WASS, CONSULTING EDITOR

Bard—Medical Ethics in Practice
Benoliel—Death Education for the Health Professional
Bertman—Facing Death: Images, Insights, and Interventions
Brammer—How to Cope with Life Transitions: The Challenge of Personal Change
Cleiren—Bereavement and Adaptation: A Comparative Study of the Aftermath of Death
Corless, Pittman-Lindeman—AIDS: Principles, Practices, and Politics, Abridged Edition
Corless, Pittman-Lindeman—AIDS: Principles, Practices, and Politics, Reference Edition
Curran—Adolescent Suicidal Behavior
Davidson—The Hospice: Development and Administration. Second Edition
Davidson, Linnolla—Risk Factors in Youth Suicide
Degner, Beaton—Life-Death Decisions in Health Care
Doka—AIDS, Fear, and Society: Challenging the Dreaded Disease
Doty—Communication and Assertion Skills for Older Persons
Epting, Neimeyer—Personal Meanings of Death: Applications of Personal Construct Theory to
    Clinical Practice
Haber—Health Care for an Aging Society: Cost-Conscious Community Care and Self-Care
    Approaches
Hughes—Bereavement and Support: Healing in a Group Environment
Irish, Lundquist, Nelsen—Ethnic Variations in Dying, Death, and Grief: Diversity in Universality
Klass, Silverman, Nickman—Continuing Bonds: New Understanding of Grief
Lair—Counseling the Terminally Ill: Sharing the Journey
Leenears, Maltsberger, Neimeyer—Treatment of Suicidal People
Leenaars, Wenckstern—Suicide Prevention in Schools
Leng—Psychological Care in Old Age
Leviton—Horrendous Death, Health, and Well-Being
Leviton—Horrendous Death and Health: Toward Action
Lindeman, Corby, Downing, Sanborn—Alzheimer's Day Care: A Basic Guide
Lund—Older Bereaved Spouses: Research with Practical Applications
Neimeyer—Death Anxiety Handbook: Research, Instrumentation, and Application
Papadatou, Papadatos—Children and Death
Prunkl, Berry—Death Week: Exploring the Dying Process
Ricker, Myers—Retirement Counseling: A Practical Guide for Action
Samarel—Caring for Life and Death
Sherron, Lumsden—Introduction to Educational Gerontology. Third Edition
Stillion—Death and Sexes: An Examination of Differential Longevity Attitudes, Behaviors, and
    Coping Skills
Stillion, McDowell, May—Suicide Across the Life Span—Premature Exits
Vachon—Occupational Stress in the Care of the Critically Ill, the Dying, and the Bereaved
Wass, Corr—Childhood and Death
Wass, Corr—Helping Children Cope with Death: Guidelines and Resource. Second Edition
Wass, Corr, Pacholski, Forfar—Death Education II: An Annotated Resource Guide
Wass, Neimeyer—Dying: Facing the Facts. Third Edition
Weenolsen—Transcendence of Loss over the Life Span
Werth—Rational Suicide? Implications for Mental Health Professionals

CHRONIC SORROW

A Living Loss

Susan Roos

Brunner-Routledge
New York and London

Published in 2002 by
Brunner-Routledge
29 West 35th Street
New York, NY 10001

Published in Great Britain by
Brunner-Routledge
11 New Fetter Lane
London EC4P 4EE

Brunner-Routledge is an imprint of the Taylor & Francis Group.

10 9 8 7 6 5 4 3 2 1

Cataloging-in-Publication data is available from the Library of Congress.

ISBN 1-583-91320-3 (hb.)—ISBN 1-583-91321-1 (pbk.)

CONTENTS

Series Editor's Foreword   IX
Author's Foreword   XIII
Preface   XVII
Acknowledgments   XXI

1

Introduction   1

Historical Overview   4
    Ancient Periods   4
    Medieval Times through the Renaissance   5
    Europe and the New World   6
    The Twentieth Century   9
Chronic Sorrow as a Paradigm Shift   21

2

What Is Chronic Sorrow?   23

Proposed Definition   26
Comparisons and Distinctions   26
Clinical Significance of Recognition   35
Extent of Chronic Sorrow   40
Proposed Model of Chronic Sorrow   42

3

Interpreting the Loss   47

Subjectivity of the Loss   47
Gender Differences   50
Self-Loss and Other-Loss   55
Real Loss and Loss of Fantasies   63

V

4   **Living with Chronic Sorrow**   **69**

Personal Accounts   **69**
Fictionalized Works   **82**
Critical Stress Points   **87**
Victimization Anxiety   **89**
Author's Observations   **92**
    Life Markers   **96**
    Triggers   **96**
    Attenuation of Affect   **98**

5   **Families, Loss, and Chronic Sorrow**   **103**

The Family Life Cycle   **103**
Family Stress and Loss   **107**
Family Coping and Adaptation   **113**
Siblings   **118**
Depleted Caregivers   **124**

6   **Existential Issues**   **131**

Disillusionment   **135**
Aloneness   **137**
Vulnerability   **140**
Inequity   **143**
Insignificance   **145**
Past Temporal Orientation   **147**
Mortality   **151**

7   **Complicating Factors**   **153**

Stress   **154**
Guilt   **159**
Identity   **161**
Symbiotic Enmeshment   **162**
Disordered Intimacy and Attachment   **164**
Anger   **165**
Depression   **168**
Loss Spirals   **173**

8 **Professional Support and Treatment** 177

Basic Assumptions 180
Desirable Attributes of the Professional and Therapist 183
Suggested Goals and Objectives 186
Diagnostic Assessment and Interpretation 186
Affect Modulation 190
Trauma Resolution 195
Restoration of Self-Efficacy and Control 198
Relinquishment of Fantasies Invalidated by the Loss 199
Embracing What Is 203
Reexamination and Update of Belief Systems 203
Prevention of Maladaptive Coping Styles 207
Hazards and Pitfalls 210

9 **Implications and Directions for Research** 215

Reinterpretation of Existing Studies 216
Independent Variables 218
Person Variables 218
Nature of the Loss 221
Treatment Effectiveness 223
Other Independent Variables 226
Dependent Variables 227

10 **Trends** 229

Professional Education 230
Shift toward Depathologizing of Grief 232
Psychotherapy 234
Increasing Prevalence of Chronic Sorrow 236

Epilogue 241
References 245
Index 259

SERIES EDITOR'S FOREWORD

Perhaps paradoxically, I find writing a foreword to Susan Roos's *Chronic Sorrow: A Living Loss* to be a difficult task. It is paradoxical because I found myself engrossed, excited, instructed, and often moved during my immersion in the book, so much so that I suspended many other pressing obligations to take time to savor it on its own terms. Ordinarily, I find that rapt engagement with the work of others leaves me quite eager to write—glowingly or critically—about the object of my attention, but in this instance, I find myself curiously hesitant. Thus, this foreword is as much a note to myself as to the reader, as I "think aloud" about the sources of my uncharacteristic restraint to add an orienting commentary on the book, something otherwise in keeping with my role as Series Editor.

In part, no doubt, my reluctance to editorialize about the volume owes to the vast sweep of Roos's scholarship. From her compelling (and often chilling) recounting of the historical mistreatment of the mentally and physically disabled—ranging from ancient Greek and Roman practices of infanticide through twentieth century sterilization and euthanasia—to her subtle exploration of the psychology of chronic sorrow and its treatment, Roos is as authoritative as she is readable. As someone who reads widely in the field of grief and loss, I was consistently impressed at her ability not only to summarize intelligently literatures that I myself would find relevant to her topic, but also to draw on other quite diverse research to flesh out the medical, nursing, psychological, familial, and sociological dimensions of living in the presence of unending losses sustained by the self or a significant other. Virtually no aspect of the topic is neglected. As a result, the reader will encounter both detailed discussions of "microscopic" treatment issues relevant to working with persons with disabilities and their families, and "macroscopic" projections of the scope of this problem in light of future trends in science and society. It is the rare author who can integrate such diverse literatures, and Roos is that author.

Complementing the sheer sweep of the book is its novelty. Again and again, the reader is treated to innovative "takes" on familiar topics, prompting a deeper look at such traditional issues as grief resolution, the nature of stress, the meaning of adaptation, the role of hope and fantasy, and even the definition of humanity. In the course of exploring the core experience of chronic, episodically intensifying sorrow in the face of relentless loss, Roos introduces a host of useful new concepts, from the "loss spirals" occasioned by reminders of that which has been or will be forfeited, to the problem of living a "marker bereft" life story, in which one's very sense of time blurs with the loss of typical life cycle transitions. The richness of her theorizing reflects Roos's integrative inclination to draw equally on the professional literature that empirically documents many of the correlates and consequences of chronic sorrow, and the first person narratives of persons affected by disabling conditions and their caregivers. The result is a new window on an old problem, which reveals novel angles from which meaningful engagement and intervention might proceed.

A further dimension of this work that bears comment is its depth. The reader who expects some sacrifice in profundity to achieve the scope of this volume will be surprised by Roos's ability to transcend the obvious and offer penetrating analyses of the "everyday life" of someone contending with chronic sorrow. In my view, this ability to ponder problems in a way that was both deep and broad owes to Roos's obvious comfort in invoking and innovating upon constructivist and meaning-making themes to reveal the often invisible struggles of persons living with loss. Thus, she provides both compelling evidence of the need of such persons to narrate their experience in meaningful terms to themselves and others, and insightful analyses of the traumatic disruption of life scripts that makes doing so a challenge. The integrity of the book emerges fully at such junctures, as Roos embellishes familiar but highly cogent existential themes bearing on our human fragility and ultimate aloneness with contemporary narrative scholarship.

Perhaps most basically, what emerges forcefully for me in reading the book is Roos's personal "presence" in the text. At times, her experience as the parent of two severely disabled daughters—one of whom died as a toddler, and the other of whom has lived to adulthood—is foregrounded, as in the evocative personal passages with which the book opens and closes. But more commonly, this personal history provides a subtle but significant background, an "apperceptive mass" through which voluminous theories, data, and stories are filtered, and given coherence and direction. Rarely have I seen an author draw so well, and so nonindulgently, on her own experience to inform and illustrate otherwise elusive ideas. I am left with the conviction that no mere professional, however compassionate or dedicated, could have written this book, which so obviously benefited from the fusion of personal and professional perspectives that Roos so capably brings to bear.

And so, I am left meditating upon my own initial hesitation to comment on this encyclopedic, informative, and ultimately wise book. What takes shape for me as I do so is a sense of quiet *awe* at Roos's generously shared vision, and the uncommon eloquence and grace with which it is offered. Significantly, after completing so thorough and beautifully crafted a volume, Roos herself closes with a reflection on the inadequacy of (her) language to convey the pain and poignancy of the human experience of chronic sorrow. Perhaps it is only appropriate, then, that I struggle with a similar sense of "wordlessness" as I try to articulate my appreciative response to her masterful efforts.

Robert A. Neimeyer, Ph.D.

AUTHOR'S FOREWORD

Once in a golden hour, I cast to earth a seed.
Up there came a flower. The people said a weed.

—Tennyson

"If a way exists to console myself, I think I would have found it by now," I told my therapist. "I'm too productive to claim to be seriously depressed, and I can feel happy or amused at times, but life just seems wrong." I realized I was being too nonspecific for him to understand that I had been swimming upstream for a very long time and that I really could not go on much longer without some hope that the gray wrappings squeezing my heart could be loosened. For several years I had thought about seeing a therapist for help in lifting what seemed to be an ever-present malaise, a pall on the world, a numbing of my senses. I had recently seen a movie, *Ordinary People*, and it had triggered a sudden and very alarming deepening of sorrow. I was hurting, and I had been crying off and on for days. Crying was almost unheard of for me then, about twelve years ago. I seldom cry.

As a very young adult I had been in analysis for two years, and I had participated in two therapy groups for over a year. I had made favorable alterations in perspective and behavior, and I had a rational approach to life. But now I knew that I had come to some sort of emotional impasse. I was plagued by pain and sorrow. I had decided there was nothing to lose in giving therapy another try and had selected a therapist who was trained in Gestalt techniques since I felt that dynamics-changing approaches were called for. I had achieved certification as a Gestalt therapist when I was in graduate school working toward a master's degree. I regularly applied Gestalt principles in my work with clients in my private practice, and I knew this type of therapy could be very effective.

I was so tired. The idea of bringing forth an array of old hurts, losses, and sorrows, enlivening them, dealing with them through dialogue in the present, and working toward completion of "unfinished business," was difficult even to imagine. Yet I had used insight and cognitive approaches for years, and I reasoned that experiential work with a qualified therapist might help. There were good things in my life, so why couldn't I be happier? Why didn't I get excited about things that others seem so "turned on" about? Why were my emotions—both good and not-so-good—experienced in such a muted way? These were some of the questions that inhabited my conscious mind.

At the end of my first session with the therapist, I felt both discouraged and hopeful. I grouped my feelings under the heading Cautious Optimism. I had explained to him that I was "at a loss" as to how to go about feeling better about living, that when I focused on my life I found perpetual dismay. He made notes of some of my history and was empathic in his responses. During my second session, I began to be fearful of the possibility that I would become "unglued" during experiential work and that I wouldn't be put back together again. I asked if he thought he could help me learn to give up some of my sadness and begin to feel some contentment and pleasure in life. I joked about wanting a guarantee. He quickly responded with reassurances that I would be much better as a result of my work with him, and he stated that he could "guarantee" this would happen. I was nonplussed at his enthusiasm but decided to get down to work on "this thing."

After a few more sessions, during which I asked for guidance about how to go about our work together, I began to sense that this therapist didn't know how to deal with me after all. I was needing structure and some indications that he had some kind of plan in mind. I needed these things as evidence of safety. I wanted to know that I would not be entirely alone in entering the darkness and that, if I got lost, he would be able to help me find the way out. I needed a knowing, steady hand to guide me and to quell some of my fears. If I could feel secure enough, I would be able to go into the darkness.

He seemed to forget most of my history from session to session, and I would have to remind him that I had eight pregnancies, not two or three. My first daughter had died when she was three years old, not three months old. When I pushed for direction, he would halfheartedly (I think) conduct me through a dialogue with ego states or with the representation of one of my daughters (either Karen who died or Val, my living child who is severely retarded, autistic, and has a seizure disorder). The dialogue instruction usually was not clearly specified, and I would find myself imagining the babies I had lost through miscarriage or terminations, and Karen, and Valerie, in alternating patterns or all at one time. I felt confused, and I knew that I was not able to address my grief for all these losses simultaneously. My thoughts and feelings differed for each of these losses. I was at peace with some of them, and I didn't want to dredge them up again. I became vaguely aware that a major part of the impasse that had brought me to therapy was that my grief had become "all one thing," so huge, so complex, and so painful that my life had become overwhelmed with it.

My sessions led to more self-understanding, and I appreciated the therapist's sensitivity and attunement and his care in not putting his own spin on things. He was right about not rushing the work. I realize now that I did not provide him with responses that would have helped in guiding and integrating the process. Since I was unable to separate and verbalize my intense thoughts and images, he could not know the extent of the bombardment I was feeling. After a few more sessions, I told him I had decided to discontinue therapy.

A year and a half later, I went to another therapist. He was able to help me effect changes resulting in cessation of flashbacks and other post-traumatic stress disorder symptoms related to the death of my little daughter Karen. I was helped to express my grief and my pain in an emotionally congruent way for the first time. Although I sometimes experienced this work as mental torture, I knew the process was no longer frozen but moving, and pain related to the internal representation of Karen began to lessen as her representation became "softer." I was supported and guided in a way that helped me feel secure. We did no direct work regarding any other losses, including those pertaining to Val. Grief work conducted in this way had been much more manageable than dealing with "all one thing." After that, I began to have feelings about my little girl that were less intense, more peaceful even.

Just as important, I began to understand that feelings of sorrow are normal in some circumstances and that expecting and working toward an end to these feelings may not result in adequate or permanent solutions. While *complicated mourning* (as reflected by my lingering responses to Karen's traumatic death) is subject to some resolution and a lifting of symptoms, *chronic sorrow* (relevant to Val) often is not. I have come to realize that chronic sorrow may be present in many persons who may or may not seek therapy. In either case, chronic sorrow is often both unrecognized and misunderstood by professionals in the mental health field as well as other fields that touch the lives of persons affected by a living loss. Chronic sorrow, a normal grief response, is not the same as grief at the finality of death, where the person who is loved will be forever absent. Chronic sorrow is not about endings; it is about living with unremovable loss and unmending wounds. It is about losses requiring—and demanding—energy and persistent courage to cope with crises and making the adaptations necessary in order to live a life of one's own. It is about year upon year of dealing with the inevitability of a loss that continues and of finding a way to achieve some balance between reality and losing one's grip entirely.

I hope to shed some light on the phenomenon of chronic sorrow so that human service professionals will recognize it and understand its pervasive and profound influence in the lives of those who experience it. I hope thereby to protect those who are beset with chronic sorrow from being unwittingly, though unintentionally, harmed by those to whom they look for help. I hope that those who are affected by chronic sorrow may be able to find some solace, or at least a lessening of feelings of isolation, from reading this book. I hope they can confirm for themselves their own expertise, and I hope that professionals will be helped to know that these persons are not usually "crazy" or "clinically depressed" or pathological in other ways. They are, rather, in the throes of a human condition that is draining and inevitable and normal.

PREFACE

In recent decades a burgeoning interest in grief and loss has produced a widening knowledge base of empirical research and scholarly theory, as well as systems of care. Grief and loss are of concern to a number of professional disciplines (among them, nursing, social work, family therapy, psychology, psychiatry, law, religion, philosophy, medicine, rehabilitation, education). Thanatology has become a recognized field of study, and a plethora of grief material in the form of books, articles, videotapes, web pages, and so on, has become available across professional disciplines as well as to the public. Concepts (disenfranchised grief, traumatic loss, complicated mourning, and so on) have been developed so that the complexities of human responses to heartfelt and wrenching loss can be more clearly understood. Although our understanding has increased significantly in virtually all other areas of grief and loss, chronic sorrow has till now received relatively scant attention. The purpose of *Chronic Sorrow: A Living Loss* is to begin to fill in the gaps caused by professional neglect of the topic and to secure a place for chronic sorrow within the larger multidisciplinary field of grief and loss. To the best of my knowledge, this book is the first professional effort to comprehensively analyze chronic sorrow and its many implications.

The concept of chronic sorrow is not new. It was introduced by Simon Olshansky in the 1960s. Olshansky (1962, 1966, 1970) used the term to refer to the normal, profound, and pervasive grief responses of parents following a diagnosis of a child's mental retardation or other severe developmental disability. Since the child continues to live and to require of the parents constant adaptations to meet his extraordinary needs, grief is ongoing and parental wounds are often unmending. The loss is a living loss, a loss without foreseeable end. After Olshansky surfaced the concept, research studies followed. Most of them attempted to validate the concept and to correlate it with certain response variables. In keeping with the original intent of Olshansky's application, this work focused on parents of children with severe impairments. Then there was a virtual absence of chronic sorrow from professional literature. A renewed interest is now in evidence, however, especially in the field of nursing, and the concept is being expanded and validated in populations other than the parents of children who are developmentally disabled. The concept has been extended to persons with a variety of chronic, debilitating conditions and to those who love them; that is, to family members and caregivers.

In most respects, chronic sorrow is disenfranchised. Clinicians, when they recognize it at all, continue to confuse chronic sorrow with other types of grief and mourning and also with pathological conditions, such as major depression. Clinical nonrecognition and misunderstandings have often resulted in serious mishandling of those who are affected. For that reason alone, *Chronic Sorrow: A Living Loss* is long overdue. Furthermore, there is evidence that chronic sorrow is increasing because of longer life expectancies and because persons who once would not have survived catastrophic injuries, strokes, diseases, severe congenital anomalies, and so on, are now living many years, with some continuing to live a full life span. While cautioning against overuse of the concept, I propose yet a further extension of the concept to situations in which there is no way to know whether a person to whom there is a deep attachment is still living or dead or permanently absent. In these cases the loss cannot be verified; therefore, closure is not feasible, and the loss cannot be grieved in any conventional way. Instead, persons coping with the loss are placed in a position of dissonance and chronicity.

Chronic Sorrow: A Living Loss has ten chapters, an author's foreword, and an epilogue and includes research and clinical case material throughout. Identifying characteristics for persons depicted in clinical case material have been altered so that anonymity is preserved. Case dynamics, however, have not been changed. Chapter 1 introduces the context for the emergence of the concept of chronic sorrow, including an extensive history reflecting societal attitudes, marginalization, annihilation, abuse, abysmal neglect, and general stigmatization of persons with severe impairments and their families. This context powerfully underscores the timing and significance of the emergence of the concept and identifies it as a paradigm shift. Chapter 2 proposes a definition of chronic sorrow, and describes its salient aspects, and discusses the clinical significance of its recognition and its extent. A five-dimensional model, consistent with its definition, is presented. The model is designed to facilitate assessment and to foster research. Interpretation of the loss is considered in chapter 3, including aspects of subjectivity and gender differences. The terms *self-loss* and *other-loss* are proposed, and distinctions between *real loss* and *loss of fantasies* are discussed. To compensate for the severe lack of longitudinal studies, nontechnical literature is included in chapter 4, describing the experience of living with the permanence of chronic sorrow. Personal accounts as well as fictionalized works are depicted, the intent being to foster the reader's vicarious understanding of the lifetime process of chronic sorrow. Critical stress points and periodic resurgence of intensity of grief responses are identified, and a section is devoted to victimization anxiety. I contribute a brief personal narrative, including observations on life markers, triggers, and attenuation of affect.

Chapter 5 addresses loss and chronic sorrow within the family life cycle. Family stress, coping, and adaptation are described, and the effects of chronic sorrow on siblings and depleted caregivers are discussed. Existential issues inherent in chronic sorrow are considered in chapter 6. The importance of fit between beliefs about life and situations of chronic sorrow is highlighted, and the daunting challenge of revising world- and self-views to accommodate the reality of ongoing loss and chronic sorrow is emphasized. Chapter 7 describes complications related to chronic sorrow, including chronic and episodic stress, guilt, anger, depression, identity issues, symbiotic enmeshment, problems with intimacy and attachment, and loss spirals. Professional support and treatment are addressed in chapter 8. While recognizing that each case is unique, I have included suggested goals and objectives related to general circumstances and hurdles that are common to chronic sorrow. I have included interventions for (*a*) diagnostic assessment and interpretation, (*b*) affect modulation, (*c*) trauma resolution, (*d*) restoration of self-efficacy and control, (*e*) relinquishing the fantasy and embracing what is, (*f*) reexamination and updating of belief systems, (*g*) prevention of maladaptive coping styles, and (*h*) professional hazards and pitfalls. Questions for meaningful research are outlined in chapter 9. Chapter 10 describes observable trends related to future developments in grief theory and interdisciplinary practice as they relate to the increasing incidence of chronic sorrow in our culture.

Studies of grief and loss are more and more becoming a part of academic professional curricula and continuing education. It is my sincere hope that chronic sorrow will take its rightful place within these studies so that helping professionals will be more likely to recognize it and deal with it appropriately. Chronic sorrow affects the lives of countless individuals and families who look to us for assistance. I hope that *Chronic Sorrow: A Living Loss* can serve as a resource in both formal and informal professional training and that it will add to our growing knowledge base. I hope it might stir up questions and concerns for research-minded colleagues and that it will motivate longitudinal studies and other meaningful research in this area of grief that is wide open to creative exploration across a multitude of variables. There is work to be done.

ACKNOWLEDGMENTS

I deeply appreciate those persons who have left their marks on my mind and in my work on chronic sorrow. My dissertation, completed in 1994, was the first attempt at writing about this subject, and I am grateful for my wise, astute, and extraordinarily supportive doctoral committee: Professor M. Willson Williams, Core Faculty Advisor; Professor Hal Kirshbaum, Second Core Reader; Rae Dezettel Perls, Adjunct Faculty; Joanna Freeze, Adjunct Faculty; Philip Hanson, and Ruthann Fischer Balas. For their steadfast encouragement and validation through the subsequent long haul, I wish to thank M. Willson Williams, Joanna Freeze, Janice Lord, Linda Hartling, Judy Sterling, Woody Sterling, and Natasha Lvovich. For their patience and practical assistance, I wish to thank Shelley Hill and Laura Windsor. Their help was unfailing and invaluable. I thank my husband Philip who encouraged me and contributed to the completion of this work through challenging some of my ideas and through understanding when I needed space and time alone. Bernadette Capelle, acquisitions editor for Brunner-Routledge, kept the project afloat, and for that I thank her. I have been supported by her positive energy, her relational style, and her consummate professionalism.

I have been inexplicably blessed with treasured friends and colleagues who have significantly impacted my personal and professional development. They have truly made my life path and my professional work richer and more intricately textured, and they have helped to make me a better person than I could ever have been without them. I dare not attempt to list them here for fear of leaving someone out. But their influences are woven into the way I think and write and, therefore, into this book. I also include for acknowledgment my daughter Valerie who hasn't a clue about my writing and who, for good or bad, has contributed the absolute most to the shaping of my life, my work, and the person I have become.

Completing *Chronic Sorrow: A Living Loss* is a bittersweet experience. Joanna Freeze, acknowledged above, was a clinical psychologist, a gifted psychotherapist, and my very close friend. Her playfulness and her psychological depth were great gifts to me. She understood the forces informing my desire to get the word out about chronic sorrow. She died unexpectedly at about 1:30 A.M. on May 23, 2000. Her spirit is with me, but I am sad that she cannot be here in the real-life dimension to see and to share in the publication of this book. Unbelievably, Woody Sterling, also acknowledged above, died suddenly and unexpectedly in much the same way that Joanna did, at about 2:30 A.M. on January 22, 2001. Woody did not realize how important he was to so many others, how much he contributed, and how much he was loved. I am glad that he and his beautiful life spirit are at least mentioned here.

CHAPTER

Introduction

The concept of chronic sorrow was first proposed in the 1960s by Simon Olshansky, a rehabilitation counselor and leader (Olshansky, 1962, 1966, 1970). He observed this pervasive and persistent psychological and emotional response in parents of children who are mentally retarded. He stressed the normality of this response, describing it as an understandable and natural reaction to the tragic fate of having a child who is seriously impaired. When impairments are permanent and the child continues to live, the loss is continuing; therefore, sorrow persists. The person who is grieved is not dead or gone as, for example, in death or divorce, where there is finality. The loss is a living loss. There is a great discrepancy between the child who was dreamed for and expected and the child who actually exists.

Olshansky advised professionals not to expect parents to resolve their grief and adjust to their loss in a time-limited manner or in a certain number of counseling sessions. Parental grief continues to exist for a lifetime, whether or not the child lives with the parents. Unlike reactions to other losses, chronic sorrow is not resolvable so long as the source of the loss continues to exist. Moreover, periodic resurgence of intense pain and grief is to be expected. Additional stress, often severe, will result from crisis management and the need to care for the child.

Olshansky's compassionate introduction of chronic sorrow was a comfort to parents who were coping with the trauma and grief of having a child with permanent developmental disabilities. The depathologizing of their pervasive reactions was a salve for their injuries. The concept came at a time when parents were in need of an understanding voice from a professional community that had often viewed them as difficult, morose, neurotic, self-pitying, and unaccepting of their child. Parents were given very short shrift when they received any attention at all. Frequently, professional attention, including literature, took the form of criticism. If the child had autism, parents (especially the mother) were thought to be the cause of this severe disorder. The assumed prototype of these parents was characterized by overintellectualization and emotional coldness. Mothers were often labeled "autistogenic" and "schizophrenogenic."

Psychoanalytic interpretations of parental responses also cast parents in an unfavorable light. It was common for mental health practitioners to view parents as (*a*) chronically depressed due to internalization of hostility and death wishes toward the child; (*b*) overprotective of the child (or excessively demanding about obtaining services for the child), as a reaction formation stemming from ambivalence and repressed anger toward the child; and (*c*) having a negative and angry attitude toward professionals as displacement of anger was displaced from the child to others.

It was common in the 1960s for parents to be advised to place their child in an institution as soon as possible, before they became "attached." Often this advice was proffered soon after the birth of the child, especially when the disabilities were obvious and severe. Lacking other options, and sometimes because of stigmatization and shame, parents often complied with this professional advice, going against the wisdom of their own hearts. The existence of the child was sometimes concealed from friends and even from family members. Parents were also encouraged to "forget" the child, to go on with their lives, and to have other children (or even to adopt), as if their child were replaceable. Some parents chose to go against this professional advice and to care for their children at home. Some of these parents, fearing ostracism and social stigmatization for their children and themselves, kept their children hidden from the community. These children were sometimes referred to as "attic children."

Even today it is not very unusual for a fully credentialed health care professional not to have had exposure to mental retardation, autism, and other developmental disabilities, despite years of education and training. Professional curricula in the 1960s, even in medical schools, usually omitted these impairments from study. Parents who could not bring themselves to place their children in state residential facilities were confronted with a scarcity of professional expertise and interest, especially in small communities. Many physicians and dentists—often for good reasons—were unwilling to treat children with significant developmental anomalies. Respite services were virtually nonexistent. Children falling in the severe and profound ranges of mental retardation usually did not meet the criteria for inclusion in systems of public education. Parents of these children sometimes discovered that, while they were paying school taxes for educating other people's children, they were obliged to pay privately for the education and training of their own. Nevertheless, some dedicated, compassionate, and creative professionals were challenged by the formidable tasks of expanding and developing the knowledge base and the concomitant skills that were so desperately needed.

Olshansky was a writer, researcher, thinker, and innovator in the rehabilitation field (Goldberg, 1992). He understood system embeddedness and interrelationships, and he contributed significantly to the shaping of policy and services in the areas of mental retardation as well as mental illness. His research and publications were applicable to "real life," demonstrating his genuine empathy for those struggling with the hardships of handicapping conditions. He was not at all "politically correct," however, and his honesty and candor led to his ostracism by the bureaucracy and some of his colleagues for a number of years. At the time he introduced the concept of chronic sorrow, he had reentered the fold. Recognized and esteemed as a pragmatic realist, he understood fully the stigma attached to disabilities such as mental illness and mental retardation. He knew, for instance, that the community would not welcome mental patients when they were discharged from treatment facilities. Well before "passing" had become acceptable, he advised many former patients to do all they could to pass for normal, to avoid exposure of their psychiatric hospitalizations, to learn job skills, to get jobs on their own when possible, and to become a part of the life of the normal community.

Richard Goldberg, Olshansky's colleague for over 25 years and author of his obituary in *The Journal of Rehabilitation*, described his friend's character as follows: "Concealed behind the curmudgeon side of his personality, there lay a witty, gentle man whose vision of the future encompassed many of the current trends of rehabilitation. . . . He saw the need to support people with disability in their own living environment without the constant encroachment of professional staff. . . . He saw the need to empower the person with disability. . . . He had the vision of a humane society where every person with disability could obtain appropriate services commensurate with his need, but not excessive or unwanted services. . . . He was the greatest critic and the greatest friend of rehabilitation I have ever known" (p. 5).

☐ **Historical Overview**

Ancient Periods

From the beginning of time, people with mental retardation and their parents have not had an easy existence. Trace archeological evidence indicates that in hunter and gatherer groups infants with birth defects and severe handicaps had very short lives. Many of these groups practiced infanticide. In the New Hebrides, not only was the deformed infant killed, but the mother was killed as well (Sumnar, 1906). There is evidence too that some groups cared for their handicapped members (Scheerenberger, 1983). Historical records, beginning around 3000 B.C., allude to conditions that are associated with mental retardation. The ethical and legal codes of the period contain some protections for persons who were helpless and dependent.

The Greek culture became the foundation of our current values and ideas about life. During the formation of the Greek city-states, about 1300 B.C., philosophers and leaders showed little sympathy or patience with those who violated Greek standards of aesthetics, physical proficiency, and intelligence. Those early Greeks had no compunctions about killing offspring who were defective and unwanted (Gerdtz, 1993; Langer, 1974; Scheerenberger, 1983). In Sparta, infanticide was extensive. Any child who was ascertained to be defective was thrown from a cliff to be killed by the jagged rocks below (Scheerenberger, 1982). Plato and Aristotle advocated that only citizens epitomizing Greek ideals of physical beauty and cognitive astuteness should have children and that children with handicaps or deformities should be killed or removed far away from the larger community. The rationale was that only those who could contribute to society should be allowed to participate.

Many of the Greek cultural foundations were assimilated or adopted by the early Romans. The killing of weak and deformed infants was both allowed and encouraged. A salient component of Roman culture was the centrality of the family and patriarchy, with power over the family unit being vested in the father. Under the doctrine of pater potestus, the father could do whatever he wanted with his children, including mutilating, beating, killing, and selling them into slavery (Lagaipa, 1990; Mays, 1993). There are historical examples of the wielding of this power, but there is also little doubt that many parents loved and cared for their children with disabilities (Langer, 1974; Scheerenberger, 1983). In fact, archeological evidence from Pompeii reveals that children with severe anomalies were well cared for by their parents. There is also some evidence that a type of charity or welfare system was begun, and some children and adults with mental retardation probably benefitted from services provided by the government. When the Roman Empire officially embraced Christianity, infanticide was denounced. Some churches provided refuge for homeless and dependent persons. Some physicians took an interest in child development, childbirth complications, and care of people with mental retardation and mental illness (Scheerenberger, 1983). People with mental retardation were also kept by some of the upper classes for amusement.

Medieval Times through the Renaissance

Gerdtz (1993) identifies the medieval period as encompassing the fifth to sixteenth centuries. He indicates that although cultural, social, and technological development occurred during this time, most people had brutishly harsh lives. Large numbers of children were abandoned during the decline of the Western Roman Empire, which was marked by plagues and warfare. Housing for these children was provided by some governmental entities and by church authorities. There were many beggars on the streets of cities, and it is thought that children and adults with mental retardation were among them (Scheerenberger, 1983). Church-sponsored hospitals and residential facilities associated with monasteries were our first mental hospitals. With the advent of the Inquisition, persons thought to be a threat to society were tortured or killed. Witches were blamed for all and sundry misfortunes and catastrophic events. Epilepsy, frequently associated with mental retardation, was thought to be evidence of witchcraft, and people with seizure disorders, mental retardation, and mental illness were the focus of witch hunts and persecution. Thought to be possessed by the Devil, they were singled out for torture and death.

Interestingly, the care of persons with mental retardation was appreciably better and more humane in Islamic cultures during medieval times. The Islamic physician and philosopher Avicenna (980–1037) and the physician and chief rabbi of Cairo, Maimonides (1135–1204), were knowledgeable about aspects of neurology, human development, and mental retardation. They advocated for compassionate care of persons with impairments. Maimonides, who was regarded as the outstanding Jewish philosopher of the Middle Ages, did not view people with severe mental deficiency as hopeless but recommended educational programs for them.

With the Renaissance, beginning about the sixteenth century, successful revolts were mounted against the Roman church. Services and housing that had been provided by the church were decimated along with monasteries and other church-sponsored houses. Wars were fought between Catholic and Protestant states and nations. Hunger, disease, homelessness, and abject poverty were rampant. Those accused of being witches were tortured and killed in both Protestant and Catholic nations (Gerdtz, 1993). Reformers, including John Calvin and Martin Luther, contended that people with mental retardation were subhuman. Although most children and adults with disabilities lived with their families, those without resources were placed in hospitals and workhouses. Conditions there were horrendously cruel. As many as 90 percent of the children in these facilities died, according to Scheerenberger (1983).

Some leaders did attempt to improve the situation. Vincent de Paul, for example, claimed that those with mental retardation and mental illness were not devil-possessed witches but innocent victims who had a right to care and protection. The philosopher John Locke helped to instigate logical, more factual ways of evaluation and problem solving. He advocated for a just society, and he recognized the differences between mental retardation and mental illness (Scheerenberger, 1983).

Europe and the New World

During the 1600s European nations established settlements in the New World. Persons with mental retardation and other disabilities were among those living in the first colonies. Early laws and ordinances were drawn up for the protection of those with "naturall or personall impediment . . . defect of minde, fayling of sences, or impotencie of Lymbes. . . . Children, Idiots, Distracted persons . . ." (Eliot, 1938, pp. 67–68). In practice, however, persons with mental retardation and mental illness were viewed as inferior human beings and were treated no better than criminals. The family unit was the primary social resource. If an individual with debilitating handicaps did not have a family, a family would be found to take the person in and provide shelter, supervision, and guidance, for which the foster family would be paid. Almshouses, hospitals, and correctional facilities were also developed during colonial times, and those with mental deficiency were often confined with criminals and indigents (Scheerenberger, 1982). These facilities were dumping grounds for deviant people, and conditions were brutal.

Scheerenberger (1983) has documented the first residential education program for children with mental deficiency in 1818 at the American Asylum for the Deaf and Dumb in Hartford, Connecticut. As a rule, however, children and adults with mental retardation—along with alcoholics, those with mental illness, deaf mutes, epileptics, homeless people, and other social misfits and nuisances—were to be found in government-sponsored hospitals and workhouses. Families who had the means probably cared for their children at home. In some places families could bid for the right to house individuals who were homeless and dependent.

These families were paid by the government. It is virtually certain that some were not motivated by altruism but, instead, exploited those they took into their homes, using them as slaves and as objects for their gratification. In many respects these government-sponsored "solutions" to the plight of vulnerable, weak, and dependent persons were of poor quality by design; what they offered was not in the least desirable. Community leaders and officials greatly feared attracting people to a life of indolence at public expense.

In western Europe and America a concern for disfranchised and neglected people surfaced during the late eighteenth and early nineteenth centuries. A few notable individuals began to change society's perception of children and adults with mental retardation through their work. Jean Itard, a French physician and director of the Institution for Deaf Mutes in Paris, took on the challenge of training a so-called wild boy who had been found in 1798 living as an animal would live in the forest near Aveyron. It was believed that this naked, mute boy had been living most of his life devoid of culture and was an example of man in his natural state. Some of Itard's colleagues believed the boy to be a hopeless idiot. Itard, who was influenced by John Locke's view that people become what they are through environmental determinants, disagreed. He believed this wild boy could acquire the skills and sensitivities of a civilized person if he was provided with a systematic program of sensory training and education. For the five years Itard worked with him, he achieved success in dressing, eating with utensils, object recognition, toilet training, some language comprehension, and so on. However, Victor, as the boy was named, could speak only two words. Itard acknowledged that his work demonstrated that improvements could be effected, but he was disappointed that he had been unable to bring about the kinds of improvement that would allow Victor to live independently.

Thirty years later, Edouard Seguin, a student of Itard's, began work with an idiotic boy, employing techniques of muscle stimulation, sensory training, and activation of the "will." Seguin dedicated his life to persons with mental retardation, and he assisted with the development of several institutions in the United States. At the end of his life he operated a day program in New York City. Both Seguin and Itard demonstrated that children with mental deficiency could be taught to do much more than anyone had previously thought possible (Ingalls, 1978).

Reports of Itard's and Seguin's work fed hope for improvement in all types of handicapped people. Samuel Howe, the director of the Perkins Institution for the Blind in Boston, advocated for the rights of handicapped persons to be educated and to receive humane treatment, and the state allocated funds for him to open an experimental school for idiots. This school proved successful, and in 1855 it was incorporated as the Massachusetts School for Idiotic and Feeble Minded Youth. Later it became the Fernald State School (Kanner, 1964). Howe was influential with his colleagues, and optimism grew about the possibilities of training children with mental retardation to have more meaningful and productive lives.

Early institutional programs were designed for children with mild and moderate levels of mental deficiency. Most institutions of the time restricted their admissions, refusing to take children with epilepsy, hydrocephalus, and other cranial anomalies. A classification system was developed in Europe for diagnosis and assessment of levels of severity. Recognition of the distinction between mental retardation and mental illness was growing, and it influenced development and separation of services for these diagnostic categories.

An institutional movement was taking place in America, especially in Massachusetts, New York, Pennsylvania, Connecticut, and Ohio. By 1898 a total of 24 publicly funded institutions for persons with mental retardation existed in 19 states (Kanner, 1964). These institutions were designed to provide training and educational programs that would return habilitated individuals to the community where they could work and live independent or semi-independent lives. Because of the abuses in local almshouses, hospitals, and foster homes, reformers such as Howe, Hervey Wilbur, Dorothea Dix, Horace Mann, and others, advocated for state-sponsored institutions. The Massachusetts School for the Feeble-Minded at Waverly and the Syracuse School for Mental Defectives became examples of what institutions could accomplish. They paroled a significant number of their residents to live and work in homes and on farms. Some parolees worked in offices and factories.

Training in these institutions emphasized punctuality, a positive attitude toward hard work, and clean habits of living. The training program in Rome, New York, focused on two types of labor; girls were trained for domestic services, and boys for farm work. In 1919 there were eleven farm colonies, each consisting of 20 boys and a farmer and his wife. There were seven urban colonies, supervised by a matron and a social worker, which included a total of 172 girls (Tyor & Bell, 1984). A model outpatient clinic at the Massachusetts School for the Feeble Minded at Waverly provided, at no cost, diagnostic evaluations, information, and advice. A team was comprised of a psychiatrist, a social worker, a psychologist, and a teacher. Clinics were conducted throughout the state to provide assistance to parents and guardians based on the premise that a diagnosis of mental deficiency must be accompanied by recommendations on how to improve the child's condition. Walter Fernald, the superintendent at that time, was considered an innovative visionary in the field of mental retardation services.

The promising foundations on which institutions were based soon began to crumble. Many residents returned to communities that did not want them. Many had no homes to return to. No matter how well-trained a person might be, jobs were not available when communities were unwelcoming and economic conditions poor. Societal attitudes continued to be condemnatory and rejecting. Community leaders usually viewed mental retardation as a growing and frightening social problem. Rather than returning residents to the sad fate that awaited them in the community and—often worse—in almshouses and other local facilities, superintendents began to request their retention in the institution. Thus a residential population began to grow in the state schools. At the same time, institutional administrators came under pressure to admit "custodial" cases, children and adults with severe and profound defects, and others who were felt to be inappropriate for education and training—the so-called subtrainables. Admission criteria were generally expanded to include individuals with seizure disorders, cerebral palsy, deformities, and other complications.

Institutions began to retain increasing numbers of people who had been trained to work. These people became unpaid workers or "inmate helpers" within the institution rather than being discharged to the outside world. The idea of permanent, lifelong institutionalization had emerged. A few communities began to develop special education classes for higher functioning children through their public school systems. Scheerenberger (1982) has noted that the first special education program in this country was probably developed in 1896 in Providence, Rhode Island. By the early 1900s, the concept of public special education programs had been accepted nationwide, but these programs were implemented very slowly, even in large urban areas. Sadly, it was generally accepted that children who were in special education classes in the community would enter institutions after leaving school.

The Twentieth Century

Strong negative public opinion about persons with mental retardation continued into the twentieth century. Children with mental and physical defects were frequently viewed as retribution or punishment for parents who had committed grievous sins. It was commonly thought that people with mental deficiencies were a threat to the community; they were a danger not only because of their behavior, but because they could have children of their own. There was an emphasis on the segregation and institutionalization of females of child-bearing age.

Institutions were located significant distances away from urban areas, and parents were generally discouraged from visiting or taking their children home for short visits since this would interfere with the child's and the parents' "adjustment." Families were fragmented, and parents were placed in a double bind. They could visit their child, leading to the child's becoming upset when he could not return home with them (this option would engender staff disapproval), or they could minimize or discontinue contact with their child, leading to feelings of guilt and torment because of their abandonment of the child. Trent (1994) has observed: ". . . Many parents, especially in the first year of their child's institutional placement, felt great loss and concern. They worried about little things—things that, nevertheless, sustain intimate relationships—a warm coat for winter, comfortable shoes, properly fitted dentures, and countless other matters they had once taken care of themselves . . ." (pp. 112–113).

Pressures on the institution to increase admissions in general and to admit more persons with serious and multiple disabilities greatly increased the workload of attendants. After 1890, care was the central mission of the institution. Giving primary emphasis to training and education was no longer realistic. Attendants, together with their inmate helpers, were the principal caregivers and shapers of the lives of great numbers of persons with mental retardation.

The early 1900s marked the development of standardized tests of intelligence. Special education and clinical psychology were growing professions, and research was under way about the nature and etiologies of mental retardation. Henry Goddard, head of research at Vineland Training School (New Jersey), obtained the Binet-Simon, an IQ test that was being used in France to screen and assess children in the public school system. He used the test in studies he conducted at Vineland and introduced the term *moron*. Goddard viewed the moron as presenting more danger to the community than any other type of feebleminded person. Goddard (1912) is best known for his study of the "Kallikak" family and for the so-called eugenics movement. Based on his multigenerational study of the Kallikaks, Goddard implied that immoral or criminal behavior and mental retardation were genetically linked in families through a number of generations. Goddard (1912) also contended that families like the Kallikaks were multiplying at twice the rate of the general population. The menace of feeblemindedness was not just in degeneracy and evil deeds, it lay also in the numbers of morons who were living in the community and could procreate.

Many professionals disagreed with Goddard's conclusions. They saw his research as highly anecdotal, severely biased, and seriously unreliable. However, Goddard and his followers were urging restriction on marriage, segregation from society, and sterilization. Goddard proposed that segregation and sterilization could, in only two generations, significantly reduce the numbers of dependent, criminal, and immoral people, save society the expense they incurred, and eliminate degeneracy and disease. Goddard (1917a, 1917b) also claimed that immigration caused much of the increase in feeblemindedness in America. With funding from volunteer sources, he began to administer the Binet to immigrants on Ellis Island, and in 1917 he presented alarming data that ostensibly revealed that as many as 50 percent of immigrants were feebleminded. The idea of a culture-fair IQ test did not exist, and although Binet insisted that intelligence was flexible and could be increased by favorable conditions, it was believed by many, certainly including Goddard, that IQ was fixed and constant.

Concerns increased about the connection between familial prevalence of low intellect (or "constitutional inadequacy") and criminality through a number of generations. The eugenics movement flourished in the United States and in Europe. The objective was to limit procreation so that only people of "good stock" could marry and have children. The feebleminded and those with disease, handicaps, or criminal and immoral behaviors were not fit to be a part of society and should not have children. Unless these misfits voluntarily refrained from having children, it was the duty of the state to prevent their doing so. Greater efforts were made to admit and retain adult women of child-bearing age in institutions, and laws were enacted to enable surgical sterilizations. Involuntary institutional placements increased significantly, as did involuntary sterilizations, especially of women. Some institutions in Canada required sterilization as a condition for admission. Many women who were sterilized were told that they were having appendectomies. Some never realized what had been done to them. From 1907 to 1958, thirty states had laws permitting sterilization of persons with mental deficiencies (Davies, 1959). Populations of institutions grew, and institutions became more crowded.

IQ tests were used more extensively, both in institution and public school settings, for purposes not intended by their developers. Most test developers had meant them to be used in the diagnosis and evaluation of intellectual level and in recommendations on special education, training, and treatment. Some developers had stressed the danger of using IQ tests as the criterion for rigid classifications or as a method for denying services. Their warnings were well founded. Public schools throughout the country were beginning to use the tests to single out and exclude children with more severe handicaps. Many large school districts used an IQ score of 40 or less to deny services, and this score was later increased to 50 (Scheerenberger, 1983). Parents of children with severe and profound mental retardation were left with two options: (*a*) caring for their children at home without educational or other services, or (*b*) placing them in institutions. Despite the use of IQ tests by the military to prevent the enlistment of men with mental deficiencies, many such men served their country in World War I (as in past wars). A number of these men served with distinction, only to be returned to institutional life after demobilization (Scheerenberger, 1983).

Knowledge about mental retardation was increasing and a number of causes had been identified, but conditions, attitudes, and fair treatment for children and adults with mental retardation and their families were deplorable during the first 30 years of the twentieth century. The situation was to become even worse. The Great Depression spread misery throughout the United States and into the industrialized world. Government-funded programs were reduced or eliminated. Financially ruined and desperate families could no longer care for members who were seriously impaired. Large state institutions were deluged with applications for admission. An angry and terrified world sought targets for blame. Anti-Semitism worsened. Political hate groups were formed. People living off the government dole, including those in institutions who were mentally ill or mentally retarded, were resented.

The Germans were especially hard-hit by the economic chaos that followed their defeat in World War I, and—abetted by popular literature of the day—intense resentment was focused on what was believed to be large numbers of institutionalized people who were living luxuriously at government expense while so many (the "deserving") were struggling to stay alive. This distorted belief could not have been further from reality. Burleigh (1991), a British historian, has determined that, in Prussia alone, about 45,000 institutional residents starved to death during World War I.

Adolf Hitler's obsession with racial superiority and the preservation of the purity of the Aryan race was promulgated by his book *Mein Kampf* and the Nationalist Socialist German Workers Party. Burleigh (1990) has documented Hitler's recommendation, as early as 1929, for the removal of weak and disabled persons from German society. As chancellor, he saw to it that laws were passed for the involuntary sterilization of persons with hereditary "diseases" such as mental retardation and mental illness. As reported by Friedlander (1997), decisions were based on medical examinations and specialized IQ tests. Hereditary health courts reviewed the cases and forwarded their decisions to hereditary health appellate courts whose verdicts were mandatory. About 300,000 individuals were sterilized before World War II. Sterilization was often only a "first stage" for patients with mental illness and mental retardation. Persons with mental defects were considered to be "superfluous beings," and were the population most at risk. Propaganda films and tours of institutions were arranged to disseminate the "right" ways of thinking about "freakish" people with defects. Euthanasia as a "solution" had also been suggested by Hitler, and mental patients were gradually concentrated into large state-operated institutions. SS officers were added to the staffs of private hospitals.

In March 1937 *Das Schwarze Korps* published an article praising a father who had killed his handicapped son (Friedlander, 1997). In the fall of 1938, the father of a baby who had been born blind, retarded, and without arms and legs, petitioned for a "mercy death." Hitler's personal physician, Karl Brandt, went to Leipzig where he performed the euthanasia. By late 1939, at Hitler's direction, Brandt had initiated a program whereby authorized physicians were permitted to "euthanize" infants with a variety of handicaps by means of injection or starvation. Midwives and doctors were ordered to report any infants born with defects. Within one year, over 5,000 infants had been killed (Burleigh, 1991; Friedlander, 1997). The program soon expanded to include the killing of children and adolescents with handicaps, and soon after to include adults with mental retardation and mental illness. Burleigh (1991) has documented enthusiastic support for the euthanasia effort from a number of prominent German academic psychiatrists and other physicians. Goldhagen (1996) has documented that this physician-implemented killing campaign took the lives of over 70,000 people who were deemed as having lives unworthy of living because of mental infirmity and congenital physical defects. The program was known as Aktion T-4, the address of its headquarters in Berlin.

Other killing programs were also in force. SS and Wehrmacht troops killed over 10,000 psychiatric patients in Poland and the occupied regions of the Soviet Union. In addition to the children and adults who were victims of these programs of mass murder, Burleigh (1990) has listed other groups who were exterminated: forced laborers from Eastern Europe who had become ill or had "breakdowns"; their racially inferior (but otherwise healthy) newborn children; and inmates of orphanages and camps for juveniles. He describes a morbid example of a type of poetic justice: a number of SS troops ultimately suffered nervous breakdowns, were placed in psychiatric hospitals, and were killed along with the other patients (Burleigh, 1991).

There were courageous parents who spoke out, protesting the "disappearance" and deaths "from natural causes" of their children in institutions and asylums. Their outcry spread throughout Germany and garnered support from some religious leaders. The Roman Catholic bishop of Münster, Count Galen, publicly protested the murder campaign. He also attempted to take legal actions to stop the killings. Galen was considered too popular for the Nazis to kill. Therefore, his public protests were counteracted by intensification of propaganda to justify the sterilization and euthanasia programs. Prominent stage and film stars participated in the development and dissemination of propaganda materials and presentations. Arguments advocating sterilization and euthanasia included economic reasons and the rationale that people with handicaps could only have lives of suffering and were "better off dead." These individuals were also depicted as a source of great misery for their parents and family members and burdens to those who had to care for them in homes or in institutions. The most powerful argument, however, may have been that people with handicaps did not contribute to society but only took resources away that were needed by others (for example, health care, housing).

In yet another killing program, Germany's special education programs were systematically infiltrated by Nazis, as were the professional associations of teachers. Some leaders of these associations, especially those who supported Aktion T-4, were instrumental in assisting the takeover of these groups by the Nazis. Special education programs were designed to train the higher functioning children to do useful work (farming and factory assembly). Children who could not be trained for work due to the severity of their handicaps were usually sent to asylums where they were put to death. Some teachers resisted the Nazis by attempting to help their students score well on the IQ tests administered by Nazi state physicians. They would provide answers to psychological tests in advance to those about to be tested. As a rule, these efforts were failures, since teachers could only provide answers to available standardized tests of intelligence, and the state physicians used "Form 5A," an unstandardized and arbitrarily "stacked" test for the diagnosis of mental deficiency.

In the years immediately after World War II, parents in the United States and elsewhere were becoming more vocal as well as more organized in their efforts to reverse, through educational outreach, the strong prejudicial attitudes of the public against their children. These parents were saying that they could no longer endure the status quo, either for their children or for themselves. Inalienable human rights granted by the Constitution belonged equally to their children as human beings and as citizens. They proclaimed that these children are as precious as other people's normal children, that they are just as human, and that their needs are just as important as anyone else's needs. Parents were also beginning to demand quality services.

Professionals became increasingly concerned with the deleterious effects of institutionalization, and research findings began to support negative impacts such as a decline in IQ, decline in verbal abilities, decline in self-help skills, increased negative attitudes toward self and others, and so on. Programs providing a more homelike environment and stimulating interactions with staff produced improvements in functioning and significantly higher IQs. The belief in a fixed, unchanging IQ had been disconfirmed by several studies, especially those by researchers in Iowa (Skeels, 1966; Skodak & Skeels, 1949). Many professionals and concerned citizens voiced criticism of the large, overcrowded, understaffed facility with rigid procedures and a milieu of depersonalization. Institutions after World War II tended to house fewer higher functioning residents while retaining a greatly disproportionate number of residents with severe and profound disabilities, such as severe motor impairment and cranial anomalies. Tyor and Bell (1984) report that in New York during the mid-1950s seven of every 10 residents were classified as being in the lower range of mental functioning. Many profoundly impaired persons were languishing interminably in institutions providing no human interactions other than those involved in biological and life support. Some were referred to as "vegetative" or even as "vegetables" or "puddings." Factors in the apparent increased prevalence of mental retardation in the United States included the higher birthrate during and after the war and medical advances leading to survival at birth and to longer life spans for children who were severely and profoundly impaired.

Grassroots organizations of parents, family members, friends, and concerned activist professionals grew in numbers and in strength. These groups began to join together in setting priorities and in coordinating objectives and strategies. Of major importance in the field of mental retardation was their formation in 1950 of the National Association of Parents and Friends of Retarded Children (later renamed the National Association for Retarded Children, then the National Association for Retarded Citizens, and now known as the Arc). The emergence of this national organization symbolized a change in parental status and self-image from that of marginality, concealment, and shame to that of empowerment and legitimacy. Some parents of considerable national prominence "went public," disclosing for the first time—often in the form of a confessional—that they had children with severe impairments. Parents were no longer accepting of "solutions" based on a strategy of "out of sight, out of mind." Many parents were no longer willing to have their children thought of as less than human or unworthy of happy, productive lives. They began to advocate for ordinary civil and human rights for their children and to protest abridgment and denial of those rights. No longer were parents pleading; they were demanding.

Attendant personnel in institutions began to describe (usually anonymously) overcrowded, violent, and inhumane conditions there. They revealed beatings, emotional abuse, and deprivations. But the picture that emerged most was of benign neglect, a lot of it. Direct caregivers formed a coalition and lobbied for better staffing and higher wages to attract more skilled, dedicated, and compassionate workers. Understaffing and demoralization had led to most of the direct care being provided by higher functioning residents. Most institutions operated on extremely inadequate appropriations that had worsened during the Depression and World War II. They had become hardly more than repositories for what Spitzer (1975) has called "social junk." Trent (1994) has reported that between 1946 and 1967 the populations of institutions for persons with mental retardation increased from 116,828 to 193,188 (a 65 percent increase and nearly twice the rate of increase in the general population during the same time period).

Shortly after Olshansky's characterization of parental grief as chronic sorrow, there were exposés of the intolerable conditions in institutions. Two of these exposés were especially notable. Blatt and Kaplan's (1966) *Christmas in Purgatory*, a photographic essay, revealed graphically the horrors of institutional life. It was a startling work. Fred Kaplan had worn a camera hidden in his belt buckle and with it had secretly obtained photos inside a huge, overcrowded New York State institution. Burton Blatt, a highly respected mental retardation specialist who directed the Division of Special Education and Rehabilitation at Syracuse University, wrote the text. He noted, "Scratch an institution and pus oozes . . . insofar as our victimized brothers are concerned—the inmates, the so-called retarded and mentally ill, any people who are denied essential human rights—I said in complete seriousness that I would rather support a cabala than what we now have" (p. 991). *Look* magazine subsequently reproduced this work, and the public could no longer ignore the abhorrent way in which the country was "solving" the "problem" and "menace" of mental retardation. The public was also educated by a TV exposé when Geraldo Rivera and a disgruntled former employee of the state of New York barged into the living units of Willowbrook, a New York State institution, video camera in hand, and recorded scene after scene of children and adults who were severely and profoundly retarded and who were living in filth, many naked and deprived of even minimal human dignity. Through these and other investigations, it was revealed to the public that many thousands of unempowered, vulnerable, disfranchised, and handicapped people were existing in conditions that—by any standard—were unconscionable and deplorable. These human beings were compelled to live in cruel and lifelong nothingness.

Federal funding began to supplement institutional budgets, making possible innovative programs and training for residents. Job training was augmented by training focused on personality development and enhancement of self-esteem. Parents and professionals found agreement in emphasizing the importance of doing all that was possible to achieve some level of social competence in those with mental retardation so that they would be more acceptable to the community. Habilitation implied acceptance of the person's disabilities while gently elevating the person to higher functional levels. Habilitation also meant the removal of obstacles to progress wherever they existed and the development of protection and support. Sheltered workshops, therapy, recreation centers and leisure-time programs, such as dances and clubs for adults, began to be community based. Measures to protect people with impairments from ridicule and exploitation surfaced as a focus of concern. Slowly the public image of people with mental retardation was shifting away from that of a "menace to society" to that of environmentally damaged persons who had done nothing to warrant denial or abridgment of human rights and dignity and who were worthy of full membership in society.

President John F. Kennedy had a personal understanding of the impact of retardation on a family—his older sister was retarded—and he was aware of the scarcity of resources, the poor conditions associated with residential options, and the general prejudice and invidious treatment of persons with mental retardation in the United States. The Kennedy administration set goals of prevention, treatment, humane conditions, and a variety of remedies for ameliorating the lives of citizens who were mentally retarded. Mental retardation, at last, was a federal health policy and a priority for social reform! Although several political leaders had been advocating for reform and endorsing cooperative federal and state systems of care, usually linking mental health and mental retardation, the president's message to the country was a galvanizing force to reverse the nation's neglect and disfranchisement of so many of its citizens. The resulting changes were far-reaching and instructive of what can be accomplished by one charismatic leader.

The Kennedy family had established the Joseph P. Kennedy, Jr., Foundation in the 1940s in honor of the oldest son, killed in World War II. The family agreed that the foundation's major work would be in mental retardation. Eunice Kennedy Shriver worked actively to direct the foundation's objectives. Many advisors to the foundation were superintendents of state schools who were well aware that mental health interest groups and psychiatry at that time cared very little, if at all, for mental retardation. The consensus was that funding would go to medical research not connected with mental health interests. University-based research was shortly under way on the causes of mental retardation and on training and treatment approaches, and the foundation presented awards to university researchers who made significant contributions. President Kennedy formed a panel on mental retardation made up of professionals. Mental retardation had come out of the closet, and the national consciousness was changing.

The concept of normalization, imported from Scandinavia (Nirje, 1969), took hold in the United States. The concept postulates assumptions and principles that apply to all individuals with mental retardation, wherever they reside. In brief, the concept entails providing and assuring as normative a life as possible, even for those with severe and profound impairments. The implications of the concept are sweeping, and they represent a clearly articulated statement of the basic rights and privileges of each person with mental retardation. These rights are the same as for other citizens. Class-action litigation was also initiated to secure guarantees of certain constitutional rights that had been denied, that is, the right to (a) treatment and habilitation, (b) individualized programs, (c) freedom from harm and abuse, (d) due process, and (e) freedom from involuntary servitude or peonage. Involuntary sterilization was ruled to be an unconstitutional infringement of a fundamental freedom. Other constitutional principles were likewise litigated, resulting in mandates on facility standards and the quality of care: (a) adequate nutrition, (b) adequate staff-patient ratios, (c) the right to choice, (d) the right to the least restrictive environment and to an array of services and environments that are similar to those afforded nonhandicapped individuals.

Professional groups such as the American Association on Mental Deficiency urged their members to find or to develop a social conscience that would translate into their participation in advocacy and legal actions to make right all the wrongs that had been perpetrated on citizens who were the most vulnerable among us (Rosen, 1974). Some professionals called for the closing and abolishment of all large state institutions. Deinstitutionalization of persons with psychiatric disorders had already begun. It was soon obvious that not enough community facilities and services for the mentally ill population were being developed to treat, support, and accommodate people who were literally being discharged to the street. As deinstitutionalization of persons with mental retardation became the "new solution" to replace the grave errors of the past, many parents grew anxious that an even worse fate than for the mentally ill awaited their family members, who were even more helpless and more subject to exploitation. Aging parents especially were frightened that their severely impaired children would return home, and that they would be unable to meet their needs—just as they had been unable to cope with these needs when they had originally resorted to placing their children in institutions. The institution, once viewed as virtually permanent, had been seen as an answer to aging parents' prevailing concerns about continuing care for their children after their deaths. While all parents tended to endorse a full range of community services, younger parents and those who lacked knowledge of past models of care tended to push for closing all institutions.

Counseling services for parents emerged, and parents themselves began to form support groups. The Arc's Parent-to-Parent program is an example of parental networking and mutual support. Increasing numbers of parents currently elect to keep their children at home, and needed services, therapies, and training/education are home-based in the early years of their children's lives. Small community residences in various neighborhoods are being developed. Progress in their development has been discouraging for two reasons: (*a*) the need for many community homes in some communities and (*b*) frequent intense public opposition to these homes. Typical rhetoric acknowledges that "something should be done" to care for people with mental retardation, but they should be in residences in "a more appropriate place" and "not in my neighborhood."

Prejudicial attitudes are alive and well in America. Parents and families of children who have mental deficiencies are aware of the risks involved in community living. Even today, there are those of us who believe (even if we don't speak openly about it) that seriously impaired people are better off dead. The arguments are the same as those used by the Nazis: (*a*) death is more merciful for the person and for the family, (*b*) the cost to society is unwarranted, given the limited gains that are possible, (*c*) money can be spent on "better causes," and so on. Parents of children with mental retardation who are "seasoned" by many years of experiencing the waxing and waning of ideas, services, and public attitudes, are often distrusting, wary, and fearful of bureaucratic and political promises about the care of their children. Some feel they can "never be paranoid enough" and that, if they turn their backs for a moment or become complacent in any way, their children will be deliberately hurt, rejected, exploited, or deprived of any quality of life they might now have. Wariness and paranoia are especially prevalent in parents and family members of children and adults who have little or no expressive language. They cannot know what their children cannot report to them.

The institutions that remain in operation are now housing significantly fewer residents, and they have been modified to be more homelike. Large wards and dormitories are no longer the rule. Living units are small, usually with six or eight beds at most, and they are designed as houses with comfortable living rooms, dining areas, kitchens, and bathrooms. Residents are taken into the community daily for some services (medical treatment, therapies such as language development and physical therapy, haircuts, shopping, dining out, excursions, and so on). They are taken to their jobs in sheltered workshops in the community. Some services remain within the institution, especially for residents who have severe medical conditions. Institutional family associations are usually quite active in monitoring major areas of programming and care, raising funds to fill in gaps not addressed by the usual budget, lobbying for increased staff, educating state legislatures about mental retardation and the need for adequate appropriations, and so on. Historically, it has been because of the efforts of families, through advocacy groups such as the Arc, that conditions have improved and services have developed.

It is a mistake, however, to assume that all families embrace the same opinions, goals, needs, and desires. These families are not amalgams of commonality. Some stress the need for as many options as possible to care and provide for their members with disabilities, including the retention of the institutional model—albeit a greatly improved, reformed model—as a stable, permanent resource and also as a readily available respite care facility when parents are exhausted or when there are family emergencies. Many aging parents are crumbling under the load of having an adult child who has never left home, while they are now additionally tasked to care for their own aging parents. Some stress abolishing the institution entirely in favor of a unitary continuum of community-based care and services for all children and adults with mental retardation, believing that with exposure and time, the community will come to accept and value citizens who are intellectually deficient. Parents differ in what they see as most important and beneficial. Family situations and needs vary greatly, and there is often significant disagreement among families as well as within families.

The history of mental retardation is so vast and so complex that a comprehensive presentation is beyond the scope of this work. Parallels can be found, however, in histories of other human frailties (mental illness, blindness, deafness, mutism, epilepsy, cerebral palsy, physical deformities, paralysis, and so on). Bell (1980) has referred to repetitive cyclical patterns and trends with regard to the history of mental illness and mental health care in America. The same patterns hold true for children and adults with mental retardation from the 1800s to current times. He outlines these patterns as (a) tenacious societal rejection and fear of those with mental aberrations, (b) the exposé of horrendous conditions within the institution, (c) the "discomforting anonymity" of patients (or of those who violate the cherished values of society and are deprived of status), and (d) isolation-segregation of these societal "misfits" in keeping with a tacit policy of "out of sight, out of mind" (p. 181).

There is already evidence that some of the gains made in the past few decades are beginning to erode. The emphasis of managed care companies on cost containment is a factor. Institutions are losing professional staff through budget cuts. There has been a general loss of funding for community programs, and there is a current trend toward privatization of community services. Community group homes often experience frequent staff turnover, changes in ownership and management, and inconsistent quality of care and staff–resident interactions. The atrocities that have occurred in large, crowded, understaffed institutions can as easily occur in community centers. Recently, in Choctaw, Oklahoma, at the 100-bed Choctaw Living Center, a mentally disabled woman died (ostensibly of a seizure) and her body was not detected until six days later. A cleaning crew (not direct care staff) chanced upon her body. According to the report in the *Dallas Morning News* of January 16, 2000, at least six former clinic employees have faced prosecution for mistreatment of residents. Another employee was convicted of raping a resident in 1991. There are observable reversals in normalization patterns; for example, (*a*) many services take place in the home setting, and some families are stressed by the resulting lack of privacy, (*b*) skilled and reliable home health care workers are scarce in some communities, resulting in frequent family crises, and (*c*) jobs in the community are often scarce, and many employers, though denying their actions are discriminatory, continue to refuse to hire persons with disabilities.

☐ Chronic Sorrow as a Paradigm Shift

Although people with mental retardation and their families may be better off now than at any time in the past, chronic sorrow for parents and other family members remains constant. Olshansky (1962) suggested this reaction to be nearly universal among parents of children who are severely or moderately retarded, that is, those children who would be considered mentally defective in any society or any cultural group. He defined chronic sorrow as understandable and nonneurotic. In a later article (Olshansky, 1966), he referred to mental deficiency as a family tragedy. No matter what one might do or say, the tragedy remained. He clarified that he was not referring to an impoverished child who is defined as mentally retarded based on some inappropriate IQ test. He was speaking about a permanently and significantly impaired child. For parents the impairment served as a "many-faceted symbol," standing for personal defeat, an angry God, cruel fate, marital conflict, guilt, anger, genetic contamination, punishment, and so on. He understood the sorrow to be chronic and unremovable, except possibly through the death of the child. He observed that there are qualitative differences in how the sorrow is experienced, some explainable and some not explainable. He admonished professionals to be patient and to be clear about goals in their work with parents. He stressed the ineffable fact that some parents require a lot of time to learn how to tolerate their "unmending wounds."

As the author of Simon Olshansky's obituary (Goldberg, 1992) implied, the pervasive grief response of chronic sorrow is applicable to other permanent losses of an ongoing nature. He further stated: "How often mental health professionals criticize parents of mentally ill adult children, finding fault with their inability to accept their child's handicaps. I was trained in the era when professionals discussed the 'schizophreno-genic mother' who was blamed for the illness of her child. Although we look back on this era with shame, we still refuse to accept chronic sorrow as a normal psychological reaction, and we still hold parents of children with mental retardation to an impossibly high standard . . ." (p. 4). There may be more hope today that professionals will recognize, accept, and understand chronic sorrow. After a sustained period of relative profes-sional disregard of chronic sorrow, a renewed interest in the concept is evidenced by the recent development of empirical research studies and exploration of chronic sorrow's applicability to other populations.

The concept of chronic sorrow represents an important paradigm shift, a new synthesis. As a paradigm shift, (a) it recasts what was considered pathological as normal, and (b) it encompasses a form of grief that differs from the classic model in that it has no end point and the intensity of grief continues to be resurgent. This paradigm shift is analogous and relevant to the paradigm shift that has occurred in counseling and psy-chotherapy. Classical psychoanalysis, psychotherapy, and spiritual healing involved a "magical covenant" between the powerful authority figure-healer and the person seeking relief and healing (Lee & Martin, 1991). The person with the need (the analysand, patient, or supplicant) shared a requisite faith or belief system with the healer, and power was vested in the healer to intercede for or otherwise bring healing to the one who was suffering. If the process failed, fault lay with the person seeking help; she was deficient in faith, was resistant, failed to do all that was required, had not atoned for sins, and so on. A paradigm shift occurred with the introduction and acceptance of alternative theories and models of human development, behavior, and relationships. Although elements of the magical covenant survive, the emphasis now is on the therapeutic alliance in which responsibility for needed change and healing is shared collaboratively and more equally. It is the "real relationship," not the "transference," that is crucial for the amelioration of pain and improve-ment in functioning and emotional well-being. Power is vested in the person needing services as much as in the caregiving professional.

In like manner, the concept of chronic sorrow is a paradigm shift away from negative and pathological labeling, and it incorporates a shift away from disregard or unequal status in relation to professional caregivers. Empowerment, self-advocacy, and human dignity are at the heart of this paradigm shift. Therapeutic services and relationships that are based on equal power, collaboration, and mutual respect are direct implications of a concept of normal, pervasive, ongoing grief responses to a living loss.

What Is Chronic Sorrow?

Simon Olshansky first developed the concept of chronic sorrow in the 1960s (Olshansky, 1962) to refer to the observed psychological and emotional reactions of parents of children who were mentally retarded. He characterized these reactions as natural, understandable, and nonpathological, and—since the child lives—as enduring for the child's lifetime. He believed that periodic and inevitable exacerbations of intense emotional pain are characteristic of chronic sorrow. Shortly after Olshansky's surfacing of chronic sorrow, studies validating the concept and assessing some of its aspects were forthcoming. Subsequently, interest faded, and for more than a decade professional literature was practically devoid of its mention. In 1982, when Collins conducted research for her dissertation on parental mourning reactions to a child with visual handicaps, only one study of chronic sorrow employing empirical design could be found (Wikler, Wasow, & Hatfield, 1981). However, professional interest has been reemerging, especially during the decade of the 1990s and most notably in the field of nursing. The aggregate of existing studies unquestionably validates the concept of chronic sorrow. More than 20 of these studies have used empirical statistical design and analysis. Many of these studies have been published since 1990 and have been conducted by members of the Nursing Consortium for Research on Chronic Sorrow. Descriptions of chronic sorrow appearing in professional literature are consistent enough to determine that researchers and writers have been referring to the same area of study. Definitions have been consistent as well, although some authors have emphasized certain features over others.

A very important recent trend has been the expansion of the concept. This expansion is based on recent observations, primarily from the field of nursing, that the concept is applicable and useful for populations other than parents of children who are mentally retarded. Studies suggest that chronic sorrow may exist in any condition that permanently and significantly impairs functioning; for example, Parkinson's (Lindgren, 1996); multiple sclerosis (Hainsworth, 1994); some forms of chronic mental illness, including many cases of schizophrenia (Davis & Schultz, 1998; Hainsworth, Busch, Eakes, & Burke, 1995; Phillips, 1991); neural tube defects (Burke, 1989; Hobdell, 1993); and muscular dystrophy (Robarge, 1989).

The author proposes that the concept may be applicable to many persons with HIV and AIDS and to those who love them. With improvements in treatment, HIV is no longer a certain death sentence. Even when this greatly feared disease has progressed into full-blown AIDS, containment and reduction of associated life-threatening conditions is possible and more common than ever. Living for many years after diagnosis and even for a full life span is no longer so rare. Stigma, aroused by the fear and panic evoked by this diabolic virus, is not unlike the stigma attached to severe mental and developmental disorders. There are other similar elements as well, such as predictable and unpredictable crises requiring difficult adaptations, shifts in identity and self-image, alienation, resurgence of intense grief, profound secondary losses, and persistent fantasies of how things could have been and should be. Since applying the concept to a wider range of permanent impairments is of very recent origin, however, the current knowledge base continues to be derived primarily from clinical observations and studies involving the parents of children with severe developmental disabilities.

This author proposes a further extension of the application of chronic sorrow to some losses that are ongoing but *not* associated with disability, serious medical conditions, or impairments. These are losses that are considered to have many elements in common with current conceptual designations of chronic sorrow. The author proposes that similarities in circumstances and responses are sufficient to warrant their inclusion within the boundaries of chronic sorrow. Persons who remain protractedly or endlessly uncertain about the whereabouts, condition, and existence of an absent or missing loved one may experience stresses and disturbances consistent with chronic sorrow. For instance, it is well known that some mothers who have relinquished their infants and children for adoption continue to grieve for decades thereafter. This is especially the case when they have not had subsequent contact or any information about their children. These women are known to develop a visual picture of their relinquished child and to update it as the child grows older. Fantasies often continue of how life might have been and would be now had the child remained with the mother. Periodic resurgence of sadness and longing are known to occur at special occasions, on birthdays, holidays, Mother's Day, the approximate time the child would be expected to graduate from high school, and so on. Noticing children or adults who are the same age as the lost child and who have physical characteristics that the child could be assumed to have is common. For many of these mothers there is a feeling of emptiness and a sense that "things aren't right," even when they have made good lives for themselves and have other children. Millen and Roll (1985) studied 22 such women seen in psychotherapy. They had given up a child many years before coming for therapy and did not know the whereabouts of their children and had not had contact of any type. The researchers referred to the continuing grief of these women as "pathological bereavement" and viewed their losses as a "serious emotional and psychological challenge." Recommendations were made for facilitating a "healthy mourning process." This study was insightful and is an example of the elements characterizing chronic sorrow. Casting the understandable grief of these women as chronic sorrow may have changed the course of their lives and the course of their therapy.

In cases where there is no way to know whether a person to whom there is a deep attachment is still living or dead or permanently absent, the loss cannot be established; therefore, it cannot be grieved in conventional ways. Unanticipated and unexplained disappearances are examples of this type of loss. Family members who simply fail to come home one evening and are never heard of again, even years later, are sources of perpetual angst and grief for those who care deeply about them. Decades later in many of these cases there are no answers. The bodies of the missing are never discovered, and they cannot be found living anywhere in the world despite extensive, cooperative searches by experts and official agencies. In addition, when children or other family members are known to have been kidnaped, and there is no available information about their fates, their families are left to cope with a loss that cannot be alleviated or resolved in a manner providing some closure. Any similar circumstances in which the ultimate and final loss cannot be determined or confirmed can place persons who are bereft in an untenable position of dissonance and chronicity.

Families of servicemen missing in action (MIAs) may be affected by chronic sorrow. The Vietnam conflict, in and of itself a protracted and ill-defined event, produced inordinate stress on families whose husbands, fathers, sons, and siblings became unaccountably absent. Few studies inform us about the effects on those who cope with the stress of prolonged and indeterminate periods of waiting, either for confirmations or for the questionable return of MIAs. It is difficult to access research on military families. Available studies conducted in the 1970s (McCubbin,

Hunter, & Dahl, 1975; Powers, 1974; Spolyar, 1973) attempted to evaluate families of MIAs in areas such as role adjustments, physical and emotional health of the wife, and emotional adjustments of children. Although data for this particular population are scarce, and much of it is inaccessible, there are indications that chronic sorrow may affect those who have been held in perpetual limbo as a result of their family member's continuing MIA status.

The use of the concept of chronic sorrow is already expanding to include those who have lost significant aspects of themselves. In these cases, it is probable that it may be experienced somewhat differently than it is when the loss relates to a significant other. The loss, therefore, can be a "self-loss" or an "other-loss." *The author proposes these terms to clarify perspective, that is, the locus of the loss.*

☐ Proposed Definition

The definition of chronic sorrow that is proposed by this author synthesizes the variations in current use. Chronic sorrow is defined as:

> *A set of pervasive, profound, continuing, and recurring grief responses resulting from a significant loss or absence of crucial aspects of oneself (self-loss) or another living person (other-loss) to whom there is a deep attachment. The way in which the loss is perceived determines the existence of chronic sorrow. The essence of chronic sorrow is a painful discrepancy between what is perceived as reality and what continues to be dreamed of. The loss is ongoing since the source of the loss continues to be present. The loss is a living loss.*

☐ Comparisons and Distinctions

Grief is of concern to several professional disciplines (nursing, social work, psychology, medicine, psychotherapy, religion, philosophy, law). Especially since the 1970s, interest in all aspects of grief has increased, and it has become a focus of study and scholarly research. Specific, familiar types of grief experiences (anticipatory, traumatic, delayed, disenfranchised, and so on) have been identified and studied. As a result, labels and terminology have evolved and proliferated from differing perspectives. Some terms in current professional use are not consistently defined, nor are they applied in precisely the same ways across disciplines. Although all types of grief possess a repertoire of common reference points, the intensely intimate, complex, and highly individualistic nature of grief fosters "fuzziness"; terminology has come into use that is overlapping and somewhat vague. Although outside the scope of this book to do so, a more refined and consistent grief and bereavement nomenclature could be developed for use by all the various disciplines sharing this important common interest. Securing a place for chronic sorrow in this nomenclature is needed and well overdue. To move toward a more inclusive, congruent, and consensually defined terminology, multidisciplinary input, "brainstorming," and consensus would be necessary.

Chronic sorrow is not about responses to a loss due to death or to most divorces. It does not apply to grief that follows from losses where there is an end point or finality or where the absence of someone from one's life is known and permanent. It is about living with the realization of a loss that cannot be removed and that continually requires energy for adaptations. The concepts of time-bound mourning and sequential stage theory have not been found to be applicable to chronic sorrow (Collins, 1982; Oh, 1993; Wikler, Wasow, & Hatfield, 1981). Since the source of the loss continues to be present, chronic sorrow is about years upon years of living with the inevitability of loss, of continually negotiating reality demands required by the loss, and of contending with ongoing and resurgent grief responses. In the case of other-loss, there is some slight evidence that chronic sorrow is likely to continue even after the death of the person who is the source of the loss (Chomicki, 1995). One could speculate, however, that since the person is now absent and an ending has occurred, the lingering grief could—given adequate time— become either somewhat resolved or shift into a chronic pattern that is not so different from that of others experiencing chronic grief but who have no prior history of chronic sorrow. The discrepancy between the fantasy of what should or could have been and what actually was may continue, of course, but with finality, the potential for relinquishing the fantasy is greater.

Central to chronic sorrow is the role of fantasy—of what could have been or should have been (and maybe will be, after all). Activation of the fantasy intensifies painful emotions, as the disparity between the fantasy and current living reality can be cruel and wounding. Attempts to manage the crushing discrepancy between fantasy and reality can be found in the writings of individuals whose lives are significantly compromised by chronic sorrow. Jay Neugeboren (1997) has described throughout his aptly titled book, *Imagining Robert*, his responses to having a brother who is severely mentally ill. He describes his heartfelt adjustment processes and turmoil. His love for his brother has survived many crises, setbacks, and disappointments through all the many years of coping with his brother's condition. When there are periods of improvement or stabilization, he describes finding that he is "still hoping against hope" and "fantasizing a future for Robert" of a life at least somewhat better than what he has had. He writes, "I don't *expect* my dreams to come true, but I do imagine the following: that Robert will continue to make gains . . . and will, within, say a half-dozen years—when he is about the age I am now—begin to live the way many people his age live . . ." (pp. 303–304). In an earlier section of his book, he states "I still broke down after visits occasionally . . . I found myself getting through these visits by acting as if there were two Roberts: the brother I grew up with, and the brother who was now hospitalized. It was as if . . . the brother I grew up with had died . . . and now another brother had taken his place . . .who seemed, sadly, a very different person, with a much grimmer, narrower life. . . . But by imagining Robert this way I seemed, often, able to make things easier for both of us: I could spend time with him in the here and now, accepting him as he was without grieving over what had been, or what might have been, or what might never be—without, that is, having any expectations . . ." (pp. 252–253). He later describes the limited value of this coping strategy, stating, "Imagining that there were two Roberts, as it were—one who had died, and one who was [still] living—helped for a while. But it wasn't so. Robert had never died, nor had I ever, in my imagination or my feelings, killed him" (p. 253).

Janet Rife's (1994) account of the harsh realities of her son Brian's severe head injury includes remarks made by Tom, another young man with similar disabilities. Tom was a senior engineering student at the University of Virginia when he was injured. After lengthy and extensive rehabilitation, he has regained some of his abilities, including walking. He has not regained normal speech. He can make himself understood by people who know him who are patient listeners; otherwise, he uses a language board. His self-understanding is expressed this way:

> Life was very hard for me the first few years, because I denied everything. I thought the things every one of my supporters was telling me wasn't true. I thought I was on another planet. I refused to live in the real world where real things happen. I would say to myself and others, "I am not in the right body." Before the accident, a lot of the time my brain did what I wanted it to; it was very reasonable. For the first few years after my injury, I said simple things that I wanted to get done; the brain and body wouldn't let me do them. It was very depressing.
>
> How does one live in the real world and stop fantasizing? For some a change of attitude has to happen. The head injured person has to live with what they have *today*. Many think in their own minds, "I was once real smart, so I should be able to do that now," or they think, "I will do what I want to do right now, in the way I want to." On the other side of the coin, some head injured people think, "I will never be able to do that." (pp. 119–120)

In a similar vein, Craig Schulze, the father of a son with childhood disintegrative disorder (CDD), writes: "For 15 years, Jill and I have been awash in the River Jordan. Sometimes that river has been calm and beautiful; sometimes it has presented capricious twists and turns, leading to unexpected destinations; and sometimes it has raged and crashed around us, shaking the very foundations of our faith in life itself. . . . Children get sick or have accidents, behave in self-destructive ways, or even die prematurely. But rivers don't mysteriously run uphill, or form dizzying and seemingly endless eddies, or simply disappear. Children don't develop normally for two years and then suddenly . . . turn into psychotic mockeries of their former selves" (Schulze, 1998, pp. 221–222). He adds, "Even in collaboration, it is unlikely that the minds of George Orwell and Rod Serling could have come up with a more peculiar and chilling tale" (p. 222). Schulze's chapter appears as one of eight narratives written by parents of children who were developing quite normally, then suddenly began to disintegrate. As has been stated about this collection: To lose a child is tragic; to lose a child who still lives is beyond comprehension. For these parents, fantasies of what might have been (as well as the reality of what is lost) are intensified and reinforced by the documentation of the earlier normal development in family videotapes made prior to the devastating regression.

In most forms of so-called normal or uncomplicated grief, bereavement is predicated on the absence of the person to whom one has forged an important attachment. Since the person who is grieved is permanently absent and the circumstances of the loss are relatively stable, extraordinary and vastly unpredictable adaptations are not usually required during the course of grieving. Grieving can progress in the direction of some resolution or "lightening" of affect and the giving up of expectations and hopes. Positive memories can become a source of comfort rather than ambivalence and distress. The relationship with the person who has been lost can be restructured, recast, and completed. Peace can be achieved. The loss is more likely to be understandable, and timing of the loss within the developmental life context may be appropriate and expected. Support is usually available, and there are customary ways in which the loss is socially acknowledged, the person memorialized and honored, and survivors recognized and comforted. It is when loss and grief are disenfranchised that there are clearer similarities to chronic sorrow. While chronic sorrow is conceptualized as being normal and understandable, there are no formal and customary social supports and expectations, rituals, or recognitions of the catastrophic loss, since the person who is the source of the loss continues to live. Adaptations are usually drastic and disorienting. Simultaneously and absurdly, the person who is the source of sorrow may at times be socially unrecognized, as if he or she does not exist. If there is no existence, there is no loss; therefore, grief is unacknowledged and unaddressed by society.

Chronic sorrow as a normal type of grief can also be distinguished from complicated mourning, although there may be similarities in persistence, in some of the traumatic elements, and, to a lesser degree, in the pervasive nature of reactions. Chronic sorrow is usually more pervasive than complicated mourning, often affecting nearly all aspects of life. Despite its pervasiveness, most persons with chronic sorrow somehow prevail and continue to function in all important facets of their lives. Barbara Gill (1997) writes about the strength that can be discovered in the maelstrom of traumatic losses: ". . . for most of us the beginning is a traumatic and wrenching experience. Our insides are torn by such shock, grief, fear, and sense of loss that it feels like death. . . . The whole shape of our selves and our lives is being pulled into a new form. We don't think we can survive these cataclysmic emotions or take on the tasks now required of us, but we do. We have a child to care for. . . . Thrown back on our inner resources, we find we do have the strength to meet the demands of each day. . . . Always the most tangible and central thing is our child. . . . Our lives are not destroyed . . . but dramatically reshaped" (pp. 11–12).

Life circumstances associated with chronic sorrow can, however, increase susceptibility to complicated mourning and to other forms of physical and emotional fallout. Complicated mourning is a condition in which it is believed by some authorities (Bowlby, 1980; Deutsch, 1937; Gorer, 1965; Lindemann, 1944; Rando, 1993; Raphael, 1984; Volkan, 1975, 1983) that the person becomes fixated in the grief and bereavement process, with a failure to "let go." As Volkan (1975) has described the impasse that occurs, there is an intellectual acknowledgment of the loss and an equally strong emotional denial of its reality. There is a sense of being frozen at some point that is overwhelmingly conflicted and that, in some cases, involves symptoms such as flashbacks and numbness and a vacillation between being affectively inundated or flooded and being "sealed off." These symptoms are often identical to those involved in post-traumatic stress disorder (PTSD). They may continue for years without alleviation, perhaps for the lifetime of the individual. In established complicated mourning the impasse may be experienced as a desperate and insoluble entrapment between two equal forces, one driven by the need to restore the person who has died and the other driven by the need to release the internalized representation of that person, to "let the person die." Since the need to let the person die requires enormous, unbearable, purposeful energy, the perception is often that of having to "kill" the dead person. The representation is physically felt, much like a large foreign object that has become so much a part of the self that releasing or "killing" it is experienced as killing a part of the self. This is the conscious nature of the insoluble entrapment. In Volkan's (1983)

treatment of individuals with established complicated mourning, opportunities are skillfully fostered that can lead to "re-griefing" and then to
some resolution of the impasse, at which point grieving at last begins to
take a more normative course.

Persons affected with chronic sorrow may have PTSD symptoms that
are similar to those found in some cases of complicated mourning involving traumatic loss. Some of these symptoms may become protracted,
and in these cases chronic sorrow may be classified as complicated. The
life of chronic sorrow is often inaugurated by trauma, and trauma is
often imbedded in the grieving process. In both self-loss and other-loss,
flashbacks may result from trauma incurred during diagnostic assessment or at the scene of the catastrophic causative event. One does not
often have the ability to prepare for the circumstances associated with
chronic sorrow. Severe brain damage, bodily mutilation, and spinal cord
injury can occur in a nanosecond. A baby can be born with unanticipated, profound congenital impairments. Lack of anticipation and
the degree of severity of the damage constituting the loss contribute to
trauma. Only infrequently does a person voluntarily choose a life of
chronic sorrow, as, for example, when an expectant mother, knowing of
serious fetal anomalies, makes a fully informed decision to continue
the pregnancy to term. In this case, grief issues surfacing during the
pregnancy would be similar to anticipatory grief that is then followed
by chronic sorrow.

At any juncture where the mind becomes overwhelmed and cannot
take in the enormity of a tragedy and its sweeping implications, imagery
of details can be frozen for future recall. That is, details can become
vividly "wired in" and so represent the totality of the traumatic event.
They are then intrusively and involuntarily replayed as a result of triggers, both conscious and unconscious, internal and external. Once under
way, these flashbacks are usually next to impossible to interrupt. They
typically continue in a sequence that is resistant to change. Potential
triggers can be almost anything: hospital corridors and smells, certain
words, certain facial expressions, the sound of a particular voice, the
sound of a certain type of emergency vehicle, a room or a specific type of
furniture, specific thoughts and memories, and so on. Triggers are highly
correlated to the event. Flashbacks are multisensory and often include
exquisitely detailed features of the scene of the moment of reckoning
when life became drastically changed; the way the person looked in the
intensive care unit or emergency room, in a coma, or having the first
seizure; the appearance of the person after the trauma, during the first
shocking contact with the severely diminished personality; and so on. In
chronic sorrow, each subsequent crisis event may become a trigger for a
resurgence of traumatic stress symptoms.

Chronic sorrow can also be distinguished from major depression and from dysthymic disorder. Chronic sorrow can, however, indisputably lead to clinical depression (or unipolar affective disorder) and, even more often, to dysthymic disorder or to what appears to be a depressive personality, although these conditions generally have different causations. Depressive disorders are usually associated with habitual, self-critical patterns of thinking. Life experiences have usually led to schemas of hopelessness and a belief in the futility of personal efforts to improve conditions. Major depression is also associated with biological markers, such as characteristic sleep disturbances, shortened REM latency, and so on.

It is often especially difficult on initial contact to differentiate between dysthymic disorder and chronic sorrow. The clinical interview is the best means of distinguishing the two. In chronic sorrow there is a relentless and specific living loss. Unlike most depressive disorders, the level of functioning remains relatively stable in chronic sorrow even when fatigue and sadness are intensified. The person contending with chronic sorrow usually knows when the line has been crossed into major depression and will often report feeling "burned out" and devoid of positive experiences and emotions. There may be an awareness that affect has worsened, with comments such as "I don't have the energy to try to tell you about it or to even know about it myself."

Feelings of sadness related to chronic sorrow will vary and are often situationally influenced. Severity of distress depends on how the person perceives and interprets what has been lost. In the early stages of chronic sorrow, the fantasy of what should be and might be can function to delay or decrease feelings of despair and intense grief, especially if the fantasy has some realistic and believable aspects. It can serve as motivation to search for hopeful diagnoses and treatment. It can be helpful as a defense against the overwhelming onslaught of a drastically changed life. As time goes on, however, the fantasy—especially if highly unrealistic—can be a deterrent to achieving a sense of being more comfortable with life as it actually is. The fantasy can be a compelling force in "doctor shopping," which goes on for years as the person looks for a doctor who will give a more favorable prognosis. It is during this time that faith and family resources can be placed in unscrupulous authority figures who hold out false promises of dramatic improvement or cure. Over time, when all reasonable efforts have been made to restore some part of the loss, the fantasy tends to lose most of its positive functions. At that point, when the fantasy of what should be and what might have been is activated, sorrow will deepen as a result of the renewed impact of the disparity between the wished-for dream and harsh reality. The role of the fantasy in mediating emotional distress is only superficially understood at this time, as it has not been explored or researched.

Grief responses will subside from time to time and will vary in expression from person to person; however, the element of chronicity and all that it implies (permanence and periodicity, for example) sets chronic sorrow apart from many other types of grief. Most individuals with chronic sorrow continue to function well and to meet their challenges and responsibilities. Many of them would contend that "there is no other choice" due to the constancy and continuity of the source of the sorrow. There are usually relentless demands and needs and no one else to take charge and do all the necessary strategizing and caregiving. If one is the recipient of care, it is important to maintain a cooperative spirit and relational qualities as well as optimal functioning. For both self- and other-loss, putting on the "best face" is the norm.

Making constant adaptations and extracting strength and endurance from a self under siege are everyday actions of courage in a life of chronic sorrow. Jayne Marsh (1995) has included in *From the Heart: On Being the Mother of a Child with Special Needs* many examples of extraordinary stress described by mothers of children with disabilities. Grief, great fear, and feelings of inadequacy are transcended, since no other choice exists but to "handle it." Martie Kendrick, one of the subjects of Marsh's book, has two sons, Asher and Zachary, in 1995 ages 14 and 12 respectively. Asher has autism (diagnosed at age three), pervasive developmental disorder, Tourette syndrome, Asperger's syndrome, and so on. Zachary, on the other hand, is described as "terminally normal." In regard to endurance and chronicity, Kendrick states: "As most families having children with pervasive developmental disorder (PDD)/autism discover, the diagnosis is just one of the first events in a lifelong cycle of chronic crisis. Our family discovered after a time that we had become so acclimated to the unpredictability of living with a child with autism, that we had, in some way, lost all sense of the bizarre. You mean all families don't have toddlers who carry around extension cords instead of teddies, scream inexplicably for hours, and spend days raising and lowering the shades? 'Autism, the early years' was a blur of doctors, frustrated behavior-management plans, and concomitant feelings of parental inadequacy. Because loud noises, large open spaces, and a variety of unpredictable occurrences all added up to long spells of inconsolable crying and screaming, we found our lives telescoped, becoming smaller and smaller . . . our world was controlled by the desire to just 'stop the screaming'" (p. 96). She describes a slow improvement and the hopeful expectation that life will regain some predictable routine. She learns, however, that gains lead to more crises. "We are not heroes," she says. "We get up every morning, and we don't want to do it either. It is not heroic, believe me. . . . We have since decided that our lives will never slip into a predictable routine. . . . His autism is lifelong. . . . We must, therefore, always expect the unexpected. . . . We are moving against a social tide" (pp. 100–101).

Living with chronic sorrow is relentlessly stressful. While clinical observation indicates that social environment and individual resources (intelligence, health, emotional maturity, sound financial status) are important influences in adaptation, significance and meaning of the loss are highly individualistic. Eric Berne (1973), the founder of transactional analysis, referred to the importance of a person's "script" in determining life strivings and motivations. While not addressing chronic sorrow per se, he stated: "If the mother's script does not call for a physically or mentally disabled child, and the disability is so severe that it is necessarily permanent, then her life becomes a script-frustrated tragedy" (p. 191). The implication is that some parents may actually have a script that would "call for" a child who is severely disabled and that these parents might adapt more comfortably to life with such a child. This type of scripting may be a factor in those choosing to adopt a child with significant handicaps. According to this point of view, the meaning or significance of the ongoing loss is different for differing scripts. Conceptualizing chronic sorrow in the context of script analysis could be useful as a way of understanding the range of responses associated with individual perceptions of the living loss.

Using the example of grief reactions in parents of a child who is severely disabled, Davis (1987) has pointed out that a final resolution cannot be reached for two reasons: (a) The child continues to live, and (b) he or she requires infinitely more care than other children. The passage of time does not allow for permanent adjustments since there will be crises along the way that will foster review of the child's life and the parents' lives in relation to the child. The so-called state of acceptance is disallowed. One might argue that, ultimately, if we live long enough, we may all be affected to some degree by chronic sorrow. After all, life deals harshly with most of us at one time or another. Even in somewhat uneventful lives there are unavoidable losses and diminishments. Judith Viorst (1987) has written extensively about these "necessary losses." She includes among necessary losses our impossible expectations (of our parents, friends, marriage, children, ourselves, and so on). To grow and to experience gains in life and in ourselves, we must also undergo the pain of loss. Loss is the price we pay for growth and living. In chronic sorrow, however, the affected person deals with all such inevitable and necessary losses in addition to the continuing presence of an individual who cannot be fully grieved and about whom closure and resolution cannot be achieved.

Pollock (1981), in his work on life stages, identity, and "mourning-liberation" processes, states that he had discovered a mourning process for the self as one grows older and comes to terms with change resulting from the unavoidable progression of aging. He describes this process as mourning for former states of the self, as if these states represented lost objects. The inclusion of the words "as if" in his description fosters understanding regarding how the mourning process can be negotiated and how one might periodically bridge and transcend the unavoidable progression of losses. Chronic sorrow is similar in some ways to this type of ongoing process, yet it differs in that it does not involve an "as if." Instead, the object of the loss is tangible, living, and constant. In addition, adjustment processes do not usually follow a predictable, logical, and gradual course, and chronic sorrow may not provide opportunities for compensations and transformation that are as gainful and satisfying.

This is not to say that there are not profoundly meaningful lessons in living with chronic sorrow. The toughest battles can be sources of courage and resilience. Poignant moments of incredible insight and humor are possible. Outrageous comedy can emerge from truly tragic circumstances. When the one who is cherished and cared for makes some small improvement or connects interpersonally in a special, mystical way, feelings that are uniquely celebratory and joyful can be experienced.

Nancy Mairs (1989) has written about her life with multiple sclerosis in *Remembering the Bone House*. She has produced a rich array of descriptive words identifying and tracking her emotions and conveying her responses to her changing identity and to the loss of her body image and functions. She shares her despair, which has sometimes been protracted and suicidal, and she also reveals a startling sense of humor about her condition. She writes, for example: "'Oh, shit,' I yell as, catching my toe on the front edge of the elevator, I pitch toward the concrete floor of the garage in my new apartment building. 'Do you realize,' George will ask me later, 'that you might have died in that fall, and then your very last words would have been Oh, shit?' 'Ignominious,' I'll giggle" (p. 265).

☐ Clinical Significance of Recognition

Clinicians and other human services professionals frequently fail to recognize chronic sorrow and its profound and pervasive implications. These professional failures are explainable in at least two respects: (*a*) Chronic sorrow generally has not been included in grief literature, nor has it been a customary topic in continuing education formats; and (*b*) most clinical and caregiving professionals have not been exposed in their training to mental retardation and developmental disabilities (where the concept originated). *These are important omissions in serious need of correction.* The impact of chronic sorrow is immense, and professionals and clinicians who are called on for help occupy positions of importance. They are often more influential than family members in their roles as consultants, functioning in such crucial areas as assessment, communication of clinical information, advocacy, treatment planning and implementation, education, counseling and psychotherapy, crisis management, spiritual guidance, and so on. They are the ones to whom the person (with self- or other-loss) turns at the most vulnerable of times. It is with the nurse, the physician, the social worker, the psychotherapist, the minister, that the person can yield some of her responsibility. She can claim her need for reassurance and admit her fears, her fatigue, pain, loneliness, and sorrow. She can do this if she feels understood and respected.

Marsh (1994) has described several examples of professional significance and influence as expressed by mothers of children with disabilities. One mother states: "I don't know if professionals realize how much their interactions with us impact our families. Because we are in some ways, not really more fragile, but more vulnerable in certain ways because of our children's problems, professionals impact us greatly. They need to know how great that impact is and how interdependent we are. They need our information and we need their information. We need to share as mutual partners" (p. 42). Another mother notes: "It was not until my daughter was five years old and undergoing a developmental team evaluation that a doctor said to me, 'This must be difficult for you. How are you doing with all of this?' I remember feeling so surprised by this question that it brought me to tears . . . not tears of anger, but of relief that someone was looking beyond all of the deficits in my daughter's development and venturing into the realm of exploring her disability's impact on the rest of the family. I know this kind physician cannot 'fix' my feelings of grief, but . . . asking the question brought me some healing that day. It's as if my grief is a sore that I keep to myself and rarely expose. However, this physician's question gave the sore an opportunity to be open to the air and heal. On that day I did not need to 'stuff' my grief away and hide it. . . . My thanks go out to that doctor. He understood that a child's disability really becomes the whole family's challenge . . ." (pp. 43–44).

Unequivocal benefits accrue from professional recognition and understanding of chronic sorrow. Three of these benefits are (*a*) increased professional comfort, (*b*) a professional frame of reference, and (*c*) appropriate goals and interventions. Increased professional comfort conveys multiple positive messages to those who are the recipients of professional attention. Professionals, including physicians, especially when they do not specialize in areas of disability, are sometimes anxious and awkward in the presence of disfiguring and severe impairments. They are put in touch with their own vulnerabilities and with their powerlessness to "make things right." When confronted with parental denial of the seriousness of a child's obvious developmental abnormalities or when a patient's deterioration is not responding to treatment, professionals must deal with their own inadequacies, their own feelings of incompetence, their own grief responses. They are faced with human limitations, including their own. Understanding chronic sorrow can increase professional comfort with human tragedy and with responses and emotions that are expressed in professional settings. When they are less anxious and better informed, professionals can observe and listen more accurately. They can then make empathic reflections and are at less risk of committing empathic failures that are hurtful and disconnecting.

Recognition of chronic sorrow will also provide professionals with a frame of reference for what is to follow. Harm can result from nonrecognition, misinterpretations, mislabeling, and inappropriate—though well-intentioned—attempts to be of help. Manifestations of chronic sorrow can mistakenly be seen as temporary and as something the client or patient should resolve or "get over" when the crisis has passed or when the impairments are "accepted." Acceptance has long been an integral component in the conceptual framework of bereavement that is based on biological death. Many professionals are known to stress acceptance in cases of chronic sorrow, demonstrating a failure to make important distinctions between chronic sorrow and other types of grief. While accepting, loving, and caring for the person who is the source of the loss (whether self- or other-) is usually carried out with great devotion and commitment, it is unrealistic to expect acceptance of tragic and catastrophic damage. Chronic sorrow as a professional frame of reference also serves to lessen impatience with "regressions," slowness, recurring intensity of grief, and lack of straight-line progress to the "promised land of acceptance and adjustment" (Searl, 1978, p. 27). Knowing that (a) some healing is possible, (b) more comfort with grief responses and life circumstances can occur, and (c) chronic sorrow is not subject to resolution in the context of a time-bound model of grief serves to build and strengthen relationships of safety between professionals and their clients in which authenticity and understanding can grow.

Appropriate goals and interventions are much more likely when professionals recognize and understand chronic sorrow. Goals that may be helpful in other types of grief can be harmful and counterproductive in cases of chronic sorrow. It is important that professionals recognize that the nature of chronic sorrow is often such that it invalidates many of the client's previous life goals. Goals of "acceptance," as indicated above, are risky if they include acceptance of the conditions inherent in the loss (severe mental and physical disabilities, intense pain, personality-altering brain injuries, progressive neurological deterioration, being "cut off" from one's child as in autism, and so on). In considering acceptance as a goal, making a distinction between the impairment and the person is crucial. Accepting and embracing the person (self or other) is fundamentally different from accepting the destructive forces that have caused such profound damage. Interventions assisting clients in making this distinction are helpful, and often clients will report an easing of their emotional burdens once they have been relieved of pressures to "accept" the totality of their circumstances.

Other examples of goals and interventions that may be appropriate in some types of grief but not for chronic sorrow include (*a*) achieving a permanent adjustment, (*b*) emotionally disconnecting from the source of the loss, (*c*) increasing recognition of the reality of the loss, (*d*) expressing anger (including redirection of anger aimed at professionals for perceived missteps) toward the person who is the source of loss and recipient of care, and (*e*) fostering catharsis for its own sake.

A permanent adjustment is not possible, even in cases of coma, due to the unpredictable nature of the far-reaching circumstances. The goal of disengagement may be very appropriate at some point following the death of a loved one so that energy or libido can be reinvested in life and other relationships. A lessening of attachment to the fantasy of what could be were it not for this loss may also be desirable and healing at certain times in certain cases of chronic sorrow. Detachment from the living person (self or other), however, may increase negative emotions, such as bitterness, resentment, weariness, and a sense of bondage. After all, grief can be conceptualized as a manifestation of love. It is the power and energy of love that can sustain someone who is faced daily with chronic sorrow. In certain cases of other-loss, caring for the physical needs of another can become a way of taking care of the spiritual needs of the caregiver.

Goals and interventions to increase realization of the loss are compatible with most other types of grief, but in chronic sorrow a fluctuation in this realization may better serve to support optimal functioning needed in dealing with reality demands. A comprehensive understanding of the magnitude of secondary losses could be overwhelming if occurring all at once. These losses are better accommodated if they are gradually realized over time, as part of coping with the unfolding of the reality of life as it is now and as it will be. Moreover, in the initial stages of loss, defenses of denial and numbing are advantageous gifts to those who are directly affected by the tragic events.

Identifying and expressing anger is considered by many professionals to be part of grief work. Recognizing anger toward the person who has abandoned us through death and expressing it can be an important step in clarifying and ameliorating the confusion and intensity of grief. In most grieving contexts, the absence of any anger at all is suspect. There are instances in chronic sorrow where anger toward the person who is the source of the loss is appropriate and understandable, for example, where the loss is the result of voluntary actions that were known to be high-risk. In most cases, however, it is a mistake to assume that anger is present toward the person who is significantly impaired. On the other hand, a common source of difficulty in working with clients with chronic sorrow is that they may enter relationships with professionals after experiencing prior professional mishandling. They may present with anger and distrust, and anger arising from a sense of injustice may be superimposed on the anger and hostility that result from the frustrations experienced day in and day out. When anger is a factor, it is frequently connected to guilt or attempts to disguise, neutralize, or deny the unbearable sadness. Its recognition and management require careful consideration and a realistic view of the "big picture." Fostering clients' problem-solving skills is often as important as interventions for the mediation of emotions, including anger. The "big picture" involves problems that entail financial, occupational, social, family, and other dimensions. At times professionals may appropriately take active roles in advocating for and supporting clients in matters such as accessing community resources, obtaining full disclosure of information from other professionals, writing justifications for rehabilitation equipment (wheelchairs, specialized beds, communication devices, and so on) as part of applications to governmental agencies and other sources of assistance. When such obstacles are overcome, it is reasonable to expect that problematic anger will diminish.

For chronic sorrow, the goal of facilitating catharsis, in the belief that expressing emotions will release them "once and for all" and restore peace of mind, will usually result in additional stress. Achieving more balanced and flexible affective discharge requires integration of difficult emotions into psychological functioning. It is the integrative aspects of emotional expression that are essential, not catharsis alone. Interventions focused on integrating emotions and experiential meaning may have enduring effects on resiliency and can strengthen the core self.

Professionals who recognize and understand chronic sorrow are much more likely to be able to develop a strong therapeutic alliance with clients who are coping with it. Clients will feel comforted and respected in a relationship that is based on a mutual understanding that their grief responses and sorrow are normal. This type of understanding fosters client empowerment and realistic goal setting which avoids the indiscriminate application of approaches that may be desirable for other types of grief but are counterproductive in chronic sorrow. The supportive relationship resulting from professional comfort and client trust will enable the client to return for assistance as needed well into the future.

☐ Extent of Chronic Sorrow

It is impossible to obtain a reliable estimate of the number of persons affected by chronic sorrow. Inferences can be drawn, however, from demographic data on serious, disabling conditions. Figures for most cases of disability are extremely rough estimates due to (a) a lack of any statewide system of reporting, (b) several reporting systems existing in the same locality, (c) nonuniformity of reporting methods, and (d) social and political factors. When a reporting system is in place, there are problems in categorical consistency; that is, very similar cases—or even the same case—can be diagnosed differently by different clinical practitioners. In addition, since reporting is discretionary, some cases are underreported, some overreported, and some not reported at all. In severe and highly complex cases, the same person is often counted more than once; if the person has multiple disabilities and conditions, he may be included by several governmental and voluntary organizations. For instance, the same person may have severe mental retardation, a genetic disorder, hydrocephalus, epilepsy, cerebral palsy, and diabetes, and be entered into lists for each diagnosis or category. Nonetheless, estimates for some of the recognized conditions associated with chronic sorrow are provided below.

Estimates of disabilities and their effects are provided by major national organizations and the U.S. Bureau of the Census. The census report *Americans with Disabilities 1991–1992* (1994) lists statistics for people with a disability who are not residing in an institution. An individual with a severe disability is defined as being unable to perform one or more functional or daily living activities or as having an ongoing need for personal assistance. The census report for Americans meeting this definition totals 24.1 million people. The Arc, using 1990 census data, estimate that 6.2 to 7.5 million people have mental retardation. Batshaw and Shapiro (1997) report that since the 1940s the prevalence of mental retardation "requiring extensive supports" has not changed, probably as a result of a balance between improved health care and the emergence of new diseases. They indicate that "many of the causes of mental retardation requiring extensive supports result from genetic or congenital brain malformations that, as of 1997, can neither be anticipated nor treated" (p. 348). Kiely (1987) has estimated the percentages of children with mental retardation requiring extensive supports who have associated developmental disabilities. These percentages are: cerebral palsy, 19%; seizure disorders, 21%; sensory impairments, 55%; and psychological/behavioral disorders, 50%. Obviously, persons with mental retardation are especially vulnerable to serious mental health disorders. These would include organic personality disorder, bipolar affective disorder, major depression, obsessive-compulsive disorder, and schizophrenia. Mallow and Bechtel (1999) report that there are approximately 4.5 million children in the United States who have chronic diseases that adversely affect family functioning and adaptation.

The *Diagnostic and Statistical Manual of Mental Disorders (Fourth edition) (DSM-IV)* (American Psychiatric Association, 1994) specifies the prevalence of autistic disorders based on studies in England and the United States that suggest that 4 to 5 children in every 10,000 have autism. While autism was at one time thought to be more common in upper socioeconomic classes, it is now believed that previous estimates were elevated as a result of referral bias. According to the *DSM-IV*, the prevalence of pervasive developmental disorder (autistic disorder *plus* pervasive developmental disorder not otherwise specified) has been estimated at 10 to 15 children in every 10,000. In both mental retardation (as indicated above) and autism (including pervasive developmental disorder) the incidence of seizure disorders is quite high.

Torrey (1988), in attempting to document the magnitude of schizophrenia, states: "In terms of how many people in the United States have schizophrenia at any given time . . . estimates of this number vary depending on recovery rates, mortality rates, and diagnostic definitions. . . . A conservative estimate . . . based on recent prevalence studies . . . would be 1.2 million people" (p. 3). Torrey emphasizes that this figure is only for schizophrenia. Not included would be those with severe manic-depressive (bipolar) disorders, severe depressions, psychoses due to other causes, or severely disturbed children.

Waxweiler, Thurman, Sniezek, Sosin, and O'Neil's (1995) attempts at determining the impact of traumatic brain injury have included information available from the Centers for Disease Control and Prevention (derived from hospital records, vital registration data, trauma registries, and surveys). Based on this information, it is estimated that in 1990 there were approximately 2 million cases of traumatic brain injury (including 51,600 deaths). Indications from a number of other sources are that 20 to 30% of traumatic brain injuries each year are so severe as to result in lifelong disability. The highest risk group comprises young males, who are most often injured in motor vehicle accidents. The second highest risk group comprises infants and the elderly, who are usually injured in falls.

According to the United Cerebral Palsy Association (UCPA), approximately 3,000 infants are born with cerebral palsy each year, and about 500 other pre-school-age children later acquire this condition. Typically diagnosed before age five, cerebral palsy has a wide range of expression, from mild (as a kind of awkwardness) to severe (largely incapacitating the child from infancy onward). Cerebral palsy is also associated with other conditions—seizures, mental retardation, hearing and vision impairments, communication disorders, sensory disturbances, and so on. Several areas of the brain are sometimes involved. No cure exists.

As for traumatic spinal cord injury, researchers at the University of Alabama have compiled figures derived from regional spinal cord injury centers. These figures are considered to represent significant underreporting and do not include cases where death has occurred instantaneously or soon after the injury; nor do the figures include injuries having no aftereffects or having minimal neurological deficits. The estimate of new spinal cord injuries per year is 32 per million or 7,800 injuries in the United States each year.

The number of injuries sustained every year in automobile accidents in this country is astronomical. Injuries range from those that are relatively insignificant to those resulting in massive and permanent impairments. Many vehicular crashes are alcohol-related. In 1995 it was estimated that 30,000 people a year would suffer permanent work-related disabilities because of crashes in which alcohol is a factor (Miller, Lestina, & Spicer, 1996).

The National Multiple Sclerosis Society estimates that 400,000 Americans have MS, with the disease being twice as common in women as in men. The National Parkinson Foundation reports 1.5 million Americans with Parkinson's disease, or more than those with MS and muscular dystrophy combined. Although Parkinson's is considered a disease targeting older adults, about 15% of the patients are diagnosed before age 50. The National Institute of Neurological Disorders and Stroke estimates that 700,000 Americans experience a stroke every year and that 160,000 people die from them (though death rates are steadily declining).

Estimates of the prevalence and incidence of severely debilitating conditions and diseases can only hint at the number of those who may be coping with chronic sorrow in their lives. Expanding the application of the concept to other populations, such as those affected by HIV and AIDS and to situations not associated with disability, serious medical conditions, or impairments, will greatly increase these numbers. The extent of chronic sorrow—with or without expansion of the concept—merits professional concern, study, and understanding.

☐ Proposed Model of Chronic Sorrow

In so-called normal or uncomplicated grief, bereavement is predicated on the absence of the person to whom one has forged an important attachment. Several models attempt to explain the experiences and feelings associated with this type of grief and mourning. Among them are: (a) the disease or illness model (Engel, 1961; Lindemann, 1944),

(b) psychodynamic models (Bowlby, 1977; Freud, 1917; Pincus, 1976; Volkan, 1983), (c) biological models (Haig, 1990; Irwin, Daniels, Risch, Bloom, & Weiner, 1988), (d) attachment theory models (Bowlby, 1980; Gaylin & Person, 1988; Weiss, 1974), and (e) psychosocial and cognitive models (Kalish, 1985; Kelly, 1955; Parkes, 1975; Rubin, 1984). There are also stage theories, most notably the epigenetic stage model of Kübler-Ross (1969), crisis and coping models (Caplan, 1964), and existential theories and models (Natanson, 1970; Yalom, 1980). Theory building with regard to chronic sorrow is currently under way as a result of the recently renewed professional interest. Intuitively, it would seem reasonable that some understandings might be derived from existing theories and models of grief, especially those related to crisis and coping, existential issues, attachment, and biological factors.

The proposed model of chronic sorrow, presented below, is dimensional. Care has been taken to avoid constructing a model that is characterized by lists of symptoms and dichotomous decision points. Dimensions of chronic sorrow are presented as gradations or continua, providing a structure for organizing key aspects of the loss and its effects. The model can function as a framework for assessing the degree to which the person demonstrates chronic sorrow and the extent to which personal and environmental forces are affecting the person's responses. This dimensional model may be used as the basis for research as well as assessment and classification. The model is built around the five dimensions of the proposed definition that was presented earlier in this chapter.

I. Characteristics of the loss
   A. What specifically has been lost (Primary loss dimension).
      1. Is the loss a self-loss or other-loss?
      2. What is the impact of the loss?
      3. If other-loss, what is the nature of the attachment?
   B. Perception of what has been lost (Subjective dimension).
      1. Degree of trauma components, current and at onset.
      2. Personal value, centrality, and meaning of the loss.
      3. Secondary losses and impacts (past, present, future).
      4. Impacts on personal and social identity.
   C. Consensual validity of the loss (Objective/reality dimension).
      1. If presented in a variety of social contexts, would there be general, cultural agreement that a loss has occurred and that it is crucial?
      2. If so, how is the observed loss crucial?
II. Continuity of the loss.
   A. Perception of the loss as ongoing rather than terminal (Subjective dimension).

III. Initial, continuing, and recurring grief responses.
  A. Grief responses related to first learning/discovering the loss.
    1. Degree of trauma.
    2. Degree of impairment(s).
    3. Supports and unmet needs.
    4. Prior losses, concurrent losses, and grief history.
  B. Continuing and recurring grief responses.
    1. How chronic is the loss?
    2. What are predictable triggers for resurgence and intensification of grief?
    3. Effective current adjustments.
    4. Unmet needs, severity of daily stressors, and specific fears.
    5. Assets, strengths, compensations, and secondary gains (financial, disability benefits, family supports, adequate regulation of emotions, coping competency, resiliency, empowerment/ego strength, humor, quality of life, development of meaning, propensity for insight, humor, and so on).
    6. Current mental health status (comorbidity factors, preexisting and current mental health diagnoses).
    7. Factors unique to the individual and unique to the circumstances (risk factors, other sources of chronic sorrow, and so on).
IV. Discrepancy between perceived reality and the continuing fantasy/ dream.
  A. Current degree of impairment.
    1. Characteristics of the loss (for example, condition improving, progressive, stable, remitting)
    2. Effects on daily living.
    3. Degree to which personal assessment is consistent with general, consensual assessment?
  B. Current nature of the fantasy.
    1. Role of the fantasy.
      a. Positive functions.
      b. Negative functions.
      c. Degree of attachment to the fantasy.
      d. How is the fantasy activated?
    2. How realistic/unrealistic are the fantasy's implied and explicit expectations?
V. Continuing presence of the source or object of the loss.
  A. General, consensual validity of the loss as ongoing (Objective/reality dimension).
    1. Whether self- or other-loss, to what degree is the crucial aspect or the object of the loss identifiable?

2. To what degree is the loss based on a continuing, material presence that has no foreseeable end?
3. If presented in a variety of social contexts, what would be the degree of cultural agreement that the source of the loss continues to exist? Is the loss a living loss?

While similar to the theoretical model of chronic sorrow set forth by Lindgren, Burke, Hainsworth, and Eakes (1992), the author's proposed model requires continuation of the actual source or object of the loss. The model constructed by Lindgren et al. omits this requirement and emphasizes the ongoing perceptual disparity between the effects of the loss and the fantasy of how things would be had the loss not occurred. It includes: (*a*) a perception of sadness or sorrow over time in a *situation* with no predictable end, (*b*) sadness or sorrow that is recurrent or cyclical, (*c*) sadness or sorrow having internal and external triggering events, and (*d*) sadness or sorrow that is progressive and can intensify. Eakes, Burke, and Hainsworth (1998) subsequently proposed that chronic sorrow exists in situations where a person has experienced a single, circumscribed loss event rather than an ongoing loss. In this view, chronic sorrow has been redefined as the periodic resurgence of permanent and pervasive sadness or other grief-related feelings associated with *ongoing disparity* resulting from a loss experience. Chronic sorrow is described as cyclical and as existing as long as the disparity remains.

Recognizing that for many persons the grief process is not time-bound, this author's contention is that chronic grief is experienced by many people who have suffered a single, devastating loss. In these cases, grief responses are related to the absence of someone to whom there is a deep attachment. The perceived discrepancy between the fantasy of what should or could have been and should or could be may persist for the survivor's lifetime. However, the concept of chronic sorrow does not apply to these situations, since the person who is grieved does not, in fact, continue to be present. In chronic sorrow the self-loss or other-loss persists, and it necessitates, predictably and unpredictably, stressful adaptations and crisis management. To extend the definition further is to lose the meaningfulness of the concept of chronic sorrow, both as originally postulated by Olshansky (1962) and in its current, though expanded, application.

When a conceptual model is overly inclusive, it loses its meaning and its utility. The author's proposed model is intended to prevent the overexpansion of the concept of chronic sorrow so that it does not become meaningless. An example of an overexpanded definition and model is the concept of "codependency." That concept emerged as a useful way of identifying forms of enmeshment and enabling that are found in couples and families who are coping with alcoholism. It did not take long for codependency to be defined so broadly as to be amorphous and to be applied almost universally to all and sundry relationship problems and addictive patterns. If a concept can apply to almost anyone, how can it be cogent and useful? The author cautions against allowing such a valuable concept as chronic sorrow to be pushed so far afield that its structure, its meaning, and its application are lost.

Interpreting the Loss

☐ Subjectivity of the Loss

The intensity, the magnitude, and the very existence of chronic sorrow are a function of how the loss is interpreted. Factors influencing interpretations and their associated reactions include, among others: (*a*) identity development, including sense of self-worth, (*b*) current lifestyle and circumstances, (*c*) life history of losses, (*d*) philosophical and spiritual beliefs, (*e*) life dreams and expectations, (*f*) nature and extent of the support system, (*g*) degree of stigma, and (*h*) temporality within the life span. These factors are greatly intertwined. It may take many years for the full impact of the loss to be realized and even more years for it to be accommodated. Moreover, interpretations may vary over the course of a lifetime for the same individual.

What may be inconsequential to one person can be devastating to another. A parent whose fantasies have focused primarily on nurturing an infant may react differently to the birth of a child who is seriously impaired than a parent whose fantasies have centered on having high-achieving children who become doctors, lawyers, scientists, and so on. While the former may be enabled to live out her dreams of being self-sacrificial and always needed, the latter may have extraordinary difficulty coming to terms with a reality so drastically at variance with her deepest dreams and expectations.

Shortly before the 1994 Olympics, American champion ice skater Nancy Kerrigan was assaulted. She suffered an injury to her right knee (her

47

landing leg). The act was caught on camera. The videotape poignantly revealed to a nationwide audience Kerrigan's immediate existential reaction. It was the universal cry "Why?" and "Why me?" Fortunately, within a day or two the injury was found not to be so severe as had been assumed. Had the injury resulted in a permanent disability, removing Kerrigan from competition or from any skating at all, it is quite possible that she would have responded with chronic sorrow. Her identity development as a young adult had been shaped by her and her family's drives and expectations regarding her achievement of star status as an ice skater. Skating was her passion and her life focus. The impact of permanent disability would have thrust upon her a drastic revision in her identity and life path. A person who does not value athletic ability and whose identity is not especially based on physical competence would view a knee injury quite differently, perhaps regarding it as only a minor and inconvenient happenstance.

If the onset of chronic sorrow occurs after a person has had a very full, meaningful life, the loss can be weighed in the context of that life. The loss is likely to be interpreted differently, and so have a less profound impact, if the person has just embarked on young adulthood or a series of disheartening setbacks have preceded it. In these cases, the loss might be interpreted as a template for an entire life.

There are also some for whom an unending tragic loss can serve as a means for attaining significant secondary gains in other areas of their lives. Secondary gains might include, among other things: (a) attention and sympathy; (b) long-term disability and other remunerations; (c) abdication of unwanted responsibilities; (d) a sense of entitlement, that is, being taken care of beyond what is actually necessary; (e) avoidance of confusing, anxiety-filled identity decisions; (f) an ability to remain the dependent recipient of a variety of services; and (g) psychological leverage with others.

How interpretations can vary over time is seen in an example from the author's psychotherapy practice. During the first session, a client expressed great distress and described herself as being in agony, stating, "I feel like I'm shattered glass." She was in her late forties, married, and the mother of three children. The two older children, a son and a daughter, were away from home and doing well. One was in graduate school, and the other was forging a career as a financial advisor. The youngest child, a daughter 17 years of age, had sustained brain damage at birth. As a result, she had a moderate level of mental retardation. The client came from a family who valued competence and achievement above all else. She and her siblings had excelled in their areas of endeavor, and they had all "married well." They had been taught to set high standards and that "anything can be done with hard work."

Two events precipitated her coming to therapy. She had recently returned from a visit with her parents, whom she had not seen for a year. She had taken her youngest daughter with her. Her father, described as been an impatient man, had not been able to tolerate being in the same room with such a low-functioning individual. For the first time, this client had seen her father's face register dislike, if not disgust, for her child. She had felt very hurt. Adding to her injury, her mother had suggested she return home sooner than planned, which she did. Feeling humiliated and rejected, she began seeing her daughter as "awkward" and "unattractive." She realized that her daughter was "not the cute but funny-looking kid any more."

Several days after returning home, she had taken her daughter to a Special Olympics event. The daughter had been "wound up," fidgety, and difficult to manage. The client decided to take her daughter home at the end of the day before the closing ceremonies. Returning home in the car, her daughter had protested leaving and had become "wild" and aggressive. She hit her mother several times, and the client—horrified—found herself hitting back. She stated, "My spirit was broken." She indicated that she had previously considered the parenting of her daughter as "not much more of a challenge than any other." Her daughter had received "the best that money can buy." She was shocked that, "after 17 years with this kid, it's now that my whole world has changed."

This woman was in extreme emotional pain. She was contending with a confluence of several factors and events. The perceptual world that had supported and inspired her had suddenly and unexpectedly collapsed. Her recent experiences were changing her perceptions. Her hard work and devotion to maximizing her daughter's abilities had been directed by the belief that her efforts would result in overcoming important limitations so that her daughter could pass for normal. She now realized this was never to be. For the first time, she had seen her daughter, now too old ever to be a "cute kid" any more, through her father's judgmental and intolerant eyes. She was attempting to adjust her own lens so that she could more realistically understand how her daughter appeared to others. Her purposeful, optimistic approach to her daughter's problems faded as the denial that had protected her from acknowledging the daughter's marginal social status was stripped away. She became aware of her own loss of status in her family of origin as a violator of parental values and "just about everything my family stands for." She was at the brink of new understandings about her family's mythologies, including their narrow demand for excellence in all family members.

Her daughter was at the age when decisions about college and leaving home would be positive family issues if she were "as she should be." The client herself had hoped to be making plans for career development and other personal pursuits. She wanted to reestablish intimacy with her husband, to be free to travel with him, and to do a great many things they had postponed. But her fantasy of this future had been lost, and her defenses (especially denial and repression) were no longer working. Her grief was intense. Her interpretation of reality shattered, she was challenged to reconstruct a new map of the future.

For some individuals, an unending loss—even of some serious consequence—can be a source of satisfaction and personal growth. It can catalyze powerful actions and provide the opportunity to meet the adversity heroically and authentically. In these cases loss and generativity are unseverably linked. This may be the case for Jim Brady and his wife, Sarah. As press secretary for President Ronald Reagan, Brady sustained serious brain injury when he was shot during an attempt to assassinate Reagan. After a lengthy and arduous rehabilitation, which may continue even today, and a partial recovery of speech and movement, he and his wife have been at the forefront in raising America's consciousness about the need for legislation to regulate the ownership of guns. The fine actor Christopher Reeve, who was critically injured when his horse balked at a jump and threw him and who since has been paralyzed from the neck down, has very effectively directed his creative energies to promoting innovative research on spinal cord injury. With the support of his wife Dana and armed with a very strong spirit, intelligence, and voice, he accomplished more in four or five years than others had accomplished in many more. These examples of satisfaction and transcendency should not be misconstrued to mean that individuals such as the Bradys and the Reeves would prefer their losses, had they the power to undo them.

☐ Gender Differences

Even in a time when we have learned to think about male and female roles and behaviors as more or less androgynous, it remains evident that men and women interpret loss differently. This difference appears to be largely related to male and female identity development. Boys generally separate and individuate more easily than girls, and male identity is embedded in values and attributes of individualism. This is not the case for most women. In general, female identity is embedded in connectedness, affiliation, and attachment. Women are more likely than men to think of themselves as someone's daughter, mother, wife, sister, friend, lover, and so on. It follows that intimacy is easier for them, and their relationships may validate, empower, and reinforce female identity. For many men, intimacy is more difficult, and it may threaten the sense of self (Josselson, 1987, 1992). The ongoing loss (self- or other-) could, therefore, represent different meanings for men than for women. Different meanings would lead to different responses. Indeed, considerable evidence indicates that mourning and other responses to significant loss are different for men than for women (Bohannon, 1990; Haig, 1990; Martin & Doka, 1998; Rando, 1988; Smith & Borgers, 1988; Viorst, 1987).

Studies of parents of children with serious developmental disabilities, where chronic sorrow has received the most scrutiny, have consistently supported gender differences. For instance, Gath and Gumley (1986) studied a large number of families with children who had Down syndrome or mental retardation from other causes (total N = 339). They found that more mothers reported mental health problems than their counterparts in the general population. The mothers were prone to depression, mood lability, and fatigue, while the fathers were not. Families of preschool children with handicaps were studied by Dunst, Trivette, and Cross (1986). Wives reported significantly poorer emotional and physical health than did their husbands. Mallow and Bechtel (1999) studied 28 parents (9 couples and 10 mothers) having 24 children (17 boys and 7 girls) with a variety of developmental disabilities. Both mothers and fathers reported initial sorrow when learning of their child's diagnosis. Mothers experienced a greater resurgence and intensity of sorrow than did fathers. The recurrence of sorrow for mothers was related to management of a health care crisis. For fathers, the recurrence of sorrow was related to conflicts and frustrations with social norms.

Johnston (1978) concludes that the grieving process, and specifically the element of protest, are associated with maternal—but not with paternal—accuracy in assessing the social skills of their children with disabilities. Hobdell (1993) conducted an interesting study of the relationship between chronic sorrow and parents' accuracy of perception of their children's cognitive development. These children had been born with a neural tube defect. The sample consisted of 132 parents (63 couples and 6 single parents). Both the mothers and the fathers demonstrated chronic sorrow, but they differed in their expressions of it. Both mothers and fathers were inaccurate to some degree about their children's cognitive development. However, mothers had more severe chronic sorrow, and they were significantly more accurate in their assessments of their children's cognitive level than were fathers. Somewhat more recently, however, Davis and Schultz (1998) found that the intensity of grief of parents of children with schizophrenia (16 mother-father dyads) was proportional to the severity of their child's psychiatric illness, and they found no differences between mothers and fathers with regard to intrusive thoughts, avoidance behaviors, and distress connected to recall of the diagnosis.

Although existing studies on parental adjustment to a child with developmental disabilities—on any variable at all—are relatively meager, some have revealed differences between mothers' and fathers' responses. Evidence does exist indicating that both mothers and fathers of such children experience significantly more stress than parents of children with chronic illnesses (Cummings, 1976). Studies indicate that mothers of children with a variety of disabilities report significantly lower marital satisfaction than do fathers (Cook, 1988; Konstantareas & Homatidis, 1989). This finding, however, also tends to be true for married mothers of normal children (Bernard, 1972; Scanzoni, 1977; Scanzoni & Scanzoni, 1981). A study by Cook, Hoffschmidt, Cohler, and Pickett (1992), in which marital satisfaction was assessed for 131 parents of adult offspring with severe and persistent mental illness (predominantly schizophrenia), found the degree of mutual comfort, family size, income, and gender to be factors that contributed to marital satisfaction. Gender operated in much the same way for these parents as for so-called normal parent samples; that is, mothers reported lower levels of marital satisfaction than did fathers. Other factors were found to relate specifically to the perception and nature of the adult child's illness. The pattern that emerged in this study was similar to that found in other research on mothers of children with disabilities, in which women reported disproportionately more negative experiences than did men. Even when factors such as mutual comfort, family size, income, and severity of illness or disability are controlled for, mothers still report lower marital satisfaction than fathers. The unequal distribution of caregiving at all points of the family life cycle is proposed as the reason for mothers' lower marital satisfaction. Even when they are fully employed outside the home, caregiving continues to fall disproportionately on women throughout the life span. It would be reasonable to assume that women might interpret an unremovable loss as a heavy and unrelenting burden and as a major source of deprivation of freedom. Men might focus more on instrumental concerns, such as the related financial stress (Price-Bonham & Addison, 1978).

Damrosch and Perry (1989) studied mothers and fathers of children with Down syndrome (ranging in age from infancy to adulthood) on overall patterns of adjustment, episodes of intense chronic sorrow (defined as periodic reevocation of intense feelings of grief), and on coping behaviors. Distinct differences were found. Overall, fathers appeared to fare much better than mothers. Mothers reported a higher frequency of chronic sorrow, including negative affect and self-blaming. They scored much higher than the fathers on a special "feelings subscale" which included: (a) feeling burdened and overwhelmed, (b) feeling embarrassed or self-conscious in public, (c) feeling very old, (d) feeling grateful for the good things about the child, (e) feeling fearful about what will happen in 20 to 30 years, (f) feeling on guard, (g) being "fearful of what other people are saying about you," and (*h*) feeling jealous or resentful of people whose children are not handicapped.

Since, even with more androgynous functioning of men and women, the burden of caring for children and other family members with disabilities falls primarily on mothers, meeting these demands places these women increasingly at odds with their contemporaries and may foster social isolation and a sense of alienation. As Schilling, Schinke, and Kirkham (1985) point out, these mothers may receive much less recognition and support than in the past, in more traditional times. Since self-blaming is found more often in mothers than in fathers, mothers may see themselves as considerably more responsible for their children's health and achievements. When a child (young or adult) is severely impaired, parents are faced with greatly revised expectations and hopes for the future. For the mother, the perception of her inability to influence a child's success or well-being in life may be more personal and more intimate than for the father. Roskies's (1972) study of mothers of thalidomide babies found that at every stage of the developmental process the mothers' perceptions of their ability or inability, success or failure, in parenting their children with disabilities were greatly impacted by social criteria. These mothers did not experience the social approval that is customarily accorded mothers of normal children. Therefore, they did not take pleasure in their children's achievements to the same extent as mothers of normal children, and they perceived themselves as comparative failures.

An additional stress for the mother may involve the lack of time and space in which to grieve and sort through her feelings. After all, how can she adequately grieve the loss of the idealized child when the actual child exists and when that child constantly and continually requires even more care than normal children? And where is the satisfaction in providing care to be found when that care is so often fraught with aversive interactions? Many mothers of children who are autistic or who have other severe developmental disabilities are deprived of the emotional attunement enjoyed by mothers of normal infants and children. Stern (1985) and Beebe (1985) have described two mutual influence patterns that occur between mother and infant. These are referred to as coactive and alternating types of matching. The coactive pattern, in which the mother and infant join in evoking the same vocalizations or facial modes at exactly the same moment, promotes bonding, intimacy, and self-esteem. Beebe (1985) has stated: "The subjective experience for the adult partner participating in these special coactive moments with the infant is a 'high' of almost magical sharing" (p. 34). The alternating pattern is one of turn-taking between mother and infant, which contributes to rhythmic matching. This pattern of taking turns is thought to be a precursor of adult dialogue. These patterns are experienced by the mother as a very special and powerful synchrony. Mothers who care for children who cannot attune with them miss out on important satisfactions and pleasures. Often, autistic children turn away from, and forcefully reject, efforts by their mothers to connect with them. These mothers may find themselves trapped in caring for children who are emotionally hurtful to them.

The literature and clinical experience with women and men who are coping with the effects of chronic sorrow have led to the following impressions:

1. More women than men come for therapy.
2. More men with self-loss come for therapy than do men with other-loss.
3. Women tend to be better able than men to disclose and to articulate their feelings and what the loss means to them.
4. Women are likely to assess the seriousness and extent of the loss more realistically.
5. Women are more likely to own the loss, to assume unrealistic blame, and to carry most of the responsibility.
6. Women are more likely to obsess and ruminate about matters pertaining to the loss.
7. Women, more than men, engage in overfunctioning and overadaptation.
8. More women react to the loss with sadness, depression, and stress-related symptoms.
9. Men are more apt to cope through denial, distraction, displacement, withdrawal, disengagement, and low participation.
10. Men are more likely to express anger than are women.
11. Men are better able to rationalize their withdrawal and their contemplated or actual abandonment of the situation.
12. Men have more difficulty expressing their sorrow.
13. Men have more difficulty owning and expressing their fears.

Despite the available evidence and these clinical impressions, the author believes that many men experience chronic sorrow with great intensity, although they may not talk about it as much as women. Even today, permissions and support for emotional expression for men who are coping with significant, ongoing loss—or grief of any kind—are not sanctioned in quite the same way as they are for women. There is much to learn from men who are willing to risk the vulnerability of disclosing their inner struggles with loss of all types. Perhaps longitudinal studies of men who are affected by chronic sorrow will clarify their experiences. It may be too simplistic to attempt to tease out gender differences in how a loss is perceived and interpreted. Both commonalities and differences between men and women are found from traumatic onset throughout the course of dealing with chronic sorrow. This type of ongoing grief, both for men and for women, is a source of stress and can also be a source of strength.

☐ Self-Loss and Other-Loss

The terms *self-loss* and *other-loss* are used to identify the locus of the loss. They distinguish, respectively, an important loss of a part or parts of the self and the loss of significant aspects of someone to whom we are bonded or with whom we have developed an important and committed love relationship. These terms seem more desirable than others, such as "loss of self" and "loss of other," in that the loss of self would indicate one's absence in toto and loss of other would indicate the absence of another. Since the other and the self remain, the descriptors "self-loss" and "other-loss" have been selected to avoid implications of absence.

The subjective meaning of a self-loss may be different from what is experienced when the loss refers to a vital aspect of someone we care deeply about. *Stigma*, the classic work by Goffman (1963) in the field of disability, attempts to speak for the person who has lost a part of the self. Goffman refers to this loss in terms of social stigma and the self-perception as one of a "spoiled identity." Nancy Mairs (1986) has written, in her series of essays *Plaintext*, a masterly description of her life as "a cripple." Well aware of the semantics of the word, she chooses "cripple" for self-reference so as to make people wince. Mairs wants to project an image of being a "tough customer," a woman who can "face the brutal truth" of her multiple sclerosis (p. 9). She was diagnosed at about age twenty-eight, and she had been making her adjustment to the realities of her changed image for over ten years when she wrote the essay, "On Being a Cripple." Mairs demonstrates that, although she "hates being a cripple," she sees her self-loss in perspective with others she knows who also have MS. Her prior identity was one of being "solitary, sedentary, and bookish," so that she can understand that some of the effects of MS have a different meaning for her than they do for the "world-famous French cellist" about whom she has read or the woman she knows "who wanted only to be a jockey" (p. 12).

Although Mairs (1986) describes herself as having an ongoing susceptibility to "immobilizing depressions," she apparently managed to effect a good initial accommodation to the changes MS forced on her life. This was mostly due to not having any dramatic exacerbations for several years following diagnosis. Her life style was relatively unchanged during this time. She grew to be "at ease" with her situation and experienced her life as "richer." However, her self-satisfaction was derailed when she experienced a sudden exacerbation while on a trip. She describes her reaction:

> It renewed my grief and fury and terror, and I learned that one never finishes adjusting to MS. I don't know now why I thought one would. One does not, after all, finish adjusting to life. . . . It may at any time get worse, but no amount of worry or anticipation can prepare me for a new loss. My life is a lesson in losses. . . . You can't, for example, get cured. In recent years researchers . . . have started to pay MS some attention even though it isn't fatal; perhaps they have begun to see that life is something other than a quantitative phenomenon, that one may be very much alive for a very long time in a life that isn't worth living. (p. 19)

Mairs is also aware of other-loss in those who care about her. This awareness has led her to develop gentleness in herself. She expresses her gratitude for this gentleness; it is something she didn't have before MS. She writes, "It has opened and enriched my life enormously, this sense that my frailty and need must be mirrored in others, that in searching for and shaping a stable core in a life wrenched by change and loss, change and loss, I must recognize the same process, under individual conditions, in the lives around me" (p. 20). Mairs provides a well-articulated awareness that one's self-loss can result in other-loss in one or more other persons. Thus, if she is not the person she was meant to be, her husband is likely to experience other-loss if she is central in his life, which appears to be the case. Although her husband has not actually lost key elements of the self, he has lost important relationship roles. He has also assumed the responsibility and role—unwanted by both—of her caregiver. The relationship as it was "meant to be" is no longer.

Chronic sorrow and its "fallout" are powerful shapers of self and others in relation. Chronic sorrow related to reciprocal self-loss and other-loss experiences may progress in such an insidious manner that the process becomes virtually imperceptible and much more serious than one might imagine. Over time, the incremental losses add up. This quality of near-imperceptibility attached to some chronic sorrow may be important in that it functions to partially shield and protect, fostering gradual accommodations, and often allowing the person to go on.

When self-loss is primarily a product of loss of mental faculties, the impact on identity may be most severe, especially when there is awareness of an eroding of the mind, such as in traumatic brain injury or a progressively deteriorating neurological disorder. In some such cases, not only is the person aware, but he or she cannot find a way to express the awareness, so that this type of self-loss may be experienced as both a loss of mind and a loss of ability to affect others or to engage in mental sharing. The self becomes more and more isolated; therefore, it becomes more and more distorted, both to self and to others.

From the viewpoint of other-loss, Doka and Aber (1989) have used, as a metaphor, the horror movie *The Invasion of the Body Snatchers* to portray the loss of the original personality and its replacement by a "parasitic consciousness" or "unknown entity." This type of other-loss can be extremely difficult to sort out, both from the standpoint of the person who is experiencing other-loss and that of others in the social environment. The perception of the loss, on a case-by-case basis, is one of dimensionality. The continuum of this type of other-loss can range from comatose to near-comatose states to severe mental illness (such as florid schizophrenia) to substance abuse to periodic but severe personality change such as results from some types of seizure disorders (partial complex, temporal lobe seizures, for example). For some, the person (such as one in intractable coma or near-coma) is perceived as the same as dead. Kalish (1968) refers to this perception as psychological death, when the person ceases to be aware of both who she is and that she is. Social death, according to Sudnow (1967), occurs when the person, though physically alive, is treated by some who knew the former personality like a corpse. This same person may be seen and treated by others as still fully alive. In either case, there is a cessation of the essence of the individual personality that once was.

In cases of psychological or social death, fantasies of how things should be and may be again may continue in a more or less constructive manner for years. The mother of a young woman seen in psychotherapy by the author had been in a coma more than half of the client's life. The client was 13 years old when her mother sustained brain damage in an automobile crash and became comatose. The client's aunts and uncles had never stopped telling her that one day her mother would wake up and then "everything would be all right." She had been led to believe that this could happen at any time, that she had to remain ever hopeful and always cheerful around her mother when she was taken to visit her. As a result, she had disconnected from her grief. She would sometimes feel the impact of having truly lost her mother. When this happened, she would do everything possible to regroup. She would feel weak and guilty for not being able to hold fast to hope and to a future happy scenario.

She knew, however, at age 29 when she came for therapy, that her grief could not "wait outside the door" any longer. She could no longer maintain any type of positive fantasy; her hope was gone. Her mother had missed her graduations from high school and from college and her wedding. The client had a good marriage, and she and her husband wanted children. She realized that, in spite of what she had been told about imminent, hopeful possibilities, her mother was not going to be present for the birth of her children. Her mother would never know them or her husband or herself as a grown woman who was making of her life what she had thought her mother would have wanted for her. She was angry with her relatives and felt they had deliberately misled her so that they wouldn't have to deal with her grief. My suggestion that they had wanted to avoid their own grief as well was met with adamant disagreement. They had presented a very false reality to her. But since her mother is technically alive, does she have a mother or does she not? And what is a realistic fantasy and what is not? What is appropriate to hope for?

There are cases, though rare, where persons who have been in coma for many years will regain a level of contact, awareness, and consciousness. This apparent miracle leads to rekindled hope that the person will truly return and be restored. However, in most of these cases the miracle is short-lived, and the person again lapses into a state of unconsciousness. Those who care for this individual are often left in even deeper dismay; whatever coping styles they had attained are now destabilized and not so available as they once were. Previous perceptions and interpretations may require readjustments.

In cases where the personality that once was ceases and is replaced by a personality that is significantly different or "alien," then the scenario contained in *The Body Snatchers* is realized. The scenario fits for many cases of schizophrenia and for organic brain disorders. The body seems to have been seized by an unknown and alien entity that, at first, may present almost subliminal evocations of change. A deep but little-understood sense of loss may be experienced by a partner, a parent, or other family members or friends. Yet the person remains, is physically alive, and demands in any number and variety of ways to be dealt with. The loss experienced by others may be unresolvable. The way in which this type of other-loss is understood and interpreted will greatly impact decisions that must be made. Decision-making about the impaired person may be very difficult and often fraught with guilt. One reason guilt may be a problem is that negative feelings may be directed toward the impaired person, even when it is clear the person did not mean to change in this way. How then are the decisions made? Are they made on the premise of knowing what the former personality might have wanted in these conditions? Are they made on the basis of current reality only?

When psychosocial death occurs, grief responses may lead to great distress, depression, and physical ailments (Quayhagen & Quayhagen, 1988). Any and all stress-related symptoms may occur. Other grief-related responses may also be present, including anger at the victim (hence, more guilt), at a system that is ineffectual and nonsupportive, at relatives and friends "who do not understand," at seemingly uncaring, abandoning, and impotent professionals, and at fate or God. Interpretation of the loss may depend heavily on where, on the reversibility-irreversibility continuum, the condition is perceptually placed. Hope can do much to pull us through the times when devoted and earnest efforts to make things better for our loved one are taking all our energy. It can also bring about a more fervent sense of mission or responsibility. On the other hand, in a situation that is clearly irreversible, we may be able to detach a bit without feeling so much guilt; we may be able to delegate caregiving responsibilities without so much fear. In this regard, an interesting study by Liptzin, Grob, and Eisen (1988) revealed that, over a substantial length of time, relatives of people who had chronic recurring depression felt more burdened than relatives of people with dementia. Relatives of people with dementia were better able to achieve a degree of reconciliation with knowledge of the inevitable decline and deterioration, while relatives of people who were depressed felt more self-blame and were unable to achieve stable coping with conditions of such uncertainty.

The latter is also true for parents of children who are autistic. The uneven course of development associated with autism is replete with frustration and emotional wear and tear resulting from the alternation of hope and despair. The child may make some sort of contact with the parent one day, and this contact is seen as a wonderful and hard-won breakthrough. But the next day or the next week, the contact is gone. The child may one day speak a little, and with more clarity, and the parent feels a surge of hope and wonder. When language subsequently— and yet again—disappears, and there is no logical reason for the disappearance, the parent plummets once again into the abyss. The child, however, is merely being as the child is—deplorably authentic.

It is difficult for spouses of those who are chronically and severely mentally ill to accommodate to their ill-defined roles. In cases where other-loss is of aspects of the mate, the spousal role is very complex and ambiguous. Terms such as *pseudo widower* and *pseudo widow* have emerged, as well as *crypto widower* and *crypto widow*. The role of wife or husband has not been lost, but it no longer means what it once did and what it means to the larger society. The nature of the role, by whatever name it is called, is so different and so ambiguous that it can add to feelings of isolation and alienation. If the mate was previously idealized, or if he or she is perceived as having been completely helpless to prevent the "body snatching," which is often the factual case (as compared with severe substance abuse, where there are implications of conscious choice at junctures throughout the process), the spouse may be immobilized in his or her own life.

A client in the author's practice provides an example of other-loss that is taking the form of a moderate degree of "body snatching." She has been married for 15 years to a man whose erratic behaviors (probably arising from inadequacies in personality) have gradually worsened. The client is in her mid-60s; her husband is in his early 70s. She was previously married to the father of her three children, who left her for another woman after 30 years of marriage. During the past six years her present husband has become more openly preoccupied with religiosity, praying loudly in public on occasion, and attempting to tell virtual strangers (restaurant staff, store clerks, people in grocery stores) "about the Lord." As an extension of this preoccupation, for the past two years he has begun to express the feeling that God loves him more than others. He knows this is true because God is showing him favoritism through circumstantial happenings, such as providing him with a cloud for shade on hot days while "everyone else has to do without one."

When the client came for therapy, she complained of great fatigue and of feeling hopeless, depressed, and anxious. Her anxiety prevented her from sleeping well. She wanted a professional opinion about her husband's behavior. She expressed her feelings of guilt about her thoughts of wanting a divorce and felt she could not leave a sick man. She stated, "I think it would be so much better if he were dead." She admitted that she knew very little of actual fact about his background, as he had concocted several histories of the life he had before they met. His adult children stayed away and were rarely heard from, although one of his daughters had expressed gratitude to her for "taking care of Dad."

Though difficult, the author and the client were able to work together to persuade him to go to a gerontologist whom the author recommended. The physical examination was very thorough and essentially negative. An MRI revealed nothing of significance, with the exception of a sinus infection, and there were no signs of little strokes or ischemia. It seemed that he had been mentally unbalanced off and on throughout his life and that he had a longstanding, though worsening, delusional disorder. Over time, she was able to see that he had always been overzealously religious and that the difference between past and current behaviors was that he had been more able to respect personal boundaries in the past. His inhibitory functions were obviously breaking down. She was terrified by how he would "go off" at apparently minor frustrations, and she described several of his catastrophic reactions. He was "not the man I married." She was so frightened of him that she had taken guns he owned and left them, without his knowledge, at a pawnshop. She kept her handbag and car keys close to the exit door of their house so that she could leave hurriedly if necessary.

In treatment she began to see him as in no acute distress and not a tormented, "sick," or irreversibly disordered man. Since she knew through experience that it was impossible to motivate him to get help (or to be compliant with treatment), she experienced some relief and an ability to consider personal options. While she understood that some of his erratic and embarrassing behaviors might be unintentional, she now believed that many of them were at times intentional. After all, she told him repeatedly that certain of his behaviors were very upsetting to her, and he would not agree to make any effort to reduce or eliminate them. Her changed understanding of her husband lightened her chronic sorrow. The author referred her to an attorney who was also a registered nurse, an unusually well-qualified resource for this client. She learned her legal rights and how to protect them. Somewhat deceptively, she was able to move him out of her bedroom. She saw this accomplishment as providing a little relief, "but no solution." Since violent episodes increased, and since she had a different perception of his condition at the time, she moved toward more internal congruence regarding divorce.

This woman carried a heavy burden for many long years, and her body was telling her this through tension headaches, uncontrollable crying "over nothing," and periods of great discontent, anxiety, and sleeplessness. She had planned to live out the rest of her life with this man, and she had hoped for love and companionship. She feared the prospect of living her remaining years of life alone. She realized, however, that staying with him was paradoxically creating more loneliness for her. For example, since her own adult children did all they could to avoid him, she gradually experienced greater separation from them and more isolation and loss of important human contact. Her connections with friends consistently dwindled over ten years. This situation was very distressing to her and constituted an important secondary loss.

In this case, a shift in interpretation of the loss resulted in clearer understandings, based on factual evidence, that allowed her to assess the loss in ways that afforded less self-imposed (as well as other-imposed) entrapment. Her previous interpretation was made primarily in terms of her feeling responsible (though inadequate) for a person who was helpless to change disruptive and frightening behaviors that he would not have intended if he were in his "right mind." Her revised interpretation was that her husband had a serious, longstanding personality disorder, that he cared very little for her feelings, and that with gradual loss of inhibitory functions his true nature was coming out. She incorporated in her perception issues of intent or voluntariness as well as some degree of potential reversibility on his part if he were genuinely motivated.

Considerable variability in responses is evident for both self- and other-loss. While this variability results from multiple factors, it is the individual interpretation of the loss that may be the most salient in determining overall adjustment and coping. For example, it appears that, despite the trauma and the enormity of the destruction and loss that have been visited upon Christopher Reeve, he has remarkably prevailed. Only Reeve himself can know the depth of his chronic sorrow or whether it exists.

Still Me, his book published in 1998, reveals minimal evidence of deeply pervasive and established grief. In it he does, however, describe his process of becoming aware of what his life is now and will be in the future. Elements of this description indicate early responses of chronic sorrow. If, as it seems, he has managed to delay the onset of chronic sorrow, the following factors are suggested: (*a*) The self-loss has occurred in the context of a richly rewarding and self-actualizing life that includes unusual and diverse personal accomplishments, his children, and a life partner who is steadfastly devoted and resilient, (*b*) his dream of walking again some day and his work toward this goal for himself and others are based on beliefs that he deems to be realistic, (*c*) he has a fundamental appreciation of the value of life itself, and (*d*) the early, definitive responses of his wife, Dana, reestablished the bedrock on which his new life could be built. Precisely at the time when he first understood the seriousness of his condition, Dana acknowledged his right to choose for himself whether to live or die. She pledged her support and her love, and she validated his identity as enduring and unchanged. Speculatively, it is quite likely that at this tremendously vibrant crossroads, Reeve was in a trancelike state, and interpretations of reality came from a source of impeccable trust. His resonance with Dana at that moment rang true, confirmed that his essential self had not been lost, and revealed a way to go on.

As for chronic sorrow and suicide, this author's clinical opinion is that persons with self-loss are much more likely to commit suicide than those who are coping with other-loss. Those with self-loss are better able to justify the decision to end their own lives (for example, on the basis that they cannot continue to be a burden to others). For those with other-loss, justifications tend to be more complicated and difficult. At times, the author has asked clients who are experiencing chronic sorrow due to other-loss to complete a questionnaire designed to assess suicidal risk. All of these clients have produced extremely elevated ratings indicative of high risk. These clients, without an exception, have disclosed suicidal thoughts during their therapy. Some have stated that they have thought about it frequently for many years. Some have voiced the fantasy of taking both their own and their loved ones' lives. The expressed wish is "to be done with it all" and "to be free." The "stopper" is expressed as being unable and unwilling to abandon their child, spouse, sibling, and so on. The fear of what will become of the person for whom they are responsible should they die (in whatever manner) is extremely persuasive. The idea of causing the death of the loved one in order to be free to take one's own life is seen as the ultimate betrayal of the other. The action would be the antithesis of what has given a central meaning to the life of the caregiver. It is one thing to assume a right to take one's own life and quite another to assume a right to take another's, especially when the other cannot participate in even the most minimal of consents.

One client, indulging in suicidal wishes for escape and accessing considerable gallows humor, described how she wanted her grave site. The stone marker was to read: "Here Rests . . . She Is Responsible No More." Another client, astutely insightful, had been caring for her child with severe mental retardation and autism for more than 30 years. She had managed to persist in a sensitive, loving, and devoted manner. She had effectively managed, despite recurrent clinical depression. At one point, she confided, "I hate this depression and how dark my internal life becomes. But I also think I need it. I need to go flat and not feel much and to have my darkness. I think my depression wants me to be free." However, the perceptual reality for these clients coping with other-loss is that, no matter how difficult, there is no choice but to function and to care for the loved one with severe impairments. The "no choice rule" applies equally to suicidal thoughts and feelings. There is no permission for suicide. For the caregiver, the following paradoxes apply: (*a*) "The thing that drives me to suicide is the very thing that prevents me from doing it," and (*b*) "The one who drives me crazy is also the one who keeps me sane." Clinical experience regarding the issue of suicide and chronic sorrow, whether due to self- or other-loss, stands mostly alone and points toward the need for research in this important area.

☐ Real Loss and Loss of Fantasies

Josselson (1992) states: "The desire to possess the idealized other is the core of romantic love" (p. 132). She cites, as typical of romanticized idealization, Romeo's love for Juliet and his perception of her as "perfect." The expression of romantic love mobilizes the greatest hope of possessing and internalizing the idealized other. Romantic attachments may, therefore, be largely made up of fantasies we hold about the other. These fantasies lead to self-enhancement through closeness to or "ownership" of the other. They can also lead us to access our own creativity and strength and to mitigate our anxious feelings of inadequacy. As Josselson notes: "Idealization, then, is a relational process fraught with danger as well as possibility. While the idealized other enlivens the self, it requires the ability to admire without too much envy and to be vulnerable without too much shame" (p. 133). Even in relationships where idealization has been to some degree relinquished, we have fantasies about the other, about the relationship, and about the shared future.

When other-loss involves a person who has been idealized, there is a loss of elements of that other that are both real and fantasized. The future we dreamed about is no more, although it never, in fact, actually existed. The replacement future is unwanted, feared, and in varying degrees unacceptable. When the experience of other-loss involves any significant other who is central in one's life, the loss is of what would have been or what might have been, if only in one's dreams. On the one hand, shattered dreams can bring forth extraordinary inner resources, so that it is possible to feel strengthened, resolute, and in touch with previously unknown courage; on the other hand, loss of dreams may be reflected in bitterness, anger, and longing because one has been cheated. Dreams do not die easily or well, if at all. More often than not, in chronic sorrow one is forced into an almost untenable position: letting go of unrealistic dreams and images of how things should be now and should be in the future is experienced as disowning a part of a cherished identity. Since what has been cherished has been a unifying element, releasing it takes an effort of will. The effort is painful and feels so wrong that the experience seems like partaking in some sort of atrocity.

Our children are often the repositories and conveyors of our idealizations, our hopes for completeness, and our dreams and aspirations for the future. If we have developed a personal identity that includes having a child, we have spent most of our years dreaming about that child and the central role he or she will play in our life. We have assumed a close and greatly valued relationship with an imagined child. We may also have fantasies about how the child will deepen and augment our relationships with our partners or spouses and how both partners will experience the miracle of the resulting life. When the child at last comes into the world, and we recognize immediately or soon thereafter that the child is severely impaired, the loss is not so much about the child we actually have; it is about the child we have dreamed of. This situation does not imply that we do not accept and love the child we have, as most of us are able to do this. Most love the child with all their hearts. What is unacceptable is the serious impairment and how it has ruined our fantasies of a healthy, normal child who will have a full and happy life.

In times past (and even in times present) the need for "acceptance" has been seen by many professionals as the *answer* to dealing with the traumas and losses in having a child who is severely disabled. Olshansky's (1962) view differed, and his words about "acceptance" are prescriptive. He writes:

> The reality faced by the parent of a severely retarded child is such as to justify his chronic sorrow. When the parent is asked to "accept" mental deficiency, it is not clear just what he is being asked to do. The great stress professional workers tend to place on "acceptance" may suggest to the parent that he is expected to perceive his child from the point of view of the professional helper. This expectation may make him both resentful and

resistant. In our clinical experience, we have seen relatively few parents so neurotic that they denied the fact that the child was mentally defective. We have seen relatively few parents who did not recover enough, after the initial shock of discovery, to mobilize their efforts in behalf of the child. It is understandable that some parents move slowly and erratically toward recognition of the mental defect and toward meeting the child's special needs. Some of them even "regress" to the point of denying, at certain times, the reality of the child's defectiveness. On other occasions they become unduly optimistic about the child's potentialities. In our view, such regressions may help the parent to tolerate better the terrible reality that confronts him each day. . . . Why does the professional worker become so impatient with the parent's slowness or occasional regression, and why does he feel such a great sense of urgency to do something about it? After all, the parent has a lifetime in which to learn to deal with the needs and problems of a mentally defective child. In most cases one can ask what will be lost if the parent is unable for several years to view his child as mentally defective. (p. 191)

It would be almost unthinkable to expect a parent to accept serious impairments of a child who is so embedded in hopes, dreams, wishes, and fantasies. When parents do not accept the impairments, they can then focus on something to fight and to ameliorate. Much of the energy that is expended in helping the child may come from the response of nonacceptance of the serious disorder or impairment, and this energy may be needed to meet the challenges that lie ahead. It is out of this energy derived from nonacceptance that creative innovations in treatment and technology have developed. We can let ourselves imagine what the world would be like without such efforts to change the "unchangeable" and thereby conjure very grim images of hopelessness, passive acceptance, and utter defeat. It is through nonacceptance that we explore, through formal research and laborious trial and error, ways in which the dreamed-for other or dreamed-for self may be—if even minutely— restored to us. It is through refusal to accept the loss of fantasies that we find ways to make our own lives and the lives of others the very best they can be. It is also in this way, at least for some, that what is so impossible and menacing when the loss is first discovered is gradually transformed into the realm of possibility.

It is from the spirit of nonacceptance that many voluntary coalitions have emerged. People with similar losses and excruciating grief have banded together to rechannel their collective grief into a positive force for societal reforms and have thereby transformed their grief into potent consensual actions. One example, among many, is the emergence and establishment of Mothers Against Drunk Driving (MADD). Having loved ones suddenly and senselessly severely injured, disfigured, and permanently disabled or killed was so unacceptable and so traumatic that a creative drive to stop drunk driving was kicked into the very highest gear.

People respond to serious life crises with considerable variability. According to an interesting theory formulated by Klinger (1977), a person initially responds to heavy obstacles or to a seriously threatened loss of a goal (dream/fantasy) with increased effort and intensity of concentration. The aim of affecting the outcome may occupy most of the person's thoughts. If there are no positive results after prolonged and sustained efforts to achieve an outcome, the person will begin to abandon the pursuit. It is at that juncture that a "depression phase" occurs. This depression phase, in Klinger's incentive-disengagement theory, is a normal part of the response pattern. Several important implications emerge from this theory: (*a*) Clinging to the vision of "fixing it" or to the belief that the original dream of the future can yet be realized, in whole or in part, may be beneficial for some length of time in both self- and other-loss. Keeping enough of the fantasy alive, at least in the early years after the loss, may postpone incapacitating grief responses that could interfere with effective coping with major reality demands. (*b*) People who are actively attempting to cope with a major life crisis may be especially vulnerable to the effects of any additional problems or disappointments or to anything that might precipitously undermine the fantasy. (*c*) Maintaining the belief that one can favorably influence important outcomes may circumvent major depression or complicated grief. And (*d*) Support is especially indicated, and perhaps crucial, at the time of detachment from the incentive (fantasy) when the "depression phase" occurs.

Wortman and Brehm (1975) have theorized that the greater the initial expectation of control, the more controlling and intense a person will become before giving up and *the more depressed he or she will be afterward.* However, individuals who do not expect to be able to influence the situation will become depressed without experiencing the initial period of energized focus. Dweck and Wortman (1980) have speculated that "helplessness effects" such as depression may stem not from the uncontrollability of the situation but from how the situation is interpreted. Williams and Koocher (1998) have noted that in chronic or life-threatening illness, the response of a patient or family member to loss of control is highly complex. They have defined a health locus of control as "the set of beliefs that an individual holds about personal influence over the course or outcome of an illness" (p. 325). They identify three possible belief sets: (*a*) internal locus of control, (*b*) external locus of control, where the outcome is controlled by powerful others, and (*c*) external locus of control in which chance alone is believed to determine outcome. Rolland's (1987) work on family illness paradigms is referenced whereby the individual who believes the cause of the disease to be random and the outcome to be influenced by personal control is differentiated from the individual who believes the cause to have a strong element of personal responsibility and the outcome to be dependent on chance.

The author has speculated that, in general, suicide is more likely for those experiencing self-loss than for those confronting other-loss. As has been implied above, perhaps the highest risk may come at the time of disengagement from the incentive to restore at least a portion of what has been lost. The variability of causal attributions and locus of control are important factors in areas of stress and coping. The strength of the human spirit in many cases of self-loss surpasses any expectation. A professional acquaintance of the author's, a young woman in one of the medical professions, was well on her way toward actualizing many of her life fantasies when she was involved in a terrible motorcycle crash that resulted in spinal cord injury. She endured the trauma and the immediate aftermath fairly well. She showed great and consistent determination to "make the best of it." After many months of "unnatural cheerfulness," she began to realize that her condition was most likely going to remain permanent and severe. She then became despondent and preferred "actual dying to this kind of living death." She blamed herself for having been such a risk-taker and referred to herself as a "stupid example of the motorcycle syndrome." She was suicidal at times and despairing that she did not have the means or the ability to kill herself. She feared her husband would abandon her since she had "broken the marriage contract" in which she was to travel the world with him and to have several children.

About four years into her dramatically revised life and identity, she began to appreciate all the things she had learned and experienced. She now claims her life and sees herself as a much wiser person. Her husband has been loyal in every way, and she describes their relationship as deeper and more intimate. She has regained her self-esteem. Although her physical impairments are quite severe, her master's degree has enabled her to return to work. She works part-time in an administrative capacity and takes great pride in her ability to continue functioning as a health professional. She is no longer the athletic, confident, vivacious, and independent woman she once was. Her health is fragile, and her mobility is so compromised that she must plan well ahead to work out a way to go even a short distance out of town. She inhabits a small physical world. Interestingly, her husband (a man from the Middle East) reports that since the accident their marriage has been better. His fantasies and dreams of marriage and of being a husband are more consistent with their current lifestyle in which she is very dependent on him. He does an excellent job of caregiving, and he is tenderly supportive and sensitive to her needs. He describes his caregiver role as his "privilege."

And he is no longer threatened by "this wild, independent, American woman."

Self-loss, just as other-loss, involves both real loss and the loss of dreams, futures, and fantasies of the self in process of development. The idealized self is lost as surely as actual, key elements of the self are lost. Self-loss can also involve positive replacements and revisions in fantasies about the self and the self in relation. One of many examples can be found in Andreasen and Norris's (1972) interviews of severely burned patients. While many of these burn victims were depressed, some could see their losses as helping to make them "better people." They saw their experiences as "a trial by fire" or as a "purgatory through which they have passed, having proved themselves by surviving" (p. 359).

In summary, continuing loss can be interpreted in many ways. Some of the salient variables to be considered are: whether the loss is of parts of the self or of a cherished other; the degree to which the loss is real or fantasy; when and where the loss is perceived on continua of temporality, reversibility-irreversibility, and controllability-uncontrollability; the individual meanings of the loss; the degree of trauma experienced; and personality variables of the individuals experiencing the loss.

4

Living with Chronic Sorrow

Most of what is accessible about the lives of those experiencing chronic sorrow is found in nontechnical writings and several retrospective studies. These include personal narratives, plays, movies, novels, and fictionalized accounts based on actual cases. Data-based research studies are usually short-term and "single-shot," focused on quantifiable and discrete responses. While the available research is informative, it often does not, and cannot, provide a sense of what it is to live with chronic sorrow. After all, it is not designed to describe an entire lifetime of day-to-day coping with ongoing loss. Chronic sorrow cannot be adequately understood by looking at cross sections, at freeze-frames, and at certain age ranges or characteristics. Nontechnical formats, on the other hand, provide material that is strongly integrative and richly dimensional. It portrays the complexity of the human condition in its abundance. It provides a view of life as it is lived and people as they evolve, always in process of being and becoming. Chronic sorrow often relates to entire lifetimes. Some days are good and rewarding and balanced. Some days are tragic and depleting and destabilized. It is the subjective experience of these days that cannot be deciphered from currently available research.

☐ Personal Accounts

Mullins (1987) has examined 60 books written by parents about their experiences raising a child with severe impairments. She classified the impairments as (*a*) sensory problems (blind and deaf), (*b*) emotional

69

problems (autism), (c) cognitive problems (brain injury, Down syndrome, schizophrenia, mental retardation), (d) speech and language disorders (aphasia, dyslexia, speech problems), (e) health problems (brain tumor, colitis, cystic fibrosis, degenerative brain disorder, heart disease, hemophilia, Hodgkin's, leukemia, lymphohemangioma, organ transplant), (f) neuromuscular problems (cerebral palsy, epilepsy, hydrocephalus, muscular dystrophy, orthopedic deformity, osteogenesis imperfecta, scoliosis, spina bifida), (g) multiple/severe, and (h) various. Mullins considered the narrations in these 60 books as "the most authentic voices among us." The authors represent a wide variety of life circumstances; they are mothers and fathers, adoptive and foster parents, single parents, parents with large families, nonprofessionals, professionals in health fields, minorities, and they have diverse religious philosophies and orientations. A very small number of the books were written in languages other than English. A small minority also related to children with potentially fatal diseases, such as leukemia, cystic fibrosis, organ transplant, degenerative brain disorder, and so on. Mullins notes that the number of books on a subject does not always reflect the prevalence of the disorder, citing spina bifida as an example of a common birth defect about which few parents have written.

Mullins identifies four recurrent themes in this literature. She refers to them as (a) realistic appraisal of disability, (b) extraordinary demands on families, (c) extraordinary emotional stress, and (d) resolution. Resolution does *not* refer to the end of parental grieving. She defines resolution as "final judgment." Since most of the authors had written from a perspective of many years or a child's lifetime, she looked for the conclusions the parents drew.

As for the first theme, "realistic appraisal of disability," Mullins found, in general, that the books provide clear and honest appraisals of what it is like to live with a disability. Some books included valuable information about child development and a number of useful techniques for coping. As for the theme "extraordinary demands on families," many of the books pointed to a general nonrecognition by others (including professionals) of the scope of the challenge of living with disability. One example cited (Siedick, 1984) is a description of unrealistic and optimistic responses by others to a son's life on a kidney-dialysis regimen. The procedures, in fact, affected and took their toll on every family member.

Many parents were creatively coping with the disability, and most described themselves as "better people"; they felt they had been rewarded because of their challenges. Mullins also observes the "real picture" to be one of extraordinary and depleting demands on family and individual resources. Some parents described almost unbelievable professional insensitivity, poor quality of care when the child was hospitalized, and apparent medical indifference to the suffering of the child. Parents also reported eternal gratitude for the times when they were sensitively and caringly dealt with by medical and other professionals. Writings were also about lengthy and difficult efforts to secure appropriate services, conflicts with "the system," and dealing with irrational and arbitrary criteria for inclusion in programs.

Parents described severe marital conflicts and inordinate stresses on relationships. These stresses and conflicts often led to a breakdown of family support. A notable example is provided by Pieper (1976) who reported that when she gave birth to a son with spina bifida, her mother-in-law's first reaction was: "You have burdened my son for life." Siblings were reported to experience stress as well, and some worried about becoming parents. They were anxious about the possibility of carrying defective genes.

The theme "extraordinary emotional stress" may be the most relevant to chronic sorrow. All 60 books described intense emotional ambivalence and anguish at having been "singled out." Some parents, despite rational recognition that they were not at fault, described torturing themselves with guilt and blame. Some deplored the uncertainties of the future and realized they had no choice but to learn to live with extraordinary fear. One couple, the Massies (1975), noted that living with constant fear and dread of the unknown "does strange things to the personality" (pp. 173–174). A future of lifelong dependency of their child and the consciousness of never having the freedom that other parents eventually enjoy was described as a cause for envy and sadness. Parents generally found it better not to plan too far ahead. Physical and emotional demands were often referred to as negatively affecting the health of the mother. Many parents felt they were on a "different road," alienated from the rest of society. They felt they did not "fit in" any more; they were forced to live in a world that was nonsupportive and barely understood them.

The theme "resolution," which expresses the "final conclusions" of the authors, is especially interesting. These so-called conclusions ranged from the very pessimistic and bitter to feelings that life had been enriched and made more meaningful. The parent of a son who was severely autistic indicated that he would have preferred the son's not living since the quality of his life was so poor. Another author (Park, 1982) posited that if she were given the choice of accepting or refusing her experience, she would accept it, since out of that experience has come "an unimagined life."

When Pearl Buck (1950), the acclaimed novelist, wrote about her daughter, who was severely mentally retarded, she noted how difficult it was to write a true story. After a very long time she had finally resolved to write her story, to offer a partial answer to parents with a child like hers about how to "bear the sorrow of having such a child" (p. 5). Her conclusion about the sorrow is expressed in this way: "Endurance can be a harsh and bitter root in one's life, bearing poisonous and gloomy fruit, destroying other lives . . . sorrow fully accepted brings its own gifts. For there is an alchemy in sorrow. It can be transmuted into wisdom, which, if it does not bring joy, can yet bring happiness" (p. 5).

Buck wrote of her awareness of having loved her child long before she was born. She told of the first time she and her little girl saw each other and how pretty and wise the baby appeared. Buck began to worry about her when she had not begun to talk by age three. She did begin to talk later, but only a little, and she was slow to walk. It was after Buck adopted several children that she realized how different this little child was. (A careful reading of her narrative gives the impression of a child who is autistic as well as severely retarded.) Buck sought consultations with many experts of the time and was given many false assurances and inaccurate assessments.

Buck's daughter was eventually placed in a residential facility in the United States. (She was born and lived several years in northern China.) There were very few options available to parents before the 1960s. Buck is very clear in her advice to parents about what to look for and what not to accept in planning for their children in the 1950s. As for the chronicity of sorrow, she wrote:

> We learn as much from sorrow as we do from joy, as much from illness as from health, from handicap as from advantage—and indeed perhaps more. Not out of fullness has the human soul always reached its highest, but often out of deprivation. This is not to say that sorrow is better than happiness, illness better than health, poverty than richness. Had I been given the choice, I would a thousand times over have chosen my child sound and whole, a normal woman today, living a woman's life. I miss eternally the person she cannot be. I am not resigned and never will be. Resignation is something still and dead, an inactive acceptance that bears no fruit. On the contrary, I rebel against the unknown fate that fell upon her somewhere and stopped her growth. Such things ought not to be, and because it has happened to me and because I know what this sorrow is I devote myself and my child to the work of doing all we can to prevent such suffering for others. (pp. 57–58)

When Autism Strikes, edited by Robert Catalano (1998), is a compilation of narratives written by the parents of children who were developing normally for the first several years of their lives until they began to exhibit severe developmental regression. The little that is known about these cases of childhood disintegrative disorder (CDD) (or Heller's syndrome) indicates that the children's level of functioning usually drops to much lower levels than in classical autism. Representative quotations from these parent narratives follow:

> Several thoughts come to mind as I reflect over the past two years. One is how grateful I am for the support I had at the beginning of Aaron's disorder. . . . Slowly over time, though, I think people get tired, and their support fades. I do not blame anyone for that. When something like CDD strikes your child, it is not only your child who changes; you do also. I no longer have the time, nor the interest, in anything or anyone but Aaron. People who incessantly complain about trivial matters annoy me. Those stressed at selecting wallpaper for their kitchen have no idea what a real problem is. The one good thing that has come of Aaron's illness is that it helped me discover what is truly important in life. (Day, 1998, p. 88)

> A depression had slowly pervaded my outlook and I stopped worrying about death. Life seemed close to impossible and should my life have been taken, I would not have complained too loudly. It surprised me, but never did I consider suicide. . . . At present, I wanted to drop the apparently impossible challenge of bringing up a child who was impossible to control without constant one-on-one supervision, a child who showed little affection or even acknowledgment of me as a mother, a child who, despite our best efforts at behavioral therapy, continued to regress. The huge management problems associated with David's illness had knocked me over and it seemed as though I couldn't get up. This new style of parenthood where the responsibilities are grossly magnified and extend through old age to death, coupled with removal of the joys, did not suit me. (Fairthorne, 1998, pp. 138–139)

Bonnie Dunn's (1993) retrospective study focused on the childhoods of nine adults who had been reared by mothers who were seriously mentally ill. Four of the subjects were men, and five were women. All were gainfully employed, with the exception of one who had been diagnosed with schizophrenia and was unemployed. There is very little in the literature about the experiences of such children from their own perspectives. Using a three-part semistructured interview, Dunn identified five themes. These are (a) abuse and neglect, (b) isolation, (c) guilt and loyalty, (d) grievances with mental health services, and (e) supports. She uses representative excerpts from her interviews to illustrate each of the themes.

As for the theme of "abuse and neglect," Dunn reports a wide range of experiences. As children, these individuals took on caregiving roles for the mother and often for younger siblings. Although occasionally supportive, fathers were generally unavailable emotionally or physically. One father had won custody of his children. Four were alcoholics. One male subject described never being bathed and wearing ragged clothes. He did not understand what bathing was and indicated that in the fourth grade he and his siblings would drink beer before going to school. One woman, in recalling the poverty experienced when she was 15 years old, described going to school and working to support the family. Late at night she would take four subways to get home. Another woman was locked in her room as a child because the mother was convinced that people were planning to kidnap her three children.

The theme "isolation" refers to peers, communities, and the family system. Eight of the nine participants reported that family members rarely acknowledged or explained to them the nature of the mother's illness or when, if the mother was hospitalized, she would return home. Since psychotic episodes were not explained, the children experienced a confused sense of their own reality and felt isolated within the family. Six participants recalled not inviting friends to visit because of the mother's behavior, and they were aware of being ostracized by the community. Despite their feelings of alienation and differentness from "normal" people, most of the subjects did reach out to others, especially to friends, friends' families, and teachers. All nine identified one or more persons as being supportive to them and as making a real difference in their lives.

The theme "guilt and loyalty" consistently emerged, although it was not a focus of the interviews. As children and as adults, most of the participants were very loyal to their mothers. One of the participants expressed a determination not to abandon the mother, admitting that the situation was sometimes intolerable. Loyalty conflicts emerged when there were child custody issues. Related to feelings of loyalty were the subjects' belief as children that they had either caused or contributed to the mother's illness. Even when they chose to leave the mother, they felt guilty about it. Survivor guilt also emerged, expressed as guilt at being healthier and more accomplished than their mothers.

The theme "grievances about mental health services" emerged for all but one of the participants. The exception was a woman who, as an adolescent, had participated in psychoeducational treatment with her mother. She had experienced empowerment as a result of learning how to cope with the mother's illness. In general, however, direct contact with mental health professionals was described as unpleasant, guilt-provoking, and harmful. Participants felt they had been blamed for the mother's problems. Interestingly, the family-systems approach, popular at the time the participants were children, was based on a belief that family interactions could cause mental illness in one of the family members and that the system "needed" the mental illness (Bateson, Jackson, Haley, & Weakland, 1958; Wynne & Singer, 1963).

As for the theme, "social supports," all of the participants had been helped by other adults in their childhoods. Being welcomed into the homes of friends where they felt safe and where they could participate in "normal" families provided comfort and an alternative reality. Supportive contacts were more often initiated by adults, but the women in the study actively sought out support, while the men were more passive in this regard. Neighbors' and extended family's treatment of the mothers as outcasts led to self-imposed isolation by participants. Acknowledging the mother's mental illness also led to participants feeling disloyal and guilty. As adults, eight of the nine went into therapy.

Nancy Mairs (1986, 1989) has had a remarkable ability to write about self-loss and her life as a "cripple" with MS. She has candidly described her initial response to the diagnosis in *Remembering the Bone House*. She refers to the diagnosis as a "sentence" in which she will "lose and lose and lose: energy, strength, musculature, coordination, control of my bladder and bowels, eyesight, sensation" (p. 241). She acknowledges that her MS is the chronic, progressive form that "moves in only one direction. Even the little I have will ultimately be taken away" (p. 241). She further writes: "I submerge the grief I feel at my uncontrollable fate beneath a greed for bodily experience that leaves me feeling, for a couple of years, like an electrical storm spitting sparks of sexuality almost randomly in all directions" (p. 241). She goes on to mention her many infidelities, which tended to consume large amounts of psychic energy but very little time. Her husband, George, only finds out about her affairs when he has read what she has written about them years later. By then they have become so fused that the "affairs shrink, shadowy and desiccated as neglected house plants" (p. 244).

As Mairs loses interest in sexual encounters, her poetry also "fizzles," and she begins to spend most of her time and energy on her teaching and working on a Ph.D. At this time, Mairs writes:

> . . . some truths about MS are seeping through the denial my febrile sexuality once served. My body is going away. . . . Suddenly, life stretches out again before me, longer than it's ever seemed, crowded with alarming possibilities: wheelchairs and diapers and electric beds and nursing homes. George got yoked to this future. . . . It leaves me feeling sorry for George for having had the ill luck to marry me. (p. 247)

Although George later considers leaving her and returning to his roots in New England to "start over," he stays with her as the children leave home to be on their own. Mairs describes herself as becoming weaker and weaker, yet she also notes moments of great satisfaction that she has become "somebody," a real writer with published books. These moments of satisfaction, fulfillment, and happiness are transient, but she realizes that, as her physical space contracts, she has them to remember.

Much more recently, in an article on Mairs by Haederle (1997) appearing in the *Dallas Morning News*, Mairs speaks of her marginalization in a world of able-bodied persons who mostly treat her as invisible. She further laments that she has become the woman she thought she could never bear to be. As for other-loss, her husband describes his uncomfortable ambivalence as his wife's primary caregiver. He describes his role as being both the most rewarding thing he does and the hardest. As Nancy Mairs's strength continues to wane, and following many years of considering suicide, she has now apparently embraced her life. She credits her more ready acknowledgment of the inevitability of death for everyone as responsible for her current, more joyous life. The finiteness of her life makes her determined not to ruin it.

Maggie Strong's (1989) writing about being the well spouse of a man with MS is also informative. Her experience of other-loss is articulately described. She uses her experience as well as that of others to illustrate how the partnership changes. One change is reflected in the perception of time by the partners. As she describes it, the well spouse may be bound to a much longer perceptual future, while the spouse who is ill may cope on a day-to-day basis.

Strong describes a kind of schism in acting (on one hand) and thinking-feeling (on the other). She has observed that there is a tendency, in other-loss, toward one or the other during protracted crisis periods. While some may focus on all the minutiae of caregiving, arranging, planning, and keeping the family going with as much precision as possible, others may immobilize themselves with obsessive thinking. In the former case, there tends to be a blocking of emotions and cognitive processes evocative of painful feelings; in the latter case, there tends to be a blocking of actions. Some might report being numb and physically on the brink from constant exertion, while others complain that they can't seem to "get a grip." She describes one man as stating, "I can't do a damn thing; I just think about my wife all the time."

Included in Strong's account is a chapter "The Chronic Emotions." She groups these emotions into three clusters. She designates the first cluster as "mostly sadness" and includes in it (a) sadness, (b) guilt, (c) trapped, (d) loneliness, (e) jealousy, and (f) annoyance. Some of the things Strong mourns for are (a) her former lighthearted self, (b) the ability to be dependent and sometimes indulged, (c) her reduced or lost sexuality and the dilemma that ensues when intimacy and desire remain while the partner's ability to engage in full sexual activity is lost, so that a perpetual longing develops on both sides of the partnership.

The second cluster, designated as "mostly anger," consists of (a) anger, (b) isolation, (c) boredom, and (d) humiliation. Strong writes:

> Annoyance moves . . . into anger. Jealousy or competition make continual
> domestic war. Loneliness grows into an encompassing isolation; the illness

mushrooms to cover everything; economic decline provides the pincers for the squeeze from outside that completes the picture. The emotions of Cluster #2 spin the well spouse far away from the sick. (p. 113)

When financial resources bottom out, there are many opportunities to feel humiliation. Strong indicates that it is the joint humiliation that may bring the well and the ill spouse together, although there may be a time when the well spouse guiltily desires to dissociate from it.

The third cluster, "mostly collapse," includes (*a*) fatigue, (*b*) depression, (*c*) anxiety, and (*d*) a sense of being overwhelmed. Strong sees this cluster as normal for the well spouse. She describes faltering under the workload, not getting enough sleep or rest, loss of self-esteem, and loss of hope. Cumulative sadness and disappointments (and the expectation of more of the same) lead to a predominant mood. This mood becomes less flexible and less subject to change. She states that in these circumstances fantasies of double suicide are not disturbing at all. She writes openly of her own anxieties and of those of others she knows who feel the loss of a certain trust in life. For her, the anxiety stems from the sense of having no active team members. Feeling overwhelmed occurs when one is aware that all possible solutions are exhausted.

Eventually, as one's life continues to shrink, Strong indicates that many readjustments are necessary to find meaning in what is left. She stresses the importance of support groups and friendships. With the help of friends and family, one of Strong's strategies was to rent a very low-cost office away from home where she could go to write. She makes cautionary statements about therapy and gives permissions to "dump" any therapist not meeting basic requirements. Interestingly, one of these requirements is the ability to laugh, reasoning that laughter is the flip side of crying. If a therapist cannot laugh, she may not be able to understand the depression and the inevitable sorrow. Strong's work to facilitate the formation of support groups for the well spouse and her accounts of the experiences of the well spouse are useful. The range of expression of MS is highly variable, however, and it is important not to overgeneralize.

Strong describes her humiliation as originating in the depletion of financial resources. Hal Kirshbaum (1991) has written on the theme of humiliation from the viewpoint of self-loss. He is a family therapist, an activist for persons with disabilities, and he speaks from his own experience as a person coping with a progressive, disabling, neuromuscular condition. His disability occurred when he was well into adulthood. He describes the changes in self-image and family as immense, indicating that the old image of oneself is lost just as surely as one's abilities are lost. The family loses patterns that have become familiar, predictable, and important sources of structure and stability when the disabled person is no longer capable of being and doing what he could before. He understands how cultural norms impact self-concept. Since there is such a high value on self-reliance, autonomy, and independence, shame and humiliation can result from the need to depend on others. He speaks of the various ways in which the able-bodied community denies full humanity to those with disabilities, alludes to the internalization of ridicule and of being treated as inferior, and describes how persons with disabilities often participate in their own humiliation.

Jean-Dominique Bauby (1997), who was the editor in chief of the French *Elle* magazine, has authored a small and extremely sensitive and articulated work, *The Diving Bell and the Butterfly*. His wording is amazingly precise. Bauby suffered a cerebrovascular accident to his brain stem in December 1995. The result was "locked-in syndrome," which occurs when the patient survives the stroke but is then imprisoned within his paralyzed body while his mind remains intact. Bauby, who died just two days after the French publication of his extraordinary book, described his existence as being held captive within a large, invisible diving bell. What hearing remained was distorted and often painful. He could blink his left eyelid, and this was his only means of communication. This is how he managed to write his profoundly moving book. Laboriously and patiently, with the help of an assistant, he indicated which letter of the specially arranged alphabet would come next by blinking his eye.

Bauby has described awakening from his 20-day coma as "drawing nearer to the shores of awareness." He would not be told the extent of his impairments until several days later, and he clung to the certainty that he would fully recover in due course. His mind was busy with many projects, such as writing a play and a novel, travel, and inventing and marketing a fruit cocktail. But the time came for him to face reality. He describes this occasion as graduating from being a patient whose prognosis was uncertain to an official quadriplegic. This is the time when he also made the transition from the bed to the wheelchair. He writes:

> My caretakers made me travel the length and breadth of the hospital floor, to make certain that the seated position did not trigger uncontrollable spasms, but I was too devastated by this brutal downgrading of my future hopes to take much notice. They had to place a special cushion behind my head: it was wobbling about like the head of one of those African women upon removal of the stack of rings that has been stretching her neck for years. "You can handle the wheelchair," said the occupational therapist, with a smile intended to make the remark sound like good news, whereas to my ears it had the ring of a life sentence. In one flash I saw the frightening truth. It was as blinding as an atomic explosion and keener than a guillotine blade. . . . (pp. 8–9)

Bauby's ability to live so fully in his mind and his determination to do so are made evident in his composition of *The Diving Bell and the Butterfly*. He organized memories and translated them into new meanings, and he engaged in magical, fantastic journeys and forays. He had a magnificent and mordant wit. His internal life and humor shine brightly in his piece about Empress Eugenie.

After his stroke, Bauby lived in the naval hospital at Berck-Plage, near Calais. In the main hall of the hospital is a stained-glass window depicting Empress Eugénie, the hospital's patroness and wife of Napoleon III. Bauby often developed fantasies in which he joined her retinue or had wonderful conversations with her. He describes one of these interchanges as:

> . . . She ran her fingers through my hair and said gently, "There, there, my child, you must be very patient," in a Spanish accent very like the neurologist's. She was no longer the empress of the French but a compassionate divinity in the manner of Saint Rita, patroness of lost causes.
>
> And then one afternoon as I confided my woes to her likeness, an unknown face interposed itself between us. Reflected in the glass I saw the head of a man who seemed to have emerged from a vat of formaldehyde. His mouth was twisted, his nose damaged, his hair tousled, his gaze full of fear. One eye was sewn shut, the other goggled like the doomed eye of Cain. For a moment I stared at that dilated pupil, before I realized it was only mine.
>
> Whereupon a strange euphoria came over me. Not only was I exiled, paralyzed, mute, half deaf, deprived of all pleasures, and reduced to the existence of a jellyfish, but I was also horrible to behold. There comes a time when the heaping up of calamities brings on uncontrollable nervous laughter—when, after a final blow from fate, we decide to treat it all as a joke. My jovial cackling at first disconcerted Eugenie, until she herself was infected by my mirth. We laughed until we cried. The municipal band then struck up a waltz, and I was so merry that I would willingly have risen and invited Eugenie to dance, had such a move been fitting. We would have whirled around miles of floor. Ever since then, whenever I go through the main hall, I detect a hint of amusement in the empress's smile. (pp. 24–25)

Bauby has described his physical and emotional pain and his coping by accessing his beautiful mind, so full with memories, sensations, creativity, and magic. Using his great intellectual complexity and emotional depth, he determined to live fully in his mind and to stay in touch with himself and life around him. He went the distance without corrupting his mind with dark and permanent bitterness and anger. He felt great joy and deep sadness. Both polarities were described in relating to his two young children. He found an advantage in being able to cry without anyone else knowing since others assumed only that his eye was watering.

Although Bauby's account does not include a lengthy life of chronic sorrow, it does highlight the importance of early decisions and motivations in dealing with impairment. In the initial aftermath of his disastrous spinal cord injury, Christopher Reeve (1998) made a commitment to live. This decision has sustained him. He has succinctly disclosed the daily, arduous routine of his life, and he has touched on some of his emotional responses to his self-loss. He states: "People ask me what it's like to have sustained a spinal cord injury and be confined to a wheelchair. Apart from all the medical complications, I would say the worst part of it is leaving the physical world—having to make the transition from participant to observer long before I would have expected" (p. 271). He then says that "to have it all change and have most of it taken away at age forty-two is devastating. As much as I remind myself that being is more important than doing, that the quality of relationships is the key to happiness, I'm actually putting on a brave face. I do believe those things to be true, but I miss freedom, spontaneity, action, and adventure more than I can say" (p. 272).

Reeve describes his early image of rehabilitation as slowly climbing hundreds of steps upward into the clouds and reaching the top. During the following two years, he says, "I had to learn to face the reality: you manage to climb one or two steps, but then something happens and you fall back three. The worst of it is the unpredictability" (pp. 273–274). He describes his adjustments in part as follows:

> I was told by so many "experts"—doctors, psychologists, physical therapists, other patients, and well-meaning friends and family members—that as time went by not only would I become more stable physically but I would become well adjusted psychologically to my condition. I have found exactly the opposite to be true. . . . Psychologically, I feel I have established a workable baseline: I have my down days, but I haven't been incapacitated by them. This doesn't mean, though, that I accept paralysis, or that I'm at peace with it. The sensory deprivation hurts the most. . . . The physical world is still very meaningful to me; I have not been able to detach myself from it and live entirely in my mind. . . . I'm jealous when someone talks about a recent skiing vacation, when friends embrace each other, or even when Will plays hockey in the driveway with someone else. (p. 274)

Reeve describes his responsibility as a father and as a husband. He does not want to cause Will to worry about him, and, he reasons, "what kind of life would it be for Dana if I let myself go and became just a depressed hulk in a wheelchair? All of this takes effort on my part, because it's still very difficult to accept the turn my life has taken, simply because of one unlucky moment" (p. 277). He applies his skill as an actor to his life and sees no other way to survive but to live in the present. "How do you survive in the moment when it's bleak or painful and the past seems so seductive?" (p. 277).

Billy Golfus's (1994) videotape, *When Billy Broke His Head*, presents self-advocacy within the ranks of America's 43 million people with disabilities. Golfus, an award-winning radio journalist, has brain damage and very limited use of his left arm and leg as a result of a motor scooter accident. When he awoke from a coma, his "body and spirit were broken." He describes his struggles with the state vocational rehabilitation agency and his discouragement when, after more than eight years, there had been not even a single job interview. His disability is primarily invisible; therefore, he states: "Part of the fun of being brain-damaged means convincing other people that something's wrong." Difficulty in counting change, significant memory deficits, and losing things he can't name are examples of his impairments. Living a life of applying for services, being denied, and appealing the decision is a source of much wear and tear. "They give you forms they know you can't fill out." (One woman reports that she must verify her blindness every year, although nothing has changed for over a decade, nor will it.)

Billy Golfus returned to school to obtain his master's degree. Despite his difficulties with memory and concentration, he completed the program, only to discover that he was still unable to obtain employment. To get his mind back, he used the computer to write a journal of how helping systems stand in the way of persons with disabilities getting what they need. He documented isolation, segregation, and negative labels by going on the road to meet people with disabilities in various sections of the country. He captured a spirit of activism and the civil disobedience that preceded the passage of the Americans with Disabilities Act, and he discovered new, empowering definitions to replace such negative definitions of people with disabilities as objects of charity, helpless victims, drains on society, and so on. He suggested that persons with disabilities empower themselves by identifying themselves as a part of America's largest political minority. Anger is justifiably the dominant emotion expressed in Golfus's videotape. A scene in which he goes to the government's disability office to appeal a "spin down" in his benefits epitomizes the frustrations of a life of dealing with bureaucratic decision makers. Since he has finally managed to find a way to make $500 per month, two-thirds of his benefits have been taken away. The agency staff person explains how this is done through a series of calculations that Golfus, because of his brain damage, cannot comprehend. All he knows is that he does not have enough money to live on.

This videotape captures the struggle for an enfranchised identity following a life-changing injury. It is an excellent vehicle for understanding the effects of social stigma in the lives of people in America who are trapped by governmental rules and legislated poverty. It presents the ground upon which the Us/Them dichotomy is maintained and how the obstacles to inclusion operate to demean and to further injure those with disabilities.

☐ Fictionalized Works

Many fictionalized works have been based on actual cases or case composites involving ongoing self- and other-loss. These works, including novels, plays, movies, and televised programs, often provide valuable insights into living with chronic sorrow. Movies such as *My Left Foot, Flowers for Algernon, The Elephant Man* (also produced as a play), *Lorenzo's Oil, Born on the Fourth of July,* and *Passion Fish* and made-for-television movies such as *Teacher, Teacher* and *Family Pictures* have been important because they foster vicarious experience in the audience, thereby evoking empathic recognition of chronic sorrow. A part of the empathic understanding that results is increased tolerance or acceptance of a very diverse—and sometimes bizarre—coping repertoire.

In *Family Pictures* (1990) from which the television movie was made, Sue Miller chronicles 40 years in the life of a fictional family, the Eberhardts: mother Lainey, an artistic and emotionally intense woman; father David, a cool-tempered psychiatrist; and their six children. In birth order, from first to last, the children are Macklin, Lydia, Randall, Nina, Mary, and Sarah. Randall has autism. His effect on his siblings and his parents is profound.

Parents David and Lainey cope very differently. As Lainey puts it (to David): "The problem is, you and I are working with two different definitions of responsibility" (p. 257). Lainey is much more intensely ambivalent, self-blaming, absorbed with and devoted to Randall. David has affairs, is often away—physically and emotionally—from the family; he is more rational, sarcastic, interpretive, and more effective in crises. He moves out of the house to get away from the stress and to continue his affairs.

As an adolescent, after Randall has become frustrated and upset one evening, he shoves his mother down the stairs. Her head strikes the newel post, and she bleeds profusely and is unconscious for a few minutes. The younger daughters are terrified and call their father for help. It is at this point that Lainey admits that she "can't do it any more." They find a residential facility in another state for Randall—no small task.

Lainey makes the trip to visit Randall on a regular basis. David goes less often, and the siblings visit even more infrequently and more sporadically. Mack is rebellious and has a very turbulent relationship with his father. David moves back into the house, and he and Lainey attempt to salvage their marriage. By now they have very different perceptions of their history together, and their previously shared dreams have become so distorted by betrayal, pain, and heartbreak that they again separate.

It is Nina who takes an interest in photography and who collects the family pictures. It is she who attempts to construct the perfect family that can be concretely corroborated through archival images. And it is

Randall's death that brings the now-scattered family members physically together again. Randall's death is a shock to everyone. He was hit by a car while on an outing with other residents when he impulsively broke away from the attendants and ran into the street. The siblings are able to do some reviewing with each other of their memories of Randall and the family, and each is able to relate from a more adult perspective with the parents. It is only with Randall's death that some "unstuckness" and healing begins.

Some of the siblings subsequently make changes in their lives. One marries, and Mack rejoins the world from which he had isolated himself by living on a farm in Vermont. Lainey and David live together again for a while, and this time Lainey decides to end the marriage. David moves out, and Lainey puts the house up for sale. David resists and isn't ready to give up the marriage. Slowly, however, the "engine of their marriage" stops. In the third autumn after Randall died the marriage is over.

Lainey becomes involved in painting sets for a theatre company and takes an apartment in New York, where Nina temporarily lives with her. David remarries. Lainey is accused by Nina of not wanting to try to make the marriage with her father work. Nina also tells Lainey that Randall is the only one who got unconditional love from her. Lainey explains that she couldn't just close over the past the way David wanted to, and she didn't have the strength to give to David what he wanted from her. As for Randall, an anguished Lainey says that she wished she had been able to love him unconditionally.

> That's the only kind of love I ever wanted to feel. The other kind . . . who would want to feel that, unless they *had* to? . . . I know I wasn't a good mother. . . . There's no excuse. But I loved you all so much. Couldn't you feel it? At all? It had so much more of *me* in it. It had all of me, in all my terrible weakness. The other kind. It asked too much. It was too hard. Maybe it used up too much of me. But I gave you whatever I had. (p. 470)

David explains things differently to Nina. He states that after Randall died he just wasn't up to a high-pitched type of life with Lainey. He didn't have the power to draw Lainey back into a life with him. "Perhaps what it is is just that Lainey has no gift for what Freud calls 'normal misery'" (p. 466).

Miller presents a brilliant insight about three-quarters of the way through *Family Pictures*. Macklin is telling his mother about a dream he has had about Randall. In the dream, Mack sees Randall walking past the old house.

> He walks right past me. I'm on the front porch. . . . I called to him, but he didn't stop. So I ran and caught up with him and grabbed him. . . . I was tremendously excited, touching him. Not surprised at all, you know, just

happy. And he was looking at me with his same face, but it was, like, intelligent. Normal. And I said, "Don't you know me, Randall? I'm your brother. It's me. I'm your brother, Mack."

. . . His eyes got just very tender and concerned. And he reached over and touched my face and he said, "But what *happened* to you? What's wrong? You look so worn out." I realized he didn't know me because I was older, older than I'd been. I'd aged. And he thought it was . . . a disease or something. Anyway, that seemed funny to me; I actually laughed, in the dream. And then I said to him, "I've been alive . . . that's all." And he looked so sorry for me, like he was the one who pitied me. When I woke up I didn't remember it. But I was just so . . . glad. I knew something good had happened. . . . And then I remembered why, that I'd seen him again. That he'd talked to me. That he was all right. Cured. (p. 344)

When Mack shares with Nina his telling of the dream to Lainey, they both find Lainey's response outrageously funny, as Mack imitates perfectly Lainey's eager inflection as she says: "'Oh, what did he *say*?'" (p. 345). Nina realizes how different her parents' reactions are. Had Mack told David about his dream, David would have understood it to mean something about Mack and to serve as a clue to Mack's thinking about himself and about himself in relation to his brother. Lainey, however, was ready to believe that Mack had brought her "her first meaningful words from Randall's lips" (p. 345).

Peter Nichols's play, *Joe Egg* (1967), was first performed in Glasgow as *A Day in the Death of Joe Egg*. It opened in 1968 in New York, starring Albert Finney, and had a successful run. It was subsequently made into a movie and was reasonably successful; over the years, the film has been shown at film festivals sponsored by drama and arts departments of universities (for example, Southern Methodist University).

Clive Barnes (1968) reviewed *Joe Egg* for the *New York Times* and referred to it as provocative and moving, as "not a comfortable evening" but "very much worthwhile." The play focuses on the relationship between Bri, a schoolteacher in Bristol, and his wife, Sheila, as they attempt to deal with their 10-year-old daughter Josephine, who is, as the Viennese consultant declares, "a vegetable." Joe has uncontrollable convulsions and is virtually unable to see, move, or talk. She drools and makes guttural noises. Sitting propped in her wheelchair, she flops spastically and has occasional convulsions.

Bri and Sheila have developed an interactive pattern in which Bri gives vent to corrosive, bitter humor, and Sheila plays his games in order to soothe him. Bri refers to God as a "manic-depressive rugby footballer" in a monologue of jokes. Sheila placates him. They both understand that he is "spoiled" by his overindulgent mother and that his immaturity is an additional burden for Sheila, who is a sort of nurturing earth mother.

They act out absurd playlets in their attempts to cope with their "living parsnip." Asides and soliloquy are used, with the audience playing the role of a mass marriage counselor.

Sheila imagines her promiscuity before her marriage resulted in her being the cause of Joe's problems. Bri contends that "the doctor botched it . . . it had nothing to do with how you'd lived or whether there was a nut in the family" (p. 28). Bri mimics the Viennese pediatrician who first pronounced Joe "a vegetable." "Vell, mattam, zis baby off yours has now been soroughly tested and ve need ze betts razzer battly so it's better you take her home. . . . Keep her vell sedated you'll hartly know she's zere" (p. 35). Sheila asks why Joe's hair has been shaved off, and Bri (as the doctor) explains, "Zis vos a liddle biopsy to take a sample of her brain tissue," to which Sheila smiles and expresses relief since "I thought at first you'd bored a hole in her skull to let the devil out" (p. 35).

Bri and Sheila explain how they've given Joe dozens of personalities down the years. Sheila tells the audience that, when they were admitted to the freemasonry of spastic parents, they found that Joe had even less character than the other children, so they began to make them for her. She also shares her hopes for Joe and how she had thought Joe was actually trying to reach for something at one time; then Joe had a series of grand mal seizures and was very sick and almost died. When she recovered, she no longer had any "spark." That was when Bri lost interest in Joe, although secretly Sheila still tries to engage Joe.

The play includes friends who offer gratuitous solutions, such as adoption and getting Bri's sperm count checked so they can have another child who will be normal. Sheila responds to the suggestion with "Two children instead of one." Bri remarks, "She won't like it, Mum." Sheila says, "She likes to rule the roost, Dad" (Nichols, 1967, p. 56). The friends then suggest institutionalization, which Sheila and Bri attempted in the past but could not bring themselves to carry out. The friends point out all the wonderful therapies that would be available to Joe in an institution, such as speech therapy. Bri says, "Better not tell *her* that, eh, Mum? She thinks she's very *nicely* spoken. One thing she does pride herself on" (p. 56). Sheila thanks the friends for trying to be helpful but says that she'll have to take care of Joe as long as she lives or until she herself dies. The prospect that Joe might outlive Bri and Sheila had not been considered by the friends. When there is a medical crisis, Bri plans to move out of the house while Sheila is with Joe at the hospital. His ambivalence blocks him so that the plan becomes a failed attempt.

The play portrays a mixture of stark reality and denial. Both parents keep their fantasies of a normal child alive in a way that is both torturing and absurdly, bitterly humorous. They continually live and act out the dream of the idealized child, while simultaneously coping with the reality of the child they actually have. This type of coping can be a step toward increased adaptation, but Bri and Sheila seem to stay stuck in their oscillations and are prevented from going beyond the impasse toward an integrated realization that the child they wanted and fantasized about does not and will not exist. *Joe Egg* was a drastic departure from conventional drama in the late 1960s. Some theatergoers "just didn't get it." That it ran for any time at all surely means that there were some universal meanings, fears perhaps, that pressed for some sort of social expression and confrontation. This author offers her suggestion that *Joe Egg* might have been a type of counterphobic intervention for some people who experienced it.

Carrie Brown's (1999) novel *Lamb in Love* is a finely crafted story of two lifelong acquaintances living in a small English village at the time of the first walk on the moon. Vida Stephen has been the lifelong caregiver of Manford, a boy with mental retardation and mutism who has now become a young adult. Manford's father is an architect who is greatly in demand internationally. He specializes in churches and cathedrals. Manford's mother died when he was born, and his father moved from the United States to England, settled in the village of Hursley, and hired Vida to care for his son. Over the years, the father spends less and less time at home, and Vida has sole responsibility for mothering a child who cannot speak. She is in every way, except biologically, his mother. The author describes Vida's worries, her fears, her constancy, and her love for Manford. During 20 years of rearing Manford, and now in her 40s, Vida has missed out on opportunities (for travel, for moving away, for frivolities, for love affairs, and so on). Norris Lamb is the postmaster for the village. He is the village church organist and a stamp collector. He has not had much experience in courtship, and he is a 55-year-old bachelor.

Brown is exquisitely insightful regarding Vida, Manford, and Norris, and she realistically describes the unfolding of Manford's developmental delays, the search for reasons, and hopes for improvement. When Norris takes real note of Vida, he is smitten with her and falls deeply in love with her. He sees her as a genuine person and senses her courage and her bravado. He sees her fragility and loneliness as matching his own. His attempts to get close to her and to let her know he loves her are fraught with awkwardness and blunders. The bridge between Vida and Norris is Manford. When Norris first meets Vida and Manford on one of their evening walks, he says, "It's funny . . . I've never seen you walking in the evenings." Vida says, "Well, that's because we're invisible, Manford and I." The author continues, "She expects him to laugh, but his face has grown quiet, and she sees that he understands the truth of this, that people in a bright room at night can't see out the windows. In fact, what you see if you look out is only your own face staring back at you. It's not a fiction, not a fancy, she realizes. They *are* invisible, she and Manford, passing along the street in the darkness. No one ever sees them. It's as if they weren't there. 'Come on, Mr. Lamb,' she says then, and reaches for his hand across the long space of the air between them. 'Come along with us. Perhaps you'll be invisible too'" (pp. 190–191). Norris begins to join Vida and Manford in their walks, and he becomes attached to Manford. When the feelings between Norris Lamb and Vida Stephen become mutual, they must consider what is best for Manford, and Vida can now share responsibility for his care with Norris.

At the end of the book, Brown describes Norris's thoughts about Vida:

> Norris sees that it is her great sympathy that has made him love her so. Her list-making and storing of provisions, her vigilance through so many nights over the boy's common colds and more, over his whole lifetime of brave, failed endeavor, her exorcism of bats and spiders and other children's cruelties, the thousand times she's thrown a ball or held his hand or soaped his back or trimmed his hair, the way she adjusts the spoon in his hand, the flower in his lapel, his hat against the sun. The way she fits herself up against him at night and holds him, loves him. Loves him. That's it. That's her reward, her privilege. She loves Manford. (p. 289)

☐ Critical Stress Points

There is general agreement that, during the lives of persons coping with chronic sorrow, there are predictable times of increased stress and exacerbation of grief responses. Wikler (1983) has identified ten critical stress points for parents of children with mental retardation. Five of these stress points relate to developmental milestones, that is, the ages at which parents would or could (if only their child were normal) expect the child to accomplish certain skills. These stress points are (*a*) walking, (*b*) talking, (*c*) going to school, (*d*) the onset of puberty, and (*e*) the child's twenty-first birthday. The five additional stress points are uniquely associated with parenting a child having significant impairments and include (*a*) initial diagnosis, (*b*) the greater developmental progress of younger siblings, when the child's deficits are more apparent, (*c*) consideration and discussions about placing the child in a residential facility, (*d*) seizure or other significant health problems, and (e) discussions and planning related to guardianship and care after the death of the parents. Stress points are often experienced as new realizations of the extent of the loss. Traumatic responses of shock, acute grief, and numbing at the time of recognition of the mental retardation have been well documented. Stress points are often the impetus for periodic resurgence of acute grief responses, and they may precipitate a crisis requiring reassessment and additional adaptations. During intensification of grief at stress points, the mediating role of the fantasy of how things should be or could have been is not well understood due to lack of research.

A master's thesis by Robarge (1989) in the field of nursing reflects the perceptions of caretakers of children with Duchenne muscular dystrophy. Robarge studied 15 mothers of children registered in a muscular dystrophy clinic. The mothers described their reactions at the time of diagnosis, and they reported episodic grieving related to developmental milestones and losses. Their pain and sorrow were chronic, and the intensity of their responses was not time related. Lazzari's (1983) doctoral thesis in the field of special education describes her study of 15 mothers of children with multiple handicaps, eight special education supervisors, and seven special education teachers. Using 12 developmental crisis points, all subjects validated the presence of chronic sorrow in the mothers (as opposed to time-bound grief). Significant differences in the three groups' perceptions of maternal distress occurred at only two crisis points: (a) management of a crisis unique to the child, and (b) the onset of puberty. The educators and teachers overestimated the mothers' distress at the onset of puberty and underestimated their distress related to management of a crisis unique to the child. The crisis points found to be highly distressful by all groups were birth/diagnosis, discussion of placement outside the home, and discussion of guardianship.

Krafft and Krafft (1998) have authored a parent narrative specifically describing chronic sorrow and chronicling their experiences as parents of a son with profound mental retardation. Their son Bryan is now an adult. The Kraffts refer to their "sadness without end" and to their life-time of losses. They point out that recurring periods of sadness are pre-cipitated by life events and by internal thoughts. They also clarify the nature of chronic sorrow by stating, "Our personal experience. . . is not . . . a permanent state of despair and pain but rather . . . a dark emo-tional 'cloud' that can quickly appear at times of crisis or when missed milestone events trigger more intense sadness" (p. 63). They describe their resurgence of grief when they drove with their other children, and without Bryan, to be with extended family the first Christmas after their son had gone to live in a residential facility. Other times of increased sadness include his birthdays, special family events, and each Christmas. They state, "There have been no opportunities to share in the milestones that a healthy child experiences, such as college graduation or a wed-ding" (p. 63).

Little is known about critical stress points for those with self-loss, and research is very much needed. For both self- and other-loss, however, stress points requiring the management of crises uniquely related to the nature of the loss (for example, obstruction or infection of the ventricular shunt in cases of hydrocephalus or other neural tube defects) can usurp large amounts of energy. These particular stress points and the distressful resurgence of grief that they engender are endemic to chronic sorrow. They are unpredictable, episodic, and draining, usually mandating decisions and action, and they compete with other priorities of living. They differ from stress points in other types of grief and bereavement, where stress points are nearly always predictable (anniversaries, certain holidays, and so on), and where they can be anticipated and prepared for. Although they may be very upsetting, stress points and emotional resurgence in grief and bereavement relative to death or finality rarely require crisis management, that is, urgent and critical decision making and actions.

☐ Victimization Anxiety

Anxieties regarding victimization are rarely discussed and virtually never considered in the literature. Only recently has an intersection occurred between the crime victims movement and the disability rights movement. The available data support this intersection. Obtained from information contained in Jane Sigmon's (1999) chapter in the curriculum prepared by the Office for Victims of Crime, U.S. Department of Justice, National Victim Assistance Academy, the following findings are listed: (a) Recent research (Sobsey, 1994; Cusitar, 1994) has consistently shown that women with disabilities (regardless of age, race, ethnicity, sexual orientation, or class) are assaulted, raped, and abused at a rate two times greater than women without a disability. (b) The risk of being physically or sexually assaulted for adults with developmental disabilities is four to ten times higher than it is for other adults. (c) Offenses motivated by disability bias are documented in the FBI's Uniform Crime Report (FBI, 1998). (d) At least 6 million serious injuries occur each year because of crime, resulting in either temporary or permanent disability. (e) Estimates from the National Rehabilitation Information Center indicate that as many as 50% of patients who are long-term residents of hospitals and specialized rehabilitation centers are there because of crime-related injuries (Tyiska, 1998). (f) Research by the National Center on Child Abuse and Neglect (NCCAN) in 1993 found that children with any kind of disability are more than twice as likely as children without a disability to be physically abused, and are almost twice as likely to be sexually abused, and of all children who are abused, 17.2% had disabilities. And (g) in a national survey (Young, Nosek, Howland, Changpong, & Rintala, 1997) it was found that women with physical disabilities were more at risk for abuse by attendants or health care providers. Other recent reports generated by state-level victims rights organizations have referred to the high rates of violent and criminal victimization of people with developmental and other substantial disabilities, including mental retardation, autism, cerebral palsy, epilepsy, traumatic brain injury, severe major mental disorders, degenerative brain disease, permanent damage from stroke, and others. They have also referred to underreporting of these crimes and to the low rates of prosecution and conviction.

Most assuredly, these data barely scratch the surface. Since the beginning of time, persons with disabilities have been prime targets for exploitation and abuse by anyone intent on finding a victim. At some level of consciousness, parents of children with major defects, especially autism and severe and profound mental retardation, worry about their children's vulnerability and the likelihood that someone will hurt them. When the child lacks the ability to communicate, parental concerns about abuse are even more warranted. Those with self-loss also have realistic fears of being harmed when their disabilities are visible and when they are unable to defend themselves. These fears are an ever-present fact for significant numbers of persons with chronic sorrow. They are a prominent feature of the inevitable anxiety that is so much a part of chronic sorrow.

The following quotations are taken from an article that appeared in the *Dallas Morning News* on August 29, 1998, reported by the Houston Bureau (Nichols, 1998):

> A New Jersey man said to have the mind of a child was lured to Texas by a woman who stole his Social Security money, then helped her son and four friends beat him to death. . . . A jogger found the severely beaten body of 59-year old Louis "Buddy" Musso in a ditch. . . . He apparently had been abused for weeks. . . . The fatal beating apparently occurred at the friends' apartment, said Assistant Chief Robert Pruett. . . . The victim broke a Christmas ornament there, and "they were punishing him with belts, baseball bats and combat boots . . . he was literally beaten to death over several days."
>
> Ms. Basso, a security guard, is accused of pilfering Mr. Musso's Social Security checks. Police were investigating evidence that she may have taken out a $50,000 insurance policy on his life. . . . At some point Mr. Musso accidentally broke a Mickey Mouse ornament. The son told police that Ms. Basso frequently "disciplined" Mr. Musso with nightsticks and handcuffs when he had accidents. They forced Mr. Musso to crouch on his knees with his face to the floor while they beat him. . . . The beating went on for several days but . . . stopped on Tuesday, when the suspects put Mr. Musso in a bathtub and cleaned him up with disinfectants. "While he was still alive they poured Lysol and Clorox in the water . . . with all those open wounds.". . . An autopsy will determine whether Mr. Musso died of the beating or drowned in the tub. Mr. Musso's niece telephoned police from

Virginia . . . because Ms. Basso had told her that Mr. Musso was missing. Ms. Basso later filed a report with police.

The sequence of events made officers suspicious, and they brought Ms. Basso and her son in for questioning. The son finally told police what happened. . . .

The niece told police she was alarmed when her uncle left an assisted-living home in Cliffside, N.J., and went to Texas with the expectation of getting married. She said she talked to him by phone several times and tried to persuade him to return. . . .

Police said they found evidence that Ms. Basso and her son had been abusing Mr. Musso for weeks. They found blood spatters on baseboards and a bloody sheet at Ms. Basso's home. . . . A neighbor told police he saw Mr. Musso recently with a black eye and bloody shirt and asked whether he could help. The neighbor "asked him if he wanted to call police or an ambulance and he said, 'No, she'll beat me again.'". . .

On February 15, 1998, in Arlington, Texas, Amy Robinson was kidnaped as she rode her bike to a new job at a grocery store. Amy was 19 years old. She was mentally retarded. She was missing until March 3, when Robert James Neville (age 24) and Michael Wayne Hall (age 19), both Caucasians, were arrested as they tried to enter Mexico. On television, they voluntarily confessed to the kidnaping and murder of Amy. They bragged and smirked. They espoused white supremacist beliefs. They reported that they were drinking wine coolers and cruising the streets of Arlington while talking of their plans to kill someone of another race. They spotted Amy on her bike, and they recognized her because they had briefly worked with her at the same grocery store. Amy was not of another race, but her disability marked her as an unacceptable human being. They knew it would be easy to persuade her to go with them because she trusted them. They took her to a secluded field where they joked with her and then proceeded to use her for target practice as she tried to run away from them. They shot her with arrows and then with a pellet gun, and they recounted how they had laughed at her. They then mortally wounded her with several shots from a .22 caliber rifle. They left her in the field but went back to see her body a few times in the ensuing days. They referred to the killing as "just a thrill killing," done for the "Adrenaline rush."

Community support for Amy Robinson's family quickly emerged. A memorial fund was established. Her grandmother, Carolyn Barker, who had reared Amy for most of her life, was the primary family spokesperson. The defendants, in separate trials, were found guilty and sentenced to death. Their bravado and arrogance receded, and Mr. Neville admitted that what he had done was wrong. Before sentence was passed, he had stated that he wanted death. Afterward, he changed his mind and stated he wanted to appeal the sentence and have it changed to life. Mr. Hall read the Bible, found Jesus, and asked the family's forgiveness. Early in the year 2000, Amy's grandmother brought suit against Amy's stepfather, Ben Grogan, when it was discovered that he had used at least $14,000 of Amy's memorial fund for his own purposes. He has admitted that he has not used any of the designated money for Amy's funeral expenses.

John Callahan (1990), the cartoonist and writer, has a corrosive and "sick" humor. He has a profound appreciation for the absurdities of life and the human condition. He is also a quadriplegic and a recovering alcoholic. His cartoons and his writing come from his resilient spirit. In *Don't Worry, He Won't Get Far on Foot*, Callahan recounts his life, his spinal cord injury, his alcoholism, and his struggles to make it on his own. His struggles have included the following:

> The trouble is, I'm not very good at being a poor person. I lack some of the necessary skills and abilities. For example, once I moved into Section 8 government housing, so I could get a rent subsidy. I had been getting a $40 "exception" for my rent, which meant I could keep that much more of my SSDI payment each month, because I needed a ground-floor apartment within a certain distance of grocery and drug stores. Now my total rent fell to only $112 a month, a big advantage.
>
> I noticed that quite a few of my fellow tenants in the government housing were wearing ski masks. That made me apprehensive. Sure enough, as soon as word got around that the new tenant was a cripple, neighbors started dropping by for a chat—and to shop for anything that might be lying around loose. They stole my stereo, my TV, my VCR, and undoubtedly would have taken my wheelchair had they known how to fence it. An able-bodied poor person would have been able to reciprocate, perhaps by carving the neighbors up with a straight razor. I lacked the necessary dexterity. (p. 177)

The above cases require no comments. Fears related to potential abuse, in both self- and other-loss, are addressed primarily through denial, suppression, and displacement. These fears are situationally activated. A lifetime of coping with such fears is exactly that—a lifetime. Fears worsen when the disability worsens or when aging caregivers and guardians become unable to assume full responsibility for their loved one and must plan for the person's care following their deaths or their own disability.

☐ Author's Observations

I appreciate having nontechnical literature and personal narratives available relating to chronic sorrow. These resources can be very helpful to professionals and to those who, in their own attempts to cope with this reality, may find a way to wrap their feelings and dilemmas in some form of cognitive understanding. In the living of a life that is often characterized by the mind's avoidance of traveling too far into the future, this type of literature can foster taking the longer view. As the mother of two incredibly impaired daughters (Karen, who died at age three, and Valerie, who is today a young adult), I can relate very well to the literature reviewed in this chapter. It supports my own center and ground regarding difficult issues. The following few paragraphs provide my own truncated parent narrative, including brief comments on life markers, triggers, and attenuation of affect.

I have frequently grown weary and irritable (and have had mean thoughts) about people who are unintentionally intrusive. This intrusiveness may only be an ordinary, innocent question: "Do you have any children?" A life can contain *so many* of these intrusions when one is forced to deal with ongoing loss. Once, and once only, my response to the question was, "No, I don't." I did not feel like going through the explanations about either of my children with anyone. Within an hour of that interaction, however, I felt intensely guilty for having denied the existence of my children. Not only had I been deceptive, I felt I had committed a betrayal of the very ones I love the most. I will not make this error again.

Weariness ensues from a litany of typical questions and comments. When people have learned that my child is severely retarded and autistic, they almost invariably ask about etiology. I tell them that, although we can now identify hundreds of causes of congenital defects, my child falls into the remaining 75% of "unknowns." I have repeatedly responded to the question "Is she Down's?" I sometimes conclude that all they (the "normals") know about is Down's. Most of the time I am then asked if I have any other children. This question continues to baffle me, although at the time I am asked, I sense that I am being asked to reduce uneasiness in the questioner. I have contemplated responding with "Oh, yes, we have a son who is Phi Beta Kappa like his father. He's at Harvard. But we really don't like to talk about him." I continue still to be asked whether my husband and I had ever thought about adoption. While suppressing an urge to scream, I have wanted to respond with "Why, no! What an amazing idea!" or "Do you really imagine that adopting a child would have fixed my daughter?"

When my daughter Val was a young child, I often avoided—at any cost—the possibility of being with people who had normal children. This avoidant behavior voluntarily isolated me from the world. There have also been times when I have stuffed my vulnerability and assumed responsibility for "educating the public" about developmental disabilities. I have not persisted in this mission in a consistent way, as I have intermittently needed to withdraw to protect myself, to reenergize and gather my resources. I have sometimes "played dumb" with people, simply to avoid prying questions and insensitive comments. I have allowed (and mostly tuned out) gratuitous "information" and lectures about people such as myself. This type of behavior is intended to be protective, but it is also nonauthentic and can lead to a destructive envy and contemptuousness of "normals." When I am with a group of people and no one knows me, I am scrupulously silent about my children. By remaining silent when the subject of mental retardation or other human anomalies comes up, I learn how others really think and feel about people with severe disabilities. I offer the following examples.

As an undergraduate, in my very first class in social work methods, the assignment was to visit one of the social agencies in the area, conduct an interview with the director or program supervisor, and present findings to the class. The class was large; there were about 75 students. One member of the class had visited the Child Study Center. She was presenting her impressions and the information she had gathered when a small group of three or four began to talk to each other and to laugh. The professor asked the group if there was a joke they wanted to share with the class as a whole. One man replied that there wasn't any joke, and the professor then asked what they were discussing that was so funny. The man replied, "Well, we just came up with the solution to the problems at the Child Study Center." The professor asked about this solution, and the man stated, "Build large ovens." Several other students thought this was indeed funny. Others were obviously uncomfortable. The professor did not confront these students, and the presentation continued. I regret that all I did was to get up and leave the class. Had I to choose my behavior again in similar circumstances, I would speak out.

Several years ago, I took a refresher course at a psychiatric hospital on the diagnostic manual. The psychiatrist teaching the course had covered several topics. When it was time to consider the diagnosis of autism, he opened with "Now, these are children whom their parents should kill and tell God they died." I was too stunned to move or to speak. At the same hospital, however, where I served in a consultant capacity, there was an admission to the adult psychiatric unit (where I worked) of a young man with schizophrenia. He was also moderately mentally retarded. When his case was first discussed in the unit team meeting, there were reports of his strange behavior and verbalizations. He soon became the focus of amusement for some of the staff members present. This time I found my voice. I said, "I'm just wondering something. I am wondering how we would feel if we were hearing this discussion and this man were our brother." As a result of hearing candid comments about disabilities, in whatever setting they occur, I have concluded that

I cannot be paranoid enough. Those who advocate for the rights of persons who are disabled should never become complacent.

Just as Bri and Sheila in *Joe Egg* had done, I have developed a caustic, twisted, and "gallows" humor. Unlike Bri and Sheila, I rarely express this humor, and then it is only with a good and exceptionally understanding friend, someone who knows my devotion to my child and whom I can trust not to denounce me or to be horrified. An example of "gallows" humor in reference to my daughter follows. An extremely elementary and short explanation of neurological development will precede the example as background.

It is now known that people with autism have a proliferation of neuronal cells, significantly more than is normal. In the embryonic development of the brain, epithelial-source cells migrate to the developing area of the brain. Neuronal cells are highly specialized and must be located in specific brain sites for normal functioning. When there are too many cells in a particular site (either the "right" kind or the "wrong" kind), there is a selection process, whereby huge numbers of cells are discarded. One theory is that only the cells that are able to hook up correctly or only those finding a supportive environment remain a part of the brain's structure. Whatever the process may be, it is imperative that cells end up in their appropriate locations, so that, for instance, retinal cells end up in the retina and not in the brain stem. Migration of source cells to their correct locations in the brain is key, and the selection process is mandatory for normal brain development. If there is a general overload of cells or if the cells are misplaced, the brain is poorly differentiated. There is mass confusion in the functioning of the brain since synapses are not making connections between cells that are compatible, coordinated, and coherent.

I was recently with a close friend, a clinical psychologist. I am comfortable enough with this friend to be entirely myself with her. The structure and development of the brain are not among her avid interests. My daughter had begun to regress, and my friend was being supportive as I was experiencing a deepening of sorrow and discouragement. After expressing these feelings, I quipped, "She has a migration problem." My friend was silent as she attempted to decipher this cryptic statement, and then she responded, "Does she have migration headaches?" We laughed hard, and I felt a release. "No," I said, "she *gives* migration headaches." My friend quickly asked, "Does she get an urge in the wintertime to go south?" To which I said, "No, not really. She went south a long time ago and stayed there." We were caught up in this dark humor, and we were attuned in an ambience of healing. This type of experience, shared with only one or two people to whom I feel especially close, is very comforting to me and serves to reduce stress.

Life Markers

Events marking transitional stages of life and functioning to organize one's recall of personal history are not so distinct for those affected by chronic sorrow. When they *are* distinct and notable, they often differ from normative patterns by being negative or painful. As described by Bauby (1997), his most dramatic life marker was his "graduation" from stroke patient with an uncertain prognosis to profound paraplegic. His life memory from that point forward would be organized into life "before" and life "after" that "graduation."

Rather than markers which format my own adult life around memories relating to my daughters' development, such as going to school for the first time, having first boyfriends, graduations, weddings, and so on, I have indistinct or often negative markers. The day Val was admitted to the residential facility was the worst day of my life, and I shall never forget it. There are no traditionally honored happy times. There was our trip to San Antonio when she was doing well (this was truly a grand milestone), and there was the time when she first began to swim and was so proud of herself. There was the time she was so cute and clever—though nonverbal—when she erased all the "Do Not Erase" areas of a blackboard in a classroom at the university where I had taken her for evaluation of her failure to develop language. Even so, circumstances in the lives of those with chronic sorrow often preclude normal organizational markers of memory and of life. We are clearly out of step. We are often less sure of dates of events than others. Time appears to be perceived differently. I refer to this dynamic in chronic sorrow as being *marker bereft* (as contrasted, I suppose, to being marker enriched). Our narratives may be "sketchier," and they may be less linear because of a severe lack of normative developmental markers. Time may not have the same relevance as a means of ordering life events in the memory and retrieval systems.

Triggers

Both expected and unexpected triggers can plague the lives of those with chronic sorrow. Triggers that precipitate sudden intensification of grief and a review of events associated with the trauma of the loss do not always have negative consequences. They may foster a review that leads to improved functioning in one or more areas. I have found that during the initial turbulence following the onset of the loss (which may last for several years), triggers may be largely self-induced, with or without intent. Rerunning sequences related to diagnosis or realization of the loss may be useful as a form of desensitization to traumatic events. Mentally reviewing the events is also useful for making sense of things in terms of explanatory cognitions and attributions, and for the development and revision of a personal narrative that may be centered in the life-changing loss. Although they invariably recycle almost unbearable pain, these self-induced triggers are attempts at mastery.

With experience, I have learned how to regulate to a large extent the trigger-induced resurfacing of my own encapsulated anguish. I visualize these intensely painful and near-overwhelming emotions as located in a container deep within me. I have never repressed these emotions. I am aware of their presence, their viability, and their source. The container is strong, flexible, and functionally well designed. There is an aesthetically pleasing quality about it. When my emotions are tapped and released, their powerful effects are reexperienced. I understand, even as I am inundated, that I can eventually manage to regroup these emotions and that they will again fit within the container. When their impact begins to wane, they begin to return to the container. At this time I have restored my influence over them. As they are nestled back into the container, I will again take notice of the container itself. It is especially well made, and the lid fits perfectly. But for all its excellence, it lacks a lock.

In some situations, I can prepare for an external trigger that will precipitate a deepening of sadness or an intensification of painful longing. At other times, often after a relatively long period of stabilization, a trigger may unexpectedly zap me and set me back for days or weeks. My daughter's annual planning conference at the residential facility where she now lives is a trigger, but I am able to prepare for it. I never miss this staff conference, as it is here that important goals are set, progress and health status reviewed, interventions selected, and living situation assigned for the forthcoming year. I realize that I will once again feel exposed as the history (however brief) is read. It will include my multiple pregnancies and Val's dead half sister and the congenital nature of Val's severe mental retardation, autism, and seizure disorder. I have managed to desensitize somewhat so that I am no longer retraumatized by this exposure, but I will have a flood of images that require some management.

An *unexpected* trigger was the high school graduation ceremony of my sister's adopted daughter. I was in a very good mood when I arrived for the ceremony. At some point during the handing out of diplomas, however, I felt light-headed and got a sudden lump in the throat. Then I realized—although I, of course, knew already—that this event would never happen for any child of mine, nor would there be *any* of the other normal life passages, with the possible exception of death. It is in this way that life markers for others can become triggers for those with chronic sorrow.

Especially troublesome as one ages is the experiencing of other people's life markers as triggers or potential triggers. These triggers are not usually evocative of extreme or acute distress, but they do activate pain and un-wanted sadness. If one's only child is severely impaired, there will be no developmental markers involving grandchildren. Grandchildren tend to be a major focus in the lives and conversations of most people who have adult children, especially senior citizens. Although it is not difficult to have and to share good feelings about others' grandchildren, the fear that ordinary contacts with contemporaries will generate triggers can create a tendency toward avoidance. Those of us with adult children who have significant disabilities continue to cope with the vicissitudes of our children's conditions and their needs for care and special services. We are worried about what will happen to our children when we can no longer care for them and—to the best of our abilities—protect them. When our age-mates are basking in their roles as grandparents and re-porting their grandchildren's development and positive "uniqueness," we are struggling with very different issues.

I do not begrudge my friends their roles and pleasures as grandparents, but I do admit to envious feelings and to a sense of alienation that I had hoped would dissipate by now. I cannot reciprocally relate to friends who eagerly share the news of the birth of a grandchild, who report on a grand-child's latest developmental milestones, or who present the most recent photographs for my admiration. So even now, I am still "out of step," and I am confronted with my differentness. I am aware that my differentness has positive valence and is a resource in my role as a psychotherapist with clients who are different, those who feel alienated from the mainstream (persons with serious deformities and visible disabilities, other parents of children who are impaired, those with gay or lesbian sexual preferences, people with HIV and AIDS, certain crime victims, and so on). Nonethe-less, a pervasive conflict or double bind has evolved; I can isolate myself from age-mates to avoid painful triggers or I can maintain and foster contacts, thereby submitting to triggers that are unpredictable, though frequent. With aging, a natural narrowing of meaningful relationships is inevitable since death becomes a more frequent visitor in one's circle of friends and acquaintances. This narrowing is augmented by the familiar sense of alienation that has often already permeated one's life and which may become even more intractable as one ages.

Attenuation of Affect

As for attenuation of affect, I believe this aspect of chronic sorrow is sometimes missed by professionals. Life just does not zing any more.

Emotional arousal and expression are blunted in any direction. One does not feel intensely and wonderfully joyful for very long, yet one can construct meaning, feel happiness, greatly enjoy aesthetic beauty, and deeply appreciate all the good things of life. Neither does one get terribly upset, disturbed or "strung out" for very long either. Sometimes I am aware of an incipient emotion or a space that it should occupy, and I wait for the full emotion to surface. For me, this pressure of expectation—of emotion in abeyance or suspension—often occurs in enjoyable situations or occasions that I have anticipated. Often this pressure of expectation is followed by a sense of muted or anesthetized emotion. This penumbral affective aspect of chronic sorrow may be functionally adaptive, but I miss being able to experience a real "high" and ride it for all it's worth. I also miss being able to cry and to wallow in sobbing emotion.

I think the apprehension and the wariness that develop with a living loss greatly influence affective states. Attenuation of affect is a defense against retraumatization. The screening of emotions so as to block thoughts and feelings connected to traumatic losses can limit the capacity for other feelings as well. Self-expression leads to an increased sense of vulnerability, and so crushing a loss leads to a fear of hope and of wanting anything for the self. But when we cut off our ability to suffer deeply—because it is too much and because we must manage the extraordinary demands associated with caring for the one who is lost—we also cut off our ability to feel ecstasy and joy.

It is well documented that trauma survivors often evidence emotional blunting, inundation, or a vacillation between these extremes (Herman, 1992; Horowitz, 1985; Litz, 1992). Losses involved in chronic sorrow are frequently introduced by trauma, which may be protracted as evaluation and assessment may take weeks to years. During this time, conditions may worsen, as in progressive neuromuscular disorders, organic brain diseases, MS, some spinal cord injuries, childhood disintegrating disorder, and so on. There is often no room for the expression of intense emotions, since the exigencies of the reality situation require strenuous coping and rational decisions. Many years may pass before it is pragmatically possible to process the traumatic events presaging the unending loss. After so long a time in which one has repeatedly circumvented or disrupted emotional expression, it is not surprising that a person emerges with attenuation of affect. Furthermore, leakage of emotion may become a signal to step up one's efforts at control.

Glover (1992) has conceptualized the "numb response" to be a psychobiologic reaction, representing an effort to diminish the psychophysiological experience of stress, and Horowitz (1976) has found that the numb response can become the most dominant characteristic of the chronically traumatized individual. One has only to view documentary films of prisoners in German concentration camps to appreciate numbing on a massive scale. Holocaust survivors have reported in various media their enduring loss of intense emotion. Cohen (1991) has reported that among survivors, feelings are so intense that they must be warded off by deadening oneself or by escaping into denial. It is immensely preferable to be dead than to feel the grief. Glover (1992) has listed terms used by traumatized persons, such as "shutdown," "numb," "ice cold," "hollow," "dead." In a study of 104 survivors of acute life-threatening experiences, Noyes and Kletti (1976) have found that half of their sample reported no emotion of any kind during the stress encounter, and the other half reported a dampening of emotions. Glover (1992) hypothesizes that emotional numbing is likely to become protracted in severely traumatized individuals because of their tendency to experience many of their life events as stressful and not within their control. This hypothesis explains why numbing is so frequently experienced as ego dystonic in that it may occur when it is no longer situationally appropriate. While these findings and hypotheses have relevance in many cases of chronic sorrow, additional theory development and research in neuroscience may shed more light on attenuation of affect in the future.

Living with chronic sorrow, though not a preferred lifestyle, can be a source of many rewards and unexpected pleasures. Survival, self-discovery, growth, and transcendence may be the yields and advantages of chronic sorrow. In both self- and other-loss, we are required to face facts, make choices, take actions, and ground our beings in a clear sense of self and a well-ordered array of priorities. Challenges are never in short supply. Meeting and resolving these challenges, making it through the peaks and valleys, and preserving a sense of humor speak volumes about the strength and tenacity of the human spirit. Many people never know the satisfactions that come from having a mission in life, but those with chronic sorrow know them. There are many avenues toward wholeness. The tragic losses, real and fantasy, that are the bedrock of chronic sorrow are not insurmountable. They help us plumb our depths, and they enlist our courage. They hone our skills and our creativity. We find our wholeness, though perhaps unrecognized by others, through integrated and keen awareness of who we are and what we have to do. We know what is trivial and what is important. We live closer to the self's essence.

There is aesthetic beauty inherent in all sorrow. Sorrow is all around us, whether it is wanted or not and despite selective inattention and the tuning out of sorrow's signals. Sorrow is part of the world and part of the human condition. Nature is filled with it. Bleak and harsh landscapes, gloomy days that are dark and overcast, torrents of rain and destructive weather, the natural selection process of predator and prey, in which one animal is sacrificed to feed another: all are examples of sorrow. Art forms that have endured many centuries tell us of past sorrows. Our most valued and affecting classical music evokes heartfelt and soulful sorrow within us. We immerse ourselves in this sorrow and feel the love, our own and the composer's, that is the companion of sorrow. Without love, how can there be sorrow? Without love, how can there be grief? Without love, how can life be lived?

5

Families, Loss, and Chronic Sorrow

☐ The Family Life Cycle

In contemporary Western culture, there are many variations in individual life cycles, and there are probably even more variations in family life cycles. The myth of Goode's (1963) "classical family of Western nostalgia" cannot apply to our postmodern family systems where individuals are moving away from relationships based on obligation and parental authority and where members make their own choices of their individual life paths. Therefore, the concept of a standard for the life span of the "normal family" is rapidly fading. Nonetheless, the family life cycle remains the primary context in which human development takes place. According to Carter and McGoldrick (1989), ". . . family stress is often greatest at transition points from one stage to another of the family developmental process, and symptoms are most likely to appear when there is an interruption or dislocation in the unfolding family life cycle" (pp. 4–5).

Since the 1960s several perspectives and schemas of the family life cycle have been proposed. A perspective of task-centered stages as suggested by Solomon (1973) has been useful as a framework for assessment and therapeutic goal setting. Emphasizing child rearing as the primary organizing factor, Duvall (1977) has divided the family life cycle into eight stages that are oriented to the arrivals and departures of members—marriage, birth, leaving home, death, and so on. A focus on

103

adult transitions for the couple over the life span is yet another way of viewing the family life cycle (Gould, 1972; Harry, 1976). Carter and McGoldrick (1989) have described six stages in the family life cycle: (*a*) launching the single adult from the nuclear family, (*b*) the addition of a new family subsystem through marriage, (*c*) challenges of parenthood, (*d*) adjustments accommodating adolescence, (*e*) the launching of children and the reordering of couple priorities, and (*f*) changes of later life. It is generally accepted that, as an organization, the family is unique in that its members (*a*) constitute an emotional and relational system that continues over a number of generations, (*b*) are generally unremovable and irreplaceable, and (*c*) assume a variety of roles and functions that change over time. The family life cycle allows for the addition of new members only through events such as marriage, birth, and adoption. Members leave the system through divorce, death, abandonment, and estrangement. Carter and McGoldrick (1989) have written:

> Although family process is by no means linear, it exists in the linear dimension of time. . . . Earlier work on the life cycle has rarely taken this complex process adequately into account. Perhaps this is so because, from a multigenerational perspective, there is no unifying task . . . if the life cycle stages are limited to descriptions of individual development and parenting tasks. But the tremendous life-shaping impact of one generation on those following is hard to overestimate. For one thing the . . . different generations must accommodate to life cycle transitions simultaneously. While one generation is moving toward old age, the next is contending with the empty nest, the third with young adulthood, forming careers and intimate peer adult relationships and having children, and the fourth with being inducted into the system. Naturally there is an intermingling of the generations, and events at one level have a powerful effect on relationships at each other level. The important impact of events in the grandparental generation is routinely overlooked by therapists focused on the nuclear family. Painful experiences such as illness and death are particularly difficult for families to integrate, and are thus most likely to have a long-range impact on relationships in the next generations. . . . (pp. 7–8)

Jeffery Arnett (2000) has recently proposed a new concept of development that he has termed "emerging adulthood" and that refers to the span between the late teens through the twenties, with a focus on ages 18–25. He argues convincingly that this period is neither adolescence nor young adulthood and that it is theoretically and empirically distinct from both. Having gone beyond the dependency of childhood and adolescence and not yet having assumed the enduring responsibilities characteristic of adulthood, the emerging adult can explore a variety of avenues in areas of work, love, and personal philosophy of life. Emerging adulthood is distinct for its lack of demographic norms. More changes of residence usually occur during this time than at any other. Demographic unpredictability and diversity reflect the behaviors having increased risk (binge drinking, substance abuse, reckless driving, unprotected sex) and the experimental and exploratory nature of this period. Emerging adults who pursue a college education often do this in a non-linear way. Demographic diversity begins to abate in the late twenties, correlating with more enduring choices in love and work. Only in the late twenties and early thirties do a clear majority of people feel they have reached adulthood. Arnett credits Erikson (1968), Keniston (1971), and Levinson (1978) with the theoretical groundwork supporting this new developmental concept.

In his research Arnett found that the personal characteristics that matter most to emerging adults in attaining adulthood are qualities of character (Arnett, 1998). The most important of these qualities are (*a*) accepting responsibility for one's self, (*b*) making independent decisions, and (*c*) becoming financially independent. Being a self-sufficient person is the most salient subjective aspect of moving into young adulthood. Arnett's review of research on family relationships among emerging adults supports some clinical observations. Although autonomy and relatedness are complementary relational dimensions for both American and European emerging adults, there are significant variations. It has been found, for example, that for American emerging adults in their early twenties, physical proximity to parents is inversely related to the quality of relationships with them. Those with the most frequent contact with parents, especially those still living at home, have the poorest relationships and the poorest psychological adjustments (Dubas & Petersen, 1996; O'Connor, Allen, Bell, & Hauser, 1996). European emerging adults who are still living at home, however, tend to be happier than those who have left home. They tend to have better relationships with their parents as well as a great deal of autonomy within their parents' households (Chisholm & Hurrelmann, 1995).

Arnett is careful to explain that emerging adulthood can exist only in cultures that allow prolonged periods of independent role experimentation and exploration. However, he speculates that, with longer life spans and increasing globalization of the economy, with the resulting technological changes in developing countries, emerging adulthood could be a worldwide, normative period of development for young people by the end of the twenty-first century. A similar prediction of globalization could be made for the trend toward increasing variability of the structure of the Western family life cycle. This variability includes intergenerational families, gay and lesbian couples and their biological or adopted children, interracial families, single parents and their children, serial marriages and the proliferation of reconstituted families, unrelated couples and families living together, women and couples choosing not to have children at all, and so on.

During the past two generations changes in the family life cycle have been dramatic. Lower birth rates, longer life expectancy, the growth of divorce and remarriage rates, and especially the changing roles of women have been central to rapid shifts in the family life cycle. In the not-too-distant past parents were occupied with child rearing during most of their adult life spans. Today child rearing is often completed less than halfway into the span of life that precedes old age. Rather than having their identities determined by their functions in the family, women have come to need and expect an identity of their own. Even with careers and full-time jobs, however, women are still pivotal in the organization and management of the family. As a result, many women experience their identities as being divided. In following a bifurcated identity path, some women are susceptible to feelings of inadequacy in both areas of their lives. Men, on the other hand, tend to experience career and family as unified and are generally subject to much less conflict and insecurity (Josselson, 1987).

In whatever way today's family is constituted, it is anchored within modernist and postmodernist Western culture, including cultural emphasis on goal-directedness, autonomous lifestyle, faith in personal effectiveness and continuous progress, and individuals in families interacting as a system. The family continues to function to sustain its heritage of cultural and ethnic identity and to transmit its unique history, traditions, and values to its members. These functions are important for fostering family cohesiveness, and they provide family members with stability, support, strength, and reliable ways of coping with daily life and the hurdles of individual development. Family routines, roles, and structures are also sources of comfort and security since they are a predictable part of the sense of "holding" that families can provide. However, this sense of holding and security may not be so generally assumed as it was in past generations. At least since the 1960s, patterns of family life have become more transient. A few generations ago, women were focused on the management of the household and the rearing of children for most of their adult lives. Today, in the "mainstream" Western family, both parents usually work for the financial benefit of the family, roles are more flexible and contingent on emergent needs of individuals, and many activities take place outside the home. Families are also more divided geographically. It is not uncommon, because of job opportunities and other considerations, for adult family members to move some distance away from locales where they lived during childhood. It is likewise not unusual for parents to move away after the youngest child has left home. Today the idea of "home" is often not related to place.

☐ **Family Stress and Loss**

Any of the extant Western contemporary models of human development and the family life cycle must be modified when applied to nontraditional families and to families who are coping with severe chronic illness and permanent disabilities. Family diversity has made it possible for today's families to define themselves in whatever way the constellation works best. An interesting example of a variant model of family was described by Donald Bradley of the *Kansas City Star* in an article appearing June 25, 2000, in the *Dallas Morning News*. Roy Hutchison was a paramedic when he saw Tiffany in a hospital in 1984. She had suffered severe brain damage at birth when the umbilical cord was wrapped around her neck, shutting off oxygen to her brain. Her hips, shoulders, and spine were deformed. She had cerebral palsy and couldn't see or hear, and it was thought she would die soon. Nobody wanted her. Hutchison, a tattooed Harley rider with a ponytail, comforted her, fell in love with her, and took her home. He made a commitment that he would always be there for her. His wife and son, Chad, agreed with him. After Tiffany had survived two winters, the Hutchisons adopted her. The couple then divorced, and Roy won custody of her. After that, Chad was killed in an automobile crash. Roy and Tiffany were on their own. Roy took Tiffany along on his dates. Tiffany's heart began to weaken. With the assistance of a hospice service, Roy saw her through to the end. She was 15 years old. He has said that Tiffany was his teacher, that she taught him about life, love, and family. His new wife has said that Tiffany taught her how little we all really need to live and be happy. Roy has also said that there were times when he thought two parents would have been better for Tiffany, but when she smiled, he knew that no one could love her more than he did.

As Carter and McGoldrick (1989) have noted, increased family stress is expected during life cycle transitions when adjustments and realignments must be made by most family members. In families coping with situations of chronic sorrow, Tunali and Power (1992), among others, have noted that stress related to transitional life stages is amplified, especially when transitions cannot be completed by the one who is the source of sorrow; that is, by the family member who cannot achieve independence. At every occasion when life cycle transitions are expected to occur but do not, family members may confront the grief they experienced when the loss was first discovered. McCubbin and Figley (1983a, 1983b) have explored familial stress and have made a distinction between essentially normative stressors (for example, life cycle transitions when family relationships change and family members attain higher levels of development) and stressors that are catastrophic. They define catastrophic familial stress as sudden, unexpected, and frightening events characterized by destruction, disruption, and loss and accompanied by feelings of helplessness and loss of control.

Figley (1983) has identified 11 criteria for distinguishing catastrophic from normative stressors. Events are considered to be catastrophic when those who are affected by them (*a*) have little or no time to prepare for them, (*b*) have little to no previous experience in handling such events, (*c*) have scant access to support and guidance, (*d*) are subjected to events that are rarely experienced by others in the social environment, (*e*) experience a period of crisis that is protracted, (*f*) have little control over events with a resulting sense of helplessness, (*g*) experience a sense of loss, (*h*) have their lives severely disrupted by destructive forces, (*i*) experience real or perceived peril, (*j*) suffer high emotional impact, and (*k*) have or acquire a medical problem. The onset of chronic sorrow perfectly fits these defining criteria.

Since clinicians rarely observe the process of family-illness interactions throughout the entire sequence of a chronic disease or impairment, Rolland's (1989) pychosocial typology of illness is especially helpful in linking chronic illness to the family life cycle and to family and individual dynamics. The typology is applicable to a wide array of illnesses and makes four broad conceptual distinctions. These are (*a*) onset, (*b*) course, (*c*) outcome, and (*d*) degree of incapacitation. Each of these variables is, in fact, a continuum. Although Rolland's conceptualizations are for chronic illness, they are relevant to virtually all conditions that are associated with disabilities.

Rolland divides *onset* into two categories: acute and gradual. Strokes and myocardial infarction are examples of acute onset. Other examples are brain, spinal cord, and other traumatic injuries that are permanent, such as severe and disfiguring burns, congenital anomalies and obvious perinatal damage, cerebral palsy, and so on. Examples of diseases and conditions with a gradual-onset include Alzheimer's, Parkinson's, MS, some forms of epilepsy, childhood disintegrative disorder (although once under way, the spiral downward is often quick and devastating), and other severe and chronic mental illnesses. Many conditions that are categorized as gradual-onset are those that are present at birth but that slowly reveal themselves over time—autism, diabetes, cystic fibrosis, some forms of blindness and other sensory impairments, mental retardation, genetic errors of metabolism, orthopedic anomalies, and so on. Rolland suggests that some families are better equipped to cope with acute-onset diseases and others are better equipped to deal with gradual-onset. Adams and Lindemann (1974) proposed that acute-onset diseases place greater strain on the family because the family divides its energy and resources between (*a*) progressive efforts for maximizing mastery through reorganization and creative problem solving and (*b*) protecting against further damage, disintegration, and loss.

Rolland (1989) describes three general types of *course* that chronic diseases take: (*a*) progressive, (*b*) constant, and (*c*) relapsing, or episodic. Progressive disease requires that the family and the individual cope with a perpetually symptomatic family member whose condition continues to worsen. Family caregivers are faced with stress that increases over time, demands continual adaptation, and affords little respite. In constant-course illness, an initial event occurs and is followed by a biological stabilization, as in stroke, spinal cord injury with paralysis, trauma with resulting amputation, and so on. After some initial recovery, chronicity is marked by obvious deficits, residuals, and functional disability. These changes remain relatively constant and predictable for a long time. Rolland acknowledges the potential for family exhaustion "without the strain of new role demands over time" (p. 436). This author contends, however, that new role demands are common in constant-course conditions since (*a*) family life-cycle transitions are more complicated and stressful, (*b*) families continue to be dynamic systems in the intervals between transitions, (*c*) family resources are variable and may be depleted over time, and (*d*) changes in individual needs of family members are inevitable (caregivers leave home, get sick, die, become mentally ill, divorce, have personal crises and emergencies, and so on).

In relapsing or episodic disease, periods of stabilization or improvement of varying lengths alternate with periods of exacerbation. Examples include MS, certain seizure disorders, hydrocephalic conditions in which there are unpredictable and recurrent shunt blockages (associated with increased intracranial pressure), chronic mental illness, autism, and so on. During periods of improvement and stabilization, families can main tain routines; however, anxiety, vigilance, and wariness characterize these periods of relative calm. It may be difficult for some families to plan ahead, and family members may learn not to count on anything or get their hopes up about the future. The large discrepancy between crisis and noncrisis is psychologically taxing. As Rolland aptly indicates, "The family is on call."

The third concept in Rolland's (1989) psychosocial typology is *outcome*. He describes an outcome continuum ranging from diseases that are not typically associated with shortened life span (blindness, arthritis, most spinal cord injuries) to illnesses that are clearly progressive and usually fatal (Huntington's chorea, amyotrophic lateral sclerosis, some cases of AIDS). In between are those conditions with outcomes that are more unpredictable, such as illnesses that often shorten the life span and illnesses with the potential of sudden death. In life-threatening illnesses, undercurrents of anticipatory grief for both the individual and the family characterize all phases of the family life cycle. Rolland describes prevalent fears for the person who is ill as (*a*) having life end before fulfilling important aspects of the dream or plan for life and (*b*) being alone in death. Family members are fearful of becoming survivors who face the future alone. All the complexities of anticipatory grief can combine with those of chronic sorrow, affecting mood, world view, intimacy, and faith in the future. In illnesses that are known to sometimes shorten life span or cause sudden death, imminent loss is more ambiguous and "farther away." Rolland indicates that the "it could happen" aspect of these conditions can foster overprotection by the family and substantial secondary gains for the ill individual.

The fourth aspect of Rolland's (1989) typology is *incapacitation*. The different kinds and degrees of incapacitation in chronic illness lead to wide differences in family adjustments. Severity of incapacitation is a significant mediator of the degree of stress with which families cope. When a family member is suffering from a highly debilitating condition (massive stroke, severe and profound mental retardation, spinal cord injury with paralysis, severe autism, and so on), issues of family identity and social stigma can become pronounced. These issues can adversely affect normal social interactions. Some incapacitating conditions are more socially disabling than they are mentally or physically limiting. Persons with craniofacial disfigurement, communication disorders, or spasticity, for example, are more subject to stigmatization than are those with less visible and "more acceptable" disabilities. Though often invisible, however, AIDS is a socially disabling condition since it is frequently perceived in connection with high contagion risk and with those who comprise highly stigmatized populations in our society.

Family appraisal of the member who is disabled and of the catastrophic event that has permanently changed the developmental trajectory of family and individual life cycles is crucial to accommodation and adjustment to the loss of normative patterns. Wikler (1986) has examined family perception regarding the degree to which having a child who is mentally retarded is seen as a threat to family status and to the family's goals and objectives. Family members may view the stressor of mental retardation in a variety of ways—as fate, an act of aggression against the family, a challenge, as God's purpose for their lives, as punishment, as shameful and embarrassing, an overwhelming burden, and so on. Differences in family perception also influence how family members view themselves, as active and empowered, as resilient and courageous, or as helpless victims. The family's social milieu has enormous impact on family identity during times of crisis. It can both assist and hinder family coping and perceptions of the family and its individual members as they relate to the social world. Writing about the difference between her experience as a parent and social constructs of disabilities, a mother whose son has Down syndrome insightfully expresses her frustration:

I couldn't see how I would ever be able to reconcile the pleasure I took in our private experiences of nursing, rocking, and singing with the way the outside world viewed Aaron and our "tragedy." I felt trapped in other people's pictures, afraid I would never get free. He seemed like such a wonderful boy; I wanted people to look past his disability and see his soul inside.

To have a child with a disability is considered tragic because a handicapping condition in America is considered a stigma. As Erving Goffman observes in his classic study of the subject, "By definition . . . we believe the person with a stigma is not quite human." Obviously, having a child who is less than human can only be tragic.

This is the social construct our culture has devised . . . and it is not easily relinquished. Never mind that a mother's actual experience of her baby is different from what society pictures it. Never mind that we parents know that the disability is not the whole child; know that the body, even the mind, are not the soul. People will work very hard to keep us fixed in their mind-sets, because to do otherwise is to give up deeply embedded social paradigms.

Trying to explain, saying, "No, no, you don't understand. It's not like that; it's like this," is to knock on the hard walls of preconceived ideas, walls that are not only rigid but extremely well defended. Often we will come away with a bloody hand, having had our experience denied, or distorted to fit the preconceived notion, or called something else—delusion, denial, false hope, fantasy.

We must reach deep within ourselves and out to one another to find the strength to hang on to our reality and insist on its truth in the face of mistaken or hostile social constructs. It took the Catholic Church almost four hundred years to admit that Galileo should not have been condemned as a heretic for proving that Copernicus was right about the sun. No matter what men believed, the sun never did revolve around the earth, and other people's ideas of our experience will never be the same as our experience. (Gill, 1997, pp. 271–272)

The differentness of the family and the sense of being misunderstood or otherwise invalidated by others (including the professionals who are now inextricably a part of family life) contribute to appraisals of the new family reality. Family identity and social ostracism are powerful forces in the development of family members who may tend to disassociate themselves from the family when in public, while others may fail to maintain maximal autonomy because of a pull toward dependency on the family for mutual support and protection.

The most universal initial response of parents, on learning that their child has a severe disability, is a combination of shock, disbelief, guilt, and an overwhelming sense of grief and loss. Denial is normal and necessary. Otherwise, shock and family stress would be so overwhelming that care for the child and problem solving for both the child and the family would be blocked, and the family system would collapse. Even with the protection of denial, severe disorganization or collapse may occur. Following a variable period of shock and denial, some family members may become depressed or decompensate in some other way. For example, some family members may relapse into former pathological behaviors such as severe obsessive-compulsiveness, anger dyscontrol, eating disorders, heavy drinking, abuse of other substances, and so on. Depression in caregivers can result from severe emotional stress combined with physical exhaustion from following through on the many recommendations, appointments, procedures, evaluations, and direct care required by the child (Dyson, 1993). Other stressors include (a) competing needs of family members, (b) spousal disagreements (regarding acceptance of the diagnosis, assessment of severity, assignment of blame, choice of treatment options, and distribution of responsibility in caring for the child), (c) financial strain, and (d) lack of a support system outside the nuclear family.

Although some marriages become stronger, others crumble under the weight of disability and chronic sorrow. Featherstone (1980) has written with great candor about marital and family issues when there is a "difference in the family," that is, when a child has significant disabilities:

> A child's disability may reveal fault lines in a marriage that no amount of effort and understanding can pave over. Some marriages collapse—and this need not be a bad thing. If a husband and wife's values differ fundamentally, if every act . . . requires an agonizing compromise, if anger washes over even the most sincere efforts at mutual support, it may be time to end things. Even a painful divorce can look good compared to inner death or a life of armed conflict.
>
> Most people do not face such irresolvable conflicts, though. Most marriages survive. . . . The bond of shared sorrow and trouble and of happiness wrung from ultimate pain can enhance a relationship. . . .
>
> Most marital problems are stubbornly complex; even when approached with energy, insight, and humility, fixed patterns resist change. . . . (p. 131)

At a time when parents are most in need of support and guidance, they may find themselves emotionally separated from friends and extended family. Friends may be unaware of the seriousness of the disability, or they may feel awkward, nervous, and very uncomfortable in the presence of a child who has severe impairments. They may not know how to offer support and comfort, or they may fear saying something wrong. Even worse, grandparents may not believe or accept that something so terrible could happen in the family or to their grandchild. If the parents do not present a unified report and back each other up, the parent who is burdened with the job of convincing the grandparents of the hard truth can be seen not only as the bearer of unacceptable news but as the source of trouble and family pain. The parent who brings such sad news to other family members is sometimes at risk of additional traumatization since she must convey in words what she herself does not want to believe. She may feel a renewal of the initial shock and pain with every telling, and she may also feel she is discrediting her own child (who needs her to make everything right instead of being the source of "bad press" about him). Truth saying promotes distancing in some families, and the truth sayer must also be prepared to give comfort to the ones who are injured with the truth—this at a time when she herself needs all the comforting she can get. Not infrequently, grandparents, in their own initial shock and confusion, may assign blame to one of the parents (commonly, the one unrelated to them) for being genetically responsible for the disability.

The onset of mental illness often occurs in mid- to late adolescence as disconcerting changes in personality and cognitive style become more and more apparent. Family members who must watch as their son, daughter, sibling, or grandchild loses life skills are faced with terrifying prospects that are soon wrapped in an ominous and dreadful diagnosis. MacGregor (1994) has described parental and family losses as internal, external, and existential. Losses considered internal include (a) self-esteem and feelings of competence, (b) dreams for the child's future, (c) control, (d) security and certainty about the illness and about the future, and (e) a positive sense of the family's history. External losses include (a) a normal and predictable family life, (b) privacy, (c) spontaneity; (d) social network, (e) faith in the health care systems and health care providers, (f) financial resources, and (g) freedom for caregiving family members. Caregiver freedom may be curtailed for life if there is a lack of financial resources with which to purchase care. Existential losses refer to the loss of the world as it was once understood. The family life trajectory has skidded off course.

☐ Family Coping and Adaptation

Families and individuals respond to the onset of disability with wide variability. Based on personal and clinical experience, this author believes that initial family disorganization, even chaos, is normal and to be expected. In many cases, a period of disintegrative family functioning and fragmentation can continue for a year or more. This is usually traceable to the nature of the disability. For example, a traumatic brain injury may involve coma and require several surgical procedures, and the person's condition may remain critical for months. Even when the person is "out of the woods," the course of the injury and extent of recovery are uneven and unpredictable. Prognostic indicators include (*a*) duration of coma, (*b*) duration of post-traumatic amnesia, (*c*) type of brain injury, (*d*) presence of multiple organ damage, (*e*) whether hematomas are epidural or subdural, (*f*) preexisting developmental disabilities, and so on. Children who come out of coma within six weeks have a good prognosis for recovery, but when the duration of coma is longer than three months, prognosis for recovery of functioning is generally quite poor (Brink & Hoffer, 1978). Lengthy hospitalization and months or years of rehabilitation can deplete financial resources. The financial condition of the family may be further depleted by costly equipment and modification of the house and loss of income if one of the parents must resign or take a leave of absence from work to be with the afflicted person. Studies have highlighted the need for early identification of families who are at risk of permanent decompensation, since family functioning, the severity of the injury, and the person's preinjury functioning are generally predictive of both the family's and the individual's functioning one year after the injury (Rivara, Fay, Jaffe, Polissar, Shurtleff, & Martin, 1992; Rivara, Jaffe, Fay, Polissar, Martin, Shurtleff, & Liao, 1993). Early professional interventions (family counseling, service coordination, referrals to potential sources of financial assistance and support groups) may prevent the collapse of the family system.

After a period of acute crisis and destabilization, most families prove that they are up to the task of coping with the stresses of readjusting their expectations for the family and for the family member who is disabled. In spite of continuing losses, most families eventually experience positive outcomes from the drastic changes in family structure and the discontinuity of the family life cycle. Families often report improved cohesion and hardiness and increased gentleness, understanding, and compassion among family members. Some families report a more meaningful and valued life (Featherstone, 1980; Gill, 1997; Marsh, 1994; Rife, 1994). Diane Marsh (1992) has catalogued the central needs of families consequential to mental retardation of a family member as (*a*) a comprehensive system of care for the family member, (*b*) information about the disability, about intervention, and about services and resources, (*c*) coping skills, (*d*) support, (*e*) meaningful involvement in intervention, (*f*) management of individual and family adaptation, (*g*) contact with other families, and (*h*) assistance in handling problems in the larger society. Goldfarb, Brotherson, Summers, and Turnbull (1986) have proposed a general typology of family needs related to disability and chronic illness: (*a*) economic, (*b*) health and security, (*c*) physical, (*d*) recreation, (*e*) socialization, (*f*) self-definition, (*g*) affection, and (*h*) education. They stress the importance of acknowledging the needs of all family members and of balancing those needs in some equitable way.

Marsh (1992) has conducted an extensive literature review, from which she has compiled three types of variables that serve as protectors, exacerbators, and mediators of family stress. Variables are characterized as individual, intrafamilial, and extrafamilial. Individual variables are (*a*) severity, (*b*) ambiguity, (*c*) etiology and prognosis, (*d*) age, sex, and birth order, (*e*) temperament, (*f*) medical, psychological, or sensorimotor problems, (*g*) caregiving demands, and (*h*) residential status. Intrafamilial variables are (*a*) life cycle issues, (*b*) transgenerational family history, (*c*) concurrent stressors, (*d*) family composition, (*e*) socioeconomic, racial, ethnic, and religious characteristics, (*f*) family systems characteristics, such as boundaries, hierarchical organization, emotional climate, and information processing, (*g*) family resources and constraints, (*h*) appraisals, (*i*) coping strategies, (*j*) defenses, (*k*) skills, (*l*) commitments, beliefs, attitudes, expectations, and values, and (*m*) resilience. She identifies extrafamilial variables as (*a*) services, (*b*) support systems, and (*c*) sociocultural characteristics.

In whatever way they do it, families have no choice but to adapt to their losses and grief and to galvanize their strengths to reorganize and to regain some control over their lives. Monat and Lazarus (1991) have described coping, defined as efforts to master reality demands that are appraised as exceeding or taxing resources, as divided into two categories: (*a*) problem-focused, referring to changing things to improve the person-environment interaction, and (*b*) emotion-focused, referring to thoughts or behaviors designed to ease the emotional impact of stress. In general, two of the most important variables in family survival and adjustment are (*a*) an unambiguous diagnosis and reliable information about the disability and (*b*) positive interactions and a cooperative spirit in the family. Families who develop a sense of being special in having a member who is disabled are also advantaged in their adjustments. As part of maintaining a positive family and individual identity, many families place great importance on "looking good." Family members may make great efforts to put on good public faces, often appearing to be coping better than they really are. Some family members in some contexts choose not to divulge the existence of a seriously impaired member. Rather than operating from shame or fear of stigmatization, the motivation in these instances is usually to protect themselves from the pain of insensitive reactions by others.

A sense of humor can be an excellent coping resource. It can be especially helpful in tempering the effects of public reactions to the person whose impairments include inappropriate social behaviors. One parent, Madeline Catalano (1998), has written:

> I have found that a sense of humor helps me remain positive. One typical
> trip to the library entailed Thomas "greeting" a large tank of fish by reaching

his hand in to remove them! When the surprised librarian approached, I nonchalantly said, "Oh, he was just saying hello to the fish." It was then necessary to tell Thomas, "We don't eat chairs at the library." Later, the librarian heard me tell Thomas to "stop licking the books" and "stop climbing up the shelves." While absurd scenes such as these are taking place, I cannot help but smile. However, I cannot tell whether this reaction comes from the obvious humor of public reactions to autistic behavior, sheer embarrassment, or some acquired coping strategy. It is more likely the latter, as an attempt at emotional detachment shields me from further psychological pain, after four years of bombardment with public disapproval and humiliation. (p. 65)

Loss of family privacy looms large and long for families with disability and debilitating chronic illnesses. Home-based services are often the most frequent current model of assistance, especially for very young or extremely impaired children. Over the course of a lifetime, families must deal with a veritable multitude of professionals. They will be subjected to home visits by state and local agencies as part of the process of obtaining certain services, financial assistance, and equipment. Strangers will know intimate details of the family's home situation, income, personal and extended family problems, individual mental and physical health status, and so on. Some intensive treatment programs that take place in the home, such as the Lovaas behavioral program for autism, require a routine of several hours a day, a number of professionals, and appropriate space and furnishings. Siblings often must relinquish their bedrooms or playroom for teaching and training sessions. Physical therapy, nutritional consultations for feeding problems, language development and remediation, skilled nursing care, and a variety of other interventions currently take place in the home. Families often feel they are living in a fishbowl, distortions included. With high staff turnover and no one person or agency to oversee things, adaptations are constant, and the family feels the strain. Recommendations and advice are often contradictory. While the principle of normalization may apply to the person with disabilities, life for other family members often becomes increasingly "abnormal." For parents of chronically ill or severely impaired children, the demands of lifelong care are tantamount to role captivity. For these caregivers, daily life is like the song that never ends.

Sue and Stephen Ferris (1998) have written about their daughter Laura's rapid regression. She was diagnosed as having childhood disintegrative disorder (CDD). A behavioral intervention team (BIT), provided by the Bureau of Community Services in Australia, worked intensively with her during an 11-week residential placement. They continued working with her when she returned home.

Laura stayed in the government house for 11 weeks, to become accustomed to wearing clothes again and to her intensive program. Although she still had tantrums, they were not of the magnitude of those she had had before going into the hospital. We agreed to take Laura back home, judging that we (particularly our other children) would now be able to cope. Laura came home on October 1, 1994. The BIT team continued Laura's intensive program in our home.

We have found having a home-based program a two-edged sword. The program has been of immeasurable help to Laura, teaching her skills ranging from constructive play to preschool skills such as sitting cross-legged on the floor to listen to a story. The staff who worked directly with Laura displayed great enthusiasm and commitment. Nonetheless, it was a great burden having nonfamily members in the house for up to 30 hours per week, even though they were very sensitive to the need of the family for privacy. Unfortunately, this sensitivity was not always shared by the administrators responsible for supervising the program. Although the government devoted many resources to the program, it did not select a supervisor with the necessary experience to actively review the program week by week. . . . The professionals who supervised Laura's program . . . were clearly amiss with respect to Laura's very specific program when difficulties presented. (pp. 175–176)

A family member who will never be able to manage even semi-independent living will require family adjustments for life. The lifelong presence of the disabled family member will necessarily impact the family life cycle repeatedly, producing nonnormative patterns. Periodic crises, recurrent intensification of sorrow, moments of despair, worries and anxieties about the future, and awareness of the tenuousness (and preciousness) of life and of health are only a part of the family's experience. Most families contending with chronic sorrow meet their challenges and recognize the power of their uniqueness. They can take joy in their relationships and in their toughness and learn the lessons of service and love for one of their own. Whether services are home-based or center-based (developmental play groups, skills-focused groups, various therapies, parent or sibling support groups, and so on), families are afforded many opportunities to enhance cognitive coping strategies. Garland (1993) has described service systems as vehicles for developing causal attribution, establishing mastery, and increasing self-esteem, especially if the systems are respectful of a family's culture and values.

Sound professional evaluation and therapeutic advice are incalculable for maximizing family adaptation and stability. That these professional inputs are often delayed or sketchy and that assessment is often imprecise is not usually the result of professional incompetence. Many conditions are ambiguous, with broad variability in course and outcomes. Featherstone

(1980) has described how the unknown aspects of the loss affect parental grief:

> Disability is never as clear-cut as death. Grief usually mingles with confusion and uncertainty. Parents of a Down's syndrome child may be told little beyond the label and have no idea what degree of retardation to expect. As they learn more, either through their own research or through professional consultation, the picture changes. As the child grows, he or she changes, too, often invalidating earlier predictions. Not knowing what fate to mourn, the parent faces a thousand alternative scenarios. (pp. 232–233)

Fostering empowerment, identifying and focusing on family strengths, and adapting flexibly to the changing needs of the family are central professional approaches to helping families endure over the long haul. Role-theory applications to the family and chronic sorrow are also useful and have been described by Warda (1992). She has relied on Nye's (1976) definition of role as relating to sets of behaviors that are normatively defined and expected of an individual in a specific social context. Roles determine what people in particular situations should do to meet their own or another's expectations. Warda describes the effects on role functioning of major situational life events in families, and she proposes that (*a*) the greater the perceived role insufficiency, the greater the negative impact on the family's ability to cope with chronic sorrow and (*b*) the family crisis associated with the onset of chronic illness is positively impacted by the family's capacity for role flexibility, role taking, and role supplementation. Facilitating role adaptation and flexibility in families is important since (*a*) chronic role strain, especially in parents, has negative impact on mastery and self-esteem and (*b*) the greater the perceived role captivity, the greater the role strain in families of chronically ill children.

☐ Siblings

Research literature is not very extensive on the experience of siblings of a brother or sister who is mentally impaired or has a physical disability. Longitudinal studies are meager. Some studies have relied on parent reports of their well children's responses and behaviors. If siblings' reports were included in these studies, they essentially echoed the parents. Studies have generally included broad diagnostic groups (mental retardation, spina bifida, cystic fibrosis, cerebral palsy, and so on), or they have lumped the diagnoses together into the larger category of "disabilities." Studies have not specified the correlation of the severity of impairment with the adjustments made by healthy siblings. Until the 1970s, professional literature generally predicted that siblings of people with disabilities would have a variety of serious problems. Achievements and character qualities such as altruism, generosity, and empathic accuracy tended to be interpreted negatively—as compensatory, a plea for attention and approval, or in some other way a pathological reaction. In any case, studies of siblings have yielded conflicting results about the kinds of people they will be as adults and how they will function.

The descriptive writings of siblings and other family members, though not plentiful, are extremely useful sources of information about the experience of growing up with a brother or sister with disabilities. Helen Featherstone (1980), as a mother, and Mary McHugh (1999), as a sister, have provided very richly textured accounts of their own experiences and understandings of the sibling effects and perspective. They have included insightful interviews and relevant research. They have gathered so much information from the literature and from direct contact with family members that the aggregate of the emerging themes from these sources is clear and well substantiated. Though there are other excellent chronicles and depictions of family life and sibling experiences, this section relies largely on their wise and compassionate work.

Featherstone (1980) has described the tug felt by brothers and sisters of handicapped children that arises from living simultaneously in two contexts or cultures: the ordinary world of classmates and activities and the world of their exceptional family. She describes the enforced role of mediator and the difficulty that is sometimes encountered when facing choices between conflicting loyalties. Siblings can become angry at the normal world, their own family, the disabled child, and themselves. She offers the account of a college student (Klein, 1972) whose younger brother had severe hearing loss and deformities of his arms:

> This past summer I worked at a playground. One day a bunch of kids and I were playing. . . . All of a sudden these little kids started dropping away from the circle. I was playing with them, so I did not really pay much attention to why some kids were dropping out. It was . . . getting more and more quiet and I turned around: my brother was standing there. Of course, this is summertime, he has short sleeves on and these kids, even now I am tempted to say these little creeps, it really upset me—they made a circle around my brother, just made a circle around him and started looking at him and I just did not know what to do. . . . I felt like saying, and it upsets me now to think that I would say what I wanted to say, "Jim, hurry up and get out of here." Even now that I say it, it is totally disgusting and at the same time I wanted to say to all those little kids, "If you don't move now I am going to throw you all over the fence." Even now I have not resolved it—more than anything else, it shows me that I have not really come to terms with the whole thing. Furthermore, it gives me some appreciation for what my brother has to go through. He has to go every place. (pp. 142–143)

This micro-event, this moment, is described by Featherstone: "Loneliness, anger, guilt, embarrassment, identification, and confusion merge and battle with one another. . . . His brother's presence set him apart from the normal children he supervised. The children's astonished horror widened the distance between him and his brother. Inwardly he raged against everybody who had put him in this uncomfortable position. . . . He reproached himself for disloyalty. Sharing his brother's stigma for a moment, he saw Jim's life through more understanding eyes. Even as the incident enhanced his feeling of identification, it shamed and confused him" (p. 143). As Featherstone implies, identification with a person who is disabled can foster vulnerability, and it can fuel protectiveness. She has described an incident when she and her husband, Jay, were asked by their daughter Caitlin about times before Caitlin was born. Jay told her he had been worried that she might be blind and brain-damaged like her brother, Jody, and he shared with her how relieved he was when she was born and he saw that she was all right. Their other daughter, Liza, stopped him and told him not to talk that way in front of Jody, that Jody could have his feelings hurt, and that they didn't know how much Jody understood.

While of necessity focusing on the child with disabilities, parents who have other normal, healthy children tend to depend heavily on their wellness. These children serve to support their parents' defenses against the implication by professionals and others that they might have caused the mental illness, autism, or other disorders of the child who is impaired. The children serve to reassure them about their parenting. When they are old enough, they help with managing the household and serve as parent surrogates to their disabled sibling. They often bolster the parents' belief that the normal children are not negatively affected by the amount of attention that goes to their sibling or to the adjustments they have to make to accommodate the disabled sibling's needs. They frequently feel that they must make up for their parents' losses and grief over the fate that has come to the family. McHugh (1999) has described the pitfalls to children who identify too strongly with a mother's grief. A child may become so obsessed with the sibling with the disability that he does not want to play with peers or go to school. She describes an 11-year-old girl, Jennifer, as a "little mother" to a brother who is deaf, blind, and profoundly retarded. Jennifer is quoted as saying, "I feed him and sit there and watch him so if he needs something, I can get it. Sometimes he cries because he's lonely and I feel bad because we can't give him all the attention he wants. I try to make him happy. Last week I felt so bad I didn't want to go to school because he was having seizures on and off, every five minutes, and I just wanted to be there with him because if anything happens, I know what to do" (p. 18).

As Jennifer's situation also indicates, some siblings—especially those who are older than the child who is disabled—experience a double loss. They have lost the sibling they expected, and they have lost the parents they once had. McHugh (1999) describes her own childhood after her brother Jackie, who had cerebral palsy and mental retardation, came into the family. She states: "I remember feeling that I had lost the mother I knew. She would look at me without seeing me. She didn't smile anymore. She always looked worried. I wanted my other mother back again" (p. 20). One of McHugh's interviewees, Ahadi, now in her twenties, was five years old when her sister was born with epilepsy. McHugh quotes from her interview with Ahadi: "It's not just that I lost my mother's attention—you always lose that when a new sibling is born. But a great deal of my life was consumed by my sister's illness. I often woke up in the middle of the night to be sure she was all right. I went to the hospital with my mother, and later when my mother was with her in the hospital, I tried to take care of the house and myself as well. You're not only losing a parent, you're also losing some of your own time and your own experience as a child. I did lose an aspect of my childhood—some of the carefreeness. Most of my friends have never even been in a hospital. You realize that your life is so different" (pp. 20–21).

A study conducted by Coleman (1990) lends support to the view that a healthy sibling tends to compensate for the parents' grief over the sibling who is seriously impaired. As might be expected, this tendency is apparently increased when the healthy sibling is the only other child in the family. Coleman found that as the academic achievement of healthy siblings increased, their self-concept decreased. The study also indicated a greater need for achievement among siblings of persons with mental retardation than for siblings of those with physical disabilities. Guilt can be a tenacious influence on achievement throughout childhood and into adulthood. It can impel achievement that is motivated by a desire to make up to the parents what they have lost in the brother or sister, even as it can reduce the sibling's pleasure in those accomplishments by comparison to what the sibling with disabilities can do. McHugh (1999) has highlighted guilt for twins of persons with disabilities. "The feeling 'Why should she have a disability and not me when we were born at the same time?' causes that guilt" (p.103).

> Andrea says her relationship with her twin began to change when Andrea got her driver's license and her sister could not get one because of the frequency of her seizures. Until that time, Andrea says, she actually tended to depend on her twin. "I was quiet and shy," she says. "She was more outgoing. I was nervous about college and chose the same school she was going to. She had a hard time adjusting to college life, largely because of her seizures, and she dropped out. Our lives changed just that much more

because I graduated and she didn't. I got a master's degree, married and had children. She has decided not to have children and that makes me very sad. . . . I wonder, how did I luck out?" (p. 103)

McHugh also reports an exception. One of her sibling interviewees expressed gratitude to her mother for saving her from guilt about her sister with cerebral palsy. Her mother sent her to college at sixteen. She told her: "Get out of here and don't move back home because this is not a good life for you. You've got to go out and make your own life" (p. 106). This sibling indicated that her mother did everything to prevent her feeling guilty even for a millisecond. She refers to her mother as "amazing."

Siblings have reasons for their sorrow and anger, but they often feel guilty about their angry feelings. Siblings experience the profound unfairness that is part of their daily life. Their families must live with blindness, autism, retardation, schizophrenia, debilitating disease, or cerebral palsy, while other families are unscathed. They must take care of themselves as best they can and also take care of their sibling when they are very young, even before they start to school, while they see their peers avoiding most responsibilities throughout their childhoods. They notice that most of the family's available money and time are going to treatment, care, and services for their disabled sibling. It's easy to feel resentful and selfish, and then guilty for these feelings. Siblings with brothers or sisters with temporal lobe epilepsy, autism, or other neurological disorders sometimes must cope with having their toys, dolls, and other possessions damaged or destroyed. They learn that getting attached to things is fraught with the likelihood of destruction. They sometimes learn that their own needs come last. Since family plans are so often postponed, canceled, or reversed, they learn not to expect too much and to dampen anticipation. They are constantly faced with unfairness and with their sorrow, anger, and guilt.

Siblings in McHugh's interview group indicated their need for information about their disabled brother's or sister's condition. When very young, they need the basics; when older and more capable of understanding, they need clear, structured, and definite explanations. They want books, magazine articles, videos, and professional counseling for specific answers to their questions. Having sound information about their siblings' disabilities helps to allay anxiety. They also need the information so they can explain to their friends exactly what has gone wrong with their disabled siblings. Their friends will be more comfortable knowing and, therefore, not so fearful. A common fear of young siblings is that they, too, will develop a disability. Young children can make very faulty assumptions, for example, that standing too close to a sister or brother with seizures will spread the disorder to them. But, understandably, parents are often reluctant to talk with their healthy children about the disability. They may want to protect them as long as possible, and they may find it unbearable to speak the inescapable truth when the impaired child has a very poor prognosis. Parents may want to keep their own denial intact. It takes time to be able to say the terrible words that validate what is already known.

The sibling with disabilities is often a catalyst for parental conflicts that can become the source of anxiety, guilt, loneliness, and insecurity in the well children. Although current marriages and partnerships are moving away from models of strict, socially constructed gender roles, patterns based on centuries of tradition are very powerful and are apt to creep into the relationship when it is under great stress—which is the case when there is a child with significant, permanent impairment in the family. When Mary McHugh (1999) asked one of her interviewees whether she would have preferred not to have a brother with mental retardation, the response was "What I really wanted was for my parents to have a good marriage. My brother's disability drove them farther apart until they finally divorced" (p. 36). McHugh found that, if the parents fight most of the time, boys are more likely to be aggressive with peers and with the sibling with the disability. Girls tend to become withdrawn and anxious. In families where there are children with mental retardation, disabilities, or illness, Stoneman and Berman (1993) have found that troubled marriages lead to fewer parental rewards, an increase in punitiveness, and a decrease of reasoning in discipline strategies.

McHugh's (1999) interviews were revealing of the stress on healthy siblings. She states:

> It takes a strong marriage to withstand the drastic changes in daily living that occur when a child is born with a disability. When any baby is born, it affects the marriage because the mother's time is taken up with the new child—time that she used to spend with her husband. So you can imagine the amount of time a child with an illness can take up. That's hard for a man to deal with. He has lost much of his wife's companionship and he has lost the healthy child he expected to enrich his life. The mother has lost too, of course, but somehow she is expected to cope and handle her marriage, a child who needs her twenty-four hours a day, and the other siblings. Many of the siblings I talked to mentioned the strain on their parents' marriage, and many said their fathers left because of it. (p. 37)

McHugh includes a statement from one of her interviews: "I think my father is the biggest unresolved anger I have. That is something I need to work on. He and my mother were divorced when I was four, partly because he couldn't handle having a son with autism and my mother was totally involved in the fight to help her child in every way she could. . . . I have a long way to go in dealing with him" (p. 38).

For young children, the perception of time is much slower than it is for adults. It may seem an eternity for a child when family chaos continues for months or years following discovery of a serious disability in a sibling. Life with a child with autism can be extremely chaotic as a result of the child's destructiveness, the unevenness of the disorder, and the bizarre behaviors. Almost half of all persons with autism never speak. One of McHugh's sibling interviewees said this of her childhood with an autistic brother: "It's like a three-ring circus day to day. There is no way you can ignore somebody who has motor oil for blood, doesn't sleep so nobody sleeps. There's constant turmoil in the house. It's not a healthy way to grow up, but you learn to cope with it. You either accept it or you flail against it your whole life" (p. 73).

Older girls appear to carry the brunt of sibling responsibility for a sister or brother with disabilities. Some theories suggest that the child who is born after the disabled child is the most at-risk child in the family because attention and emotional supplies are being depleted by the older brother or sister. Mothers may also be depressed at this time so that bonding and attunement may be significantly diminished. A study by Cleveland and Miller (1977) found that older female siblings were more likely to go into helping professions than other siblings and that only sisters of children with mental retardation were most influenced by the retarded sibling in their career choices. More recent studies have yielded conflicting results. It would appear that adult siblings of disabled persons have more ambivalence and reluctance to have children than other adults who have not grown up with disability in the family, but studies are not available to support this reasonable assumption.

☐ Depleted Caregivers

Parent issues are central to chronic sorrow and are addressed throughout the book and will not be readdressed here. But concerns and issues of aging that are unique to parents and caregivers of older persons with major disabilities will be covered in this section. As caregivers age or wear out, family dynamics undergo significant change. If siblings and other relevant family members of persons with disabilities have managed to avoid confronting their own issues vis-à-vis the disabled person's impact on their lives and on their personal development, planning how to care for the person when parents or other caregivers are unable to continue may reactivate these issues. Siblings who were ashamed or resentful of their disabled sister or brother and who avoided closeness may face some difficult soul-searching. The feelings that family members have about one another and family ideology will greatly influence decision-making processes. If family beliefs are based on the value of "taking care of our own" and of family duty and loyalty, discussions and decisions will differ from those of families who hold grudges, do not forgive and let go, and manage intensity through distance and disconnections.

Because the subject of dying and transferring responsibility for the person with disabilities to others is so daunting, caregivers will frequently deny the problem or postpone planning for these events. Others may assign the future of their loved one to fate or to God. Some siblings find it very difficult to persuade their parents to make provisions for their brother or sister while they are still alive and thinking clearly. Some parents are so fearful that their child will have an unacceptable quality of life after they are gone that they make great sacrifices in their late years to make sure that they have done everything possible to assure that this does not happen. Some older parents recall the television documentaries on abuse in state institutions where residents lived in cold, filthy buildings, naked, bruised, and overmedicated. They are terrified that these conditions might await their child. Some parents may have done all they can to set aside money for the care of their child, only to find that one or both of them needs it for their own care in the months or years preceding death. If financial resources are not available for care after the caregivers have died, siblings who take on this responsibility may have to assume both emotional and financial burdens. If siblings and other relatives are unwilling or unable to take these on, the situation may be disastrous as the person with disabilities is left alone, without a home, without money, and without anyone who cares or knows to take the reins.

Family discussions about future planning may become arenas in which past angers, resentments, and grief are expressed. Parent caregivers who are attempting to provide as secure a future as possible for their child may experience additional distress through complaints, accusations, and bitterness from other family members who may be verbalizing their feelings for the first time. As parents age, they are also likely to engage in life reviews, in revisions of their personal narratives, and in exacerbated existential anxieties. This is a time for a resurgence in the intensity of chronic sorrow. McCullough (1981) made some startling discoveries about family planning for persons with mental retardation and physical disabilities. Both parents and nondisabled children were prone to make assumptions about future care without ever actually talking about it. More than half of the parents McCullough queried reported they had made no plans at all. More than half of the siblings thought plans had been made. Sixty-eight percent of parents reported they had not made any financial arrangements. Some parents may assume that a particular family member will volunteer to assume guardianship for their child, only to encounter a deeply disappointing refusal. And some will find themselves agitated and worried at the end of their lives, unable to die peacefully in the knowledge that their child will be in trustworthy hands.

If a sibling does take over the care of a brother or sister, that sibling is most likely to be a sister. The pattern of women doing the great majority of caregiving shows no sign of change. As recently as 1993, Krause and Seltzer found that more than 75% of siblings who were planning to share a household with the sibling with disabilities were women. One of McHugh's (1999) interviewees, an only sibling who has a brother with autism, explained that she and her mother agree that the brother will be placed in a group home, but she reported:

> Nothing has come to my attention that sounds even remotely like the place that I want for Simon. . . . This is the heartbreaking part. He has such an enriched environment now. He is a musical savant and can play anything he hears on the piano. I am really committed to finding a place for him that is enriching. But I will find just the right home for him. He's the most important responsibility I have. My mom had a heart attack recently and I went to a lawyer and became Simon's guardian. (p. 189)

Finding a well-managed, caring, residential facility for a person with severe mental illness, mental retardation, or autism is extremely difficult. Taking on such a task can be frightening and disheartening. Challenging as well is the task of convincing some caregivers who are aging or in declining health that the time has come to relinquish their day-in and day-out responsibility. There are cogent reasons for keeping the person with disabilities in the family home for as long as possible, and there are often equally convincing reasons for moving the person out of the home while caregivers are still fit and healthy. Conflicts among family members and the competing needs of individuals and values can be extremely complicated and resistant to negotiation. Depleted and aging parents may find that their social support system has dwindled as lifelong friends age and die, so that intrafamilial disagreements are more distressful since there are no friends available for encouragement, haven, and reality checks.

The problem of how to provide care for the disabled family member after the death of parent caregivers is highlighted by an article in the *New York Times* (Felton, 2000). According to this article, there are at least 480,000 adults with mental retardation who live with parents who are 60 or over. The article presents a prototypical case of Jimmy, a 58-year-old man who lives in a group home. His parents died within six weeks of each other in 1975. They had been very diligent in their planning for

Jimmy and had managed to set aside $140,000 to cover their son's financial needs. They had believed this amount would see him through to the end of his life. As of July 1999, this nest egg, which was invested in money market funds, had shrunk to $269. His sister, four years younger than Jimmy, has stepped in to take responsibility for him. The county has begun to pick up most of the $93 per day cost of residential care, and the remainder comes from Jimmy's $680 social security check. His sister is obliged to pay $271 per month for clothing, medical care, and other necessities. When she realized two years ago that Jimmy's inheritance was running out, she began to save some money on her own, but she has managed to put aside only a few thousand dollars. Financial planning is fraught with difficulty. Most families do not understand the need to preserve eligibility for benefits, and they do not know how tricky it is to manage this. According to Felton's article, the most fragile of benefits is Supplemental Security Income (SSI) which is generally available to those who are over 65 or who are disabled, provided their assets are worth less than $2,000. The total assets exclude such items as house, car, and burial plot. The monthly SSI check can be as much as $512, with states adding some moneys to that amount. If inheritance is left directly to the person who is disabled, SSI benefits are not available. As Felton further explains:

> Some families sidestep the issue of trusts and government entitlements altogether by handing all their assets to their offspring who are not disabled—along with the burdens of long-term care. That . . . can be a bad move. For one thing, there is nothing, other than good faith, to prevent those children from using the money to make a down payment on a home or pay off debts. (p. 9)

On the other hand, when special-needs trusts are properly drawn and funded with most of the estate going to the care of the child who is disabled, the nondisabled children may feel slighted, especially if they harbor unresolved resentments from the past or are enduring financial hardships of their own.

High socioeconomic status does not necessarily protect caregivers from burnout and depletion. Skilled home care and respite services are not guaranteed commodities. The buck stops with the parents. Through the New York Times News Service, the *Dallas Morning News* reported on December 29, 1999, the apparent abandonment of a 10-year-old boy by his parents at a Delaware hospital. More information was reported in an article by Libby Copeland in the December 30 issue of the *Dallas Morning News*. Steven is the son of a 62-year-old chief executive officer of a Pennsylvania chemical company and his 45-year old wife. The $500-million-a-year company is the world's largest producer of sodium silicates.

Steven has very severe disabilities, including cerebral palsy, frequent seizures, and difficulty breathing. He cannot speak, and he requires a respirator. He requires 24-hour nursing care, including diapering, bathing, feeding, cleaning his nasal passages and tracheotomy, and so on. He has been hospitalized countless times during his life. The parents were reported to be devoted to Steven, and his mother is well known for advocacy. She served on a board that advises the state on ways to better serve the disabled.

Steven's parents reportedly wheeled him into the hospital emergency room, telling a receptionist they wanted to admit him. They left a note saying they could no longer care for him and explaining his medications, his favorite toys, and what he liked to do, and they left boxes of his belongings. It appears that their actions were a last resort. Nonetheless, they were charged with child abandonment. Public opinion was mixed; there was outrage as well as sensitivity and compassion. A report on the days preceding Steven's being left at the hospital revealed that the 24-hour in-home care provided by a nursing company had been discontinued. The company had told the boy's mother that nurses were not available through the Christmas holidays. The parents had attempted to obtain help from other sources, but none was available. The parents alternated shifts between them so that Steven would be continually cared for around the clock, but their endurance ran out.

Newly emerging resources for aging caregivers and families include books and organizations. Estate planning and the establishment of trust funds that do not disqualify persons with disabilities from receiving essential benefits are important considerations. A 1993 publication, *Planning for the Future: Providing a Meaningful Life for a Child with a Disability after Your Death*, by Russell, Grant, Joseph, and Fee, is an excellent example of the types of written resources that are becoming available. It was reviewed by this author in the *MADDvocate* (S. Roos, 1996). As recommended in this and other publications, the drafting of a letter of intent by parent caregivers is worth the time, emotion, and effort. The letter of intent regarding the future life of the person who is disabled forms the basis for subsequent actions and fosters development of coherent, well-developed strategies. It can be invaluable for the nondisabled siblings or others who will be taking up where the parents have left off. Parents can include in the letter such details as the person's developmental and medical history, photos taken at different ages, information about medications, allergies, and vaccinations, descriptions of the person's abilities and what he or she enjoys. It can include favorite foods, what is known to work when there are specific problems, ways to communicate with the person, how to comfort the person, and so on. Through the letter of intent parents can describe the kind of life they want for their son or daughter.

They can identify the person who has agreed to assume guardianship and how this is specified in their wills. The naming of a successor guardian, should the person first chosen or appointed not be able to function in this role, can provide another layer of protection and some peace of mind for the parents. In all respects, the letter of intent increases personal clarity about what matters most in providing for children who are disabled. Actions are then informed and empowered by this clarity.

Families coping with ongoing loss and chronic sorrow have unique challenges and opportunities. Balancing what is best for the family member with disabilities with what is best for the family is not always feasible. Positive changes, such as inclusion of children with disabilities in mainstream society, early intervention, parent support groups, and mandated parent involvement in treatment and educational programs, have made it easier for families to be more open with themselves and with those outside the family about the family member who is disabled. When families are able to find meaning and purpose in their loss, and when they are able to approach their situation as manageable, although difficult or tragic, they can be strengthened both individually and as a family system. Families that function cooperatively and develop resilience are those who avail themselves of services, who empower themselves with knowledge, who maintain a sense of humor and perspective, and whose members demonstrate a healthy internal locus of control. Families are complex entities. They are constellations of persons who are wounded, sorrowful, and sometimes overwhelmed, and they can inspire others through their courage, their wisdom, their consideration of one another, and the care that comes from their hearts for their member who is chronically ill or permanently disabled.

6
CHAPTER

Existential Issues

The traumatic onset of a life beset with chronic sorrow marks the beginning of instruction in the strong hand of fate. The world as it was previously experienced and understood no longer exists. There are feelings of betrayal and of alienation from a world that once was familiar. Part of what is so traumatic is the inability to find coherence and meaning in a dimension that is beyond comprehension. Existential questions will plague the conscious mind. How could a God who loves me allow such devastation to occur? Is this profound loss a punishment? What crime has been perpetrated that deserves such a punishment? I've sacrificed, and I've lived by the rules, so how can this happen to me? I've been believing a lie about living and working and doing the right thing. Can the universe be so uncaring and so random in meting out tragedies? How can I continue to believe that there is some benevolent purpose to life? I am no longer the person I was, but who am I now? Who will I be? Can I learn to live with this terror of what's ahead of me? The psychological pain and stress of chronic sorrow, and the need to achieve an accommodation to the nature and circumstances of the loss, will lead to deeply troubling existential conflicts and turmoil. Existential issues can become intrusively foreground. For many, the work of making sense of the loss and of integrating it is a lifelong endeavor.

A person who suddenly finds herself unable to make even the simplest of ordinary movements because of spinal cord damage can see her physical world reduced to small spaces and the ministrations of others who maintain, clean, and position the body. Her identity is assaulted. She no longer knows herself. Her world becomes a strange and confusing set of routines. Erving Goffman describes in his work *Stigma* (1963) the lament of a woman whose legs were paralyzed by polio at age 24. "I was like everyone else—normal, quarrelsome, gay, full of plans, and all of a sudden something happened and I became a stranger. I was a greater stranger to myself than to anyone. Even my dreams did not know me . . ." (p. 35). The parent of a toddler who "doesn't look right" and who sees his child changed by the rapid, unstoppable, and pervasive disintegration of previously acquired speech and motor abilities will enter a world filled with treachery and fear. His mind may not be able to open to what is taking place inexorably and relentlessly right there in front of him. The belief that he can control, provide, and manage the circumstances that will equip his child for successful competition as an adult is rendered absurd. The belief that he is the most significant author of his life is replaced by an awareness of cosmic injustice and cold indifference. It is as if an earthquake had occurred. The world and the self in the world are forever changed.

Even in normal and conventional lives unmarked by disastrous loss, the many harsh realities of the world foster the development of extensively elaborated perceptions and responses to cope with existence and the human condition. Since we live within our individually and socially constructed realities, the so-called real world may remain comfortably on the edge of our perception for disproportionate periods of time—perhaps most of our lives. Our predominant realities function beneficially to protect us from overwhelming and crushing perceptual inputs; as a result, we can adapt to a world which enables us to enjoy life and our achievements. We can face life and ourselves with a sense of integration and wholeness. The world is experienced as familiar, predictable, comfortable, and secure. Our overriding mythologies about the world and about ourselves provide comfort, rules, principles, and beliefs about outcomes that are understandable and just. They provide impetus and frameworks for acceptable methods of problem solving, for social roles, and a variety of comforts and protections. In self-reflective individuals, there may be occasional moments of contact with essential aloneness, vulnerability, isolation, and the indifference of the universe. At such times "recovery" can take place through reclaiming or modifying and reempowering constructed beliefs and necessary mythologies about one's place in the world. It is then that stability and structure can return, and we can get on with our lives.

Awareness of mortality bestows many challenges on us all. It has been said that we all know we will die; we just don't *believe* that we will. Even when our deepest beliefs and values support us in our lives and enable us to live without becoming immobilized by hopelessness and fear, revisions are sometimes necessary. We will need to readjust belief systems in order to cope with new or more mature understandings and percep-tions of ourselves and the world we live in. Existential management, for most of us, is an ongoing process. Since many, if not most, of the ways we protect ourselves from overwhelming existential angst and fear are primarily unconscious, when we experience a significant, life-altering loss, we often find ourselves confused, lost, ungrounded, and disoriented by the intensity of our anguish. The very things we had considered fun-damental, permanent, crucial, and precious can suddenly vanish. The experience is disintegrating and so powerful and overwhelming that the soul cannot make an image of it. The mind cannot make sense of what is actually happening. We are like pilots of aircraft lost in a fog and with-out visual cues. There is no horizon, and we no longer know if we are flying up or down, right-side-up or upside-down. The world as we have known it has vanished.

We may be unaware of just how powerful the influences are of our social, cultural, and subcultural values, beliefs, attitudes, and behavioral prescriptions. They have been transmitted to us from a past about which we may have only vague and imperfect comprehension. We often do not realize how dearly we treasure these values, beliefs, attitudes, and be-haviors until we are forced to confront them. They are so much a part of our identity that they are only obvious to us when we are inundated with demands to cope with a drastically changed world. A traumatic and catastrophic life-changing crisis is a formidable challenge to our cher-ished beliefs about our existence. Many of our beliefs will no longer fit us. Serious and threatening existential conflicts, previously kept at bay (through repression, denial, reaction formation, "normal" delusional think-ing and dissociation), present themselves to us as we begin to realize some of the effects of the loss. Existential conflicts differ sufficiently from other conflicts and crises that they stand apart, while also affecting —and often determining—our thoughts, emotions, and behaviors.

Existential themes and the struggle to reestablish some coherent and acceptable meaning in life can be found in nontechnical literature, espe-cially the writings by persons who are striving to make sense of their lives in the context of chronic sorrow. Mairs (1986, 1989, 1993) has written about the existential conflicts in her physical deterioration from multiple sclerosis. She has described her intense and recurring thoughts about end-ing her own life and has only recently transcended her suicidality and embraced her life as it exists. Strong (1989) has written about her role as the well spouse who experiences a narrowing and disappearing future because of her husband's MS. Rife (1994) has journaled her son's struggle to survive traumatic and severe brain damage. Her account of his coma, reawakening, rehabilitation, permanent disability, heartbreak, and frus-tration, charts her own existential challenges and her spiritual growth.

Jay Neugeboren (1997) has chronicled the life of his brother, who is chronically mentally ill. He describes his own periodic despair and existential torment. He writes, for example, ". . . and would he ever recover . . . and had I done the right or wrong thing . . . and *was* there a right thing—and why was he shut away in a lunatic asylum when people far crazier (and more mean- and evil-spirited—the shits of the world—were getting on with their lives . . . preying on those less powerful (but far worthier) than they were . . .?"(p. 166).

Narratives written by professionals who are parents of children with severe developmental disabilities (Park, 1982; Roos, 1977; Turnbull & Turnbull, 1978) are revealing of existential themes, as are more generic parent narratives (Daly & Reddy, 1991). An earlier parent narrative was movingly written by Pearl Buck (1950), the author of widely acclaimed fiction. Buck's daughter, though born physically healthy, was soon diagnosed as having severe mental retardation. Through her book, *The Child Who Never Grew*, Buck accessed at least two means of assuaging her own existential concerns. She was able to see to it that any profits from the book would go toward her daughter's support in a residential facility. This provision ameliorated to some extent her fears for her daughter's welfare after her own death. The book also assured that her child's life would be of use to her generation and not an unnoted or wasted life. Oliver Stone's film *Born on the Fourth of July* is a well-constructed chronology of one man's existential crisis. Ron Kovacs, a Vietnam veteran, returns home from the war as a paraplegic and finds himself utterly without a script in an incomprehensible world. He experiences a sense of being forsaken by all the beliefs he has so fervently and unquestioningly held. His identity and his world, once unassailable, are now reduced to the unknown and alien, the hostile or indifferent.

It is important that professionals not overlook existential implications in the lives of those experiencing a living loss. It is also important that they learn about the enormousness of reality demands and situational stress on most persons coping with an ongoing loss (especially, for example, when that loss entails 24-hour caregiving responsibility). Professional insensitivities in certain existential areas are somewhat understandable, even somehow forgivable, since most of us do not relish having our own fears and dilemmas stirred up, reactivated, and brought to consciousness. For very good reasons, we prefer to remain existentially unmolested, keeping our own conflicts safely dormant within us. Furthermore, speaking of the invisible and the often unnamed and immaterial within us is extremely difficult. We are often more comfortable and confident in speaking of the visible and the named. As professionals, we have an extremely lengthy tradition of naming phenomena and etiologies; we believe that if we can name it, we can understand it, achieving some mastery over it. We have become enamored of labels, jargon, and proliferating terminology. We shore up our competence and our self-confidence with test scores, empirical evidence, correlations, and other quantifying data.

The central position of computer technology in our postmodern world has further underscored and defined our perception and understandings of life events as being measurable and subject to analysis that is often removed from personal involvement. The medical profession has an enthusiasm for technology such as noninvasive visualization and biochemical measures. For many of us who work in hospital settings, the chart can become our shelter and the focus of our interest and maintenance. ("I don't know how the patients are getting along, but these charts look great!") Physical therapists focus on such quantifiables as range of motion, muscle tone, eye-hand coordination, and so on. Psychologists concern themselves with test scores and subscales. Nurses meticulously monitor intake-output ratios, vital signs, and symptoms. Human service and health professionals need to be able to concretize, name, and master what would otherwise be overwhelming and confusing. Focusing on the material world serves to reduce tension and anxiety and to free up energy that can be channeled to the immediate task. Professionals can likewise unintentionally distill or reduce a human being to a series of historical milestones, functional assessments, and categories of diagnostic indicators, descriptions, and names.

In those coping with chronic sorrow, prior existential adjustments become stressed and sometimes fractured. Rando (1988) has described existential turmoil following a significant loss and identifies this turmoil as a major secondary loss. There is both real and symbolic value in wholeness, intactness, and integrity of the body-mind. When the self or other to whom one is emotionally attached is substantially and permanently impaired and diminished, an intensification and reactivation of existential anxieties will occur. While there can be considerable overlap, some of these responses are discussed below.

☐ Disillusionment

A great gap may occur between actuality and what is thought to be a reasonable expectation of self, life, and others. A profound sense of disparity and failure may be present. Disappointment and disillusionment in self and in one's expectations and dreams are often inevitable; however, the nature and intensity of the disillusionment is considerably more problematic in chronic sorrow. Disillusionment can permeate nearly all of life and is sometimes only a step away from despair. Furthermore, it is not necessarily the case that the unexpected and unimaginable realities of living will invariably lead to emotional or spiritual growth. As children, we have typically developed expectations of parents (usually as wise, loving, always there to protect and guide), selves (as currently or potentially lovable, as capable—given ordinary opportunities—of full and satisfying lives), mates (who will hold us forever in high esteem, and who will love and protect us unconditionally), and children (who will be nearly perfect, and who will love us and help us fulfill—by extension—our longings for realization of our aspirations for achievement, importance, happiness, and permanence). We have also developed an expectation of fate, God, or the higher power in our lives. This expectation is usually—though not always—one of beneficence.

During the course of living, and with growing experiential awareness, a series of normal disillusionments will occur. Judith Viorst (1987) has described some of these disillusionments in terms of "necessary losses." Parents are "dethroned" (through a sequence of events allowing for revision of perceptions in the direction of more reality). Mates do not ameliorate all our distresses; they do not even heal and make up for all the slights, hurts, and injuries of our childhood. They may even abandon us, just as our parents might have done. We are also our own disillusionments. We are not as attractive, as brilliant, and as powerful as we "need" to be. Rejections and loss of self-confidence are suffered. Cherished goals (many of which have been set by families and parents, as we are our parents' hope for a future beyond themselves) fade from actualization, so that we disappoint ourselves and significant others.

When we become permanently incapacitated in some way, or when a child or mate becomes physically or mentally disabled, a momentous and penetrating loss of our original dreams and expectations occurs. We are confronted instead with a substantially different, often unacceptable, outcome. Reality will overwhelm our defenses. The framework upon which a life has been constructed will now seem to have splintered. There will be a growing recognition of a twisted confluence and consummation of disappointments. In this now emergent and deeply flawed world, the inevitability of tragedy is realized. If we are to withstand the deep sense of disillusionment, we must eventually abandon these essential yearnings and dreams. Life's meaning can only be regained by ceasing our resistance to the new reality, not by clinging to fantasies that the old reality may not be gone forever. This is a hard truth. We will need to redirect ourselves in a search for other avenues, and we will need to define and revise our hopes, dreams, values, and expectations more realistically. This type of redirection will not only serve as a way to survive but eventually compel us to learn to live more creatively with our loss. This may be a very lengthy process, and it is complicated by the need to manage and deal with constant and excessive demands and burdens related to the ongoing loss.

☐ Aloneness

Perhaps the most painful of our existential realizations is of our ultimate and essential aloneness. We are inescapably alone; no one can transcend his or her individual boundaries. An unmitigated and unqualified sense of aloneness is a consequence of the human condition. The need to fuse with another human being, to belong to someone, to be a part of a group from whom we derive closeness, support, and validation: all are attempts to find solace, to soothe or block our sense of separation and aloneness. Under the effects of relatively normative stress and strain, we are able to maintain our defenses in order to cope with our aloneness and to avoid full awareness of it. Even in these circumstances, however, there may be occasions when we realize that, no matter how close we may feel to someone, we are still alone and responsible for our own lives. When confronting a serious life crisis of any kind, we are subject to intimations and glimmers of aloneness that will increase our anxieties and may obstruct our progress.

From the beginning of time, cultures have developed and devised ways to cope with aloneness and to make awareness of it manageable. There are resources to which we can turn for affiliation and for support and comfort. Feeling that we are a part of a larger and more meaningful whole can be a source of personal security and protection. Religious beliefs and spiritual development can be very effective conveyors of hope and alleviation of aloneness and isolation. Families who truly work to support one another can provide a haven to a family member who is in trouble and who needs something beyond the self to make it through. The need for intimacy is thought to be virtually universal, since intimacy provides us with fantasies of merging with another who loves us and who places us at the center of his or her life. The striving for reuniting or joining with another is extremely strong and tenacious. It is so powerful that there are some who manifest an addictive pursuit for fusion and oneness with another. Often this type of addictive interpersonal relating is associated with fantasies of an ultimate rescuer. The threat of experiencing any awareness at all of the essential aloneness of the self is deeply terrifying to many of us. Once a person has experienced existential aloneness, that person is never quite the same; it is impossible to go from knowing to not knowing.

Those affected by chronic sorrow may have a perception of being so different from others and of having a personal reality that is so unrecognized and misunderstood that they may feel they have crossed the line into a parallel universe. They feel a protracted and difficult disconnection from others. In describing her realization of serious impairments in her baby, one mother wrote in *Changed by a Child* (Gill, 1997), "We have been struck by something unexpected, unwanted, undesirable . . . a grievous thing, an event that marked us out and separated us from the group. To be alone in the sense of not belonging is terrifying. Our trauma may make us feel disconnected not only from society, but also from time, from the flow of our life . . ." (p. 18).

A recurrent motivation or life theme may be to rediscover human connections, to find a place to belong. Those experiencing ongoing, un-removable loss will long for (and often distrust) relational opportunities and a place where they can feel safely understood and accepted, a place where they do not always feel several hundred light years removed from other human beings. For some caregivers who are ministering to the person who is the source of sorrow, disconnection from others may be secondary to an even more painful disconnection from the one who is lost. Intimacy in any context is increasingly problematic and complex when the one to whom the heart is given has rejected us. Secunda (1997) has reported difficulty in intimacy as a key issue in siblings and offspring of the severely mentally ill. Intimacy can be a major issue for anyone who is coping with chronic sorrow. Rejection by the one who is lost can occur at many levels, from a failure to recognize the caregiver to being incapable of responding reciprocally to expressions of love to angry and physically assaultive reactions (such as in certain organic brain syndromes). The caregiver may experience, especially in the latter case, the "intimacy of rejection." The caregiver and the receiver are emotionally isolated from each other. This type of dual isolation and perpetual aloneness is a major tragedy of autism and certain other brain disorders. The caregiver may learn that any urge to express heartfelt love and affection triggers a fear of rejection, trauma, and injurious loss of meaningful connected-ness. Feelings of love and affection are associated with emotional pain and are experienced as stressful and risky. They are not to be trusted, and elaborate defenses must be crafted. One must walk a very fine line in order to maintain a "comfort zone" in relationships.

Chronic sorrow can dissipate fantasies of being watched over by a lov-ing and caring God, or of having friends or family members who will truly understand and be fully present. These fantasies may be extremely difficult to restore. While some will find their religious beliefs strength-ened, it is not at all unusual for persons experiencing a catastrophic, ongoing loss to feel intense anger—even hatred—toward fate or at God. The concept of a supreme being who is loving and personally concerned about one's state of being may have been the crucial shelter from aloneness.

When God is perceived as abandoning or cruel, the recourse may be to disown God, either out of retaliation or out of despair. There is no longer believable imagery of a protective and caring deity. Many will eventually be able to restore and restructure their spiritual lives, their roles, and their connections with a higher power. Others may never again be able to sustain a belief in God or a life force that is benevolent and caring, preferring to keep the heart and soul protected from devastating betrayal or wounds perceived to come from powerful sources outside the self. In this case, a primary way to achieve some mitigation of aloneness is foreclosed. Helpful and normal fantasies of sheltering relationships on any level may fade as a consequence of growing awareness of essential and utter aloneness. In chronic sorrow, exacerbated aloneness may reappear over time as a dominant issue because of the discontinuity in adult identity development and in phases of the adult life cycle. Crises, deterioration of condition, and additional important losses over the life span will increase the probability of intense psychic pain related to ultimate aloneness.

People whose lives are based on a fatalistic philosophy may have fewer spiritual conflicts and significantly less distress, and some may be able to make the tragedy of the loss fit more easily into their belief systems. In the Islamic faith, for example, life circumstances are understood as the will of Allah. Emphasis is placed on truth, which is the basis of all understanding. It is important, therefore, to know the truth about catastrophic conditions. The suffering inherent in disabilities and illness is believed to be physically and spiritually cleansing. As Allah has determined the tragedy that has befallen the individual, then it must be accepted, and trust must be put in Allah. Putting one's trust in Allah, however, does not mean indifference or lack of responsibility. An Arab parable sums up the operative concept. A man traveling with Muhammad asked, as they were stopping for the night, whether he should tether his camel or trust in God. Muhammad replied: "Trust in God—and tether your camel" (Lippman, 1995, p. 76). It is thought by those in most Islamic cultures that very few individuals are meant to have lives characterized by an abundance of success, material wealth, and other good fortunes. Those who are blessed in this way have had great *baraka* bestowed on them by Allah. They are special people who have been given unusual benefits. They are the ones with good luck in life. Islamic communities may accept and support those with very poor luck, maintaining social connections in a shared belief system that is less stigmatizing and more affiliative.

The nature of the loss that generates chronic sorrow, in and of itself, often leads to a significant reduction of opportunities to temper the sense of isolation and aloneness that accompany debilitating conditions. For instance, impaired communications and conditions that violate specific cultural values of human attractiveness and social acceptability are likely to lead to negative responses or ostracism. A self-loss which includes major craniofacial distortions or other conditions of a "spoiled identity" will inevitably lead to social responses of uneasiness, even revulsion or feigned nonperception. That is, the person will either be treated as an unacceptable alien or as if he or she does not exist. Since, as Irvin Yalom (1980) has stated, the "major buttress against the terror of existential isolation is . . . relational" (p. 363), efforts will need to be made to overcome obstacles (internal and external) to bridging interpersonal gaps. Yalom refers to the central issue in relationships as being one of negotiating the polarities of fusion-isolation. It is in facing our aloneness that we are ultimately able to engage with another in a deep and meaningful way. Out of our aloneness can come a reaching out to others and the development of compassion for others who are facing their own fears. Although no relationship can abolish isolation, it is the facing of our separate aloneness that can enable some of us to share our aloneness in such a way that love compensates for the pain.

Those dealing with the circumstances of chronic sorrow are aware of their differentness. It is often difficult to find a common ground with others. Isolation and aloneness may be intensified by the narrowing of mutually shared intersections between self and other. However, a by-product and benefit of confronting existential aloneness that often has positive payoffs may come from learning not to care so much about what we imagine other people to be thinking about us. Awareness of aloneness may also instruct us to give up pretense and artifice and to see certain attitudes and fears as frivolous and just so much wasted energy. The discovery of resources and strength can emerge. If being alone and experiencing the dread of aloneness is what is feared the most, the onset of chronic sorrow will provide many opportunities for confronting this core terror.

☐ Vulnerability

If we cannot control or contain a life event so major and reprehensible as this traumatic loss that has initiated us into the world of chronic sorrow, then what control over our lives do we actually have? Having lost so many of our infantile illusions of omnipotence already, we may have clung to the belief that in adulthood we would regain a sense of autonomy and control. We have learned that authority figures as well as the self are not so powerful, and our concept (or projection) of God may have changed and become less powerful or extremely confusing. By the time we have reached adulthood, we have already had our earlier impressions and fantasies of omnipotent protection and ultimate rescue shattered, in a gradual and tolerable way perhaps. We have seen and felt our own dependencies, and we have learned that our parents, once perceived as all-knowing and all-powerful, are really ordinary people with their own insecurities and conflicts. We have inevitably experienced a series of disappointments, and even our heroes and role models have usually shrunk proportionately. Injury, personal losses, failures in important relationships and personal goals, illness, and other assorted evidence of our tenuous control over the world have usually been assimilated to some degree.

With the initial confrontation and the subsequent persistent stress of managing a loss that cannot be removed, we are repeatedly confronted with the fragile nature of life itself. We realize that anything and anyone is subject to destruction, without warning, and that we are without the power to prevent or impede the process. There is no way ever again to be wildly naive. When there is a living loss, the sense of dyscontrol and of helpless vulnerability can be immense. For those with self-loss who must look to others for survival and affectional needs, vulnerability is seldom subject to denial or to disregard. When there is a dependency on home health providers, trainers, physical therapists, and other health care professionals, caring and caregiving family members and the person who is the focus of care are confronted daily with possibilities that necessary support will not show up. Sometimes the fear that help will not be forthcoming will be the subject of repetitive bad dreams. Anxiety regarding potential abandonment may become thematic.

During the time when there is a search for a diagnosis, which may last many months or even many years (sometimes it never comes), the anxiety of vulnerability often peaks. There is a desire to know the worst, and simultaneously there is the need to maintain hope. As Featherstone (1980) has written, there is a pressing need to put an end to the anxious waiting, "to exchange butterflies in the stomach, if need be, for a lead weight on the heart" (p. 96). But once the diagnosis is made, the most crucial questions may go unanswered, and overwhelming fears may not be addressed. These uncertainties may foster a kind of panic or terror. Some previously successful ways of coping with crisis may not only be ineffectual, they may increase the realization of powerlessness to change the course of truly tragic circumstances.

A mother of a child with serious impairments, fighting for appropriate services and running into brick walls, wrote: "Yesterday my husband became emotional at my daughter's PET meeting. I think he was feeling helpless (I know I was) about how one teacher was stonewalling. . . . So his eyes welled up and his voice cracked, and then he stopped to regain his composure. The group was awkwardly speechless, but it sure did get their attention. . . . My husband has just become aware of the issues . . . we have a six-year-old daughter who is nonverbal, and he's just now starting to get it . . . five and a half years behind me. . . . He's been moved to tears three times this month in different groups talking about Jess's disability. He's just now tapping into the vulnerability that this stuff brings up" (Newman, 1995, pp. 114–116). Aloneness with the vulnerability, as experienced by this mother since her daughter's infancy, can heighten the sense of being unprotected.

Vulnerability is more problematic in chronic sorrow than in many other types of grief. After all, vulnerability cannot be prevented, for it has been confirmed already by the catastrophic, life-changing, ongoing loss. The anxiety of vulnerability is both sustained and elevated since (*a*) the loss is permanent and lives on, providing constant and unmitigated evidence of vulnerability that precludes efforts at denial, repression, and resolution, (*b*) there are constant reminders of how things "should be" or "should have been," and (*c*) the actual vulnerability of the individual who is the source of the loss can be magnified for that individual and can foster a reciprocal and vicarious (or empathic) vulnerability in the caregiver.

The nature of the loss involved in chronic sorrow is likely to promote a type of worry, agitation, and fearfulness that one will not be prepared for what lies ahead. Will I be able to deal with this for the rest of my life? When I can no longer do this, who will care for my loved one? Who will love her enough to do all the things I do to help her have a decent life? Who will love her at all? Conversely, who will care for me if something happens to my spouse, my mother, or the nurse who knows me so well? What if someone doesn't know what to do if I get an infection? The need to somehow be prepared for anything that might threaten to devastate the vital and delicate system of care often leads to fatiguing and futile worrying involving what-if scenarios. In an already anxious person, these fantasies can grow to include a wide range of potential horrors—fires, depletion of financial resources, random violence, abuse, heartless neglect, various types of injury, and so on. Many parent narratives about their lives with severely impaired children reveal their intense fear about the uncertainties of the future and their realization that there is no other option but to learn to live with extraordinary fear. For the sake of mental health, some of these parents caution against planning too far ahead. Strong (1989) has written about her anxieties and those of others she knows who have spouses with MS. A primary source of increased vulnerability she cites is having no active team members and no one to fall back on (that is, no Plan B).

There are many mechanisms by which we can attempt to reduce or conceal our anxieties related to vulnerability, ranging from addictions, obsessions, and interpersonal enmeshments, to projections, identification with perceived power, personal grandiosity, protective religious beliefs, overfunctioning, judgmental attitudes, controlling and manipulative behaviors, and so on. Anger can function to obfuscate feelings of weakness, helplessness, and dependency. Anger can help us feel stronger and more forceful. Since it can also serve to alienate those persons who are our often meager sources of support, an overuse of anger can unintentionally increase our vulnerability, both actual and imagined. For those experiencing the grief of chronic sorrow, defensive mechanisms are frequently of limited value.

The ability to tolerate a heightened awareness of vulnerability is crucial to resiliency and endurance. Some perception of power in the sense of having influence in interpersonal relationships is crucial to the maintenance of self-esteem. Having the opportunity to ventilate feelings of anxiety to someone who is able to listen empathically and who can skillfully (without minimizing the fears) function as a trusted reality check can be an important anchor. Validation of current coping style and tangible evidence that past crises have been resourcefully and creatively addressed are helpful in providing a more balanced view of the problem situation. Stress management that is realistic in terms of prevailing conditions and time constraints can be useful in preventing decompensation, in restoring confidence, and in giving both caregiver and care recipient permission to insist on personal time and comforting interruptions in the daily demands. Respite services, an empowering kind of encouragement, and a willingness to be available are gifts of compassion that can soothe the tortured soul.

☐ Inequity

The moral and ethical dilemmas that accompany chronic sorrow are usually more conscious and more consciously repetitive than other existential issues. They are closely allied with disillusionment and are usually the first to emerge and the easiest to verbalize. In the author's clinical experience, the work of psychotherapy is often to address a client's attempts to fit her life experiences of injustice and inequity with cherished beliefs about fairness, rewards associated with hard work and good intentions, and "playing by the rules." We have often internalized, from our earliest childhood, important and supportive myths or beliefs such as Good is stronger than evil; Justice will prevail; We reap what we sow; Love conquers all; A greater power or wisdom will mete out rewards and punishments according to merit even if we cannot determine that fair treatment is currently available.

Philip Roos (1977), writing at that time as national executive director of the Associations for Retarded Citizens—U.S., referred to the overwhelming sense of inequity that a parent of a child who is severely mentally retarded faces. In a parent's search for answers, she or he is "likely to entertain two possibilities: either s/he deserves the 'punishment,' because of grievous 'sins,' or the world is neither fair nor just. The former alternative generates guilt, remorse, and self-recrimination; the latter endangers fundamental ethical, moral, and religious beliefs" (pp. 103–104). Under stress, a person confronting ongoing loss may opt for both explanations, of course. Whatever the case, the person is thrown off the path and into the ditch. He will be forced to grapple with fundamental questions: "Why me?" "Is there a God?" "Does God know or care about what is happening to me?" "Why does God allow this to happen?" "Have I actually done something so terrible as to deserve this?" In the case of the child who is severely damaged, the question may be "How could God do this to a child who has surely done nothing wrong?"

Perceptions of great inequity can impel us to actions intended to make right the terrible wrongs. Where fault can be assigned, the injured party or family members may decide on civil remedies such as personal injury or medical malpractice litigation. When the severe and permanent disabilities have been caused by criminal negligence or reckless disregard for life and safety, or by other criminal behaviors (such as in drunk driving, aggravated assault, shootings, attempted homicide, or hit-and-run), participation in the state's prosecution may help in restoring some semblance of justice and in gaining some control. Providing the prosecutor with information to develop testimony, becoming knowledgeable about criminal proceedings, direct testimony, and so on, may reduce the sense of having to passively take whatever comes. Victim impact statements can also function to validate the hurt that has been done. Victims and their families often feel that they have done the "right thing" and that they have discharged their responsibility when they take active roles in legal proceedings. Feeling purposeful and not ignored or dismissed can be empowering. However, there are also costs in looking to the courts for justice. Engaging in personal injury litigation or assisting in the criminal justice system can bring additional stress to people who are already at the limit of endurance. If there has been an unrealistic view of legal outcomes (that is, that they will "fix things"), there may be ever increasing grief and angst when justice is not perceived to happen. Legal proceedings can take years, and the process may intermittently reactivate the initial trauma of the loss, since certain details will need to be kept fresh in the mind.

There are sound reasons for using the courts to decrease feelings of inequity, but there are no guarantees that this will occur. Lack of control over the process can intensify feelings of powerlessness and vulnerability. The process itself may take on characteristics of unfairness. For instance, the defendant may receive more consideration than the person who will contend with disabilities for the remainder of his life. If criminal prosecution results in a conviction, some monetary restitution may be ordered by the court, thereby holding the guilty party personally accountable. However, actually receiving the ordered restitution is highly unlikely. Perhaps most important, directing energy into extracting reparation can usurp internal resources that might be otherwise galvanized for the formidable task of integrating and accommodating the loss.

Issues related to inequity may be prominent for a long time. Estimates of the incidence or prevalence of a particular incapacitating condition (1 in 10,000) are not comforting. For the person suffering a chronic and recurring loss, the incidence is 100%! Unfairness is all around us. The person with other-loss who is essentially held prisoner by the need for constant and intricate caregiving has only to see her neighbors freely leaving and returning to their homes. The person with chronic mental illness who is discharged from yet another inpatient facility with no place to go and no plan at all is a sad contrast to someone who is malingering and has been milking the disability system for years. The indifference and randomness of the universe are hard to accept.

Having one's beliefs about fairness assaulted will affect how events and circumstances are interpreted. The meaning of life itself is at stake. Bitterness can set in and harden. It takes some time to realize that railing against injustices and rip-offs accomplishes one thing only: it makes us feel worse. Contending with the impact of ongoing, unremovable loss, especially in the early stages, severely narrows the focus of the mind. The perceptual world is filled with the loss. After some sense of mastery and effective problem solving have been achieved, a larger vision of the world can emerge. Recognizing that the underlying principle of fairness continues to shape the workings of the culture and is a coherent force in our system of government is reassuring. In the context of the bigger picture and a lifetime, positive beliefs about justice and equity—restructured to be sure—can be restored. For the parent or partner caregiver, however, another realization may eventually occur: that there is no one now and there may be no one in the future who will care for the caregiver as he or she is now doing for the one who is ongoingly lost.

☐ Insignificance

As adults, we begin to realize that we are only obscure (and temporary) players in the human universe. Some of us will make more of an impact than others. Through experience, most of us have learned to give up our infantile perceptions of importance and centrality. Only a very small minority of the human population achieves greatness. The remainder of us must learn the art of muddling through and to be content with replacing early fantasies with more reasonable expectations. Through compromise with earlier aspirations, we can direct our efforts to achieving meaning and importance by assuming certain social roles. We can be recognized for certain accomplishments in our work. We can contribute to the community by taking an active role in a wide variety of social institutions and by volunteering our skills in schools or hospitals. We can find personal satisfaction through our work in a church or through the political process.

Perhaps the most satisfying of roles are those of father, mother, husband, wife, sibling, close friend, and lover. We can find significance in knowing that we matter to someone we care for, someone who is deeply important to us. These primary roles give us a purpose in life and the feeling that our lives are worthwhile. Significance, self-esteem, and personal power are closely linked. They require each other. They help us to relate effectively to others, and they are necessary for integration of the self. Unless we feel that we count for something, we are adrift and bereft of meaning.

Disappointment in social roles can result in painful reactivation of feelings of insignificance. For instance, disappointment in the role of life partner can occur when the mate, as a result of severe cerebrovascular insult, may barely be able to recognize his partner. A severe violation of expectations has occurred. Disappointment in the parental role that results from having a child with autism or other severe developmental impairment can intensify feelings of insignificance by denying the parent ordinary opportunities to experience personal importance to his child. In any context, the role of provider of lifelong care for a loved one tends to be inadequately recognized, minimally understood, and underappreciated by the greater society. Far too often, the one with self-loss becomes invisible to the community. Her caregiver may not be thought of as a separate person when social identity becomes fused with the one who is cared for. If the person with self-loss cannot participate in the larger community, it may be assumed that the caregiver is also unable to participate. They become an invisible *unit*. The caregiver must work hard at having an identity separate from the care receiver in order to have some recognition beyond the confines of this caregiving unit. If a sense of significance accrues relationally only from caregiving, there is a better than average chance of burnout and clinical depression.

Moreover, the longing for some sign of recognition or appreciation from the loved one for the devotion and personal sacrifice attendant to lifelong care—willingly given though they may be—may trigger guilt in the caregiver. How dare she want something, anything at all, from someone so damaged, someone who hasn't the capacity for independent life or, in many cases, for any meaningful attachment. Some might say that gratitude as an emotion would not exist if we did not make it exist through early stages of learning and development. Its perpetuation may be due to ethical teachings and "payoffs" in adulthood. Appreciation and gratitude, however, are powerful reinforcers to most caregivers and can greatly enhance their satisfaction with their roles. It may be adaptive for many caregivers to suppress or repress their longings for some awareness of their devotion so as to avoid further guilt and to forestall surges of grief related to the loss of even that response in her lifetime. A parent of a severely impaired child, already denied the usual opportunities to experience personal importance to the child, cannot even share with other parents, in the conventional way, the child's accomplishments. In the larger social reality, that parent and his parental mission are largely ignored or deeply discounted. There is a failure of fit.

Persons with socially stigmatizing conditions, already challenged in most aspects of life, are often placed in situations of marginality; that is, they are frequently "not seen" by others. Experiential exercises that send students in various fields of therapy and rehabilitation into urban areas with mock physical disabilities prove very enlightening and informative for these future professionals. Some will report "not being there," that people removed themselves from close proximity or expressed aversion or distaste. It is not surprising that persons with disfiguring or other stigmatizing conditions, who live every day with these reactions, are at risk of internalizing this negative mirroring of themselves. Marginality fosters existential questioning such as What is the worth of my life? Does it matter? What is its meaning? And what purpose does it have?

Chronic sorrow can swiftly take away one's life purpose, but it can also give or replace it. The significance and meaning of life are not "out there," someplace; they are in the life that is actually being lived every single day. Significance can be found in the realities of courage and self-transcendency. Much could be done to develop theory about the psychology of service. Those with other-loss whose lives are characterized by dedication, commitment, and devotion know many things that others would be better off knowing as well. Learning the value of service to others, fighting for a cause, discovering personal tenacity and patience, loving without the conventional rewards: all of these actualizations of the self are integrative, significant, and meaningful. They also require no justification.

☐ Past Temporal Orientation

An important aspect of the human condition is the wonderful ability to transcend time. We can revisit the past through memory and artifacts. We are able to project ourselves into the future, where we can mentally rehearse various scenarios. Projecting oneself into the future is characteristic of those who are optimistic and planful, whereas avoiding the present and future through retreat into the past is associated with a number of psychological and emotional disorders, including depression. Most of us can reasonably look forward to happy times, to a future with improvements, growth, achievement, and other satisfactions. Those who are affected by chronic sorrow, however, will find the future to be filled largely with dread and apprehension. Thinking too far into the future will activate anxiety.

A family with whom the author worked several years ago in her practice illustrates a cumulative and interactive existential crisis that threatened the entire family system. This family included a mother and a father, in their late 30s; the oldest child, a 12-year-old son who had Down syndrome; another son aged nine; and a little girl, aged four. Over the course of about two years, the author intermittently saw the father, the mother, and the nine-year-old son. They were seen individually and in various combinations. The father made the initial appointment for himself. He was seen individually for a number of sessions before other family members were included.

This man had done "all the right things." He had worked extremely hard to move up the corporate ladder and had done well in his career. He loved his wife and derived considerable satisfaction from his family and from an active role in the community. As a couple, he and his wife were very dedicated advocates for people with developmental disabilities. Together, they had creatively worked out many perplexing problems related to the oldest child. They had not, however, grieved the loss of the child they had expected when this baby was born. They had stoically "faced the facts." Now the time was nearing when the son would move to a group home and live away from the family. The anticipated change—although the father felt it to be a positive one—was affecting all family members. The son was needing a lot of reassurance and encouragement from his parents and his siblings, especially his younger brother, in order to make the move effectively. The parents had not expected any of their children to leave home in this way. This was not what should have been. The parents were apprehensive, and neither wanted to think too far ahead, to "wade into the swamp." They were especially worried about the quality of the staff and the chance that the group home might be bought by another health care company or that it would not be well managed. They were worried about the home's continuing existence, in view of the prevailing focus on the "bottom line," that is, that the home make a profit. The future was unpredictable and frightening.

The mother had worked very hard, both inside and outside the home; she had been active in the community and had held a full-time job until the birth of the youngest child. Shortly after that child was born, she began to have "odd symptoms," such as blurred vision, some clumsiness, and occasionally some difficulty writing. She had been diagnosed as having multiple sclerosis about a year before the father made his appointment for therapy. The father was struggling with his conscience, as he was having urges to "run away." He did not want to think about the future and was immobilized. He was clinically depressed (sleeping fitfully, eating poorly, losing weight, essentially anhedonic, unable to be sexual with his wife, and frequently tearful). He had begun to volunteer for company trips and to fantasize about moving out of the house (the beautiful house he and his wife had designed and built only three years before). He was mentally rehearsing a future that would be free of worry. He felt alone with his guilt and repulsed by himself. He had even begun to think of divorce, and he was ashamed of these thoughts. He was overwhelmed by his future. He wanted to "stop the clock."

After several months of very difficult work in therapy, he invited his wife to join him in his sessions. They worked diligently to do what they could to reconstruct their relationship. They expressed their sadness at the loss of the future they had expected with each other. Both realized that they would have to move out of their dream house. It was not at all workable for the wife to manage and negotiate a multilevel living space. The house had ceased being a realistic house. It was, however, a house steeped in symbolism. To let go of their dream and to transfer it to others was extremely painful. Symbolically, the nurturing container of their rightful future would have to go to someone else who would thereby claim what should be theirs. They were bitter and angry; they cried together over the loss of their denied future. They recognized the important endings that were occurring in their lives. Her MS symptoms were rapidly worsening, and she often needed help just to get out of the bathtub. As they grieved the loss of their house (their future), they grieved the loss of the idealized firstborn. They were emotionally attuned and together at this crossroads. They reminisced about the good things in the past. Neither could project into the future beyond the sale of the house.

A few months after they left therapy, they brought the second oldest child, by now age 10, to therapy. The son himself had asked to see me. His older brother was living in the group home and was very homesick, although he visited the family home every other weekend. The little sister was in preschool and very happy and carefree. The house was for sale, and things were being packed up in anticipation of a move. This son asked his parents to stay for the first session. He described a vague sort of anxiousness. He had developed the habit of going to bed at night, and then—after his parents were asleep—he would get up and walk through the house many times, checking on his parents and his little sister. He essentially kept watch over the night. He had become very tired and was fighting to stay awake when he was in school.

It soon became clear to all of us that this child had taken it upon himself to do the worrying for the entire family. His parents, in their efforts to protect him, had not shared with him their many deep concerns. They were attempting to keep things light and "cheerful" and encouraged him to be playful and fun-loving. Their protective efforts had left him with the impression that they were oblivious to the potential problems of the future. Before the older brother moved to the group home, the younger son had often had responsibility for him, and he was distressed that his brother was not adapting well to the new residence. His little sister was far too young to understand the serious implications of the mother's MS. *Someone* had to take care of this family, and the ten-year-old had taken on that job. During his therapy with me I insisted that his parents explain the assumed nonlethality of the mother's condition. I asked them to explain to him that they had thoroughly thought through what could happen in the future and that there was a plan for how to manage if his mother became more seriously disabled. The parents were also encouraged to develop a letter of intent and a plan just in case "something" should happen to both of them. They did this, and they shared the main points of the plan with him. Other strategies, systems, and interpersonal interventions took place during his therapy. For instance, I suggested that he experiment with getting up only on Wednesday, Friday, and Saturday nights, and that he put all his worries into those three nights and see how this worked for him. He accepted this suggestion with alacrity and found that he could sleep well on the other nights. On his own, he further reduced his getting up and checking behavior and then gave it up altogether. He was able to get back on track. He could look to the future without great sleep-depriving anxiety. He could free up and play again, and he could sleep well again. He could go on into his future, even without guarantees.

He brought a large volume of Georgia O'Keeffe art with him to his last session. We sat close to each other on the sofa and shared the beautiful colors and shapes. He described what he saw in some of the larger abstract works. He was relaxed, and it was a mutually special time, tender and trusting. His projections and imagery stimulated by the art were generally positive and associated with calm or blithe affect. With certainty, this family would face future difficulties, but for now the members were no longer frozen in place and time.

The mother of a young child who once was apparently normal in every way, only to rapidly go into a spiral of deterioration (childhood disintegrative syndrome), wrote of her fears of the future in *When Autism Strikes* (Goldstein, 1998). She describes her son's condition and prognosis as extremely poor. Evaluative tests and examinations had been exhaustive, and his condition had steadily worsened. She and her husband were at the point of having to make impossible, heartbreaking decisions.

"If Abe and I wanted a normal home life for ourselves and Lea, Ben could not live with us beyond age 10 or 11. Although my feelers are out for living situations for this Ben of the future, I do not have a great desire to find out about what is available for a child with Ben's limited skills. . . . I feel our greatest challenges are still ahead. When Ben bounces out of bed at night, who will lie down with him if we do not? I think I know the answer, and it scares me" (p. 220).

When the future is "loaded," that is, when it holds little promise for improvement in the one we care for, or for ourselves, we will tend to block the future, shifting our focus to a past where we may have once experienced hope and happiness, a past when the future was not so threatening. For those affected with chronic sorrow, there is a sense of being prematurely old so that the future is viewed very much like an elderly person might view it. However, the ability to construct a future that contains something—even a small, simple pleasure—to look forward to can be an antidote for depression. Careful planning for the future is incumbent on those experiencing ongoing loss, even when planning becomes difficult because there is a need to avoid the anxiety generated by projections into the future. The author has observed that many persons affected by chronic sorrow process time in a somewhat different way than others. Life is lived on a different time trajectory than that of "normals." Life markers are more indistinct, distorted, and unpredictable when they exist. For example, customary times for starting to school, for leaving home, for various developmental milestones, and for celebrating rites of passage, may be quite different in cases of chronic sorrow, when life phases and patterns are not at all in keeping with cultural and societal customs. Life may be measured and noted instead by crisis markers (before or after a person began to have seizures; before or after a certain emergency hospitalization, before or after the need for a wheelchair, and so on). While most persons can report a sequentially coherent personal narrative, complete with dates and ages of major players, a person experiencing chronic sorrow may have much more difficulty estimating dates or numbers of years that have elapsed since the occurrence of certain events associated with their lives. Past, present, and future are not clearly demarcated. Many aspects of life remain constant, including the disability of the person who is the source of sorrow. The author has suggested the term *marker bereft* to refer to this phenomenon.

☐ Mortality

Death is inescapable. We are all terminal cases. Death lies in the future for us all. No matter how many kidney or heart transplants we get, we will die eventually. The anticipation of death tends to be a major source of existential concern and anxiety. It is the knowledge of our finiteness that may underlie certain phobias and other irrational fears. Options do exist for mitigating our fears, including knowing that we will live on through our children and their children. However, for parents of children who are severely impaired and for others when the severity of the disability precludes having children, achieving such symbolic and genetic immortality through one's offspring is unavailable or seriously compromised. If the severely impaired child is an only child, this particular avenue toward immortality is removed and gone. The only child's parents are faced with the prospect of the ultimate obliteration of their identities. Achieving a way to make known, after life ceases, that one has existed for a while on this earth is likely to be impossible.

There are related concerns for caregivers who are often tasked with caring for their loved one who will, in all probability, outlive them. The fragility of life and the concern for what will happen to one's partner or child in the event of one's death, illness, or disability, can be a source of great stress. Anxiety for the frailty of life itself can be pronounced when there is a significant health problem in the caregiver. The overriding question then becomes: Will I last long enough to care for the one I love? As the caregiver ages or when he or she begins to weaken because of poor health, it is not so unusual as we would prefer to think for the caregiver to harbor fantasies of a double or simultaneous death (that is, a murder and a suicide). Worry about what will happen to the one who is the receiver of care after the caregiver dies is both disturbing and realistic. The awareness of mortality and ultimate personal powerlessness can be experienced as "always there" for many who cope with chronic sorrow. If the loss is a self-loss, chronic anxiety and concern for the lives of those who care for you may become focal and draining.

In a complex society such as ours, there is usually little tolerance for deviations such as exist in ongoing loss and chronic sorrow. Existential conflicts have no easy answers, and many professionals find themselves very wary of wading into these waters. Nevertheless, serious existential anxieties and conflicts related to chronic sorrow may become overwhelming. Unless they are recognized by helping professionals and addressed in some way, they may block efforts in problem solving, planning, grief work, and adjustment. After all, we are born in pain and often die in pain; therefore, it is only logical that we should also learn to live in pain. We can learn to live so as not to frantically reject or attempt to avoid pain at the expense of living fully, developmentally, and generatively the life we are given.

Complicating Factors

While chronic sorrow per se is a nonpathological, pervasive response to a continuing loss, circumstances can considerably complicate that response. These complications can result in decompensation of prior levels of functioning and may lead to (a) major depression, (b) regression to earlier and more primitive coping, (c) affective overload, (d) immobilizing guilt, (e) anger dyscontrol (f) increased number and severity of stress-related physical ailments with decreased efficiency of the immune system, (g) emotional numbing, including dissociative symptomatology, (h) protracted individual and interpersonal systemic disorganization, and (i) psychotic states. Although positive strengths and qualities often emerge from the development of personal resources, those who experience chronic sorrow have an increased susceptibility and reactivity to additional stressors. The delicate balance they have achieved often belies how little it might take to topple it. What may seem to others to be a normal, or even an advantageous, life event may be experienced as traumatic and pernicious by those experiencing self- or other-loss. For example, culturally valued celebrations (Christmas, Easter, Mother's Day, Father's Day, graduations, birthdays, anniversaries) may be times of dread, vulnerability, and increased stress. Even apparently minor additional stressors may precipitate pathological conditions. The impact of these stressors may best be understood in terms of what they mean to the individuals and how they operate contextually. Case material included in this chapter will illustrate the usefulness of this type of assessment.

□ **Stress**

A lifetime of chronic sorrow is a lifetime of stress, both chronic and episodic. Events experienced as stressful are not only the major or cataclysmic changes but also the routine hassles of day-to-day living (Lazarus & Folkman, 1984). Viewing loss of ability in the context of chronic sorrow, described as a recurrent stress pattern, Hewson (1997) has proposed an episodic stress model as an alternative to models of grief that are based on death and dying. She indicates that a similar range of responses is observed both in those who sustain a loss of ability and in their close family members. She lists in this range of responses: (a) emotional states such as shock, sadness, anger, and guilt, (b) physical responses such as feeling hollow, headaches, and fatigue, (c) cognitive responses such as denial, questioning, confusion, rumination, and a sense of going crazy, and (d) behavioral responses such as social withdrawal, sleep disturbances, restless overactivity, and crying. Hewson's episodic stress model makes a useful distinction between primary and secondary stress episodes. Primary stress episodes are related to extreme emotional and life-changing events, such as the time of first diagnosis (when recognition and adjustment are demanded) and when there are subsequent major crises. Secondary stress episodes refer to periods when the appraised stress is not as inherently challenging to daily routine and the future (cumulative stress, constancy of reality demands, fatigue, lack of support, emotional reactions to triggers such as developmental milestones which are not achieved when expected, and so on).

Symptoms of post-traumatic stress disorder can be observed in some parents of children who are severely incapacitated by autism and also in foster and adoptive parents of children who have attachment disorders caused by trauma, abuse, and severe neglect in infancy. Without any warning or preparation, many foster and adoptive parents of attachment-disordered children have found themselves in what has been called a war zone. The discrepancy between parental hopes and expectations and the reality of a child who believes the new parents are the enemy who will cause him unbearable pain can be devastating. Having had no basic training for helping their children or themselves, parents can feel abandoned, alienated, deceived, confused, demoralized, and inept. Adoption Quest (2000, online) indicates that parents of attachment-disordered children cannot avoid being adversely affected and that their ongoing stress can threaten their psychological and physical health.

For these parents the symptoms of post-traumatic stress disorder include (a) flashbacks and intrusive thoughts and images, (b) feelings of detachment or estrangement from others, (c) restricted range of affect, and (d) increased arousal, such as difficulty sleeping, irritability, angry outbursts, hypervigilance, difficulty concentrating, and exaggerated startle response. Secondary symptoms include: (*a*) realization of changes in self and the world, (*b*) decreased ability to enjoy social interactions, (*c*) feeling different from others, (*d*) lowered self-esteem, (*e*) feeling out of control emotionally, and (*f*) physical symptoms. Existential changes include (*a*) high attunement to potential dangers, (*b*) selective perception, (*c*) loss of the illusion of security, (*d*) loss of meaning, (*e*) deempowerment, (*f*) depression, and (*g*) stressful relationships with significant others.

Stress has been linked to a variety of mental and physical disorders. It is not yet understood how much a person's stress contributes to vulnerability to diseases that would normally be deflected by the immune system. Generalizing from studies that demonstrate a linkage between "something that increases or decreases stress and some disease or mortality outcome," Sapolsky (1998) describes the linkage as a four-step process:

1. We differ as to the pattern and frequency of stressors to which we are exposed.
2. These variations will determine the magnitude and frequency with which we turn on the stress-response (glucocorticoids, epinephrine, and so on).
3. The magnitude and frequency of the stress-response regulates immune competence.
4. Our level of immune competence, in turn, determines what diseases we get and how readily we resist them. (p. 140)

It is commonly recognized that the stress response (the body's physiological responses) is well adapted for dealing with physical demands on a short-term basis, that anxious worry turns on the stress response, and that this response can be very harmful when it is evoked on a prolonged or chronic basis. In this case, the stress response does not become depleted, but rather, with extensive activation the response itself can be damaging. As Sapolsky (1998) points out, "If you experience every day as an emergency, you will pay the price. . . . If you suppress immune function too long, trouble will surely follow" (p. 13). In describing the effects of a stressor, he writes:

> The idea of temporarily perking up your immune system with the onset of a stressor makes a fair amount of sense (certainly at least as much as some of the convoluted theories as to why suppressing it makes sense). As does the notion that what goes up must come down. And as does the frequent theme of this book, namely, that if you have a stressor that goes on for too long, an adaptive decline back to baseline can overshoot and you get into trouble. (p. 116)

Social isolation and bereavement are associated with the stress response and with diseases traceable to immune dysfunction. People who have few social relationships tend to have shorter life expectancies and be affected more severely by various infectious diseases (House, Landis, & Umberson, 1988). Becoming isolated from one's significant other (for example, during the process of divorce or marital separation) is very stressful and is associated with worsening immune functioning (Herbert & Cohen, 1993), and depressed immune function has been found in people who have high scores on loneliness scales (Kiecolt-Glaser, Garner, Speicher, Penn, & Glaser, 1984). These findings on the effects of social stressors apply to both men and women, and the impact of social relationships on life expectancy appears to be as large as the impacts of smoking, hypertension, obesity, and physical activity. Bereavement has been correlated with increased risk of dying in a number of studies (Kiecolt-Glaser & Glaser, 1991; Levav, Friedlander, Kark, & Peritz, 1988). In these studies, significantly higher mortality rates were found when bereavement was coupled with an already existing loss and bereavement process.

These studies apply to chronic sorrow in several ways. Social isolation (as well as alienation) is common in persons with self-loss and with other-loss. Social support and protective relationships can be of great protective importance in chronic sorrow, whatever the locus of the loss. Since grief responses are at the heart of chronic sorrow, it is reasonable to assume that added significant stressors—especially stressors related to other losses—can result in decreased immune efficiency. In parents of children with serious developmental disabilities, studies have generally documented more reported, stress-related symptomatology in mothers than in fathers (S. Cummings, 1976; Damrosch & Perry, 1989; Dunst, Trivette, & Cross, 1986; Gath & Gumley, 1986). More recently, in a longitudinal study reported in *The APA Monitor* (Sleek, 1993), researchers have found that aging adults who have spent prolonged, burdensome periods caring for an ill family member continue to suffer stress-related physiological damage long after their loved one has died. Participants in this study, conducted in the psychiatry department at the Ohio State University School of Medicine, experienced lasting depression and impairment in immune system response. They, in fact, reported significantly more incidents of infectious illness than control subjects, even though they typically had fewer social contacts by which viruses are commonly contracted.

Mitigating factors that may reduce the effects of chronic sorrow have been identified. Some studies have found that a close caregiver-patient relationship is associated with less perceived burden (Williamson & Schulz, 1990) and less perceived stress (Horowitz & Shindelman, 1983) by the caregiver. Lower levels of caregiver depression have also been found when there is an affectionate relationship with the patient (Schulz & Williamson, 1991). Uchino, Kiecolt-Glaser, & Cacioppo (1994) have found that family caregivers of Alzheimer's patients who reported having higher affection for the patient before the onset of Alzheimer's had lower resting diastolic blood pressure and lower heart rate reactivity to the experimental stressors than caregivers who reported relatively low pre-illness affection.

Researchers have recently found that people who have experienced serious adverse life events often report benefits as well as harm from these events. Models based on understanding how people withstand the effects of adversity include (*a*) self-efficacy (Bandura, 1989), (*b*) Kobasa's (1979) theories on hardiness, and (*c*) studies and interventions based on resilience (Fraser, 1997; Werner & Smith, 1992). Effectively coping with adverse life events can result in stress inoculation effects leading to enhanced self-efficacy, coping skills, and an ability to prevent or reduce future stressors. Other benefits from adversity cited by McMillen (1999) are (*a*) positive changes in life structure (Lehman et al., 1993), (*b*) becoming more empathic and kinder (Tedeschi & Calhoun, 1995, 1996), and (*c*) transformation through finding meaning (Frankl, 1962, 1986; Silver & Wortman, 1980; Tedeschi & Calhoun, 1996). Those adversities that are relevant to chronic sorrow and for which benefit has been reported (McMillen, 1999) include AIDS, the birth of a seriously ill child, stroke, and caring for an ill relative.

For many persons with chronic sorrow, the wear and tear of stress related to daily living clearly add up. Since the stress response is activated not only by stressful events but also by worrying about them, there is ample opportunity for decreasing the immune system's effectiveness. Christopher Reeve (1998) has described the early aftermath of his spinal cord injury when he could not take a single breath on his own:

> . . . the connections of the hoses on these ventilators are tenuous at best. The nurses put tape over the joints, but they don't always hold very well, and you lie there at three in the morning in fear of a pop-off, when the hose just comes off the ventilator. I had several. After you've missed two breaths, an alarm sounds. You just have to hope that someone will come very quickly, turn on the lights, figure out where the break is, and put it back together. . . . So when you have a pop-off, there is no air in your lungs except for a tiny amount in the nooks and crannies. If you're pretty healthy, the percentage of oxygen that is getting to your brain can probably stay in the seventies, which means you can last a couple of minutes, but those are very, very anxious minutes. The nurses' station was not far away, but I was never sure how closely they were paying attention. They had many patients, I was alone in my room, and I had absolutely no control. . . . (p. 44)

Reeve also explains how he must be aware of his body at all times so that he can head off some emergencies before they have a chance to occur. When he was in Kessler for rehabilitation, he was required to read a manual about spinal cord injuries. He writes:

> It was the last thing I wanted to read: a book about my fearful present, my dismal future. But she made me read about bowels and sexuality and dysreflexia. Dysreflexia is a condition that results from a clogged bowel or urinary tract . . . or a kink in the catheter. It often happens quite suddenly, causing high blood pressure, and in some cases a heart attack or a stroke. It is particularly dangerous because a patient may not become aware of it until it is too late. The worst situation is to have it happen in a place where people know nothing about it. One day some of the rehab staff at Kessler took me to Newark Airport to learn how to board an airplane . . . I was relaxing and drinking a ginger ale when suddenly I felt my heart pounding . . . my heart was just booming. I asked Sylvia, "Could you take my pulse, my blood pressure?" My blood pressure was 140 over 100. Usually it's about 110 over 70. And my heart rate, usually about 68, was up to 135. Then I started to have an excruciating headache . . . and we knew I was experiencing my first bout of dysreflexia. (p. 113)

Reeve and the rehab staff members were in a public place without a catheter irrigation kit or nitro paste to lower his blood pressure. There was a kink in his catheter. The airport EMTs were called and, since it took them a half hour to arrive, Reeve's blood pressure rose to 210 over 150. He describes his fear, explaining that "when you are paralyzed you don't know when clogging is taking place. And many hospitals don't even recognize it when it happens. If you went to the emergency room of the average hospital with dysreflexia, they wouldn't know what you were talking about" (p. 114).

The daily stress for caregiving family members is intensified by wariness, vigilance, anxiety, and worry. In an interview with Marsh (1992), a mother of a child with developmental disabilities describes her constant stress:

> I wouldn't ever choose to have a retarded child. It's not fair to the child. It's a lifetime of agony. I never worry about my child. She's fine. It's the normal people on the street I have to worry about who would abuse her, would hurt her, take advantage of her, cheat her, not help her. She's just a wonderful person. Why anyone could reject her or should reject her I just can't understand. There's a lot of anger, a lot of sleepless nights. (p. 3)

Siblings and children of persons who have severe mental illness, Huntington's chorea, Alzheimer's, and other heritable conditions can ponder their own risks at length, and they can directly observe what it is they fear. Secunda (1997), in her study of family members of persons with mental illness, states: "The most pervasive legacy that looms over the lives of the siblings and offspring is the possibility that they, too, will become mentally unhinged. 'Anniversary reactions' punctuate their calendars—five, or twenty-five, years from now, I'll be the same age my relative was when he or she got sick. Family members constantly monitor themselves for signs of madness: If I have a fantasy, might it really be a hallucination? If I lose my temper, will I ever be able to stop? Am I a psychological time bomb?" (p. 9). Secunda also describes the stress of junior family members who attempt to compensate for the fallen relative by being perfect and becoming high achievers, taking on unreasonable challenges and putting themselves at risk of burnout or breakdown.

☐ Guilt

Guilt may be considered along a three-dimensional continuum: (a) guilt that is primarily based on rational considerations (for example, a mother's remorse over having a child with fetal alcohol syndrome), (b) a transitional area of guilt (for example, arising from inaccurate information provided by authority figures or from an inability to determine the cause of the loss), and (c) irrational guilt (for example, accidental injury or serious illness that is perceived as the basis for self-blame, leading to beliefs and cognitions of *shoulds* and *if onlys*, and other regrets and attributions of responsibility). There are many reasons for reactive guilt in those with chronic sorrow. Some guilt may be reasonable, and it is often a positive contributor to moral development and socialization in childhood. In chronic sorrow, however, guilt can lead to an impasse. It can prevent caregivers from doing what is in the best interests of those involved, and it can also foster a continuation of unwise actions, which tend to persist so long as the person feels guilty about them. In self-loss, the person may feel responsible, directly or indirectly and at varying levels of rationality and consciousness, for his or her own impairments. Such feelings of guilt are compounded by having needs for which others must now provide. Conversely, in other-loss, the spouse, parent, or other family caregiver may feel that he has caused or worsened the loss in some way.

Caring for the severely ill or impaired person is often highly overdetermined. Feeling tired, resentful, or irritable may foster even more guilt so that providing for the other may, in part, be an attempt at atonement or expiation of guilt. In this case, caregiving is experienced as an obligation and a duty to the person one has "wronged." Simultaneously, care is provided out of genuine affection, compassion, and commitment. Survivor guilt needs considerably more investigation. It is clear, however, that it can be a consistent source of angst. Bleuler (1974) conducted an extensive longitudinal study of over 200 families of persons with schizophrenia and referred to survivor guilt as the "shadow" that is cast over the lives of children of schizophrenic parents. Secunda (1997), referring to the children and siblings who were subjects in her research, states that one way children make sense of tragedy is to feel they caused it. She found that this belief often continues into adulthood. It can affect self-image and lead the child to doubt that there is a right ever to be happy. Though not intending to address guilt, Dunn's (1993) retrospective study of nine adults who had been reared by psychotic mothers revealed that themes of guilt and loyalty, pronounced in childhood, continued to be issues in adulthood. Survivor guilt may apply most to those who were with their loved one at the time of the tragic event that caused the person's permanent physical incapacitation or the person's "personality death." Could they have done something differently to avert the disaster? Do they have a right to their own survival? How can they be happy or pleased with their accomplishments without feeling guilty so long as the other cannot be restored or repaired?

An example of an especially complicated guilt response, with survivor overtones, involves an acquaintance of the author. This acquaintance is in her early 70s and has been caring for a daughter with multiple physical disabilities and mental retardation for at least 40 years. She also is the mother of two other adult daughters. One of these daughters has removed herself from any responsibility for her severely impaired sister and has disavowed any involvement in her care. The other daughter had willingly assumed the role of future guardian and caregiver for her sister when the mother died or could no longer carry the full load. About three years ago, this daughter died suddenly from an asthma attack. The mother of these three daughters has been unable to disentangle her feelings of grief, anger, despair, and guilt. She has admitted to being intermittently suicidal. For several months she did not visit her daughter with impairments because she felt so resentful and defeated in continuing to be charged with her care. She felt immense guilt for this neglect on her part. She continues to have thoughts that generate intense guilt. These thoughts are: (a) it should have been the daughter with the severe impairments who died, as this would have been "the solution," (b) she herself should have been the one who died, since this is the only thing that makes sense, (c) if one of her normal daughters had to die, it would have been "better" if it had been the daughter who would not become involved in her sister's care, and (d) she has failed in her commitment to see to it that when she dies, her impaired daughter will be cared for. She has not been able to find any peace and often resents the fact that she is still living. She has "run out of steam."

Guilt, survivor or otherwise, can be a major complication in chronic sorrow. It can overshadow mood, decision-making abilities, resilience, health, and even—when it is possible—potential resolution after the person who is the source of chronic sorrow is gone. A type of "until" scripting may be enacted (Berne, 1973; Steiner, 1975), based on the belief that one is not allowed to have a good life until the person to whom there is an attachment or obligation can have one or until all that can possibly be done to ameliorate the situation has been done. This belief, often largely unconscious, is a derivative of the concept that mandates no playing until all work is done. The "until" often becomes "never," wherein the person, much like Tantalus, is aware of all the good things he or she is missing but will never have.

☐ Identity

Complicating identity factors may be so subtle that their effects are difficult to isolate. Goffman's (1963) work continues to be useful to clinicians by underscoring the humiliation aspects of a "spoiled" identity in self-loss. Its stigmatizing effects may be internalized so that the person's identity is experienced as fundamentally flawed. Shame may be evident in both self- and other-loss, and shame-avoidant behaviors may evolve as major impediments to living life as fully as possible. In other-loss, much of the self may be defined by the totality of restrictive roles that relate to the loss. Roles and identity are often indistinguishable, so that the person assumes a largely unidimensional identity. The loss looms larger than self, and the mind is so crowded with the loss that it touches virtually all facets of life. The world and the self in the world can become increasingly distorted, leading to frequent misperceptions and faulty interpretations of experiences. Emotionally painful sequelae may then result, leading to maladaptive behaviors and mind-sets.

When the onset of the loss occurs in early childhood, late adolescence, emerging adulthood, or at any time the individual is confronting major identity decisions (that is, when the person is in a moratorium [Josselson, 1987]), the loss may become a solution in providing the person with answers to perturbing and anxious questions about what to do and be in life. Resolving identity questions in a way that is absolving of responsibility for choices may have some advantages, but it may also lock in an identity that will be inflexible to revision and avoidant of options that may be useful and somewhat freeing. Kohut and other theorists in the area of self psychology (Kohut, 1980, 1983; Ulman & Brothers, 1988) define the self as the core of the personality that can be reflected in the introspective ability to know who one is. The nuclear self is the most enduring part of the self. A similar conceptualization of the nuclear self is that it consists of the original program that was laid down, which is largely unconscious. This conceptualization implies that the nuclear self has a destiny that it tries to fulfill. Since both self- and other-loss can be formidable impediments to the self's original program, a perpetual frustration and dismay may result. It may not be entirely possible to comprehend and articulate the nature of the frustration and dismay since the original plan may not lend itself to conscious awareness.

☐ Symbiotic Enmeshment

In chronic sorrow, complications arising from symbiotically enmeshed relationships are common, and in some cases they are intractable. Enmeshed relational patterns are often unavoidable, and they are inseparably connected to identity and role. An argument can be made that symbiosis for mother and child is normal during infancy. In normal child development, the mother-child relationship gradually gives way to separation and individuation. When the severity and permanence of the child's impairments are such that he will always require care in order to continue living, normal developmental sequences do not occur, and symbiotic enmeshment may be difficult to interrupt. The foundation upon which all other parenting commitments rests is that of life sustenance and growth. When the mother or parental unit is assailed with a child's extraordinary needs that require priority attention, a frantic quality may permeate the interactive process. Over time, a symmetry of relatedness evolves, and the interaction is characterized by the blurring of the receiving and providing roles. Tension and relief are experienced on both sides of the symbiosis through the providing and receiving feedback loop. Attunement becomes so much more than attunement; it becomes a symbiotic enmeshment (or, perhaps more accurately, a secondary symbiotic system). A morbid joke about "codependency" begins to fit the situation. The joke refers to being in a near-death situation and having someone else's life flash before one's eyes.

The living of another's life leaves little space for a life and identity that is entirely one's own. The self, if experienced at all, may be experienced as being inhabited by another who displaces the self. Symbiotic enmeshment may endure throughout the lives of children who are severely disabled and their parents. Similar enmeshment may occur in the lives of partners and other persons in primary relationships where there is self- or other-loss. While protracted and intense affective resonance can provide a sense of solidarity, intimacy, and security, neither of the individuals will be able to achieve self-containment without undue anxiety unless boundaries are established.

Social contacts outside the symbiosis with severely enmeshed persons can become mere stages upon which the enmeshment is enacted rather than genuine interpersonal interaction. In one-on-one encounters, it is as if a third person is present who intrudes into every topic of conversation. It is virtually impossible to engage in a conversation that does not include repeatedly hearing of the one with whom the person is symbiotically attached. The enmeshed other is the reference for practically all other aspects of life. The author has observed in these instances that the symbiotically enmeshed person will grow increasingly agitated or anxious during those times when the content of the interaction cannot be construed to relate to the enmeshed other. As these intervals stretch out, an interesting type of separation anxiety occurs. As anxiety rises, the person will be compelled to bring up the name or some other identifying aspect of the enmeshed other. Then anxiety is immediately reduced, and allostasis is reestablished. This type of interaction inadvertently discourages attempts by others to connect with the person and may actually drive them away.

In extreme cases of symbiotic enmeshment, disturbance of the symbiosis creates a sense of threat to one's life, of impending death, and of an unbearable severing of life forces. The overwhelming sense of tearing or wrenching is doubtlessly a factor in cases where a partner dies or commits suicide soon after the death of the loved one. An extreme symbiosis was reported by Wallace (1987) who described twins in England who, from infancy onward, developed their own private language that was unintelligible to others. Even when they engaged in homicidal fantasies, threats, and injurious assaults on each other, life without the other was seen as intolerable and entirely untenable. Because of their repeated criminal misdemeanors, they were placed in a residential center as adolescents. One of these twins died in the early 1990s, and the surviving twin has reported knowing the thoughts, feelings, and physical experience of the other in her agonal death throes. It was reported that the survivor twin was being assisted to reframe and to interpret her sister's death as a gift from her sister that was meant to free each from the other and that because of the nature of the gift, it mandates that she continue to live.

Symbiotic relationships may continue even after the death of one of the individuals. The survivor may refuse to recognize the death and material absence of the other. Restructuring the relationship to accommodate the new reality may not be possible or wanted. Therefore, complicated or established pathological mourning may be more the rule than the exception after the loss of one with whom there has been symbiotic enmeshment. The survivor may repeatedly enter an impasse where the need to "let go" is experienced as not only "killing" or rejecting the other but also as the killing or rejecting of the self.

☐ Disordered Intimacy and Attachment

In many cases of self- and other-loss, there are virtual bombardments on primary relationships, and they suffer terribly. Several studies (Freeston, 1971; Marcus, 1977; Tew, Laurence, Payne, & Rawnsley, 1977) have reported increased marital breakdown and higher divorce rates in families dealing with a severe chronic illness or disability. But available studies do not fully reveal the impact of chronic sorrow on partnerships and on individual abilities to achieve and maintain intimacy and to forge relationships based on reciprocal authenticity. They do not fully reflect what is seen by clinicians who work with those who are beset with chronic sorrow. On the other hand, studies also have found remarkable strengthening in family relationships (for example, Wikler, Wasow, & Hatfield, 1983). That relationships are sometimes strengthened and that they endure at all are tributes to human courage and commitment.

As Kernberg (1980) has pointed out, real intimacy is possible only when people are truly separate individuals. When we are clear about who we are, we can be free to risk ourselves in relationships. Josselson (1992) has stated:

> Increasingly, we understand psychological conflict as resulting from distortions in relatedness, from being haunted by inner representations of past painful interactions with others, and from failures of the effort to have one's needs met. Inner conflict may also result when a person is overwhelmed by another's insatiable or inappropriate needs or is inadequately responded to by important others. (p. 18)

In clinical practice, the author has frequently worked with clients who have traced their disordered relational patterns directly to early experiences with parents who were psychotic, chronically ill, or otherwise severely disabled. One client, who was seen a few years ago and who had vegetative symptoms of chronic clinical depression, described her mother (who died from drowning) as having been diagnosed with bipolar affective disorder and alcoholism but as probably also suffering from schizophrenia. This client had no idea who her father was. The mother drank heavily and was often abusive and floridly delusional and went into psychotic rages. This client lived sometimes in children's homes, sometimes in foster homes, sometimes with neighbors or relatives, and sometimes with her mother. The mother had numerous husbands and boyfriends, some of whom sexually molested the client. She stated that she felt she had always been old, that she had always been alone, and that she had always been depressed.

This client had managed to complete high school, and she was proud of her accomplishment. Both as a child and as an adult, she felt responsible for her mother. As an adult, until her mother died, she was a primary agent of her care. She had the courage to marry. Her husband drank and used drugs and was shot to death in a drug deal that "went wrong." She now lives alone. This is her conscious choice and her preference. She is employed and is a conscientious worker and a valued employee. She did not come for therapy to increase her capacity for intimacy. Her stated reason for therapy was to obtain help with distressing job-related issues and decisions. Her closest attachment is to her dog, a little mongrel she brought back from Mexico several years ago. Her only family consists of an aunt, her mother's older sister. This client is anhedonic and wary and expresses no interest in attempting an intimate relationship. She is "content" with superficial interpersonal contacts.

The author's belief is that most individuals who have coped with the ongoing, unrelenting loss involved in chronic sorrow have developed some problematic responses that lead to some degree of difficulty in intimacy and attachment. Loving and caring for those who are severely limited in their abilities to make interpersonal connections (persons with autism, severe brain damage, severe and profound mental retardation, progressive neurological disease, those in coma, and so on) is fraught with potential for developing fears and anxieties leading to approach-avoidance behaviors with regard to other relationships. Loving someone who is sometimes open, sometimes rejecting, and sometimes unpredictably assaultive can eventually lead to a pairing of feelings of love with fears of imminent pain and injury. Unevenness of emotional supplies, disproportionate power, dwindling energy, the constancy of excessive reality demands, loss of self-esteem, diminished opportunities and means for mutuality, increased vulnerability, chronic anxiety and apprehension —all these factors contribute negatively to the achievement of satisfying intimate relationships. Some persons realize that interpersonal wounds related to trauma and to ongoing losses have influenced conscious decisions to avoid closeness and attachment in order to prevent the recurrence of intense emotional pain from potential future losses.

☐ Anger

It is difficult to imagine situations of chronic sorrow that do not include anger. Certainly one has the right to feel and express anger at the perceived injustice of a life of continuing loss. Furthermore, anger can be functionally valuable in (a) mobilizing our resources, (b) fostering communications, especially for relationship readjustments and "fresh starts," (c) redressing wrongs, (d) making demands, (e) organizing behavioral responses, (f) energizing constructive actions, and (g) clarifying and strengthening the self. However, anger can become a "racket" emotion (Berne, 1973), that is, an emotion that automatically replaces other emotions that either feel worse or that have frequently evoked responses of disapproval or indifference. The emotions that have been replaced (sadness, guilt, shame, vulnerability, fright, and so on) may eventually fade away. When a hint of sadness, for example, begins to enter awareness, it is immediately repressed or suppressed. Anger is quickly galvanized as a substitute emotion. Sadness is a passive response to loss, and when the loss is considered irrevocable, sadness is often experienced as weakness. By replacing sadness and other emotions associated with anxiety and helplessness, we protect ourselves from our fears. Anger can easily become a type of conditioned reflex, and as the preferred or favored emotion, it can intensify as well as generalize. Unfortunately, many complications can result from using anger as the "do everything" emotion.

Johnson (1990) has suggested that anger may be both a necessary response to chronic illness (and by extension, severe impairments) and an exacerbating agent in the illness or impairment. Coyne's (1976) interactive model of clinical depression, wherein depressed individuals produce a self-fulfilling cycle of negative interpersonal expectations through alienating behaviors that result in rejecting feedback, is analogous to what can occur when anger is the overriding emotion. Reactive depression may be seen as more understandable, and it may foster support and empathy. Conversely, expressed anger may be much less understandable and considerably less tolerated by others.

As theorized by Hobfoll (1989), loss per se is the central element of stress. His Conservation of Resources (COR) stress model challenges other conceptualizations (Selye's General Adaptation Syndrome, event-perception viewpoints, and so on). Germane to the COR model is the idea that people actively interact with their environments to increase their possibilities of reinforcement (Bandura, 1977). Success is more likely when individuals can create and maintain personal characteristics (self-esteem, efficacy, and so on) and social circumstances that increase the likelihood of reinforcement and protect against loss of such characteristics and circumstances (resources).

Hobfoll's (1989) definition of psychological stress is: a reaction to the environment that (*a*) causes a loss of resources, (*b*) threatens the loss of resources, or (*c*) results in a lack of gain from the expenditure of resources. Environmental circumstances can threaten or cause depletion of resources (for example, status, abilities, loved ones, beliefs, self-esteem). Chronic stressful events, such as in chronic sorrow, can lead to severe losses of current and future resources. Anger may then become the dominant emotion. Research testing Hobfoll's COR model (Lane & Hobfoll, 1992) has supported the theory that, in patients with chronic debilitating diseases, anger increases in proportion to the intensity and the number of symptoms and to losses resulting from chronic disease. Lane and Hobfoll found that when patients expressed their anger, their supporters reacted with anger. Hence, expressed anger led to alienation of support resources. Chronic stress was seen to deplete both personal and social resources, thereby increasing patients' vulnerability to additional (and inevitable) stressors. Reactive anger or, more specifically, expressed anger may be especially critical in chronic sorrow. It can be a formidable obstacle because (*a*) it is so personally distressing, and (*b*) it can alienate whatever scarce support that may exist at times of intensified need.

Paradoxically, anger as a "hot" emotion may be a major factor in symbiotically enmeshed relationships and a key ingredient in the glue that binds. As a racket emotion, anger is often valued and perceived as protective and necessary. Without it, the person feels threatened by a loss of self-esteem, acute humiliation, and terrifying vulnerability. In symbiotic relationships, anger is often felt by the recipient as being a real or incipient disconnection. The recipient (often in tandem with the other) is then tasked with taking immediate action to restore the symbiosis. These actions can be direct or indirect. Direct action is illustrated by the person's becoming apologetic, making amends, negotiating solutions, and so on. Indirect action is illustrated by the person's increased neediness, development of new or more intense somatic or psychological symptoms, and other forms of "graymail." Symbiotic relationships can become prisons of hostile dependency, experienced as ever more painful and as ever more gridlocked. The longed-for intimacy is not to be, and the relationship is characterized by angry interactions and resentments and a sense of being propelled into ever worsening miseries from which there can be no liberation.

Diffused anger is often pronounced in the initial stages of grief. Unfocused, enraged responses are common when the loss is unexplainable and when there is no one and nothing that can be singled out as accountable for the loss. The more senseless the loss, the greater the likelihood of diffused anger and rage. When there is no reasonable target for anger, problems can develop on all fronts. The anger will leak out in a way that promotes envy, bitterness, alienating actions, self-punishment, hatred, and the assumption of a perpetual victim position in life. Rage requires inordinate amounts of energy. Displacement of anger onto others or onto the self is destructive because it blocks self-efficacy and fosters unreasonable expectations, additional disappointments, and interpersonal disconnections. A person who is caught up in diffused anger is difficult to reach and, therefore, to help. Considerable time may elapse before the person becomes interpersonally accessible and ready to find new and different ways of being, doing, feeling, and relating to others and to the

loss. When the cause of the loss is identifiable, anger can be construc-
tively and appropriately channeled. Examples of causes that often define
and promote the constructive use of anger are: when permanent, serious
disability results from someone's choosing to drive while drunk and when
clear medical malpractice has occurred.

Featherstone (1980) has candidly described the problematic relational
aspects of anger related to having a child with disabilities:

> Parents of handicapped children have . . . many reasons for feeling angry
> and few arenas for expressing that anger. . . . Various sorts of consideration
> can prevent an open confrontation with . . . adversaries—particularly the
> child.
>
> When caution or inhibition shields the true target of frustration, feelings
> usually bounce off in another direction. One of my friends tells me that
> when she has a bad experience at the hospital, she comes home and tells
> her husband about it. She cannot yell at the doctor: she needs his services;
> anyway, she is instinctively polite to strangers. When her voice rises an
> octave, her husband feels she is blaming him . . . in fact, he does take the
> brunt of her outrage. . . .
>
> Suppose a boy knocks his cup off the table, spilling cocoa and broken
> shards over the floor, the newspaper, and an older sister's science project.
> His mother snaps at her husband for using a china cup and for setting it too
> close to the edge. . . . Is she misdirecting her anger? It's hard to tell.
>
> When a little girl's shrieks ruin the evening meal, does her tired father
> feel angry? Does he blame the child herself, the mother who fails to quiet
> her, or the malign fate that linked his destiny with both of them?
>
> When a ten-year-old ruins expensive prostheses, does his mother blame
> the boy's carelessness or the father who took him boating? . . .
>
> As Jay and I struggle to understand the anger we felt toward one another
> in the second year of Jody's life, it seems to us that our inability to focus
> our frustrations on Jody himself might have contributed. When our dreams
> lay in fragments at our feet, when a crying baby interrupted every activity,
> fury and frustration were inevitable. But how could we blame Jody, who
> suffered, through no fault of his own, more than anyone else? Longing
> for solutions that no one could provide, we turned on one another. (pp.
> 97–98)

☐ **Depression**

Not surprisingly, the normal responses of grief in general and chronic
sorrow in particular frequently beget dysthymic disorder, and they often
lead to major depression as well. Stress and the onset of depression are
inextricably linked. Sapolsky (1998) has offered his definition of a
major depression as "a genetic-neurochemical disorder requiring a strong

environmental trigger whose characteristic manifestation is an inability to appreciate sunsets" (p. 230). Major depression is an amalgam of psychological, biological, and cognitive factors. Research on psychological stress and depression (Seligman, 1975; Hiroto, 1974; Hiroto & Seligman, 1974) has identified dominant features of psychological stressors as (*a*) a loss of control and of predictability within certain contexts, (*b*) a loss of outlets for frustration, (*c*) a loss of sources of support, and (*d*) a perception of life as worsening. A major depression can be the outcome of life events and severe stressors that are outside our control. It is known that people who are exposed to clusters of life stressors are significantly more likely to succumb to depression than are their counterparts who are experiencing "ordinary" stress, and persons who are suffering their first major depression are more likely to have recently undergone a significant stressor. Unfortunately, stressors (and the stress response) are implicated only in the first few episodes of depression. In the fourth depression or so, depression appears to take on a rhythm all its own, recurring no matter what is going on in the person's life (Anisman & Zacharko, 1982). It has become "hard wired." According to Sapolsky (1998), a "mad clockwork" takes over.

Recent innovative work discussed by Jacobs, van Praag, and Gage (2000) provides information on leading-edge discoveries related to stress and neurological changes in depression. Neurobiologists once believed that adult brains did not produce new neurons. Today we know that this is not the case. Gould and others (Gould, Beylin, Tanapat, Reeves, & Shors, 1999; Ericksson et al., 1998) have reported the birth of new neurons in the hippocampus of adult rats, monkeys, and human beings. The hippocampal region of the brain is located beneath the cortex in the temporal lobe. Most neurons in the mammalian brain and spinal cord are produced during prenatal and perinatal development, but it is now known that neurons continue to be born throughout life in the olfactory bulb and in the dentate gyrus lying in the lower, middle area of the hippocampus. The reason for neurogenesis in these areas is not known, but it is thought that the olfactory bulb (which processes scents) and the dentate gyrus may need constant renewal to process and store new information, while other regions of the brain might require a stable population of neurons.

Nerve cells in the hippocampal formation are among the most sensitive to the negative effects of stress. It has been found that both the administration of corticosterone and the occurrence of naturally stressful situations clearly suppress the rate of dentate gyrus cell proliferation in adults of a number of species. The suppression of neurogenesis is likely due to increases in brain glucocorticoids. Jacobs, van Praag, and Gage (2000) do not suggest that this new discovery is the only change in the brain associated with depression. Other studies, however, confirm the connection between depression and decreased hippocampal volume. Temporal-lobe epilepsy also points to the connection between hippocampal damage and depression. Temporal-lobe epilepsy involves a significant loss of cells in various structures in and around the hippocampus, and persons with temporal-lobe epilepsy suffer from depression more than persons with other forms of epilepsy and more than patients with comparable debilitating diseases. The supporting evidence for the link between stress and depression is growing ever stronger.

A multifactorial case example of chronic sorrow and the development of a severe major depression with psychotic features comes from the author's experience a few years ago as a group therapist and consultant on the adult unit of a psychiatric hospital. This woman, in her late 40s, was newly admitted as a transfer from a general medical and surgical hospital where she had undergone successful surgery, a hysterectomy, nine days earlier. She was assigned to the author's process group, and she was also referred to the author for individual therapy. Her post-op recovery was progressing satisfactorily, but she had become despondent, agitated, and confused and was often unable to distinguish her dreams from reality. She had many of the biological markers for depression. Her dreams were vivid, and her REM latency intervals were very short. (They occurred within a few minutes of sleep onset and continued at a pace of 20 to 30 minutes from one REM cycle to the next.) She slept fitfully and was having terrifying hypnagogic imagery. She had reported to the surgical nursing staff that she was sometimes unable to rest or to sleep because she could hear low voices. Their words were indistinct, but their tone was argumentative. She was understandably upset. At first it was thought that her symptoms were the transient effects of the anesthetic in combination with other pharmacological agents, but her symptoms had not abated.

Her husband was the informant for the psychosocial history at the time of admission. She had no prior psychiatric history. Her husband described her as "unemployed," "not very social," "joyless," compulsive, and perfectionistic about the management of their home. He stated that she "preferred a reclusive lifestyle." The husband traveled frequently in his work. He had looked forward to having her with him on some of his trips when their three children had left home, as they now had, and he expressed anger and frustration that she had been refusing to accompany him. There was now "no reason" for her to remain so homebound and so uninterested in being his travel companion. He was very unhappy and was considering divorce.

This woman appeared physically and mentally exhausted. During her first week on the psychiatric unit she spent much of her time in bed. She was sometimes encouraged to participate in activities, but since she was recovering from surgery, she was not pushed to do more than she felt she could handle. She would come to my group, in her robe, without urging and would attend to the process for a while before dozing off or leaving the group well before the session ended. During her second week she began to tolerate staying for the entire session, and it was during this week that I began to see her individually. She had become more coherent, and her hallucinatory symptoms had begun to fade, either spontaneously or as a result of psychotropic medication. In her first session with me, she shared her distressing inability to make sense out of what was happening to her. She had looked forward to having her children out of the house and had dreamed of the day when her time would be truly her own. Now that this had happened, she was distraught and shattered.

She had three children, two sons and a daughter. The older son and daughter were doing well. They were both pursuing college degrees, and the daughter was engaged and soon to be married. The youngest son was 18 years old. He had multiple disabilities, including severe cerebral palsy, scoliosis, and epilepsy, and he had been profoundly mentally retarded from birth. At age 12, this son had brain surgery to remove a tumor. For her this had been a traumatic event that she felt she could never resolve. Things had gone badly during the surgery, and her son had been near death. His condition remained critical for three weeks, and she had not left him for more than an hour at a time. His seizures had worsened in frequency, duration, and intensity, and he required a gastrostomy for food intake since he could no longer swallow properly. His seizures had continued to be only partially controlled. This son had lived at home and had been in her care until six weeks prior to her hysterectomy. At that time he had been placed in a nursing home that was apparently well equipped to deal with his needs. She was reasonably secure that he was receiving good care. "So why am I falling apart?" she asked. "Instead of being happy to have some freedom and to live, I'm suicidal and crazy!"

Multiple impacts, both symbolic and real, had coalesced to bring about this woman's decompensation. I assumed a fairly active and relational role, and as we sorted these factors out together, her agitation and tension quickly diminished. Factors included:

1. Major identity crisis, triggered by loss of role.
2. Departure of youngest child from the home in a way which underscored his abnormalities. (This is not the way in which most 18-year-olds leave home, nor was it was the way her other children had left.)
3. Demands by her husband that she join him in *his* life rather than endorsements of her right to a life of her own choosing.

4. Guilt about the relief she felt about placement of her son outside the home.
5. Increased ambivalence toward the son, whom she now both "needed and missed terribly" and "wanted to be free of."
6. Multiple triggers in the hospital surgical setting of her hysterectomy, which had precipitated flashbacks to her son's nearly fatal brain surgery (which had left him even more impaired and compromised so that the gastrostomy had been necessary).
7. Fantasies of the hysterectomy as "punishment" (that is, the necessary removal of the offending, malevolent part of herself).
8. Guilt about wanting to relinquish all her burdens and responsibilities for her son's life.
9. Self-blame and self-directed hostility for feeling envious of her daughter, whom she imagined to be able to have the life she herself had wanted but had irrevocably lost.
10. The perception that, for the first time in her adult life, she could get sick or have personal needs without guilt or untenable repercussions.
11. Resentment of her husband's life of relative freedom as compared to her own "lost years."
12. Resentment of her own extended family and her in-laws for non-support and virtual abandonment.
13. Normal cumulative and episodic stress and fatigue.
14. Biochemical and physiological shifts arising from surgery, anesthesia, and hormonal adjustments.

As if these issues were not enough, an additional factor to be considered was the adaptive functional value of her decompensation and incapacitation. For nearly her entire adult life, she had been "selfless." She had served others and, of necessity, overadapted to their needs. She could now put those others to the test and see for herself whether any of them (especially her husband) would actively care for her and allow her some centrality of their concern. In fact, she stated that she had "always wondered" if any of them would "inconvenience themselves" to respond to her needs. She could, as well, now give vent to her grief. She no longer had to be strong (though "joyless"); she could collapse without fear for her son's life and welfare. She at last had some freedom and some internal permissions to go crazy, to need, maybe to want, and perhaps even to die.

This woman was strongly motivated to improve her life and to make some changes in it. As she began to understand herself better, she became more empowered. Individual therapy continued for several months after her discharge from psychiatric care. She worked hard to develop a support network. She involved herself in a church where she participated with other women in educational and recreational activities. She began to express her needs and her wants to her husband. As her son appeared to be receiving satisfactory care, she decided to go on a trip after all. This was her first trip in more than eight years. It was not, however, with her husband; it was with a group of women in her church-affiliated group. It is not known whether her marriage has survived. However, if it continues to be viable, it has doubtlessly changed form as a result of her commitments to herself and her ability to translate commitment into action. She has had countless days and countless hours to develop life-affirming actions for her son. These days and hours are the foundation and the source of her own self-help and changed life trajectory.

☐ Loss Spirals

The concept of loss spirals is introduced here by the author. They are suggested by the author as distinct from reactions described in chapter 4 under the heading of "Triggers," but the distinctions are subtle. As described in chapter 4, trigger-induced responses are associated with the traumatic aspects of the onset of chronic sorrow (and often contain PTSD type symptoms such as flashbacks) and with reminders of the specific loss or losses that result from environmental cues and stressors. Reminders include special occasions and unmet developmental milestones. Loss spirals might be considered a subset of all these sudden, intensified reactions. Loss spirals emanate from new losses that result in new and additional grief.

It is at times of loss in other areas of life as well as those related to chronic sorrow that loss spirals may occur. Current loss places one at risk of rekindling affective flooding as one is launched into a review of virtually all past losses, the current loss, and anticipated losses well into the future. The spiraling goes into the past and into the future. A "rubberbanding" effect occurs in which a new loss—sometimes not even a very serious one—serves to activate old pathways to old wounds and their associated emotions. The experience is one of unintended and unanticipated emotions and imagery. An example of a not-so-serious current loss activating a loss spiral would be the cancellation of plans to attend a concert. The response of disappointment, instead of quickly dissipating, escalates and rekindles memories and emotions related to other losses. A spiraling downward evokes a stream of consciousness that revisits, mostly in amazingly accurate sequence, old losses and old grief. The spiraling then twists upward into anticipated losses.

The current loss, which is the impetus for a loss spiral may be, yet again, a loss of a fantasy. The partner of a person who has become permanently and severely brain damaged in an automobile crash, for instance, may simply accept a dinner invitation from an old friend. He begins to drive to the friend's house when he realizes that his dream of sharing friendships and small pleasures with his partner is forever gone. This realization may be the spark for a loss spiral into the past and into the future. Sometimes the person experiencing the temporary despondency and flooding of a loss spiral will have to work hard to become aware of the stimulus for these responses.

There are times, however, when loss spirals can be expected as a virtual certainty. This is the time when all progress stops, after years of vibrant hope and of sincere and fervent efforts and after some recovery, growth, and development were observable. There is a slow but clearly emerging realization that whatever the hard-won gains, they are virtually all that ever will be. The most reasonable hope now is to prevent regression, to "run in place." This new realization is, emotionally, a new loss. The heart breaks again, and loss spirals are evident. For example, fantasies that have functioned to keep a person with self-loss hopeful and focused on the hard work of rehabilitation will begin to fade and disappear after years of minimal further progress. The person will then one day admit, "After all my hopes, my lofty goals, my sweat and tears, this is about as good as it can ever get." Not only is the hope or the dream to which it was attached lost, but there is a realization that this hope or dream was an unwanted—though embraced—substitute for most of one's original dreams (those existing prior to the disability). The "window of opportunity" has passed, and "even this I cannot have." And loss spirals will ensue.

The parents of a daughter with autism may have worked diligently and devotedly to achieve contact with their child and to promote the development of language. When she has reached early adulthood and looks like an adult rather than a child, the parents may gradually become aware that even their reduced and minimal expectations and hopes are not to be realized. The daughter has achieved whatever contact and whatever language she is likely ever to master. Some of the growth and development that have occurred, moreover, may disappear either periodically or entirely. There will be no major "breakthroughs," no miracle cures, no remarkable developments in expressive language.

While adaptations to a new loss may seem a matter of relative simplicity, the new loss evokes a maelstrom of images along the loss spiral, backward and forward in time. The replaying of an entire series of personal losses may lead to moments or days of affective overload. A suggested theory that is based on cognitive therapy is that loss may be the central aspect of certain schemas, and the current loss event may tap into the brain's confirmatory function. It is the brain's confirmatory function that crystalizes schemas about losses. Spirals can also lead to maladaptive avoidant behaviors. Once having experienced a loss spiral, prevention and avoidance are likely to become strong influences in a person's life. Life decisions can be based on an overriding fear of potential losses and fears regarding one's ability to withstand or manage loss spirals in the event of recurrence. A fear of not being able to recover, of being permanently lost in the spiral, may also become a preoccupation. These fears can easily lead to fears of intimacy and interpersonal closeness, emotional spontaneity, personal achievements, positive expectations, emotional attachments to places and things, and many feelings of want and desire. Both loss spirals themselves and their aftermath can become problematic. Relationships may become more intensely ambivalent and disordered. Relationship patterns arising from the goal of avoiding loss spirals may in fact lead to further losses, thereby increasing loss spirals rather than preventing them. In many ways, unless awareness and change intervene, the patterns that emerge resemble a repetition compulsion, a transfer of the past onto the present and the present onto the past (when present circumstances become the lens through which the past is recast).

A positive side effect of loss spirals is the strange awkwardness that occurs after one unexpectedly gets what one wants!

Chronic sorrow itself is a natural, normal set of responses to a loss with no foreseeable end. The stress and vicissitudes inherent in chronic sorrow are strongly influential in the development of complications resulting in pathological conditions. The discussion of complicating factors in this chapter is an attempt to further clinical understanding. The intent has not been to emphasize deleterious factors, since strength, wisdom, resilience, and wonderful appreciations can also come from the depths of chronic sorrow. There is nothing to compare with hearing a son, who has not previously been able to use expressive language no matter how hard he has tried, manage to mutter a phrase. There is nothing to compare with the elation that comes from being equipped with a language board for the first time in a long life of paralysis and spasticity. There are terrific "wins" among the losses, and they are even more precious and cherishable in the context of human ruination.

8
CHAPTER

Professional Support and Treatment

Professionals will be involved at many points in the lives of persons with self- or other-loss. Families and individuals will face numerous critical incidents, as well as times of increased stress from the nature of the loss and the process of chronic sorrow. Professional assessment and reevaluation will be required at various life junctures in connection with acquiring appropriate services. Assistance will be needed for problem solving in difficult circumstances, including emergencies and crisis events, and for longer-range planning, even beyond death. Professional assistance will be required both predictably and unpredictably from a variety of disciplines (social work, psychology, medicine, education, nursing, rehabilitation, clergy, law, and so on). Although chronic sorrow is a normal, pervasive response to ongoing loss, the author refers to "treatment" as a generalized concept to which most disciplines can relate and use to construct models of important client-professional interactions. In no way is "treatment" meant to convey that chronic sorrow is a pathological condition or a process requiring treatment in the traditional sense. In fact, as has been noted earlier, if the professional fails to recognize the normality of chronic sorrow and its unique qualities, there is risk that the client might incur more suffering. There are, however, ways in which the intensity of the response can be ameliorated, adaptation enhanced, and painful patterns modified or prevented. *Treatment*, then, refers to *all professional interventions designed and intended to help individuals and families deal with chronic sorrow and with its complications.*

In general, studies have demonstrated that bereaved individuals who participate in treatment have a reduction in depression and anxiety and in symptoms such as avoidance and intrusion. Studies have also shown that treatment is associated with improved functioning in various role domains and with enhanced quality of life. Types of treatment for grief that are known to have value are (*a*) brief psychodynamic therapy, (*b*) behavioral exposure-based treatments, (*c*) family therapy, and (*d*) interpersonal therapy. The common element in these treatments is their emphasis on facing the reality of the loss and processing the loss (Exline, Dorrity, & Wortman, 1996). Studies comparing the effectiveness of different types of treatment are very scarce. There is a consensus, however, that bereaved individuals are best helped by an eclectic orientation. This is a logical consensus, since grief is so individualistic. Different approaches are appropriate for different clients, different symptoms in the same client, and for the same client at different times.

Wolfelt (1998) has proposed a "companioning" model for the bereavement counseling relationship associated with the death of a loved one. The model is one of parity. The imagery inherent in "companioning" is very different from imagery evoked by a "treating" model. There is much to recommend Wolfelt's model as a guide for professional-client collaboration in the context of chronic sorrow. Replacing the medical model of treatment with one that is growth-oriented has significant merit, especially in empowerment of the client and in normalizing grief responses. Wolfelt's position is that growth means change, and he indicates that we are forever changed by traumatic pain in our lives. Further, growth and transformation are different from "resolving" grief. Basic to companioning are the following: (*a*) honoring the spirit (not focusing on the intellect), (*b*) curiosity (not expertise), (*c*) learning from others (not teaching them), (*d*) walking alongside (not leading), (*e*) being still (not frantic movement forward), (*f*) discovering gifts of sacred silence (not filling every painful moment with words); (*g*) listening with the heart (not analyzing with the head), (*h*) bearing witness to the struggles of others (not directing those struggles), (*i*) being present to another's pain (not taking the pain away), (*j*) respecting disorder and confusion (not imposing order and logic), and (*k*) going with another into the soul's wilderness (not being responsible for finding the way out).

Since chronic sorrow is about a loss that continues to live, this author proposes that a supplemented companioning model may be very beneficial for those experiencing this type of loss. Companioning that is supplemented by skilled interventions and techniques—as they are needed and mutually agreed upon—provides a comprehensive, client-centered, and empowered format for healing. When specific techniques are indicated, they are conceptualized as coaching. The model, therefore, is one of companioning with coaching. Coaching can occur from either side of the relationship. For example, a client with spinal cord injury and paralysis may be distressed by flashbacks of scenes and events occurring in the hospital during the terrifying days when he realized he could not fully recover. Six years after the injury, the flashbacks are no longer so disorienting or so frequent, but they persist and seriously undermine self-confidence. In the context of a companioning relationship, the client asks the professional (social worker, rehab counselor, psychologist, therapist, psychiatrist, and so on), for information and help that might reduce or put an end to these disturbing intrusions. The professional contributes her knowledge about trauma-related flashbacks and, accessing her technical skills, works with the client to achieve the client's goal. The client provides important details of the flashbacks, the meaning they have for him, and what he has discovered to be antecedent triggers. He gives feedback to the professional during and after specific interventions. This is how the client actively coaches the professional.

The supplemented companioning model is very well suited to chronic sorrow when the person has become worn down and worn out. In her discussion of making appropriate referrals, Marsh (1992) has described the anguish and hopelessness as it is expressed by a mother whose son has profound mental retardation:

> He was down at the hospital. The doctor was accusing this nun of not feeding him. They walked out, and I had this pillow in my hand. He was laying there crying. And I said, "If I could just put this pillow on your face, nobody would fight any more about how bad you're suffering." I just couldn't take it any more. That pillow was shaking in my hand. I just wanted to end it all. I wanted to end the nightmare. I wanted to end the crying and the suffering and the pain that he had gone through for so long. (pp. 207–208)

Being nonjudgmental and truly alongside this woman as she enters the wilderness of her soul and struggles for control would be an offering of great acceptance and solace. At the same time, a search for respite services and for volunteers to stay with her son and do what they can to care for his needs, comfort him, feed him, and bring new energy to the situation would be acts of mercy reflective of an accurate assessment that the mother is verging on incapacitation and requires active interventions that will not further deplete her coping abilities.

Most of the literature about professional handling of persons who are coping with chronic sorrow pertains to management of the initial diagnostic assessments, their interpretation, and recommended follow-up support and treatment interventions. Obviously, first professional contacts may be among the most critical in the forever-changed life of the individual or family; therefore, these contacts merit considerable thought and attention. Serious blunders here are apt to have far-reaching consequences. There is, of course, no substitute for personal and professional maturity and for years of in-depth training in various assessment and therapy modalities. A multitude of factors go into the making of a seasoned, competent, and clinically astute professional who is theoretically well grounded and who possesses technical expertise and fluency. With apologies to these seasoned, well-trained, and attuned clinicians, the author will from time to time in this chapter point out common professional mistakes and pitfalls.

☐ Basic Assumptions

No one school or methodology can serve to do all that is needed to assuage the pervasive distress of chronic sorrow. Likewise, there is no one plan of intervention applicable to all situations. A relational approach, characterized by professional flexibility, empathic attunement, and a spirit of collaboration with the client, is fundamental to establishing a therapeutic rapport and alliance. Making every effort to join the client where she or he is, especially in the days and weeks after the first realization of the loss, sets the tone and potential quality of the helping-healing relationship. It is at this time of catastrophic crisis that the professional can become a calm presence in the midst of chaos. In meeting the client on the client's own ground, the professional respectfully works from a position of integrative eclecticism and flexibility. It is not usually necessary for the client to learn the therapist's or professional's favored system, vocabulary, and philosophy. Being alert to the client's values, strengths, and previously effective coping strategies can, from the very beginning, empower both client and professional.

As recently as 1990, Turnbull and Turnbull have reported communication problems between parents of children with disabilities and professionals. These communications are described as often stressful and flawed for both. Problems tend to emerge from the expression of professional dominance, paternalism, and control, and from a variety of power issues. Parents consistently report that they need every scrap of information they can have about their child's impairment or diagnosis. Professionals who treat parents evasively are usually met with parental resentment or with increased fears for the child. Many parents express relief when there is, at last, a diagnosis. What *is* shared by professionals and parents at this time is the frustration and sense of helplessness to "fix it." The Turnbulls indicate that professionals are primarily responsible for methodology, and parents are primarily responsible for goals.

Use of the model of chronic sorrow proposed in chapter 2 can greatly enhance professional assessment and selection of treatment approaches. The model includes the following dimensions: (*a*) characteristics of the loss (subjective and objective reality), (*b*) continuity of the loss, (*c*) initial, continuing, and recurring grief responses, (*d*) discrepancy between perceived reality and continuing fantasy or dream, and (*e*) continuing presence of the source or object of the loss. Ongoing assessment and sensitivity to shifts in client adaptation and circumstances can be guided by the model.

Whether self-loss or other-loss, the worst-case scenario, based on this model, would likely include the following elements: (*a*) the impact of the loss is catastrophic, and if the loss is other-loss, the nature of the attachment is profound (such as a mother's attachment to her child), (*b*) subjectively, the loss is highly traumatic, central, and is perceived as tragic; it impacts all aspects of living and is the determinant of serious secondary losses (past, present, and future); and personal and social identity are dramatically and negatively changed, (*c*) objectively, there is cultural agreement that the loss is real, catastrophic, and pervasive, (*d*) the loss is subjectively perceived as unending, (*e*) the loss was intensely traumatic when first realized; the impairment is profound; support was scarce; many needs were unmet; and there are a number of significant prior and current losses and an extensive grief history, (*f*) the loss is unrelentingly chronic, with predictable triggers; current adjustment is poor and characterized by numerous unmet needs, severe daily stressors, and specific fears; there is a paucity of ego strength and assets, and there are identifiable secondary gains; comorbidity is problematic, with a number of risk factors and prior mental health diagnoses; and there is at least one other source of chronic sorrow, (*g*) there is a wide discrepancy between perceived reality of the loss and the continuing fantasy, and there would be consensual agreement regarding this discrepancy, (*h*) the fantasy has more negative functions than positive ones; there is a strong attachment to the fantasy, and it is largely self-activated and extremely unrealistic, (*i*) there is a general consensus about the continuation of the loss; the loss is obvious and stigmatizing, has no foreseeable end, and is a living loss.

Ongoing assessment of family and individual strengths increases professional flexibility and informs interventions and responses. Of his work with traumatized families, Charles Figley (1989) states: "I am concerned with equipping the family with the systemic resources not only to speed their recovery to the current trauma but also to help them avoid future ones or to recover more quickly" (p. 36). He states further: "I strive to assess the degree to which family members are currently supportive to one another, the degree to which they really *want* to be supportive, and the degree to which they are *capable* of being supportive. Through modeling and training in some basic family relations skills, social supportiveness can be increased significantly" (p. 36). Fostering these skills can enhance (*a*) exchange of information between family members, (*b*) problem solving, and (*c*) conflict resolution.

Fundamental to the therapeutic relationship are parity and empowerment of the client. Goals are jointly selected by the client and the professional; the professional does not impose her own agenda on the client. Selecting goals with clients who are coping with chronic sorrow often differs from work with those who are struggling with losses that are potentially resolvable. The importance of mutual goal setting is humorously depicted by John Callahan (1989). Callahan is quadriplegic as a result of a spinal cord injury, and he is a recovering alcoholic. After his discharge from rehabilitation, he continued to drink heavily, until he decided to join Alcoholics Anonymous and achieve sobriety. He was feeling desperate about his life. He recounts:

> AA took a very broad view of spirituality. It had been founded, in the 1930s, by a surgeon and a stockbroker and about a hundred other ordinary drunks who discovered that by working with each other they could stay sober. Like many of them, I was hungry for tools and impatient with religious hocus-pocus. Once, ready to try anything, I made an appointment to see an Indian guru on the other side of town. Heavy Metal Mike drove me over. The guru came out and we talked for a while. He said, "Listen, my son. You are fortunate."
> "What do you mean?"
> "You are in an excellent position for spiritual growth."
> Fuck spiritual growth, I thought. I wanted to feel my own body, jump around, and be free of these crazy attendants. (p. 120)

In many cases of chronic sorrow, expecting the client to complete a plan of treatment within a specified period of time may not be appropriate unless the goals are discrete and reflective of steps toward healing. It is important to assume that healing can and does take place, even in the midst of great and continuing distress and despite the periodic resurgence of intense grief. In chronic sorrow, the client may have an entire lifetime to achieve higher levels of accommodation to the ongoing loss and its changing dynamics. This view of available time, however, does not absolve the professional or therapist from doing as much as possible during a particular time allotment or restricted number of sessions. It is helpful and considerate of the client, however, not to pressure the client to conform to the therapist's restrictions regarding end points of contact.

Clients are more likely to feel safe enough to proceed with therapy when the professional can provide a secure "holding" environment and when the therapist models attributes that are comforting to the client. Structure is crucial to the client's feeling of personal safety and the ability to risk self-disclosure and to enter a new and frightening internal landscape. Structure includes mutual agreements on circumscribed and manageable segments of work. Other "holding" structures include such logistics as predictably stable appointment times, a calm setting conducive to the work of therapy, guidelines regarding phone calls, canceled or missed appointments, therapist reliability in organizational matters and time management, and so on. For many clients, a sense of safety is enhanced by a display of credentials (degrees, diplomas, licenses) on the wall, symbols of expertise and experience. Consistent with empowerment of the client are (a) the professional's definition of roles and responsibilities, (b) her acknowledgment that the client has more expertise in the reality situation than does the therapist, (c) her expressed belief that the client already has many resources that can be identified, accessed, and put to beneficial use, and (d) that it is realistic to expect an improved level of adaptive functioning. The therapist contributes skill and proficiency in clarification, in assessment, and in the appropriate selection and timely implementation of a wide range of therapeutic techniques. The therapist is held responsible and accountable for ethically engaging in the work of therapy, including management of boundaries, roles, issues of consent, confidentiality, privilege, and so on. The therapist is sensitive to transferential issues in the therapy relationship and is aware of their associated preclusions and of their limiting and empowering aspects. Persons with chronic sorrow frequently present for therapy having already developed a negative transference. The therapist's capacity for vicarious introspection (that is, empathy) can "save the day" and offset the potential for distrust and other obstacles to productive collaborative work.

☐ Desirable Attributes of the Professional and Therapist

Different clients will have differing impressions of the same professional and will have differing attributional preferences in the selection of a therapist. As in work with all types of grief and loss, there are some general desirable therapist variables. Some of these variables are alluded to in the above discussion of basic assumptions in therapy. Berne (1973) and Crossman (1966) spoke of the three P's of therapy; these are the determinants of the effectiveness of the therapist. They are potency, protection, and permissions. Although these attributes have been narrowly defined and discussed strictly from the viewpoint of transactional analysis, they can be defined more broadly as essential therapist qualities, regardless of theoretical stance, treatment modality preference, and skills.

For therapy to be effective, in process and in outcome, the therapist needs potency (the first P). The easy way to explain this is: The therapist should know what she is doing and do it with confidence. Probably all therapists and other professionals who have some years of experience have seen clients who have been ineptly treated by prior therapists who have lacked basic expertise. Kindness and a sympathetic attitude are certainly positive attributes in a therapist; however, if the client begins to experience the therapist's lack of authoritative know-how, he will begin to back off and may feel a sense of betrayal. Insight, skill, the ability to communicate a clear understanding of issues and options, and technical competence are essential. In chronic sorrow, therapist awareness and knowledge of the nature of the loss is fundamental to potency. If the loss is neurological, knowing something about neurology, at least to the extent that the client is not forced to educate the therapist from "square one," can foster client confidence in feeling understood. If there is a severe craniofacial defect, the client is helped if the therapist knows something about related underlying defects and implications, as well as something about craniofacial and plastic reconstructive surgery.

A therapist who demonstrates (a) an ability to maintain focus, (b) a consistency with regard to goal-directed work, (c) a spirit of rational confidence, (d) perceptive and empathic accuracy, (e) the respectful acknowledgment of pain, and (f) competence in timely and parsimonious interventions will be experienced as trustworthy and as a source of hope for the client. The client can then feel secure that risking, openly sharing, and working with the therapist are worthwhile endeavors, and there is reason to believe that things will, in time, be better.

Protection (the second P) is viewed by this author as a subset of therapist potency. Protection is the underlying principle of ethical codes of conduct. Herman (1992) has described the core experiences of psychological trauma as disempowerment and disconnection from others. The protections of a safe haven and a therapeutic alliance can foster reempowerment and new connections. The therapist's ongoing assessment is protective, and it is conducive to work that does not involve a risk of preventable harm. When a client is in the initial throes of chronic sorrow, or experiencing an intense resurgence of grief, or is coping with additional losses, or in any way indicates she is cognitively and affectively flooded, careful assessment may lead to interventions of organization and prioritization of issues. They can then be addressed individually and systematically, and the client can be supported by the sense of security that comes from protective containment and active structuring of the therapy process. Protection follows as well from the types of structure and reliable parameters that are set and maintained, even in the face of the client's own provocations and maladaptive behaviors. Careful and consistent management of interpersonal boundaries is crucial to the client's sense of safety, as is skillful support and modulation of affect. In order to make progress, the client may have to endure new understandings and realizations that evoke great pain, anger, or anxiety. The therapist's capacity to anchor the client in the therapeutic window between "too much" and "too little" affective charge for certain dynamics-changing work is a very important protection. Pacing and appropriate timing of interventions, interpretations, and reconstructions that are made as reflections (and not as explanations), and not pushing the client toward problems she is well aware of but—for very good reason—unprepared to address are therapeutic protections and enhance the client's perception of being understood and respected while working to find meaning in a new and unanticipated life journey.

Permissions (the third P) refers to the therapist's ability to convey acceptance and approval of the client's coping attempts, even and especially when the client is deviating from customary and past ways of managing life. The conditions of chronic sorrow often call for innovative actions. New and frightening thoughts and decisions may be sources of strain, and the client may do well to "break the rules" that were learned in the family of origin. A wise therapist, much like a wise parent, does not proffer indiscriminate permissions. Instead, the therapist challenges destructive impediments or behavioral injunctions from a grounding of well-considered rationales and intentions that are congruent with the client's higher sense of "what is right." As a result, the client may be enabled to surpass previously established coping strategies, generating the development of more available choices and behaviors. Permissions are characteristic of a therapist who assumes therapeutic neutrality with regard to content, even during disclosures of harsh and bitter feelings. Neutrality goes hand in hand with caring and the acceptance of the client as a person of unquestionable positive worth.

Hayes, Gelso, Van Wagoner, and Diemer (1991) conducted a study of expert opinion with regard to managing countertransference. Thirty-three expert therapists identified the five most significant therapist qualities as (a) self-integration (associated with role congruency), (b) self-insight (associated with the ability to recognize personal strengths and weaknesses), (c) empathic ability, defined as the ability to "see from another's eye sockets," (d) skill conceptualization, based on adequate training to select appropriate skills and to understand why various skills may be effective, and (e) management of anxiety. In a larger study involving 93 reputed expert therapists and again focusing on countertransference, Van Wagoner, Gelso, Hayes, and Diemer (1991) contrasted these experts with therapists assessed as average. The experts (*a*) had more insight into and rationales for clients' feelings, (*b*) had greater capacity for empathy, (*c*) were better able to make distinctions between the needs of clients and their own needs, (*d*) were less anxious with clients, and (*e*) were more adept at conceptualizing current and past client dynamics.

☐ Suggested Goals and Objectives

Individual circumstances and client variables will naturally lead to goals and objectives that are unique to the case. However, there are several general circumstances and hurdles that are common to chronic sorrow. Presented below are suggestions of recurrent problems and opportunities that warrant professional intervention and support.

Diagnostic Assessment and Interpretation

It is usually most effective to adopt a crisis-oriented approach at the time of initial evaluation of the loss. The rewards of careful (and successful) management of this highly charged, dreadful, and frequently traumatic experience will far outweigh the expenditure of additional professional effort and time. The initial diagnostic assessment is most often conducted by several professionals, each with her own area of competence. A person who has suffered a stroke, for instance, may be evaluated by a team consisting of a neurologist, neurosurgeon, psychologist, rehabilitation specialist, physical therapist, social worker, nurse, speech therapist, and others. Much confusion can be prevented by the simple implementation of adequate communication among professional team members so that coherent explanations of diverse findings (and vocabularies) may be developed prior to presentation to the client(s). One way to accomplish this is for one of the team members to assume the task of collecting the evaluative reports, clarifying discrepancies among them, and highlighting all salient aspects of the assessments. Preparing statements of one or two sentences about each of the significant findings and printing copies for each team member and the client can facilitate a sense of the "big picture" regarding a "real person" for the professionals and the communication of information that is most relevant to the client. The use of a checklist can guide this process.

It is both humane and pragmatic to suggest that the client have someone, such as one or two family members, a minister, or a trusted friend, with her at the time of assessment interpretation. In some circumstances this type of support is warranted for both immediately obvious reasons and for managing the hours and days which follow the diagnostic interpretation. If a client conference is held in a professional team setting, careful consideration of seating arrangements can do much to convey important nonverbal messages. It is important to avoid, if possible, the presence of a Zeus-like authority figure, flanked by "junior" professionals, seated in the "power chair" at the opposite end of the room facing the client. For the client the situation is fraught with fear already, and the sense that she is entering a chamber to face sentencing by judge and jury is not emotionally supportive; the setting impedes comprehension and fosters additional trauma. Instead, holding the session around a large table (convenient for note taking and for sorting through reports) or in a circle of chairs with as much eye contact as possible is preferred. This type of configuration conveys that the client is on an equal footing with staff.

The client may feel more secure when, at the very beginning of the conference, a social worker or other professional support person individually connects with her and explains the format of the meeting and encourages the client to speak up about anything that she is not understanding and about what she wants from any of the professionals present. The client can be told that she is a respected member of the team. Input and clarification that is actively solicited from the client—and noted— can also let the client know that she is valued and cared for. The author's experience as a parent in such settings as the annual planning conference has been variable. At times she has felt validated and respected, but all too often the staff have moved right through the agenda without asking for any input at all. When, as a parent, the author has shared a particular insight or has offered important new information, the parental voice has often been treated as if it were some type of background noise in the room. When the author speaks as a professional colleague in similar meetings, perhaps expressing the exact same thoughts, the response is quite different. In the latter case, colleagues typically listen with interest and often make notes.

The client will need simple explanations of the validity and reliability of specific evaluative findings. While being sensitive to the client in every sphere possible, the rule of thumb here is: If the client expresses a need to know the worst potential scenario, professionals should be forthcoming about it. Many clients will want to know every detail of the evaluation; others will want only the information that is useful for planning in the immediate future. Professionals, even when conveying extremely discouraging diagnostic impressions, should organize, position, and present findings in a way that is least likely to shock or overwhelm. Emphasis on what can reasonably be expected or positively accomplished is much more workable than going through a list of cumulative deficits and prophecies of gloom and doom. For example, an assessment statement that says, "Your daughter has more potential than these tests can detect, and even now we can say with a high degree of certainty that she will be able to dress herself, feed herself, and do a lot of things that will give her a sense of pride and fun in living and doing" is just as accurate as "Your daughter will never go to a regular school or learn to read or do more than count to ten." A statement (with regard to self-loss) such as "We can't predict the rate of loss of functioning, and you may find that most of the time you will hardly notice the changes since they will be so gradual" is as truthful as "You have already lost many of your higher functions, and this will only get worse." Honest assessment is more often wanted and appreciated than not. In most cases, the client will already be aware of serious problems and will suspect others. She will feel validated and supported by having this awareness confirmed, named, and outlined in a beneficially open manner.

Various degrees of protective denial can be expected. Far from being detrimental, denial—both at the time of diagnostic assessment and perhaps for years afterward—can be useful to the client by facilitating the management of current reality demands. It is unrealistic and harmful to attempt to elicit the client's full realization of the loss at this time. In the months and years after diagnosis, the client can often handle crisis situations and other stress quite adequately for the very reason that she is able to fractionate and to maintain only partial conscious awareness of the extent of the loss. Many clients will exhibit signs of shock, and trance-like behaviors may occur. It is important to recognize this state of altered consciousness and its protective functions. Ericksonian hypnotic approaches (Erickson & Rossi, 1979) use such altered states for deescalating emotional arousal and for restoring effective cognitive functions. These approaches would include (*a*) pacing and leading, (*b*) utilization, (*c*) permissions to absorb, manage, and use new information and learnings in the client's own way and own time, (*d*) interspersal of suggestions about the client's strengths and resources, and (*e*) perhaps a future-pacing technique, such as evoking imagery or an expectation that the client will be able, within a certain period of time, to make important decisions that she will know to be "right" or "good."

The client will often be searching for something to interpret as positive or stabilizing—something to "hang on to." Many clients report, months or years afterward, that something was said (or, more accurately, heard) during the conference that took precedence over all else. This type of reported experience often relates to the brain's confirmatory function; that is, the brain will recognize certain data, from a particular universe of data, that serve to confirm and reinforce preexisting beliefs, schemas, and understandings about life. In this way, the client manages to protect the self and to remain in a familiar world. The client may begin to feel some pressure, as well as confusion, about constructing a plan of action, and it is tempting at this point for some professionals to make predictive statements that could come back to haunt them. If predictions fall ridiculously far from the mark, they will, without doubt, haunt the client. The client is likely to take in segments of presented information concretely and globally, leading to misinterpretations. This is the nature of trance.

Depending on the level of functioning of the individual, it can be very useful to conclude the conference with helpful prescriptives. Suggestions regarding specific things the client may wish to do in the immediate future are often a way to anchor abilities, resources, control, and empowerment. Providing the client with copies of reports or with the previously prepared list of primary aspects of the evaluation can reduce confusion and serve as rationales for certain actions. Providing the client with a list of appropriate resources, contact numbers for support groups, and direct referrals is stabilizing and comforting. Behavioral assignments that are presented in the context of client choice can activate a sense of hope and competence to influence the future. The social worker, therapist, or other liaison professional can expect follow-up contacts that will refer directly to the diagnostic assessment. The client will need to have information repeated, clarified, and explained more than once. Affect management may be needed. Professional availability is crucial. Professional abandonment in the immediate aftermath can have devastating effects and can lead to a multitude of future complications.

Professionals can expect that clients will find fault with some of the evaluative assessment. No matter how thoughtful and competent the process, the client cannot be happy with the reality of his loss and with the inescapable truth of his forever-changed life and self. The client may have extreme difficulty in accepting the inadequacy of professionals who cannot cure or even substantially alter the course of the loss. It is not unusual for clients to lash out in anger at the message carrier. Some client anger directed at professionals may be well deserved, and if the professional can remain objective and nondefensive regarding this type of anger, a helpful alliance can be preserved. Some anger is likely to be displaced. The professional who is able to accept and deal well with expressed anger may be able to galvanize the energy available in that anger to achieve positive goals. But rejection and disavowal of the client's expressed anger, especially at the time of diagnostic evaluation, may be experienced by the client as disapproval and as an aggressive disconnection and, therefore, may lead to a number of negative outcomes (for example, increased aloneness and alienation, severe depression, cognitive dissonance, loss of self-esteem).

Burke (1989) has documented how mothers of babies who were born with a myelomeningocele disability regarded helpful factors during the initial diagnostic assessment. Receiving accurate information and encouragement from professionals were highly rated, as was a positive professional attitude. A professional's minimizing the problem, however, led to mixed messages and confusion. One mother recounted:

> The doctor said that it was "a minor problem with the spine." The next thing we knew, the neurosurgeon was calling for permission to operate on her immediately. When we said we needed to talk it over, he said that we could decide not to operate and just "let nature take its course." When we asked what that meant, he said, "I mean let her die." (p. 131)

Twenty-six percent of the mothers in Burke's study identified another early professional factor as being a source of anguish. After delivery of an impaired child, these mothers had been placed in rooms with mothers of normal babies. One mother recalled: "I was in a room with three other mothers, and seeing them with their babies was awful. I used to close the curtains and cry. I had to stay in the hospital for a week because of the C-section, and I felt like I was being punished the whole time" (p. 134). On the other hand, isolation from the normal may pose its own problems. The author has had clinical experience with mothers of children who were born with severe anomalies who have reported being placed in a room somewhat remote from normal obstetric activity and being assiduously avoided by nursing staff. These mothers also felt they were being punished, and the punishment was perceived as ostracism.

Affect Modulation

Emotional expression is the link between the self's internal experience and the environment. Whether or not expression or nonexpression is adaptive or maladaptive depends on context. A person may be nonexpressive for several reasons: (a) he may have feelings that are unrecognized or misinterpreted, (b) he may recognize and correctly interpret his feelings, but value self-containment, control, and stoicism as identity attributes and as adaptive coping skills, (c) he may feel cut off from others whom he perceives as indifferent, or (d) he may want to express his feelings but stop himself for fear of burdening someone or of being misunderstood, rejected, devalued, or condemned. Although our culture takes a mixed view, emotional expression is often promoted, and a clinical bias toward expression may be prevalent. The emotional content of chronic sorrow is enormously complex and often very disturbing. Processing and managing emotions that are sometimes perceived as overwhelming can result in reactions ranging from raw and unrestrained venting to highly inhibited or "numbed out" expression.

Kennedy-Moore and Watson (1999) recently synthesized extensive theory and research on emotional experience and expression. Regarding clinical work with clients who are struggling with problems related to emotional behavior, they state:

> In general, therapists need to help clients find a delicate balance in their emotional expression, so that clients can (1) understand their feelings rather than be overwhelmed by them, (2) harness the energy of their emotions for planning and action rather than be either thoughtlessly driven by it or paralyzed by it, and (3) communicate their emotional experience to others in a way that enhances interpersonal functioning rather than impairs it. This delicate balance entails using expression as a means of gaining self-understanding and relating to others in life-enhancing ways. It involves reflecting upon emotional experience and integrating it with other aspects of the self rather than either acting impulsively or shutting oneself off from experience. (p. 7)

Kennedy-Moore and Watson have summarized four major functions of emotional expression as (*a*) arousal regulation, (*b*) self-understanding, (*c*) coping and emotional processing, and (*d*) adaptive social communication. Both expression and nonexpression affect arousal. Expression, in whatever form it takes, tends to be adaptive when it fosters the return of arousal levels to "baseline." It tends to be maladaptive when it intensifies or when it is so protracted and unremitting that it compromises health (Siegman, 1994). The enhancement of self-understanding is a very important function of emotional behavior. Excessive expression and excessive nonexpression can obliterate potentially adaptive information inherent in emotional experience. Emotional understanding requires being aware but not overwhelmed by feelings. Clients "need to experience and express their feelings vividly, but with enough distance that they can thoughtfully examine and interpret these feelings" (Kennedy-Moore & Watson, 1999, p. 299).

Expression can facilitate coping and emotional processing, but too little or too much expression can be immobilizing. Working through and making sense of emotions is helpful in shaping adaptive behavior. Kennedy-Moore and Watson (1999) state: "When expression is part of adaptive emotional processing, it carries a sense of movement and change, involving new, deeper understanding and readiness for action. In contrast, ruminative expression is stagnant. Repetitively expressing 'I'm miserable; I'm always miserable; I'm just plain miserable' doesn't enhance coping. Instead it rehearses and intensifies distress, and it interferes with the implementation of active coping strategies" (p. 300). Regarding the function of expression in adaptive social communication, Kennedy-Moore and Watson stress its critical importance for well-being. Nonexpression in the social context interferes with the development of authentic relationships and blocks the availability of social support. Maladaptive expression, on the other hand, can destroy relationships and drive people away. For example, no matter how much significant others may care for someone, if that person's expressions are consistently of distress that is intense and enduring, others may not be able to tolerate dealing with them indefinitely.

Kennedy-Moore and Watson have described three characteristics of adaptive emotional behavior that can be used as guidelines for clinical interventions. These are (a) integration, (b) flexibility, and (c) interpersonal coordination. Integration refers to the ability to identify, name, and interpret affective experience and to incorporate it within the personality and view of the self; that is, such "individuals have an ego-syntonic way of acknowledging, articulating, and communicating their feelings. This aspect of integration in emotional expression involves finding and using one's true emotional voice" (p. 301). In experiential work with clients, emotional expression is not an end in itself. Integrating rational-cognitive and emotional response systems is central and results in integration of emotional behavior with self-view. Cognitive-behavioral approaches can also be effective in integration. Therapist flexibility is important in working with the client's own style of expression. Coercing tears from someone who values stoic self-containment is counterproductive. Clients may need time to build trust and to become comfortable enough to openly share their feelings.

Adaptive emotional expression is also characterized by flexibility. Rigid, maladaptive ways of interacting with others yield repeated disappointing and hurtful results. Interpersonal approaches, including group process, can be helpful in recognizing destructive patterns of relating. Cognitive-behavioral therapies are very effective for building behavioral response repertoires that foster increased client choice and adaptation. Interpersonal coordination refers to the person's ability to communicate in the desired way. To get her point across so that it is understood, the client must be able to speak clearly and congruently about her feelings, while taking into consideration other people's viewpoints. Clarity about goals directs the interaction. Those coping with chronic sorrow can be empowered by making their feelings known without alienating others by excessive displays of distress or by being so emotionally flat that responses are not elicited. The teaching of simple assertiveness skills validating both cognitive and emotional systems can do much to bolster the self and the self's effectiveness.

Writing one's thoughts and feelings can activate parts of the brain that are not so closely associated with intense emotional content and expression. Structured writing can foster movement toward self-under-standing and strengthening. It can also serve to access internal resources that contribute to meaning and to new adaptive capacities. For example, writing about (a) the antecedent or trigger for the emotion (anguish, pain, flooding, guilt, anger, and so on),(b) the meaning of the antecedent or trigger, (c) evoked feelings, (d) possible alternative meanings of the antecedent or trigger (reframes), and (e) changed perceptions, actions, and decisions that might influence future emotional reactions can ameliorate disturbing and painful responses. This type of structured writing in no way trivializes the client's experience or the reality of severe stressors. Instead, it serves as a way to acknowledge the reality of the client's life, while generating choices that may improve the self-regulation of emotions.

In chronic sorrow, the destructive expression of anger is usually directly related to the client's interpretation of the loss. Anger dyscontrol tends to occur when (a) the person has a sense of threat and harm, (b) coping capacity is overwhelmed, and (c) there are anger-enhancing attributions. Feeling threatened and harmed can result when goal-directed efforts are blocked, when there are major boundary violations, when post-traumatic symptoms are figural, when promises are broken, when expectations are shattered, and so on. Coping abilities are undermined when the person feels victimized and helpless or when the person believes she should not be the one who has to deal with certain provocations. Anger-enhancing attributions that are often present in chronic sorrow include (a) malevolent intent; that is, some person or some life force deliberately caused the problem, (b) the loss was preventable, (c) the loss and associated problems are unjust and undeserved, (d) someone or some situation is blamed and deserving of punishment, and (e) anger is believed to be the way to get what one wants or needs. Maladaptive anger includes overt injurious aggression (verbal or physical), passive aggression, an automatic pattern of defensiveness, and other behaviors such as getting drunk, driving recklessly, impulsively leaving, and so on.

Professionals who are overly anxious in the face of anger and who habitually avoid real or potentially angry situations may have difficulty in helping clients with anger management. Professionals who are not overly judgmental of clients with anger problems, who demonstrate a gentle tenacity, who model rational, problem-focused behavior, and who are confidently proficient in anger reduction skills can greatly help a motivated client who owns anger as a significant personal problem. Outcomes are not so favorable when anger is (a) a component of another disorder (for example, a delusional system, a neurological syndrome, or a personality disorder), (b) long-term and violent, (c) denied as a problem, (*d*) congruent with role and self-concept, (*e*) condoned, rewarded or reinforced, and (*f*) associated with underlying guilt, humiliation, fear, and so on.

Cognitive-behavioral therapists have developed a number of empirically based anger strategies. Some work better in some cases than in others. The author has found the use of time-outs and the "stop, think" approach to anger dyscontrol are usually welcomed by clients who see these strategies as something they can actually do, even when they are extremely agitated and upset. As anger builds, the client can visualize a red stop sign (or some other clear signal) to interrupt the escalating anger "right now!" The client directs himself to "Stop!" When his emotional arousal has eased, he directs himself to "Think!" He can focus on what he wants to accomplish and weigh the costs of his angry outbursts. He can identify his underlying fears, asking himself if there are other, more constructive ways of expressing himself, of achieving his goal, or allaying his fears. Adaptive uses of anger can be taught as well. These would include behavioral skills building such as (*a*) assertiveness, negotiation, and improved communication, (*b*) limit setting, (*c*) establishment of stable personal boundaries, and (*d*) problem analysis and solving strategies. Relaxation interventions can reduce the physiological arousal associated with angry emotions.

In obsessive, ruminative emotional experience, the client can also use a "stop, think" method of gaining control over her emotional life. Self-assignment of a "worry time" is coupled with the "stop, think" directive. In this case, for example, after the client has been able to interrupt her obsessing with "stop," she then directs herself to think about something she has planned in advance, such as a song, a poem, a scene, or a certain memory. She then directs herself to a specific "worry time." She might say, "At 10:15 this evening, I will think these terrible thoughts for at least ten minutes. I will think nothing but these thoughts, even if I want to stop before ten minutes have passed. I will think these thoughts for ten minutes or until they make me feel sick." Some of the body therapies, such as techniques from bioenergetics, yoga exercises, and massage can also be useful in reducing or preventing draining and immobilizing emotional discharges.

Heightened grief reactions are likely to occur during diagnostic assessment and at other stress points (for example, when developmental milestones are not achieved, during holidays, at puberty, in medical crises). Anticipating these life events can circumvent or lessen emotional costs. Problem solving that involves support, respite, increased socialization, constructing a life narrative, addressing existential issues, or taking an action that has symbolic value can often prevent responses that are despairing or excessively angry, bitter, and resentful. Standard stress reduction techniques are also appropriate for affect modulation. Progressive deep muscle relaxation, diaphragmatic breathing, meditation, and other uses of trance (such as quietly imaging shelter in a personally constructed place or assuming a position of observer), if used consistently, can lead to improved sleep, increased efficiency, and calmer mood.

Assisting the client in maintaining a sense of self-efficacy, empowerment, and control is basic to affect regulation. In this respect, it is not necessary for the client to actually *have* control over elements of the situation itself; what is necessary is the *impression* of control. As in virtually all work with persons who are experiencing profound losses, interventions can only be effective when they occur at a level where healing is possible. The client and the professional may not be able to influence most critical realities of the loss, but together they can identify other loss-related consequences in which comfort and healing are feasible. For example, a client with a progressive debilitating condition may not be able to slow the disease process, but she *can* claim control by achieving a more supportive environment, making peace in an important relationship, finding new ways of soulfulness, constructing personal meanings for her life, and so on. Sometimes control can be experienced in very small ways as well. Asking the client, for example, whether he wants a door open or closed and then doing as he wishes is one way of suggesting control.

Trauma Resolution

The effects of trauma are insidious. Trauma affects important psychological abilities, such as (a) the ability to temper or modulate strong feelings and the associated ability to soothe and comfort oneself, (b) the ability to maintain interpersonal connections, and (c) the ability to sustain a positive self-image (Briere, Grant-Hall, Pearlman, & Laub, 1992). In some cases, traumatic aspects of the loss can be resolved, but in other cases the trauma will be intractable. Much can be done, however, to reduce the frequency, intensity, and duration of post-traumatic symptoms. Charles Figley's (1989) extensive work with traumatized families has led to a five-phase model, based on empowerment, for addressing the destructive consequences of traumatic incidents for families. In Figley's model, there are eight treatment objectives: (a) rapport and trust building between therapist and the client family, (b) defining the therapist's role, (c) eliminating unwanted effects of the traumatic experiences, (d) strengthening of family social support, (e) developing new rules and skills of family communication, (f) promoting self-disclosure, and (g) building a family healing theory. The five-phase model is similar to human development models in which developmental tasks in one stage are completed before going on to the next stage.

Phase one, the foundation of the model, is the building of commitment to agreed-upon therapeutic objectives. If phase one is not completed, even with further negotiations on the objectives, then proceeding to the next stages is unwarranted. Phase two consists of framing the problem. In this phase the family tells its story and describes the problems of family life in need of change—a family member's PTSD symptoms, hardships, adjustments, breakdowns in the system, and so on. When problems are identified to everyone's satisfaction, phase three consists of reframing the problem. If the family process is productive, family members identify ways of thinking about the family predicament that are better tolerated and more adaptive.

Figley (1989) points out that new insights developed in phase three usually include the basic ingredients for a family healing theory, which is the task of phase four. The theory emerges from continuing discussion among family members and consists of an explanation of the current family predicament and a family prediction about the future. Phase five, consisting of closure and preparedness, ensures that treatment objectives have been attained for all client family members and, very important, that they are well prepared for future adversities and crises, including potential future trauma. This model is applicable to the trauma involved in most cases of chronic sorrow. Further, it fosters family cohesion, builds intrafamilial support, and provides a forum in which each family member may have a say about how the trauma is perceived and what it is like to live with the changes brought about by the loss.

There is obviously much more to therapy than the mechanical application of techniques. In work with trauma, the therapist is often challenged to develop pragmatic approaches on an ad hoc basis. The effectiveness of interventions depends on variables such as (a) the setting in which they take place, (b) appropriateness and personal "fit" of the intervention, (c) the style and finesse with which the intervention is carried out, (d) relationship variables, (e) therapist variables; and (f) client variables. The author has found Gestalt approaches, if tolerated by the client, are helpful in reducing or eliminating flashbacks and other intrusive symptomatology. The flexibility of experiential techniques is conducive to ongoing therapist assessment and client input. The therapist can mold and adjust her guidance and support so as to reinforce client choice and stability. "Speaking to" instead of "speaking about" aspects of the trauma can reduce the effects of entrenched internalized "videotapes" of the catastrophic event. Dialogue with discrete elements of the flashback can reveal their intrinsic meanings and disempower their forcefulness. For example, a client may continue to have intrusive images of the split second in which he and his life were forever changed. Dialogue with elements of that split second and the self within that moment may bring to light certain impressions that can be reframed in the present. The client may also be helped to realize or construct symbolic meaning of the image. It may represent, for instance, his last glimpse of himself as able-bodied.

The intrusion of the image as if it were happening in the present may be partially driven by an unconscious magical reasoning that the loss can be prevented or undone. But when the scene continues to its inevitable catastrophic outcome, it tends to intensify the terror of the loss. A sense of helplessness and a feeling of being inextricably trapped in a life of inevitable losses may increase. In this case, it may be appropriate to assist a man in voluntarily "running the tape" from the moment just before he was changed and then, instead of stopping, as the image has always stopped, encouraging him to continue the tape well into the future from that moment. Therapeutic modulation of the intense emotional responses (the affective bridge) can both sustain connection to the event (important for achieving change) and reduce its painful impact. The goal is to help the client reexperience the memory of the event in a safe setting with the therapist's skilled guidance and support and to help him develop a different or novel element or viewpoint. When continuing the "tape" past its previously fixed end point, the client can see and append an image of his survival, and he can be encouraged to say or do something that he needed at the time of the trauma. He may also be helped to experience himself as empowered to deal with the aftermath rather than as beaten down by tragedy. This type of work helps to break up fixed images and can submit them to conscious control while, at the same time, facilitating a disengagement of intense affect from the memory. The client is then no longer immobilized by the memory, and it loses its autonomy.

So long as intrusive imagery continues without successful intervention, the client may continue to develop additional symptoms associated with avoidance of possible triggers. His life and his interactions may narrow considerably. He fears doing something that might inadvertently invite the reexperiencing of the imagery, and so he finds himself in a double bind. He may feel desperate for help, but he is terrified of the memories of the trauma. He is therefore wary and afraid of therapy (and therapists) as he feels at great risk of incapacitation if his fragile defenses are disturbed. Client readiness and commitment are crucial, and the therapist will have to carefully assess client resources in preparation for the work. Usually the client will be unable to address many important aspects of his loss until trauma symptoms are significantly reduced or resolved. When the impasse created by the trauma is resolved, therapy can move on to specific grief issues and other problems of life.

Existential therapy and interpersonal approaches that facilitate the construction of a meaning for the traumatic loss are useful in generating cognitive coherence; that is, some way of making sense out of the trauma within the framework of the larger picture. Incorporating the loss into the personal life narrative so that it is viewed as a major agent of tremendous life challenges rather than as an unsurpassable disruption of life can serve to contextualize the trauma and reduce its impact as a perceived uncontrollable and alien force that can never be accommodated.

Hypnotherapy techniques, such as those involving visual-kinesthetic dissociation (Bandler & Grinder, 1979) and variations of spot reparenting are also useful in work with trauma. Eye movement desensitization and reprocessing (EMDR) (Shapiro, 1995) appears to be compiling a reasonable record of success in reducing or eliminating the intensity of affect associated with traumatic memories. Other debriefing techniques such as traumatic incident reduction (TIR) (Gerbode, 1989) and thought field therapy (TFT) (Callahan, 1985) work well for some cases. Art and music therapy, usually as components of psychotherapeutic approaches, are also known to be effective for ameliorating trauma. The techniques that are currently promulgated for relief of post-traumatic symptoms have commonalities. It could well be that it doesn't matter much which technique is selected. What may matter most is pairing the review of the traumatic event and its associated affect with a different, neutral (or affectless) task that requires some attention. Whether that task is eye movement, tapping on acupressure points, viewing from a different vantage point, or running the scene backward may not be so important as the fact of pairing. Comprehensive trauma work includes integrating the trauma into the client's world- and self-view. Relief of post-traumatic symptoms can reposition the client to address important issues and to generate adaptive changes in other facets of his life.

Restoration of Self-Efficacy and Control

The traumatic loss that is central to chronic sorrow frequently results in drastic damage to self-esteem and self-confidence. The chaos and strain resulting from the loss constitute an assault on capacities for self-reliance, trust, autonomy, initiative, and—perhaps most important—identity and relationships. The situational context combined with dynamics of the individual mediate how and when self-efficacy and control can be restored. Judith Herman (1992) states that healing cannot occur in isolation. The companioning model of professional assistance (Wolfelt, 1998) promotes parity as the basis for the client-professional relationship. Wolfelt (1998), Herman (1992), Figley (1989) and others have developed models of help that challenge the utility of the medical model for the very reason that it undermines equality and the restoration of self-efficacy.

Empowerment has been defined as "the convergence of mutual support with individual autonomy" (Stark & Flitcraft, 1988, p. 141). Restoring self-efficacy, then, requires relational support, validation of the client's experience, respect for her competence, assisting but not directing her life decisions, and an alliance grounded in equal power. As Herman (1992) indicates, "Others may offer advice, support, assistance, affection, and care, but not cure. Many benevolent and well-intentioned attempts to assist the survivor founder because this fundamental principle of empowerment is not observed. No intervention that takes power away from the survivor can possibly foster her recovery, no matter how much it appears to be in her immediate best interest" (p. 133). In exceptional circumstances, however, where there has been a total decompensation, or in crises mandating emergency intervention (with or without consent), others may have to take unilateral actions. Even then, if it is at all possible, the person should be consulted. As the client regroups and gathers her internal resources, it is advisable to return responsibility to her at the earliest reasonable time.

Self-efficacy and control are greatly bolstered by accurate information. Clients who immediately and actively inform themselves tend to lose less momentum during diagnostic assessments, crises, and treatment. They are better able to interact with professionals from an empowered position. Information expands options, and choices are more confidently made. Some clients spend many hours searching the Internet. Support groups can be not only sources of emotional comfort and encouragement, but also places for the interchange of information and resources. Following the precept that "anything that helps the person who is the source of chronic sorrow helps the system" can also foster restabilization. Other positive influences are (a) establishing a structured daily routine as quickly as possible, (b) framing requests for help as self-efficacy behaviors, and (c) reviewing times of stress and identifying strengths and creative client coping in those situations. In the latter instance, imaging and accessing the thoughts, feelings, and actions that were evoked by the client in successfully coping with the situations can be strengthening and reassuring in the present.

Relinquishment of Fantasies Invalidated by the Loss

In their review of research on bereavement, Exline, Dorrity, and Wortman (1996) found that as many as 40% of the bereaved may develop full-blown clinical complications after a major loss. Although there is a paucity of research specific to chronic sorrow and clinical complications, it is reasonable to assume that, since chronic sorrow usually endures for a lifetime, a significant number of people coping with self- or other-loss will suffer from such complications, some repeatedly. It is widely understood that a major contributor to psychological difficulties in all forms of bereavement is the impact of fantasies about the loss. The author's belief (supported by her clinical experience) is that, in chronic sorrow, these fantasies are likely to endure longer and to be reevoked much more frequently than in other bereavement. The ever-present fantasy of how life should have been and perhaps still could be significantly influences the client's affect management skills and difficulties. The role of the fantasy in the extended course of chronic sorrow, though recognized, has not been systematically studied or researched. It appears, however, that the effects of the fantasy are extremely complex, that they can be both positive and negative, and that the fantasy is usually extremely tenacious.

The fantasy of restoring all or some of what has been lost can support and energize efforts to obtain extensive diagnostic evaluations and expert opinion. It can motivate the very hard work of treatment and rehabilitation and can serve to open the mind to new and creative possibilities for potential solutions. At times, usually during the initial years after the loss, the fantasy may fuel the pursuit for information, and it may help in staving off depression and other clinical complications. Keeping the fantasy alive may fend off debilitating and overwhelming despair. However, it can also lead to inordinate doctor shopping and to endless searches for more hopeful treatment and prognoses. It can foster denial and selective attention so that information is distorted; that is, bad news is not heard, and some unfavorable information is interpreted as favorable. It can overshadow pleasure in the person's hard-won accomplishments, when these achievements are even more precious, given the ground from which they emerge. The fantasy can make perfect targets of those with chronic sorrow who want to believe in miracles and who are prey to charlatans who promise undeliverable goods. A therapist's suggestion that the client relinquish the fantasy can be experienced as a threat of losing all hope. But the questions are: How much hope should a person cling to, and what should one hope for? When does the fantasy become an impasse to making the most of what actually is? When does it impair decision making and planning for care?

Giving up fantasies related to the loss may be more difficult when (a) the loss is the result of someone's negligence or criminal behavior or it is believed that the loss could have been averted, and (b) giving up the fantasy also means giving up other things to which one is significantly attached or which are identity-related. These things might be a house, an automobile, membership in an esteemed group or club, travel, certain hobbies, careers, and so on. Relinquishing fantasies in some instances of other-loss is much more difficult when the subject of the loss often appears normal. For example, parents of children with autism may not be in a position to give up their fantasies until their child has reached adulthood. The fantasy may grow more painful and wrenching with time, since when they look at their aging child, they may more easily see both the child who is and the child who was meant to be. When the child has become an adult and the parents realize that "this is as good as it gets," and the fantasy no longer holds promise, they may grieve their loss intensely and more deeply than ever before. Loss of the fantasy before this time, however, may be fraught with more serious complication.

Premature interventions to "take away" life dreams and fantasies can be just as injurious as insisting that the client realize all her losses. MacGregor (1994) describes the development of serious mental illness in one's child as causing the same parental grief that is caused by the death of a child. The goal of her article is to assist professionals in recognizing grief responses of parents of children who are mentally ill, to view these responses as normal, and to validate and address them. For this reason, MacGregor's article is extremely valuable. However, there are differences between interventions that are appropriate regarding death and interventions that are appropriate to a living loss. For example, assisting parents of children who are mentally ill to "realize the multitude of losses they are experiencing and to assist them in recognizing their partner's grief" (p. 163), may be appropriate in a few cases; more often, this intervention may only serve to strip away coping strengths and abilities. Why must a parent be required to realize, in any meaning of the word, the *multitude* of losses? It is often quite enough to realize a few at a time. Moreover, it would be unusual not to recognize a partner's grief; however, recognizing it does not necessarily bring the partners closer to one another. Recognizing, supporting, and respecting differences in grieving styles may be more desirable as a goal. Even then, a partner may be more supportive by choosing *not* to impose a great outpouring of grief and painful recognitions. In short, there is no single prescription for the management of grieving, shared or not.

A skilled and caring therapist will often notice characteristic, recurring patterns of behavior and affect in her clients that will relate to the client's staunch attachment to the fantasy. When client and therapist determine that the time is right, a major piece of grief work in chronic sorrow is saying good-bye to the dreamed-for, expected, and now forever lost self or other. This releasing process is incomplete unless it includes letting in and embracing the self or other who actually exists. This type of work can be excruciatingly difficult for the client (and sometimes for the therapist). It is best done when the client has sustained significant periods of adaptive functioning, when he has done some soul-searching, and when he has found value in his present situation and existential position. The therapist can be the source of gentle guidance toward the time and place to say good-bye. Preparatory work will include mutual understanding of the goal and the eventual therapeutic implications of this type of core grief work.

The specifics of this work depend on the client's internal resources, coping style, and strategic systems. The work can be done in one session or in several or many sessions. Two important components in the letting-go process are (*a*) the client experience of congruence in her emotions, words, thoughts, and actions, and (*b*) achievement of integration and internal ecological balance—a sense of fit. The client may feel more anchored if, as part of preparation, she makes an outline of all she wants to express to achieve closure. She may need assistance in selecting and clearly imaging her fantasy of herself or other so that she will feel she is in contact with the essence of the fantasy. During the work she can then clarify what she is relinquishing. Gestalt dialogue with the representation of the loss can be facilitated and guided. Structure is helpful in providing safety so that the client is less likely to experience traumatic images and affective flooding. Without structure, the client can too easily stray off course and into unsafe territory. An example of structure is the use of sentence stems such as "I regret . . .," "I resent . . .," and "I appreciate. . . ." The client is given space and time in which to express her feelings of disappointment, grief, love, anger, and so on. "I am deciding . . ." statements can then be empowering.

Often at least one impasse emerges during this work. Without it, the work would not be so compelling. Ego state work, such as Gestalt and Ericksonian interventions, and cognitive therapy can be employed to work through the impasse. If successfully resolved, a sense of relief and a "knowing" will take place in which the client will feel changed and aware of having let go of a cherished, yet impossible, dream of self or other. This work may qualitatively shift the client's grief in the direction of greater comfort and increased internal consistency. The process may continue for hours or for many days and weeks following the work. New insights are not uncommon. It is important to avoid intellectual discussion of the process after its completion. Analysis, interpretation, and review of what has happened may depotentiate the work. Considerable time may elapse before the client can meaningfully articulate the changes that have occurred and may still be occurring.

The inclusion of a shift that is affirming of the real self or the actual other involving expressions of caring, acceptance, sadness, commitment, or other positive statements of intent are also important for a sense of completion. Connecting with the self or other without the intervening veil of the fantasy may result in reduced distortion and in perceptions that take into account the whole person. For the first time, it may be possible to see the person who is the source of the loss much as others see him. Feelings of compassion may be evoked, and greater intimacy may be felt.

Embracing What Is

An improved capacity for owning and valuing the self or significant other in the context of loss can result from surrendering the fantasy. Expressed heart-felt commitment to a clearly envisioned, internalized representation of the severely flawed, but wholly lovable, self or other can (a) mark the closure of the process of relinquishment of fantasies and (b) strengthen and energize the bond with the existing self or other. A distinction must be made between embracing and accepting the person and accepting the cataclysmic events of and surrounding the loss. The person need not accept the latter. It is entirely appropriate and frequently constructive for the client to express anger, sadness, and other strong emotions related to the unacceptability of the loss itself. Future-pacing techniques may be indicated. For example, the client may be helped to project himself into his life a year hence and visualize positive changes, such as more comfortable coping, decisions which will have been made that improve lifestyle, feelings of self-satisfaction for having obtained certain services, and so on.

Helping the client to take some time out in the days after intensive experiential therapy can protect her and safeguard the process. An analogy of needed recuperative and restorative rest after surgery is often useful and indicates to the client that healing is already taking place. Metaphorical communication with some clients seems to have a stabilizing effect. Some clients may benefit from keeping a journal or writing poetry at this juncture of their lives. The therapist might suggest opening stems for journaling that are tailored to the individual and designed to carry the process along.

Reexamination and Update of Belief Systems

Since serious loss often challenges core beliefs, helping clients to reevaluate and modify beliefs is often a key element in therapy. In most clients, beliefs about the fundamental existential dilemmas, discussed in chapter 6, will require reevaluation and some revision. Approaches based on unconditional positive regard, such as client-centered therapy, and assistance from clergy, can do much to support the client in finding his own life path in a context of modified cherished beliefs and values. The client may discover new options as a result of reinterpretation of major components of the self, how these have developed, and what needs to happen in light of current reality. Ericksonian working assumptions (Erickson & Rossi, 1979), especially those that point to the uniqueness of the individual, the generative nature of personal resources, and assistance focused on course alignment (rather than on course correction) can provide the basis of support on which the self can change and grow. Cognitive and cognitive-behavioral interventions can address attributions of causality of losses and their influence on the present and future. The helper's positively biased view of personal autonomy can contribute to a reordering and shift in the client's rules for living. For some clients with propensities for insight, dream work can be helpful and personally validating. Dreams can be used to foster growth, clarity, change, and reframing of core struggles. Some clients are benefitted by identifying and understanding the teleological aspects of some of their dreams. While probably not predictive or auguring in a prognosticating sense, dreams can reflect and illuminate one's current concerns and dilemmas and point toward a future that is somehow different.

Assisting the client in moving away from beliefs of self-blame while fostering control may be a central concern. In many circumstances, it is not necessary that the client have actual control, only that she *perceives* herself to have control (Miller, 1980). Attending to those aspects of life where client control is feasible and including these as part of priority setting (that is, identifying and addressing what the client actually needs and what is important *today*) can reduce confusion and support course realignment. The anxieties inherent in chronic sorrow tend to reinforce client worry about potential uncontrollable events. Clients often worry about things that might happen far into the future. These fears can be reduced by decreasing the tendency to "put the cart before the horse." Clinical depression may be reduced by modifying the tendency toward self-blame and by modifying values and beliefs which lead to pervasive helplessness (Seligman, 1975).

The following case illustrates a client's reevaluation and updating of values, life principles, and self-view. Therapeutic approaches were primarily experiential and cognitive. The client had been admitted to a psychiatric hospital as a transfer from a general medical and surgical hospital. He had nearly killed himself with an overdose of Valium and alcohol. This man, in his late thirties, was extremely bright and enterprising, and he had previously displayed high levels of creative and productive energy. He had galvanized his considerable assets and had made a good deal of money in entrepreneurial pursuits. At the time of admission, he was full of rage and despair that he had survived. He was assigned to my process group, and he later requested that I see him individually as well. For several days he could not move in any direction from his anger and despondency. At that time, several years ago, the therapeutic milieu of the adult psychiatric unit in this hospital was extremely stable, and a large percentage of the patients had a propensity for insight and empathic attunement. After his second weekend among a cohort of caring, astute patients, he began to participate in the therapy group.

At the time, he was struggling with a progressive neuromuscular disorder of unknown origin that had become noticeable three years before his admission. He lived alone and had been able to continue his work as a successful businessman. His wife had left him two years earlier. He had initially been extremely distressed, but he had adjusted well to his divorce and to living alone. More recently, however, he had begun to fall down frequently so that it had become necessary for him to spend most of his waking hours in a wheelchair. A girlfriend had ended her relationship with him at about the same time he began to use the chair. His father had been dead for many years, and his mother was in very poor health. There were no siblings.

His interactions in the therapy group disclosed that this man's belief systems were failing to sustain him in the changed context of his life. In the process of our work together, he realized that he had a malevolent view of the wheelchair. It symbolized failure, pity, victimization, confinement, and unacceptable diminishment as a person in a highly competitive world. He had very strong beliefs about "winning" and "success" as being predicated on beating the competition. His charismatic persona had attracted numerous followers who looked to him for inspiration and guidance. His role was to have all the answers for others. It was unthinkable for him not to live up to his and their expectations, and it was doubly unthinkable for him to be the one in need. He had never imagined that he could end up in a wheelchair. Such a happenstance was a severe blow to his self-image.

With therapeutic reflections on content and emotions, he gradually became aware of his polarized beliefs and opinions. His good self was a "winner," an imaginative, aggressive, and clever man who could overcome the odds. His bad (disowned or shadow) self was puny, weak, disgusting, and small. The wheelchair was experienced as humiliating, as exposing and affirming the bad self. It was an invasive and alien thing that adhered to him like a stigmatic disfigurement, thereby disqualifying him for meaningful participation in life. With the caring support of the group, in a Gestalt type of dialogue (the goal of which was to begin to integrate the good-bad split), he stood accusingly before the chair. Since he could stand for only a few minutes without support, a group member offered him a regular chair. He then sat in that chair and faced the wheel-chair. He called it derogatory names, and he spat on it, rejecting it force-fully and profanely, pushing it away from him. At this point, he became aware that he was expressing verbally what he had witnessed in his mother's behavior at the time of his father's death when he was 13 years old. His mother was very dependent (and parasitic). She had become chronically angry and bitter that his father had not been able to get well and that he had abandoned her through death. She had expected her son to take care of her, which he now was in no condition to do.

Identifying, sorting, revising, and empowering a new set of beliefs that could accommodate an integrated self with both positive and negative qualities, and in which the wheelchair could be experienced as a blessing as well as a curse, were very difficult yet feasible tasks. Strategies in-cluded accessing his considerable strengths and resources, all very evi-dent in his extraordinary entrepreneurship, and validating them as still parts of the changed self, just as much as they had been a part of his "good" self. He soon saw his belief systems as being well suited to an adolescent boy, and they had served him well in the years after his father's death. He had been solicitous of his mother, and he tolerated her angry, entitled demandingness through splitting (that is, she was neither all good nor all bad), just as he had tolerated—at least for a while—his own drastic changes and losses through polarization or splitting of the self. As an independent, charismatic, successful entrepreneur, he was a rescuer and a dispenser of wisdom and guidance to his friends and fol-lowers. He also lent or dispensed money to those with hard-luck stories and occasionally allowed people to move into his house until they could "get back on their feet." Some of these people eventually had to be ousted. Many borrowers had not repaid him. He realized that he would either have to attract different types of friends or redefine the limits of friendships. In fact, he was severely challenged to update nearly all facets of his life; to do so required beliefs about his value as a person of great worth, despite—and also because of—his disabilities.

Treatment lasted about 10 months. Cognitive-behavioral, Gestalt, hypno-therapeutic (trance and nontrance), values clarification, systemic, and exoneration and forgiveness approaches were used, with good results. He began to internalize a positive image of himself as the "wounded healer," and he began to accept help from others. He could understand the value of asking for and accepting help so that others could have some of the same good feelings that he enjoyed when he was helpful to them. His disabilities led to an understanding of the benefit of setting limits on the amount and kind of help that is useful and warranted. This simple understanding returned to him a significant sense of control. He also understood that, as an adolescent at the time of his father's death, he had not adequately grieved the loss of his father, since he had been expected to take care of his mother, whose angry grief was "the really big deal" while his loss was treated as irrelevant. Any dependency needs he may have had were denied. As an adult, he was able to accept dependency from others and to take care of them, often in a way that he himself had wished to be cared for. Grief work regarding previous losses, of his father and to some extent his mother, of his wife and the important girlfriend, and of certain specific losses of prior personal capabilities, was necessary as a part of reestablishing workable values and beliefs. The client's acute misery was a strong motivating factor in his progress.

Three years ago this client referred an acquaintance to the author for therapy. She informed the author that he was driving a beautiful, new, customized van, that he was doing well in business, and that he had moved his mother into an assisted living facility. His mother had indignantly objected, but he was firm, and she eventually had to see the move as a good solution. He had lost most of the function of his legs. The acquaintance reported that he had a serious relationship with a woman who was "appropriate." She described him as an inspiration to herself and others. He had continued to allow some people to take advantage of him, but he required more from these people and set limits on what he would agree to do for them. He was still working on saying no.

Prevention of Maladaptive Coping Styles

Therapists can use all therapeutic contacts as opportunities for prevention of maladaptive behavior. If the client, for instance, is seeing the therapist for affect modulation, mental rehearsals of coping with future stressful events (that is, triggers) can prepare the client and increase perception of control and autonomy. Because of exhaustion, some caregivers may need help in managing their angry and tearful outbursts. But they can also be helped by competent respite care. Professionals can assist in tracking down needed relief services, intervening at the level of the workplace when time off is warranted, and in making recommendations for time away so the client can have the opportunity to sleep, let the mind go blank, and be in the wider world. Realistic professionals will learn about services that will lighten the load, and they will advocate for them when none exist. Clients are comforted when they know that help and options actually exist, and they can temporarily delegate—even for a few hours—the responsibilities that are so draining of life energy.

Identity strengthening, clarification of issues and needs, and reinforcement of competent coping can help prevent maladaptive coping efforts.

When the client recounts a serious life crisis that has been negotiated, it can be helpful to identify what the client did (for example, how he defined the event, how he determined what could be done about it, and how he successfully resolved the event). "Wiring in" the client's perception of competence by increasing his awareness of the effective strategies he has already used can reduce the likelihood that he will be overwhelmed by his future. Encouraging the use of support networks and practical assistance to achieve balance in the major life areas, especially in cases of other-loss, can likewise do much to prevent decompensation and burnout. Permissions and solution-focused interventions can help clients assign higher priority to themselves so that some of their important needs are met. These needs may be spiritual, educational, vocational, recreational, social, sexual, creative, and aesthetic. When clients are assisted to claim time for themselves and for their own interests, tendencies toward symbiotic enmeshments may be decreased. Frightening thoughts of abandoning the scene altogether may likewise be reduced.

As Featherstone (1980) has described, parents of children with serious disabilities often question their decision to marry. Is this what they did wrong? "The vitality of healthy children reassures parents about their marriage as well as about themselves. Children are tangible, lovable symbols of their joint undertaking. In thriving they bless a parent's choices—the choice of spouse, the decision to have children, the style of parenting. When a child's development goes seriously awry, it calls the whole enterprise into question" (p. 102). She states further: "With luck, the pleasures of parenthood outweigh the loss of liberty. A child's disability can shift this balance. Concerns for the future weigh heavily on both parents. Practical responsibilities nibble away at the slim margins for recreation and leisure. Dreams of lost promise return—unreachable, but deceptively fresh and green" (p. 105). Many parents do dream of taking flight and being free of the prison their lives have become. While usually keeping their fantasies to themselves, some parents threaten to leave as a way to express their despair. Professional awareness of the strains placed on a marital relationship when a child is disabled can help to separate feelings about the relationship from those about the child and the child's impairments. Assisting parents in finding ways to interrupt triangulations and to focus on the maintenance of their relationship can prevent further deterioration of the marriage. Finding small, manageable things the partners can do to nurture each other may make an immense difference. Obtaining an agreement to make time for themselves as a couple, even if only once or twice a month, can also strengthen faith in the relationship. Some couples report they have found each other again through couple time that involves a strict commitment to talk about virtually anything *except* the child with disabilities.

Monitoring the client for adequate medical care is also an effective way to prevent negative outcomes. While some will respond to losses with increased somatic complaints, others will ignore their distress and their physical symptoms as part of their denial and fear of weakening in any way. The judicious use of psychotropic medications for depression, obsessive tendencies, and anxiety may be warranted and may make the difference between adequate coping and disaster. Exline, Dorrity, and Wortman (1996) report that in depression, psychotropic medication should help to mute the symptoms, allowing a shift away from concerns about personal sadness to issues that are more specifically linked to the loss. They explain that, paradoxically, a temporary increase in grief-related distress may be a positive result. Those with a history of depression may benefit from the continued use of an antidepressive medication for at least five years. According to Exline, Dorrity, and Wortman, this type of long-term treatment appears to be an effective means of preventing recurring episodes of depression. Antidepressants are also useful in the management of PTSD symptoms. Referral for medication evaluation can be framed in terms of increased client control.

Clients experiencing chronic sorrow may become prone to doctor shopping. They may seek out referrals to all manner of perceived expertise. This behavior is usually highly overdetermined. Professionals themselves may be guilty of referral *ad absurdum* of persons coping with ongoing and unrelenting loss. If this is the case, clients may begin to feel they are in a "hot potato" game with no ending. Some clients remain for some time unwilling to accept an initial diagnosis or assessment and may search for disconfirmations or for an opinion indicating less severity. Doctor shopping may function to delay awareness of many facets of the loss and of the necessity to take certain actions or make drastic changes in lifestyle. The professional has an ethical duty to such clients in at least two areas: (*a*) conservation of the clients' financial resources (they will need to salvage funds that will be sorely needed in the management of their future), and (*b*) prevention of obsessively driven behavior patterns. In the latter area, it may be necessary to assist the client in deciding definitively on a balance between ethical duty about obtaining the best help possible and the need to get on with the job of living. Rational assessment of proposed consultations, from a therapeutically neutral position, may prevent the seduction of some clients by opportunistic quacks who prey on desperate and vulnerable people.

Encouraging and strengthening the client's development of a meaningful life narrative can also be a means of prevention. The client may not find this type of support and validation in any other way, since friends and family usually have not faced her anxieties and dilemmas. Because she has stepped into a parallel universe, she may turn to professionals who do have experience and expertise in finding coherent meaning and integrating it into the fabric of life. The exquisite need for one's own narrative could not be described better than this:

> You hear the sound of your voice explaining what has happened, describing the events in painstaking chronological detail. The person listening wants you to jump to the end. In his tensed body you can hear the questions: So what happened? What's the point? But you need to lay it all out, to say, Well, first his blood pressure was high, but the doctor said not to worry. And then we noticed he was sweating a lot and drinking all the time. He seemed to eat constantly, but he was very thin. By now it was September. I made an appointment for a physical and we couldn't get in until October. October 12. I remember because it was Columbus Day. And then . . .
>
> You need to hear your story out loud so that you can make sense of what has happened and what is going on now. You are like a spider, your words the filaments of sound, lines you are spinning to attach the web of your experience to a corner of the world. In this way you connect the thin gauze of this new, incomprehensible event to the solid wall of what your life has been until now. In this way, telling your story heals you. (Gill, 1997, p. 24)

☐ Hazards and Pitfalls

Seasoned therapists and other professionals may not need or want information about therapeutic errors and cautionary approaches with persons coping with chronic sorrow. The following discussion, based on the author's clinical and personal experience, is included primarily for professionals who may have had relatively little experience in working with this population. It may be difficult to believe that persons with chronic sorrow have been handled (or not handled at all) in this way by the helping professions. However, it is still not uncommon for persons with serious and visible anomalies to be rejected outright by some members of the medical community and by professionals in other health care disciplines as well. Some dentists will do work for persons with severe developmental disabilities only when the patients are sedated and restrained. Some therapists insist that unless a person can think abstractly, he cannot benefit from psychotherapy.

The importance of meeting the client where she is cannot be overstated. There is a joke that illustrates this principle. In it, the client is pouring her heart out about the horrendous train wreck that took so many lives and caused so many severe and permanent injuries, including her own. She is recounting her terror at finding she could not stand up. She describes the way the paramedics, when they finally got to her, did all they could to stabilize her before putting her in an ambulance.

She describes the pandemonium at the trauma center, the moans and whimpers, how she was placed in a holding area, how the nurses raced past her, and how she couldn't feel her legs. The therapist interrupts her at this point and asks, "Was the ambulance a Medstar or a Lifeline?"

When the therapist is "out of sync" with the client, interactions can be experienced as disconnections (or worse). If the client has already seen a number of professionals, including therapists, she may not want to dredge up issues and history with which she feels she has already dealt. Rather than taking a detailed history, the therapist can ask her to tell him what she feels is important for him to know in order to be able to help her. During the course of that and subsequent contacts, he can enlarge his understanding of the history and clarify issues that "stand out" for the client. Staying with the client's process in a collaborative manner will significantly reduce the risk of empathic failures. Therapists who are wedded to a certain psychological theory and who tend to see virtually all their clients through the lens of the theory may make assumptions that are inconsistent with the client's reality. For example, a person with a progressive neuromuscular disorder who can no longer work may seek help when he fears his wife is planning to leave him. He wants his fears to be acknowledged, and he wants help in salvaging his marriage or in developing survival options so that he will not be so dependent on his wife's staying with him. He may experience even less control, as well as abandonment, when a therapist insists on doing family reconstruction work and persists in probing for family history and dynamics through three generations. A woman known by the author consulted a therapist when she felt herself slipping into a depression after it became obvious that her child had autism. The therapist wanted to know about her dreams during her pregnancy. She could not remember any specific dreams. She had been seeing a psychoanalyst at that time, and the therapist asked her to write to the psychoanalyst for his notes or his report on any dream material that was part of her psychoanalytic work. The analyst wrote to the therapist, stating that the analysand had reported dreams of seeing her child as healthy, normal, and happy, playing with other children. The therapist appeared very disappointed with this report, and the woman left therapy feeling she had fallen short of the therapist's expectations and also confused about the importance of her dreams during pregnancy.

Humor can be very healing, insightful, and a source of edifying perspective. But humor introduced by the therapist before a trusting alliance has been established, before the therapist is sure of the client's disposition regarding humor, or that goes directly to issues that are extremely sensitive to the client, can be experienced as uncaring and discounting. The same situation holds regarding the use of reframes. The rule, of course, is to know your client. Reframes that truly take into account the client's reality, reflect the client's truth, and introduce a different perspective can illuminate the client's life and expand options. But reframes that are offered as a "quick fix" (sometimes for the therapist who is extremely uncomfortable with parts of the client's content) can be received as superficial, dismissive, and reflective of the therapist's misunderstandings or lack of empathy with the client. One of the author's clients, whose husband had suffered a severely crippling accident, reported that when she had sought therapy previously, the therapist had stated: "You're fortunate, you know, when you really think about it. Your husband can never leave you now. Many women worry about their husband's fidelity, and that is something you never have to concern yourself with." She realized the therapist was only trying to help her feel better, and she pretended to be reassured, thereby taking care of the therapist as well as participating in her own sense of bewildered estrangement.

Some therapists use a standard repertoire of imagery for stress management. They may apply this imagery to their work with PTSD symptoms. The use of imagery that has not been tailored to the individual client can inadvertently trigger emotional flooding, abreactions, and flashbacks. Inadvertent triggers can be avoided through careful assessment of the trauma and its aftermath. In the case of a client being seen in a hospital setting where he is undergoing yet another of many surgical repairs for traumatic injuries he sustained many years ago, it may be safe to assume that he has already had opportunities to review the trauma and to express how he felt when he realized he and his life had been permanently changed. He may not need or want to dredge up such painful emotions again. It is better to ask the client if he feels it would help to talk about his injuries and how they happened rather than to directly ask him about the trauma and about his feelings. In a hospital setting, parents of a child born with multiple deformities can be approached in a similar manner. If the child is now an adolescent and is having another in a series of surgical procedures, asking them directly how they felt when they first saw their baby's defects may unintentionally retraumatize them. Reliving the moment at a time and in a setting out of their control may be injurious and nonproductive and may only reinforce a sense of helplessness. What may help more at this time is to be fully present with them, to convey positive feelings to and about their child, and to offer pragmatic assistance.

Professionals (and friends) who only wish to offer comfort and consolation and who make remarks that are not within the client's system can also cause inadvertent stress. In many cases, for example, saying something like "God sees you as a special person, and he gave you this child because he knows you can love and take care of him" can be confusing and alienating to someone with chronic sorrow. If outside the client's system, such a statement may be offensive and disconnecting. If the client's beliefs are compatible with such a statement, it will be gratuitous. Professionals and friends who are entirely well intentioned and compassionate may give the client poetry or vignettes essentially conveying the same message, that she is somehow "God's angel" or "special" or "chosen." Many people experiencing chronic sorrow will perceive such poems as shallow, saccharine, and unrealistic. They may also suspect that these poems or stories are intended to sugar-coat the client's situation so that the giver feels better. The message that a person with chronic sorrow is "special," "chosen," "God's angel," or saintly conveys a perception of the person as different from others and can further increase aloneness and alienation. The message itself is often unacceptable. Who wants to be chosen or special in these circumstances? Why not be normal like practically everyone else?

Preventive measures may be indicated for some professionals as well as for clients. As Exline, Dorrity, and Wortman (1996) have indicated, working with clients who are bereaved can be extremely stressful for mental health practitioners. Anguish, rage, and ceaseless crying may lead the therapist to "push the client to work through the material too fast" (p. 18). The practitioner's confrontation with his limitations in alleviating the client's situation, as well as the practitioner's own grief issues, may create difficulties in focusing on the client's needs. If the loss is traumatic, and the client's content is filled with vivid and graphic images, the professional may be at risk of "vicarious traumatization" (Pearlman & Saakvitne, 1995). It would be wise for the professional who finds himself disturbed by traumatic content to obtain close supervision with these cases. This may safeguard his own mental health.

The need for professional expertise will emerge throughout the course of living with chronic sorrow. Often the need will relate directly to the loss, but the usual problems of living (affairs, abandonment, divorce, suicidal obsessions, housing, legal complications, grief and loss, financial stress, crises of faith, and so on) occur in lives of chronic sorrow just as they do for "the normals." Working with people who are contending with chronic sorrow can be extremely stressful and challenging, and it can also be extraordinarily rewarding. For therapists, the work demands hard thinking, authenticity, wisdom, and courageous actions. The work and world of therapy are unlike the work and world of most other professions. Therapy—its study and its interactive process—is an ethical commitment, and it is an engagement in the construction of the world and the self. To engage in this work with those who contend with a living loss is also a privilege.

9 CHAPTER

Implications and Directions for Research

As a field of inquiry, chronic sorrow has much to offer. Not the least of the research questions is why so many clinicians and researchers have avoided knowledge building, theorizing, and exploration of this life-span phenomenon. Do the nature and morphology of chronic sorrow "disinvite" clinical interest and concern? Why have we tended to avoid the murky waters of unrelenting loss? Do we dread having to deal with the jetsam and flotsam that might wash up if we are open to seeing it? Why are there so many studies of other types of grief and mourning while there are so few of chronic sorrow? Western contemporary culture thrives on obtaining the competitive edge and on attainment of status and power, self-sufficiency, wholeness, attractiveness, bravado, and winning. Do we imagine that our cultural identity will be compromised, or will we ourselves become "less," if we open ourselves to knowing about human ruination and unrelenting grief? Is chronic sorrow part of our shadow identities as human beings, compeling our resistance, denial, and rejection? It was once said, "If we didn't have these mental hospitals, we wouldn't have so many mental patients." This twisted correlation has materialized. With the closing of psychiatric hospitals throughout the land, there *are* fewer mental patients; they are now among the homeless. (According to some estimates, one-third of homeless people suffer from mental disorders or mental deficiencies [Simon, 1993].) Do we, as clinicians and researchers, use this type of thinking to deter ourselves from knowing the extent and severity of chronic sorrow among us? If we don't know about it, will it shrink?

Our current knowledge base is so thin that the field is wide open to creative research across a multitude of variables. However, the type of research that will contribute most to expanded and credible professional understanding will not come from "the lab" or from analogs; it will come, instead, from real people in real circumstances. The early studies that followed Olshansky's (1962, 1966, 1970) introduction of the concept of chronic sorrow have provided support for his perceptions and interpretations of parental reactions to having a child with significant impairments. These studies validated the existence of chronic sorrow, supported gender differences in grieving, and suggested patterns of resurgence of grief intensity at certain stress points. Many professionals who were interested in chronic sorrow at that time were either directly involved in mental retardation services or were themselves parents of children with mental retardation. For more than a decade thereafter, very little on the subject appeared in the professional literature.

During the 1990s, interest reemerged, as was demonstrated by a small but growing number of dissertations and articles, predominantly from the field of nursing. Many of these studies sought to find chronic sorrow in populations other than parents of children with mental retardation. Burke's (1989) dissertation on mothers of school-age children with myelomeningocele involved a questionnaire that has subsequently been modified for use with self-loss as well as other-loss, and which has been used in studies of other chronic diseases and disabling conditions. Equally important, professional awareness of the need for longitudinal studies has been heightened. The advent of the Nursing Consortium for Research on Chronic Sorrow (NCRCS) has sparked continuing serious inquiry and theory building. This consortium may, hopefully, facilitate the development of studies of the life process of chronic sorrow. Enlarging the understanding of ongoing, ambiguous, and apprehensive grief responses can contribute to countless lives. Even when the studies do not provide definitive results, they can reassure those who cope with chronic sorrow by showing that health care professionals recognize and honor their unresolvable sadness, and that they are attempting to better understand it. In short, the field is ready for illuminating research, both prospective and retrospective, at all points of the life span on this phenomenon that is never so clear-cut or final as death.

☐ Reinterpretation of Existing Studies

As clinicians become more enlightened, the findings of studies that were not designed to address chronic sorrow may be subject to reinterpretation. For example, some studies have found that parents and siblings of children with autism display significantly more social and personality abnormalities, including communicative deficits, than do controls (Kanner & Lesser, 1958; Wolff, Narayan, & Moyes, 1988; Bartak, Rutter, & Cox, 1975). For instance, Kanner and Lesser (1958) observed that, in general, parents of children with autism disdained small talk and that their communicative style was pedantic. There is evidence as well that some parents have difficulty providing a clear account of their personal history and their children's symptoms. Speculations have included stress and genetic liability as factors in these social and language impairments. A careful review of studies such as these could lead to additional or alternative interpretations, that is, that chronic sorrow may be implicated.

An article by James Kocsis, "Is Lifelong Depression a Personality or Mood Disorder?" which appeared in the *Harvard Mental Health Letter* (Kocsis, 1991), also provides grist for potential alternative theorizing and interpretations. Kocsis refers to distinctions between "affective" dysthymia and "characterologic" dysthymia, stating that "it is often hard to say whether the personality disorder or the depression came first" (p. 8). Symptoms that may be interpreted as personality traits include (a) low energy, (b) low self-esteem and sociability, and (c) lack of interest or participation in so-called pleasurable activities. The old question is brought to mind: "Were the parents like this before they had this child, or did the child cause the parents to be like this?" More important, however, is the possibility that persons who are being proposed as having dysthymic personality disorder may include a fair number of people who have been coping with chronic sorrow for much of their lives.

Millen and Roll (1985) studied "pathological bereavement" in 22 mothers who gave up a child for adoption and who, as long as 20 or more years later, were still attempting to work through and resolve their grief. These mothers reported repeated dreams of reunion with their children, and described somatic complaints such as sleeping difficulties, headaches, muscle tension, eating and digestive disturbances, and restless anxiety. They had developed a mental image of their child, demonstrated scanning and searching behaviors, and had fantasies of accidentally meeting the child. Guilt and self-reproach had intensified with time, and they harbored bitterness toward those who had encouraged and supported their relinquishment of their babies. Millen and Roll described factors that delay or suppress grief, that is, those that contribute to grief that is pathological. "Among those factors that we have found to be most relevant to our clinical sample are the following: 1) the loss may be socially stigmatized; 2) external events prevent the expression of feelings of loss; 3) there may be uncertainty as to whether or not there is an actual loss; 4) there may be an absence of mourning at the normal and expected time; and 5) mourning rituals are lacking" (p. 417). These factors were based on the work of Bowlby (1963), Greenblatt (1978), Lindemann (1944), and Volkan (1970). Permanent loss could not be verified, since it was assumed that the relinquished children continued to live and that it was not unrealistic that the mothers might some day have contact with them. Viewed from the perspective of chronic sorrow and its aspects of disenfranchised grief, the continuing and pervasive grief responses of these 22 women would have different shadings of meaning, especially in the direction of a nonpathological definition of their continuing grief. The literature surely contains many more studies that are subject to reconsideration and follow-up. A thorough review of research in areas with potential relevance to chronic sorrow could lead to new and important theory and enlightening information.

☐ Independent Variables

Examples of some of the independent variables that are suited to research, have high priority, and would contribute significantly to the knowledge base are suggested below.

Person Variables

In addition to the customary demographics used for matching, cultural and ethnic dimensions might be emphasized. Do cross-cultural data support hypotheses that severity of loss is largely culturally defined? For example, are there some cultures in which having a child with schizophrenia would not be perceived as a loss? If so, how do these cultures differ from those in which such a child is a source of acute and chronic grief?

The effects of age at the time of the loss may be important. Research questions might include (*a*) How does age link with self-esteem prior to, at the time of the loss, and at various later time periods? (*b*) How does age at the time of the loss influence later adjustment and coping, identity development, self-image, social support or friendship networks, and so on? and (*c*) Does this variable contribute (and if so, how) to the development of strengths and resilience? A further question, possibly related to age at the time of the loss, would be: Why do some losses trigger chronic sorrow in some persons and not in others? It might be hypothesized that some people with other-loss who yearn to cling to a nurturing, caregiving role (and who may fear relinquishing that role) may react to severe disability in their child or spouse with minimal chronic sorrow. Perhaps these are the people who seek to adopt children with disabilities and who care for these children devotedly and with predominantly positive feelings. What are the salient characteristics of these people? At what age were they influenced toward choosing lifetimes of caregiving and sacrifice? What were influential factors?

What are the effects of earlier losses? Persons who have already experienced a series of significant losses would be expected to respond differently to self-loss or other-loss. What have they found or developed in themselves to make life a worthwhile endeavor? How do their grieving styles differ from others with chronic sorrow who have not experienced significant prior losses? What are their coping strategies? Is there something notable about their sense of humor? Are they significantly more depressed than others? Do their losses function as life markers? If so, how do these losses affect temporal orientation? Is suicidal ideation more frequent or more problematic in persons with significant prior losses? Is suicidal *risk* higher in self-loss than in other-loss? If so, does risk relate to prior losses?

The effects of earlier psychiatric conditions and disorders would also be an interesting area of investigation. Are these effects necessarily negative? Are earlier psychiatric disorders related to degree of support? What kinds of interventions are useful in prevention of subsequent disorders? When the self-loss is a chronic mental illness (for example, schizophrenia, severe bipolar affective disorder, highly dystonic and persistent obsessive-compulsive disorder) and there is other-loss as well, what is the nature of the interactions between losses? Does the existence of other-loss contribute positively to treatment compliance in self-loss? When there are two or more sources of chronic sorrow, how do family members manage to carry out the regular activities of daily life?

It would be valuable to test the hypothesis that chronic sorrow is more likely to increase depression (both frequency and severity) than other types of grief. This hypothesis is based on the likelihood that persons with chronic sorrow (*a*) receive less validation of their grief, (*b*) may not feel they have permission to grieve, (*c*) do not feel understood when they do express grief, (*d*) do not have cultural rituals to support their grief, and (*e*) may criticize themselves for "weakness" and experience lower self-esteem when they express grief. Longitudinal studies are needed to increase professional understanding of the linkage between chronic sorrow and clinical depression and what interventions might be useful in reducing or disengaging the linkage. Comparing persons with severe chronic sorrow with those who demonstrate minimal or mild responses of chronic sorrow and who have similar "objective" losses at equivalent times in the grieving process might identify important coping mechanisms or personality variables that mitigate the distress of chronic sorrow.

Studies of gender differences in both self- and other-loss are needed to determine whether earlier findings continue to be valid. Earlier studies have been helpful, though sometimes inconsistent. Family studies and studies of marital relationships are also needed. The hypothesis that chronic sorrow has a more debilitating impact on families than "terminal" grief (that is, grief related to finality or to the absence of someone), could be tested by periodically obtaining measures of family disturbance (marital satisfaction, conflict between parents and children, and so on) after the onset of chronic sorrow and comparing these measures with those obtained at regular intervals from families after the onset of terminal loss. Adding matched families without grief issues would strengthen the findings. Families with chronic sorrow would be expected to show more intense and longer levels of disturbance than the other two groups.

Referring to family life involving a child who is disabled, Gliedman and Roth (1980) have concluded that anywhere one looks, basic descriptive work is lacking. Further, it is inaccurate to group all disabled children together, since their disabilities are so diverse. Murphy (1982) has recommended research directed toward determining what specific factors (inability to communicate, inability to walk, unusual physical appearance, and so on) have the greatest impact on family stress and adjustment. She points out that parental stress cannot be separated from the status of the child's impairments. Longitudinal studies, employing qualitative methodology, of family and personality dynamics related to caring for a child with an atypical developmental trajectory would provide clinicians with invaluable information.

Available studies of siblings of children with chronic diseases and disabilities are especially notable for their confusing and conflicting outcomes. Bluebond-Langner (1996) describes the research literature on siblings of children with cystic fibrosis and other life-threatening and chronic diseases as replete with conflicting outcomes and explanations, and she attributes these results to differences in (a) theoretical perspectives, (b) population, (c) type of study, (d) sample size and criteria, (e) timing, (f) methodology, and (g) informants. She also indicates that much of the research was based on conceptualizing illness inappropriately in a cause-and-effect approach so that results could be quantified and specific hypotheses validated. Her selection of qualitative, process-oriented, and ethnographic methodology to study siblings and parents of chronically ill children has yielded more clinically useful results than approaches by previous researchers.

From a humane, compassionate, and ethical view, the need for studies on abuse and neglect of children and adults with disabilities is imperative. Prevention of abuse and neglect may be possible if studies can identify family and personality characteristics and environmental circumstances indicative of high risk. What is the nature of current social stigma and invidious discrimination against persons (and families) with disabilities, especially disabilities that are characterized by physical helplessness, obvious deformity, inability to communicate, and other inherent attributes that transgress cultural norms? What is the status of chronic sorrow in parents and other caregivers who are facing their fears for the safety and well-being of their loved one after their deaths or when they can no longer carry the load? What factors lead to terror and desperation of such magnitude that a caregiving spouse or parent will resort to homicide (or euthanasia) or suicide?

In some circumstances, persons with self-loss can transcend and transform chronic sorrow. When and how does this transcendence and transformation take place? One could speculate that there are circumstances in other-loss as well in which chronic sorrow can be prevented, avoided, or arrested. If emotional attachment to the person who is the source of the loss is blocked, the expectation would be that no grief responses would ensue. Detachment from the source of the loss appears to work well for some individuals. There are cases of parental or spousal abandonment where there are no signs of grief or even of remorse, shame, or guilt. In some cases, life appears to go on for the one who has detached, disowned, and abandoned, even to the extent that others in the person's subsequent life never become aware of the existence of the abandoned child or spouse. What kinds of rationalizations are made for the abandonment? Is it severely compartmentalized? And does this kind of detachment actually work? Does it work for a substantial length of time, with precipitation of grief and guilt later in life? Is there ever a desire to make amends, "pay the debt," or seek forgiveness? We need answers to these questions.

Nature of the Loss

Are the author's proposed model and proposed working definition of chronic sorrow valid? Many research questions arise from all dimensions of the model. For instance, there is a need for the development of "objective" or consensual criteria for defining losses as "chronic," ongoing, and living. Where does the larger contemporary culture place major types of losses along the continuum stretching from "chronic" to "final"? Creative research could clarify cultural criteria regarding chronicity and finality. These criteria could be used as independent variables in investigations of chronic sorrow. They would also provide clinicians with a research-based framework for assessment of the degree to which grief reactions in specific clients are culturally appropriate. Criteria derived from cultural consensus are especially useful in identifying and assessing chronic sorrow in populations and situations other than those in which chronic sorrow was originally identified (that is, in parents of children with mental retardation and other developmental disabilities). These would include the various types and degrees of self-loss as well as other-loss associated with debilitating mental illness, physical conditions that permanently and significantly impair functioning, HIV/AIDS, and so on. There are significant numbers of persons with HIV who are alive today, 10, 15, or more years after diagnosis. Identifying and studying chronic sorrow in this population could change current professional conceptualizations of grief responses and suggest new and enhanced support and treatment services. Taking into consideration family members and friends, the benefits for such a large population would be quite significant. Also included would be losses that are ongoing but not associated with disabilities, major medical conditions, or impairments, such as (a) persons who remain protractedly and endlessly uncertain about the whereabouts, continuing existence, and condition of a missing loved one who has disappeared without a trace, (b) families of MIAs, and (c) women who have given up a child for adoption who is presumably still alive but with whom there has been no contact.

The cultural criteria described above could be used to test interesting hypotheses. An example would be the hypothesis that as responses of chronic sorrow become increasingly discrepant from the "objective" (or culturally determined) assessment of chronic sorrow, psychopathology increases. In addition, is chronic sorrow the inevitable or desirable response to ongoing loss? If not, what other responses occur, and do they work better or not as well? In cases where the ongoing loss ends (for example, when the loved one eventually dies), does chronic sorrow transition into "traditional" grief, or are other patterns more common or more adaptive? How does the course of chronic sorrow compare with "traditional" grief over time? To what degree is chronic sorrow more persistent and more intense? Are there significant differences between symptoms, course, and outcome of chronic sorrow in self-loss and in other-loss? One hypothesis might be that greater guilt exists in certain cases of self-loss because of prevalent beliefs about being self-sufficient and not being a burden, as well as related taboos about having strong feelings of sorrow about oneself (characterized as "pity parties," being a "gloom dumper," a "sad sack," and so on). Cross-cultural studies could be both interesting and potentially beneficial. For instance, does chronic sorrow exist in some cultures and not in others? What are the differences in beliefs and coping styles between cultures? What can Western contemporary culture learn from other cultures?

Additionally, does chronic sorrow lead to a more negative or shortened future temporal orientation than other types of grief? Is there a typical difference in the valence (that is, the positive-negative continuum) of the projected future? Since it is still often presumed that "general" types of grief have a time-bound trajectory and chronic sorrow does not, it might be hypothesized that chronic sorrow will usually result in more negative future projections and probably will carry a more negative future projection when the projected time increases (that is, five or ten years out, chronic sorrow will lead to more negative anticipated futures than other types of grief). Variables for research would also include dimensions such as (a) relatively stable vs. progressively worsening conditions, (b) life-threatening vs. non-life-threatening conditions, and (c) the age-appropriate-inappropriate dimension. The use of Shea's (1986) four factors, or derivatives thereof, related to specific acute and chronic diseases, may be helpful as a suitable beginning structure for inquiry. These factors include (a) the nature of the disease process, (b) locus of decision making, (c) impact on lifestyle, and (d) the organization of treatment. The degree of support, as a variable for research, has countless possibilities. The dimension of intimacy could generate a great many research findings of importance.

The role and function of the fantasy of what should or could have been and might be deserves meticulous attention, since it relates to disappointment, hope, severity of distress, depression, resurgence of intensity of chronic sorrow, and so on. It is central to the discrepancy that is the core of chronic sorrow. It affects lifestyle, management of care, types of services, and timing and choice of interventions. The complexity of the role and function of the fantasy is a challenge to research design and a compelling reason for trying to understand it.

Research leading to prevention or to amelioration, at any level, of the conditions that are the source of chronic sorrow is crucial and primary. Increased and concerted professional support, advocacy, and implementation of this type of research can be generative not only of direct results but of more realistic hope for positive change in the lives of those with chronic sorrow. The concept holds true that anything that helps the person who is the source of chronic sorrow helps those who love and care for that person. For example, developing research-based interventions that improve communication in persons with autism positively impacts the caregivers.

Treatment Effectiveness

Much can be learned directly from client interviews about treatment approaches that have been helpful (or harmful). However, clients do not always recognize specific approaches and often later cannot recall the result of specific therapist interventions. Furthermore, it is extremely difficult, in general, to sort out what works and what may be irrelevant in therapy. Studies to date have often yielded confusing results and interpretations. Analysis of variance techniques, which purportedly sort out which effects are related to which interventions, are probably most suited to the evaluation of treatment effects. Interaction of effects, for example, would emerge from research that is designed along the lines of *treatments × types of loss (self- or other-) × person variables.* Evaluation of the effects of treatment would be based on rationales for selection of interventions and would most often include psychotherapy modalities, supports, and psychotropic medications. As with any type of evaluation of treatment effects, many studies and many replications of studies will be needed to reveal with confidence which interventions are helpful and how and when and with whom.

Other research might address such questions as: Is optimism helpful in reducing the intensity, pervasiveness, or complications of chronic sorrow, as is the case with depression? Or does optimism worsen the distress of chronic sorrow by fostering the discrepancy between the hoped-for fantasy and perceived reality? Christopher Peterson's (2000) article on "The Future of Optimism," in the *American Psychologist*, indicates that optimism as an individual difference can be a highly beneficial psychological characteristic since it is linked to good mood, perseverance, achievement, and physical health. He makes a distinction between two types of optimism: little and big.

> Little optimism subsumes specific expectations about positive outcomes: for example, "I will find a convenient parking space this evening." Big optimism refers to—obviously—larger and less specific expectations: for example, "Our nation is on the verge of something great." . . . optimism can be described at different levels of abstraction and, further, . . . optimism may function differently depending on the level. Big optimism may be a biologically given tendency filled in by culture with a socially acceptable content; it leads to desirable outcomes because it produces a general state of vigor and resilience. In contrast, little optimism may be the product of an idiosyncratic learning history; it leads to desirable outcomes because it predisposes specific actions that are adaptive in concrete situations. (p. 49)

Perhaps some persons with chronic sorrow maintain big optimism, adaptive for the long view and the "big picture," through very selective little optimism. Learning to select those things about which optimism is reasonable and remaining neutral or pessimistic about others may work to promote realistic problem solving and to sustain positive feelings about life in general. The function of pessimism as a protection against further harsh disappointments invites study as well. What are the advantages and disadvantages of giving up all faith in plans and expectations? Is faith of this nature at least partially restored when trauma resolution has occurred? Peterson asks important questions related to hope and helplessness and to optimism as a social value. For example, he asks: Are optimism and pessimism mutually exclusive? What is the relationship between optimism and reality, and what are the costs of optimistic beliefs that prove to be wrong? These questions are directly relevant to chronic sorrow and treatment goals. As Peterson concludes, optimism promises to be an important interest to positive social science, but it needs to be approached in an evenhanded way.

Another question important to treatment effectiveness is: Do coping mechanisms (defenses) found useful in increasing subjective well-being also reduce distressful responses of chronic sorrow? For example, Vaillant (2000) has reported that the following "adaptive mental mechanisms" relate to subjective well-being: anticipation, suppression, altruism, humor, and sublimation.

> First, how should psychology quantify positive mental health? At present, psychology has no metric except perhaps scores of greater than 85 on the DSM-IV's Axis V (Global Assessment of Functioning). If more reliable methods for assessing the relative maturity of defenses can be developed, psychology may gain a means of quantifying the theoretical formula for positive mental health that Marie Jahoda (1959) offered to psychology forty years ago. She suggested the same synthesis between affective life and practical reality that is reflected in the conceptualization of adaptive-level defenses. Jahoda suggested that mentally healthy individuals should be oriented toward the future and efficient in problem solving. They should be resistant to stress and perceive reality without distortion. They should possess empathy and be able to love and to play as well as to work. They should remain in touch with their own feelings. In short, they should manifest anticipation, suppression, altruism, humor, and sublimation. (p. 98)

Vaillant indicates the need to understand how best to facilitate the transmutation of less adaptive defenses into more adaptive ones. He suggests increased social supports and interpersonal safety as priorities, followed by fostering intactness of the central nervous system (for example, rest, nutrition, and sobriety), and he points toward integrative psychotherapies that are catalysts for change.

Of immediate importance is the impact of managed care systems on services for people with chronic sorrow, both those with self-loss and their caregivers. What are the effects of constructing rationales for services that meet the criteria for "medical necessity?" Has managed care led to increased problems of isolation and disenfranchisement? Does managed care reinforce a poor self-image and a characterization of grief responses as pathological? If so, what is the impact of these effects?

Cost-benefit types of research could conceivably lead to changes in managed care systems. These changes could favorably influence integration of services and reduce anxiety and other stressful responses currently associated with negotiating with an impersonal (and sometimes antagonistic) system for delivering desperately needed services. It would be sad to discover that persons with chronic sorrow are using notable battles for services as life markers.

Other Independent Variables

The accessibility of treatment and support services, their structure, how they are perceived and accepted by consumers as well as the general public, how and where these services are provided, and so on, are important areas for evaluation, potentially leading to empirically based recommendations and improvements. Such studies could affect community and legislative actions with regard to publicly funded programs and agencies. Many social organizations prioritize education of the public about the organizations' constituencies. How well do these educational projects work? Do they lead to less disenfranchisement? Do they increase the likelihood of employment for persons with disabilities? What impact do specific types of services have on chronic sorrow? How do respite services improve coping and reduce stress levels? Do respite services for caregivers also benefit the person with self-loss? Are benefits greater with certain types of respite, for example, in home as against outside of the home?

Support groups are increasingly emerging as primary interventions in the lives of those with chronic sorrow. Correlational studies of beneficial outcomes (or harm) with various formats and group constellations could greatly influence the conduct and direction of group support. Do benefits outweigh the cost and effort of engaging in other types of social support? Are church affiliations and attendance conducive to the alleviation of isolation and alienation? Are some religious orientations and practices more beneficial than others? What types of spiritual beliefs foster resilience and transcendency? What role do various cultural environments play in the lived experience of chronic sorrow? What are some of the culturally related attitudes (toward specific types of loss) that are associated with inclusion and support? Does caregiver employment outside the home lead to better accommodation of the loss? When do the stress and demands of employment outweigh the benefits? What are the benefits of so-called leisure-time activities—hobbies, continuing education, volunteer work, music, and art?

☐ Dependent Variables

The identification of appropriate current research instruments and the design of new ones present challenges that are piqued by the need for life span, or longitudinal, studies. A review of research literature in areas pertinent to chronic sorrow reveals numerous questionnaires, scales, and inventories. For example, Glidden and Floyd (1997) examined the psychometric properties of a five-item subcomponent (DEP5) of Factor 1, Parent and Family Problems, of the Freidrich Questionnaire on Resources and Stress. Data from more than 450 respondents were submitted to internal analysis that established that the DEP5 had adequate internal reliability and stability over two years. Confirmatory factor analyses indicated that the DEP5 measured depressive reactions as distinct from other parent and family problems. Therefore, researchers could reanalyze the Questionnaire on Resources and Stress data specifically for depressive reactions. The technique for disaggregating instruments used to obtain global ratings can be useful for application to other variables as well.

Qualitative approaches that are process-oriented and thematic and include content analysis of structured interviews are recommended for revealing nuances and change over time. Burke's (1989) Chronic Sorrow Questionnaire, developed for use in face-to-face (or telephone) interviews with mothers of school-age children with myelomeningocele disabilities, was based on a review of the literature on chronic sorrow. This basically qualitative instrument, now the Burke/NCRCS Chronic Sorrow Questionnaire, has been modified for use in self-loss as well as other-loss and has undergone fine-tuning for use with a wider variety of disabilities and medical conditions across the life span. It could also serve as a guide for the development of a more quantitative instrument. It would be very useful to modify this instrument, or develop a new one, to assess differences between chronic sorrow and other continuing grief responses, perhaps with similar characteristics, related to death and finality. Such an instrument could validate chronic sorrow in populations other than those associated with disabilities or chronic medical conditions.

Personality tests designed to describe how the personality functions (for example, the 16-PF, the Myers-Briggs) rather than to tease out diagnostic categories and other pathological features would be useful to determine strengths as well as problem areas. Projectives such as the Mother-Child Picture Test (MCPT) and specially designed sentence-completion tests may be useful as well. Currently available instruments and assessment tools also include: *DSM-IV* Axes I and II categories and codes; the GAF (Global Assessment of Functioning) Scale; the SPS (Severity of Psychosocial

Stressors) Scale; a variety of suicidal ideation and suicidal risk scales; psychological tests of many types; rating scales (for stress, marital satisfaction, depression, anxiety, cognitive distortion, self-esteem, impact of event, and so on); certain inventories (including the Roos Time Reference Inventory [Roos & Albers, 1965; Westergren, 1990]); and scales and inventories specific to grief and loss. Informal Likert ratings can be relatively nonintrusive for assessing degree of stress, pain, multiple areas of life satisfaction, severity of trauma symptoms, existential conflicts, and so on.

Symptom checklists (including a range of mental and physical symptoms) might also be devised for quick measures that can supplement other dependent variables. Tools that reveal common or relevant themes in chronic sorrow could provide further insight into the condition. For example, journaling techniques might be used—across the life span—employing structured stimulus stems, such as: "It was a time when . . . ," "What has really mattered to me . . . ," "The worst of it . . . ," "The best time . . . ," "The future . . . ," and so on. Cluster writing and other flow-of-consciousness types of writing may be a revealing source of thematic information.

This chapter has presented a sampling of research ideas that might enlarge and enrich the knowledge base of chronic sorrow. Research that includes openness to findings of such positives as strength, satisfaction, pleasure, humor, philosophical maturity, realistic perspective, and so on, will contribute to balance. Research may reveal that persons coping with ongoing loss may benefit and grow in more ways than we have realized, even in the midst of crisis and resurgence of emotional pain. Assessments of what has worked, of successful and creative problem solving, of philosophical beliefs and approaches, and of satisfactions in small but hard-won gains and accomplishments, will be informative to clinicians and clients alike. Certain paradoxes unique to chronic sorrow may appear. The nature of sanity during times of "weakening" or increased stress may evoke different responses in those with chronic sorrow. The quality of humor may be different as well, and that quality, taken in context, may be sustaining and healthy. Great latitude and opportunities exist for creative and innovative exploration and theorizing. Research prospects are exciting.

10
CHAPTER

Trends

The helping professions are intimately connected with the values and structure of the social context in which they exist. Professions are, in fact, socially determined and sanctioned with regard to their fields of interest, objectives, boundaries, and modalities. Societal trends in conjunction with professional trends shape the focus and nature of the various helping professions. For example, the trend toward deinstitutionalization of large populations of persons with mental illness and the massive downsizing and closing of state institutions as well as private, freestanding psychiatric hospitals has led to an increase of professional activity that is decentralized and community based. Night shelters and clinics have increased as a result of so many visible homeless people. Likewise, the increase in divorce and remarriage and in the numbers of working women has led to a proliferation of child care facilities, services, and agencies. It has become necessary, as a result of the global economy and widespread use of computer technology, for graduate schools to include computer competency as a basic requirement for degrees. Degree programs involving distance learning are coming into their own as well. To remain viable, a profession needs to be responsive to current needs, and sensitive to change, to anticipate it and quickly identify and replace outmoded practices and theories.

Macarov (1978) identified four major determinants of technological change: (a) scientific feasibility, (b) technical feasibility, (c) economic practicality, and (d) social acceptability. Even when scientific, technical, and economic determinants are favorable, many things that can be done will not occur in a consistent manner unless and until they are socially acceptable. According to Macarov (1978), social acceptance is influenced by (*a*) technological forces (for example, technical diffusion is changing education, medical practice, professional/community outreach programs, forms and quality of social interaction and support), (*b*) economic changes (for example, multiple changes have impacted cost-effectiveness of health care services. A primary change is managed care, a force that has curtailed many services and added many hours per month that are not direct client services to the professional workload. Many professionals who were in private practice have elected to work for agencies or have left the field entirely), (c) ideas and people (for example, Harrington's [1963] *The Other America* which was a force in the War on Poverty of the Johnson administration. Martin Luther King, Jr., Margaret Sanger, Rachel Carson, and Benjamin Spock all impelled changes in awareness and social action), and (*d*) physical changes (for example, epidemics, natural disasters, toxic waste, and deforestation lead to widespread social effects and responses. One of the most pronounced of contemporary social change agents is AIDS).

The past two decades have witnessed significant increases in scholarly and compassionate interdisciplinary studies of death and dying, loss and traumatic loss, and grief and bereavement. During the past decade, there were emerging signs of growing professional interest in chronic sorrow. Including chronic sorrow within the interdisciplinary field of grief and loss has obvious future benefits. However, trends and innovations often come and go in our culture. Predictions of durability are often biased in the direction of what seems desirable in the future rather than based on neutral or dispassionate evaluation of social influences. Predictions can be conducted in a number of ways, such as (*a*) construction of scenarios, (*b*) computer simulations, (*c*) expert consensus—for example, the Delphi method, (*d*) polls, and (*e*) prediction through extrapolation of existing trends. Relying on the extrapolation method in this chapter, the author will identify some current trends that may impact future professional understanding and interventions related to chronic sorrow.

☐ Professional Education

Until recently, chronic sorrow has received mention almost exclusively in academic curricula in mental retardation and developmental disabilities. There is today some slight evidence that chronic sorrow may have a foot in the door as part of formal professional training and continuing education in the area of grief. The best evidence comes from the nursing profession. Beginning in the early 1990s studies began to emerge in the clinical nursing literature. The establishment in the United States of the

Nursing Consortium for Research on Chronic Sorrow (NCRCS) implies inclusion of chronic sorrow as part of some nursing curricula. Work from members of the NCRCS is cited in a growing number of articles, with sources both in the United States and abroad (for example, Wales, regarding chronic sorrow in parents of children newly diagnosed with diabetes [Lowes & Lyne, 2000]). Krafft and Krafft (1998), both professionals with positions in academia (one in nursing), presented chronic sorrow as part of the educational program of the annual meeting of the Association for Death Education and Counseling (ADEC) in 1999. Chronic sorrow as a specific type of grieving was a new concept for almost everyone attending the presentation, lending credence to the belief that there is a rather large gap in the training curricula of persons who work directly with grief and loss.

It is unrealistic to expect academia or the professional training schools and institutes turning out health care and other human services providers to assimilate social trends and practice needs at the same pace. It is also unrealistic to expect training to be based on anticipated future needs at the expense of training to meet current needs. Even with the most comprehensive knowledge base, professionals require constant retraining. Whether good, bad, or otherwise, education lags behind practice, sometimes at a considerable distance. It is the actual practice in the field that leads to educational change. Educators are faced with a formidable task, that of preparing students to deal with, act responsibly within, and positively influence future changes.

There are a variety of ways, however, in which chronic sorrow can be introduced to and understood by educators. Patricia Leigh Brown's article in the *New York Times* (August 20, 2000), under the teaser, "A New Culture Moves on Campus," and titled "Viewing Ahab and Barbie Through the Lens of Disability," refers to "the next unsung frontier." The article states:

> Disability has spread from the more familiar precincts of the law, medicine and public policy into the humanities—from Richard III to labor history to discussions on whether the tippy-toed Barbie doll is technically disabled. In Berkeley, which is the birthplace of activism among disabled people, an oral history archive of the Independent Living Movement is scheduled to open this fall at the university. Professor Schweik is developing an undergraduate liberal arts degree in disability studies (the University of Illinois at Chicago and Syracuse University offer doctorates). At San Francisco State University, a diverse group including philosophers, literature professors, theater scholars, historians and others, fewer than half with disabilities themselves, recently completed a summer institute financed by the National Endowment for the Humanities aimed at creating disability studies in the humanities. And this fall the first international conference on disability studies will be held in Washington.

"The liberal arts are supposed to pose fundamental questions like, what makes a person human, and what is justice?" said Catherine J. Kudlick, a historian at the University of California at Davis, who studies the blind historical experience and who is legally blind. "Disability studies provide new ways of approaching these questions." (p. WK3)

The article describes disabilities studies, as a part of humanities, as "potentially vast," suggesting that a literature course might examine Melville's Captain Ahab or Faulkner's Benjy in *The Sound and the Fury*. Paul Longmore, a historian at San Francisco State University who is quoted in the article, refers to a breakdown of the "tragic but brave" model of disability. Douglas Baynton, a University of Iowa historian, points out that disability has been an especially rich vein and is everywhere in history, yet conspicuously absent in written histories. The article states: "New scholarship is rapidly changing that, unearthing attitudes behind laws like 19th-century Chicago's 'unsightly beggar ordinances,' which barred from public view any person 'who is diseased, maimed, mutilated or in any way deformed so as to be an unsightly or disgusting object'" (p. WK3). Brown concludes the article: "Though it seems specialized, disability studies —the corporal dimension of the human experience and its consequences— could wind up being one of the most inclusive academic fields of all. As Professor Longmore points out, 'It's a social group that all people will join if they live long enough'" (p. WK3).

☐ Shift toward Depathologizing of Grief

In the general area of grief and loss, there are indications of a dynamic shift away from stage and time-bound models of grief and mourning. So long as these models have been standards by which to measure a person's "progression" in the grief process, they have defined and implied prescriptions for the "normal" course of grief. Deviations from these standards have suggested pathology. A further implication is that something must be done to help move the process along toward "resolution." Fortunately, in recent decades, a burgeoning, multidisciplinary interest in grief and loss has produced a widening base of empirical research and scholarly theory, as well as systems of care such as hospice, support groups (for family members and persons with cancer, cystic fibrosis, AIDS, and so on), and alternative interventions. Interests and advocacy in euthanasia and assisted suicide have also grown. The larger knowledge base and caregiving experience have emphasized the highly individualistic nature of grief. What is normal and what is not normal is no longer so clear-cut. The suggested time frame for adaptation and for accommodation of significant loss is more ambiguous and continues to lengthen.

Reflective of conceptual shifts in the field, the language of grief is also undergoing change. For example, grief "resolution" and "recovery" appear less often in the literature, and they have become more ambiguous terms. More dynamic terms such as "healing," "adaptive mourning," "transcending," "transforming," and "meaning making" are increasingly coming into use. The concept of continuing bonds (or continuing attachment) is also taking hold (Klass, Silverman, & Nickman, 1996; Field, Nichols, Holen, & Horowitz, 1999), fostering grief work that includes reconfiguring or restructuring the relationship with the deceased in a way that accommodates the realization of the person's permanent physical absence while also supporting the survivor's need to get on with life. In the context of continuing bonds, "getting on with life" does not mean returning to some inner balance that existed prior to the loss; instead, it means achieving a new inner balance.

Maintaining an interactive relationship with the deceased in the realm of fantasy and memories is being viewed as appropriate and helpful for some persons. Adaptations to grief that are increasingly viewed as normal also include the use of transition objects and symbols to maintain connections with the person who is grieved. In at least one study, however, use of the deceased's possessions to gain comfort correlated with significantly greater distress and more grief-specific symptoms over time, while continuing attachment through memories was related to less distress. This study suggests that whether or not continuing attachment is adaptive depends on its form (Field, Nichols, Holen, & Horowitz, 1999). Therefore, the trend toward viewing transition objects and symbols as normal for maintaining continuing bonds could be reversed in the future. Continuation of bonds has great overlap with issues germane to chronic sorrow. Moreover, some grief theorists are now contending that mourning is never completed. Obviously, this contention is at the opposite end of the continuum from time-bound mourning, as is an unending loss that is the source of chronic sorrow.

As discussed in chapter 2, there is a need for a consistently defined, interdisciplinary grief vocabulary. The language that is applied to issues of grief greatly influences how it is handled and what directions are taken. Language that is descriptive of process rather than reductionistic, labeling, or suggestive of abnormality is recommended, and is consistent with the trend toward viewing a wider range of responses as normal. Furthermore, the trend toward extending conceptualizations of loss beyond that of a person, to include loss of a physical or mental faculty, a life stage, roles, dreams and aspirations, cherished assumptions about life, and so on, relates directly to both primary and secondary losses associated with chronic sorrow. Chronic sorrow clearly has a place within the current trend of enlarging the scope of what is viewed as normal grieving. Further expansion of the concept of chronic sorrow (for example, to conditions such as AIDS and situations where a loved one has vanished, where it cannot be determined whether the person still lives or has died, where reminders are constant, and where passage of time does not permit a determination of the loss as permanent) is also consistent with the trend.

Articulating the trend toward a perception of more grief responses as normal with the development of a system of health care services under the thumb of managed care companies is complicated at best. In order to receive services within the managed care system, pathology (or "medical necessity") is required. The client is frequently the recipient of conflicting messages. On the one hand, a client must meet the diagnostic criteria of pathology in order to qualify for services. On the other hand, he or she may be responding normally, though intensely, to a profound loss. Additionally, persons with disenfranchised grief—including chronic sorrow—who are receiving minimal to no social support may find themselves doubly disenfranchised when professional services are denied. The result may be the development of a related trend; that is, persons who are grieving may turn increasingly to nonprofessionals and to helping professionals who are not mental health service providers. Therefore, the need may never have been greater for a high level of training and retraining in grief counseling and theory of persons in non–mental health disciplines.

☐ Psychotherapy

In the early 1990s, Norcross, Alford, and DeMichele (1992) conducted a futuristic study on psychotherapy. Using the Delphi method for forecasting, they assembled a panel of 75 psychotherapists and researchers. All 75 had doctorates (70 Ph.D.s, four M.D.s, and one with both). Predictions were made through the first decade of 2000. These predictions are consistent with the trend suggested above. For example, providers in the form of self-help groups, social workers, and psychiatric nurses were expected to render an increasing proportion of mental health services. Strong positive expectations were expressed for short-term therapy, with moderate increases predicted in psychoeducational groups, crisis intervention, and marital therapy. Systemic, eclectic, cognitive, and integrative orientations were expected to increase moderately, with psychobiological, behavioral, and feminist perspectives increasing slightly. Marked reduction in psychoanalytic and other long-term therapies was expected. The trend was seen as encouraging for active, present-centered systems. In regard to trends in the nursing profession, Daniel

Pesut (2000), writing in *The Futurist*, describes the trend of more nurses earning research degrees and states that nurses who specialize in genetic counseling and nursing research will care for persons through the management of genetic information, applying scientific discoveries to patient-care problems in innovative, creative, and cost-effective ways.

The Delphi panel's forecasts appear to be accurate in the first year of 2000, especially about support groups. Davison, Pennebaker, and Dickerson (2000) have reported that more Americans are trying to cope with health problems through support groups than through all other forms of professionally designed health programs combined. Participation in support groups was measured for 20 disease categories in four metropolitan areas (New York, Chicago, Los Angeles, and Dallas), as well as on nationwide online discussion groups. For self-help groups in both face-to-face and Internet formats, support seeking was greatest for diseases considered the most stigmatizing (alcoholism, AIDS, and breast and prostate cancer). Participation in self-help groups has increased by 20% to 50% over the past decade, and it is anticipated that about 25 million people will participate in these groups at some time in their lives. Because of practical barriers, people with rare and debilitating diseases are more likely to use online groups. Concerns were expressed about Internet use as a "substitute" for "actual" emotional support. It can be said that grief counseling has become an Internet industry, with thousands of websites, hundreds of advice-filled books, and "grief facilitators." Some of these grief facilitators offer "therapeutic touching," and a few propose to facilitate a reunion with the departed.

Time saving properties of computers have inevitably found favor, and it is reasonable to assume that computer technology will continue to expand in service delivery systems. Many people are more comfortable asking computers for certain information than they are seeking help from professionals. In 1979 an interesting study by Schoech and Arangio found that computers can predict suicide attempts more accurately than experienced clinicians. Computers may shape the future of caregiving services in undesirable ways as well. For example, as Etzioni (1964) indicated, the emphasis on counting leads researchers to do countable things. In other words, computer technology may lead professionals to do more and more of what can be recorded in the computer so that practice may become less holistic (and more piecemeal). In addition, the fact that clients are increasingly able to retrieve their records from Internet services may influence what is in (and out of) the record.

Norcross, Alford, and DiMichele's (1992) Delphi panel also predicted increased emphasis on accreditation, specialization, certification, and peer review. These predictions were based on hallmarks of a mature discipline as well as the tightening health reimbursement system. It was also expected that relatively inexpensive psychopharmacology would accelerate at the expense of psychotherapy. It was noted that Cummings (1987) had predicted that over half of mental health practitioners in independent practice at the end of the 1980s would not survive. Cummings (1991) has further indicated that the industrialization of health care is manifesting two cardinal characteristics of any industrial revolution: (*a*) the producer (in this case, the mental health practitioner) is losing control over the product as control shifts to business interests, and (*b*) practitioners' incomes are decreasing since industrialization requires cheap labor.

☐ Increasing Prevalence of Chronic Sorrow

Great advances are being made both in theoretical and applied genetics, and ethical concerns about these advances are rapidly increasing. As bioethicists and philosophers, Buchanan, Brock, Daniels, and Wikler (2000) have reexamined traditional social practices and ethical theory for a world that is being remade as a result of the Human Genome Project. One of several future scenarios requiring ethical reflection is the demand by parents for perfect babies or babies with certain desirable features. It is predicted that by 2020 parents will more frequently regard unborn babies that are found to have a risk of certain cancers or Alzheimer's as "undesirable." These parents will often choose to abort their otherwise healthy fetuses. By 2030, fetuses that are projected to fall short of the highest levels of intelligence will simply be considered not good enough. In another scenario developed by Buchanan, Brock, Daniels, and Wikler (2000), job seekers will gain a genetic edge through credentials proving that they have received genetic enhancements boosting their memory skills and lowering susceptibility to colds or depression. In yet another scenario, they predict that an inexpensive blood test for prospective parents will detect virtually all serious genetic disorders and risks for various illnesses. Advocates of mass genetic screening will argue that, as a public health matter, people should not be free to inflict avoidable diseases and disorders on their children. Opponents will argue that genetic services of any kind are a matter of choice.

It is not difficult to extrapolate from these scenarios that those with conditions related to chronic sorrow will be increasingly unacceptable and ostracized. Parents of children with serious anomalies may become more readily blamed for their misfortunes. With genetic engineering in human reproduction gaining ground and with parents "tailoring" their babies to their standards, the gap between these children and children who are seriously flawed may widen considerably, thereby underscoring the unacceptability of defects. Alienation and isolation may significantly increase, and many people with disabilities (children and adults) may be stigmatized more severely. One might even speculate about the possibility of increased infanticide. Moreover, those persons who have learned of their genetic susceptibility to certain disorders and diseases may experience grief responses related to self-loss much earlier than they would today and much before the onset of the disorders and diseases. Therefore, for these persons, chronic sorrow would have extended duration.

As a result of improvements in technology and medical care, the life span of persons with severe developmental disabilities is lengthening significantly. Premature infants who once would not have survived the first day of life outside the womb are now surviving, and most will have normal life spans. A large proportion of these infants have congenital anomalies or neurological damage, some of it immediately obvious and some not apparent until they are older. Many children with inborn errors of metabolism and their many associated disabilities can be treated to lessen or prevent further damage and prolong their lives. Before open-heart surgery became available to correct congenital heart conditions, most children with Down syndrome did not reach adulthood, whereas today they can live into their 60s. Some children with cystic fibrosis and muscular dystrophy are being treated as patients with chronic disease since their lives can now stretch well into adulthood. Until ventricular shunts were developed, most infants and children with hydrocephalus languished until they died. Shunting is now routinely practiced to reduce intracranial pressure, and enormous head size is prevented; further brain damage is kept to a minimum.

Technological assistance that replaces or augments a vital body function (ventilators, artificial airways, and so on) has proliferated. Nutritive assistance (gastrostomy feeding tubes) and intravenous therapy (dialysis) are significantly lengthening lives. The need for medical technology supports appears to be increasing in children under one year of age, principally because of the improved survival of extremely low birth weight infants (Levy & O'Rourke, 1997). The survival rates of stroke victims and persons with traumatic head injuries is currently increasing, even when brain damage is quite severe. New protocols of intervention and care have made a dramatic difference in these cases. Before the introduction of antibiotics, serious injuries often led to infections that caused death. Now, the survival rate is high even among those with very extensive injuries.

The media constantly remind us of the great strides that are being made in finding cures for cancer and that researchers are on the brink of knowing how to restore motor abilities in spinal cord injuries, multiple sclerosis, Parkinson's, and muscular dystrophy. Neural implants of the future will apparently overcome the debilitating effects of many conditions. Because of future compensating technology, blindness, deafness, paralysis, and other physical conditions are purportedly soon to be essentially eliminated as functional disabilities. Promises are made daily of amazing inventions that will remove barriers to mobility and allow participation in the larger world. A vaccination or cure for AIDS is ostensibly just over the horizon. Genetic research is characterized by new findings and possibilities that were thought to be impossible only a few decades ago.

The cultural belief that money, enthusiasm, and work can find cures, prevent devastating diseases, and restore physical and mental losses is maintained and strengthened by media reports. The myth that we can forestall death, find answers, and "fix" things that are less than the desired standard is entrenched in the culture. This myth is the driving force for great medical advances and social activism. On the other hand, the myth may also lead to negative consequences for those coping with chronic sorrow. As some individuals appear to be reaping the benefits of new discoveries and innovations in treatment, others may perceive themselves as the "unlucky" ones who are left out of the loop. They may experience their marginality in the dominant culture, and they may also feel marginal (or not included at all) in the hierarchy of research and treatment related to disabilities and losses. The belief in eventual remedies may contribute to the fantasy that life can be imminently perfect and that what was originally meant to be may yet occur. Belief in the potential of restoring what has been lost may increase the disparity between the fantasy and current reality, ultimately leading to a series of profound disappointments and increased chronic sorrow. The pattern of hope alternating with despair that continues for many years on end or for one's entire lifetime can be costly. Adaptations are hard enough without these peaks and valleys.

Several projections indicate that approximately one in four Americans will be over age sixty by the year 2030 (for example, Fowles, 1986). This number will inevitably include more persons with severe and profound disabilities than ever before, and health care systems will be strained to cope with this dramatic increase. For the first time, we are faced with the needs of a sizable, aging, chronically disabled or developmentally impaired population. The aged, in general, are among the most costly of consumers of health services. Professionals will be increasingly tasked to be informed about mental illness of organic etiology, and they will need to be involved in community organization to a greater extent. It is easy to see that moral and ethical questions will challenge the country at many levels. Quality of life issues are likely to increase significantly. Professionals working with geriatric populations will need specialized training in an entirely new field, that of aging persons with autism, mental retardation, and other lifelong developmental disabilities. The need for expertise in living wills, "right to die" issues, organ transplants, legalities involved in signing over one's property or life savings in return for lifetime care (for self or other), guardianship, conservatorships, and so on, is strongly indicated.

Lengthening life expectancy means that children will be significantly older when their parents die. Perhaps increasingly, adult children—often elderly themselves—will die before their parents. Professional skills will be strained to deal with issues of increasing numbers of losses during a lifetime, revisions in family structures, and crisis attendant to death in the family when a surviving family member is severely impaired and is left without resources. Professionals may find themselves significantly stressed by having to assume roles historically and traditionally assumed by family. (Enforcing "family responsibility" has not met with much success to date, regardless of how it has been attempted.) Professionals and non-family caregivers may be more likely candidates for chronic sorrow themselves as they take on more responsibility for the lives of those who are unable to care for themselves. Chronic sorrow may be the price that is paid for the prevention of impersonal, brusque, uncaring services or for the prevention of abuse and neglect.

It is a sad speculation that as the numbers of elderly grow, especially those with severe developmental disabilities and other chronic conditions and illnesses, so too will the problem of abuse. Persons who are in a weakened position and who reside in residential facilities, or even with relatives, will likely experience a continuum of abuse, from slaps to murder, from verbal abuse to cruelty through the refusal of something needed to make life livable (glasses, a telephone, a computer, Internet connection, and so on). Professionals may need the skills of an investigator as they function as ombudsmen, caseworkers, mediators, family liaison, and so on. They will need to be more conversant in the law as it applies to diminished capacity and to abuse and the violation of civil rights. Administrative competence may become more important in professional training, since professionals may take on more oversight and supervision of direct caregivers.

The helping professions of the future will face rapid shifts and expansions in technological innovations, with concomitant positive and negative spinoffs. Many new professions are likely to proliferate as a result of increased reliance on technology. Team building and cooperation among professions will become even more important in addressing the needs of persons with chronic sorrow. The United States will continue to become significantly more multicultural. However, there are fears that, rather than becoming a true multicultural society that values people's differences, the country will become increasingly fragmented. A patchwork of subgroups may arise, each competing with the others and intent on promulgating its own self-interests and fighting to maintain its own separate identity. Grief may become important as a unifying force, globally and professionally.

EPILOGUE

Writing about chronic sorrow and its effects has led me to a number of awarenesses extending somewhat beyond the boundaries of this human response to loss. I have, for instance, a deeper appreciation of the inadequacy of language. But perhaps it is not that language fails me; rather, it is that I fail language. However, if the meaning of language is found in its use, meanings are frustratingly unreliable and ephemeral. I struggled not to become undone by frustrations brought on by language's imprecision, and I resisted submitting to brooding and to ruminative thoughts that might have seriously thwarted my efforts to develop and communicate ideas about unremovable loss.

Another awareness is of the wide range of experiences in my life that have occurred as a direct result of being the mother of a child who is "atypical." These experiences have ranged from absurdly funny to tragic. I have been wondering about others in similar circumstances, and I have developed fantasies of dialogues among us that recollect these experiences; these memories could result in huge volumes of nonsensical narratives evoking the worst and the very best in what is called human. The dialogues might also contain superimposed alternative scenarios, or subscripts, in which we empower ourselves to "say it like it is" and also to construct optional story endings. I wonder if "the normals" would be able to understand and tolerate these dialogues and this way of being. There are so many stories about my daughter that it's hard to single out just a few. These experiences are reflective samples of a life that matters and of circumstances that are complexly challenging and rewarding.

When Val was three years old, her sleep disturbance was about at its worst. She would go to bed at night without any trouble at all, sleep well for two or three hours, and then wake up and rhythmically bang her head for the remainder of the short yet long night. My husband and I tried many things to alleviate this "jarring" problem and were soundly defeated. Phenobarbital was prescribed at one point, and it made her wild. She could not stop moving. She emptied out all the drawers she

241

could access, gracefully tossing items over her shoulder onto the floor. She ripped the cover off her mattress. The frenzy went on for many hours. It is called a "paradoxical reaction" to medication. (The result would have been better if I had been the one to take the phenobarbital.) When it was all over, Val and I were exhausted. We both had dark circles under our eyes. I don't know which of us was the crazier at the time. This is the unreal, or surreal, world that comes with the territory.

At about age four Val began to sleep a little better. She also began to pull her hair out in small chunks. I deduced that the empirical treatment for head-banging must be pulling the hair out—something I have felt like doing myself! Was it possibly just this sort of empiricism that led to the development of the behavior modification technique of overcorrection? Several times I took her to the medical school. I would have to carry her up to the fourth floor as she would not get into an elevator and she couldn't do stairs. When we got to the floor, our arrival was signaled by Val's quick-as-lightning contact with a long row of light switches. The entire floor was dark until I managed to flip all the switches to on. I did not do this as fast as I wished due to the transitory tremor in my hands and arms from carrying my child up all those stairs. Although Val was growing entirely bald, I could count on her to meticulously throw the little strands of hair into the wastebasket, even if it meant she had to get out of bed at night to do this. I found this bizarre and inordinate "neatness" both astonishing and hilarious. One's perspective in these circumstances adapts in the service of coping.

When she broke the lamp in the office of the child psychiatrist in Austin (she was two years old at the time), I registered the scene in memory as a sort of comedy on the lines of an old Jacques Tati or Mack Sennett movie. There was a sink in his office that she immediately took to in her perseverative way. He seemed irritated by this. Maybe it was because she went straight to the sink as if it were an old friend she had come to visit, while ignoring him completely. He was keen on seeing us "interact," so I attempted to redirect her after a while. She then crawled over to the floor lamp, which was positioned behind and to the side of his chair. She "tested" it by giving it a little shake. The shade took on a rakish angle, and I got up several times to "interact." He observed passively.

As the lamp went over and down, seemingly in slow motion, it passed within inches of the back of his head, illuminating and sparking, diffusing his hair in a way that made it look like it was on fire. I was momentarily transfixed. Actually, I had depersonalized. There were some very awkward moments following the crash. I did have the presence of mind to unplug the lamp, and I picked up the pieces as best I could. I offered to replace the lamp or pay for it; he declined my offer. Several years later I had access to his evaluation. In it I read about "the mother's

inappropriate affect"; and the example he cited was "the child's damage"
to his office, noting that "the mother appeared to smile." I was very
pleased to read that I had demonstrated any affect at all, especially since
he himself was so inscrutable. I can affirm that my affect was quite
appropriate. Truth be known, I wanted to laugh. I wanted to break the
tension. I wanted to see this scene as a comedy. I was tired of stoicism.

Today my daughter is a young adult. She has a full head of hair. She is
neat and clean, and she doesn't unravel her socks any more. Her character is sound; she is a good person. She works in a sheltered workshop.
Without complaint, she gets up very early five mornings a week and
rides in a van to her job. She does good work and seems to enjoy being
productive and busy. She has some receptive language, and she is able to
say a few things, but the intelligibility of her speech varies from day to
day and week to week. I'm very proud of her. She knows how to put
forth her best efforts. Of course, it's obvious to anyone that there is
something terribly wrong with her, but she looks good enough to me
(sometimes very beautiful even) that when I look at her, I see her not
only as she is but as how she was meant to be. And there it is again—
that sorrow.

I have had an awareness of a different sort as well while writing about
chronic sorrow. This awareness of a "cousin" or parallel sorrow has
persisted and permeated my thoughts. This sorrow is shared by a broad
and quite cosmopolitan segment of the world's inhabitants. It comes
from knowing how we have been trashing the planet and how we as a
people hurt each other and how we do "justice" through violence. Our
planet continues, like the object of chronic sorrow that remains in an
injured or diminished form. I think many of us are worried and sad that
our destructiveness has taken on such shortsighted and heartless characteristics. In the face of scientific evidence about the effects of hacking
away at our rain forests, of polluting our atmosphere, of removing the
means for survival of many of the earth's species—plant and animal—
and of continuing to annihilate, torture, and commit other atrocities on
some segments of the human population, we continue relatively un-
checked. We are able to rationalize our actions in our human way. And
so the oceans are strewn with toxins and debris. Deforestation proceeds
at an unbelievable pace. We leave our junk even in space.

Besides doing my paltry individual efforts toward counteracting waste,
destruction, and violence, I sometimes offset this latter awareness by
focusing on the best that humankind has been able to achieve. Music,
literature, art, wonderfully designed human and animal habitations, remarkably beneficial scientific breakthroughs and discoveries—they exist
too. They represent the other polarity of human potential, highlighting
possibilities of compassion and caring, of being soulful.

WORDS

So many words . . .
Deep down in the throat,
Stuck in a lump,
Impeding breathing
And so much else.

And so much to say . . .
Start, Stop, Start,
Stop, and Stop,
And the words swirl
Mixed by hidden powers
Into spectral ribbons
Of liquid color,
None so pale as the spoken—
Featherlight representations,
Anemic sprinkles.

So many words . . .
Stuck, stored, magic
Recognized and avoided.
Make a pun
Grab a cliché
Fill the nonvoid.

The well remains
Flowing deeply
Its possibilities disturbed.
Go to the well
Surreptitiously and alone
And the swirls
Become a private universe
Where words flow
True and timeless.

—Susan Roos, 1999

REFERENCES

Adams, J., & Lindemann, E. (1974). Coping with long-term disability. In G. Coelho, D. Hamburg, & J. Adams (Eds.), *Coping and adaptation.* New York: Basic Books.

Adoption Quest (2000, on-line). Available at http://adopt.org/datacenter/bin/AQP_pts.htm.

American Psychiatric Association. (1994). *Diagnostic and statistical manual of mental disorders* (4th ed.). Washington, DC: Author.

Andreasen, N., & Norris, A. (1972). Long-term adjustment and adaptation mechanisms in severely burned adults. *Journal of Nervous and Mental Disease, 154,* 352–362.

Anisman, H., & Zacharko, R. (1982). Depression: The predisposing influence of stress. *Behavioral and Brain Science, 5,* 89.

Arnett, J. (1998). Learning to stand alone: The contemporary American transition to adulthood in cultural and historical context. *Human Development, 41,* 295–315.

Arnett, J. (2000). Emerging adulthood: A theory of development from the late teens through the twenties. *American Psychologist, 55*(5), 469–480.

Bandler, R., & Grinder, J. (1979). *Frogs into princes.* Moab, UT: Real People Press.

Bandura, A. (1977). *Social learning theory.* Englewood Cliffs, NJ: Prentice-Hall.

Bandura, A. (1989). Social cognitive theory. In R. Vasta (Ed.), *Annals of child development: Vol. 6. Six theories of human development—Revised formulations and current issues* (pp. 1–60). Greenwich, CT: Jai Press.

Barnes, C. (1968). The cast. In *Theater reviews from The New York Times. On Stage: 1920–1970.* New York: Author.

Bartak, L., Rutter, M., & Cox, A. (1975). A comparative study of infantile autism and specific developmental receptive language disorder: I. The children. *British Journal of Psychiatry, 126,* 127–145.

Bateson, G., Jackson, D., Haley, J., & Weakland, J. (1956). Toward a theory of schizophrenia. *Behavioral Science, 1,* 251–264.

Batshaw, M., & Shapiro, B. (1997). Mental retardation. In M. Batshaw (Ed.), *Children with disabilities* (4th ed.). Baltimore, MD: Paul H. Brookes Publishing Co.

Bauby, J. (1997). *The diving bell and the butterfly.* New York: Alfred A. Knopf.

Beebe, B. (1985). Mother-infant mutual influence and precursors of self and object representations. In J. Masling (Ed.), *Empirical studies of psychoanalytic theories, Vol. 2.* Hillsdale, NJ: The Analytic Press.

Bell, L. (1980). *Treating the mentally ill: From colonial times to the present.* New York: Praeger.

Bernard, J. (1972). *The future of marriage.* New York: World.

Berne, E. (1973). *What do you say after you say hello?* New York: Bantam Books.

Bleuler, M. (1974). The offspring of schizophrenics. *Schizophrenia Bulletin, 3,* 93–107.

Bluebond-Langner, M. (1996). *In the shadow of illness: Parents and siblings of the chronically ill child.* Princeton, NJ: Princeton University Press.

245

Bohannon, J. (1990). Grief responses of spouses following the death of a child: A longitudinal study. *Omega: Journal of Death and Dying. 22*, 109–121.

Bowlby, J. (1963). Pathological mourning and childhood mourning. *Journal of the American Psychoanalytic Association, 11*, 500–541.

Bowlby, J. (1977). The making and breaking of affectional bonds: Aetiology and psychopathology in the light of attachment theory (The fiftieth Maudsley lecture). *British Journal of Psychiatry, 130*, 201–210.

Bowlby, J. (1980). *Attachment and loss: Vol. 3*. New York: Basic Books.

Bradley, D. (2000). A parent's goodbye. *Dallas Morning News* (June 25).

Brier, J., Grant-Hall, R., Pearlman, L., & Laub, D. (1992). The impact of severe trauma on the self (Audiotape). Los Angeles, CA: International Society of Traumatic Stress Studies, Eighth Annual Meeting.

Brink, J., & Hoffer, M. (1978). Rehabilitation of brain injured children. *Orthopedic Clinics of North America, 9*, 451–454.

Brown, C. (1999). *Lamb in love*. New York: Bantam Books.

Brown, P. (2000). Viewing Ahab and Barbie through the lens of disability. *The New York Times* (August 20).

Buchanan, A., Brock, D., Daniels, N., & Wikler, D. (2000). *From chance to choice: Genetics and justice*. New York: Cambridge University Press.

Buck, P. (1950). *The child who never grew*. New York: The John Day Co.

Burke, M. (1989). Chronic sorrow in mothers of school-age children with a myelomeningocele disability (Doctoral dissertation, Boston University, School of Nursing). (University Microfilms No. AAD89–20093.)

Burleigh, M. (1990). Euthanasia and the Third Reich. *History Today. 40*, 11–16.

Burleigh, M. (1991). "Euthanasia" in the Third Reich: Some recent literature. *Social History of Medicine, 4*(2), 317–328.

Callahan, J. (1990). *Don't worry, he won't get far on foot*. New York: Vintage Books.

Callahan, R. (1985). *Five minute phobia cure*. Wilmington, DE: Enterprise.

Caplan, G. (1964). *Principles of preventive psychiatry*. New York: Basic Books.

Carter, B., & McGoldrick, M. (1989). Overview, the changing family life cycle: A framework for family therapy. In B. Carter & M. McGoldrick (Eds.), *The changing family life cycle: A framework for family therapy, second edition*. Needham Heights, MA: Allyn and Bacon.

Catalano, M. (1998). Searching for the blue fairy: Thomas's tale. In R. Catalano (Ed.), *When autism strikes: Families cope with childhood disintegrative disorder*. New York: Plenum Press.

Catalano, R. (Ed.) (1998). *When autism strikes: Families cope with childhood disintegrative disorder*. New York: Plenum Press.

Chisholm, L., & Hurrelmann, K. (1995). Adolescence in modern Europe: Pluralized transition patterns and their implications for personal and social risks. *Journal of Adolescence, 18*, 129–158.

Chomicki, S. (1995). Surviving the loss of a child with a disability: Is loss the end of chronic sorrow? Three case studies. *Physical Disabilities: Education and Related Services, 13*(2), 17–30.

Cleveland, D., & Miller, N. (1977). Attitudes and life commitments of older siblings of mentally retarded adults. *Mental Retardation, 15*.

Cohen, B. (1991). Holocaust survivors and the crises of aging. *Families in society, 72*, 226–231.

Coleman, S. (1990). The siblings of the retarded child. (Doctoral dissertation, California School of Professional Psychology, San Diego).

Collins, M. (1982). Parental reactions to a visually handicapped child: A mourning process. (Doctoral dissertation, University of Texas at Austin).

Cook, J. (1988). Who "mothers" the chronically mentally ill? *Family Relations, 37*, 42–49.

Cook, J., Hoffschmidt, B., Cohler, B., & Pickett, S. (1992). Marital satisfaction among parents of the severely mentally ill living in the community. *American Journal of Orthopsychiatry, 62*(4), 552–563.

Copeland, L. (1999). Case of son left at hospital puzzling. *The Dallas Morning News,* 3A.

Coyne, J. (1976). Toward an interactional description of depression. *Psychiatry, 39,* 28–39.

Crossman, P. (1966). Permission and protection. *Transactional Analysis Bulletin, 5,* 152.

Cummings, N. (1987). The future of psychotherapy: One psychologist's perspective. *American Journal of Psychotherapy, 61,* 349–360.

Cummings, N. (1991). Out of the cottage. *AAP Advance Plan*(Spring), pp. 1, 2, 14, 15.

Cummings, S. (1976). The impact of the child's deficiency on the father: A study of fathers of mentally retarded and of chronically ill children. *American Journal of Orthopsychiatry, 46,* 246–255.

Cusitar, L. (1994). *Strengthening the links: Stopping the violence.* Toronto: DisAbled Women's Network.

Daly, B., & Reddy, M. (Eds.) (1991). *Narrating mothers: Theorizing maternal subjectivities.* Knoxville: The University of Tennessee Press.

Damrosch, S., & Perry, L. (1989). Self-reported adjustment, chronic sorrow, and coping of parents of children with Down Syndrome. *Nursing Research, 38*(1), 25–30.

Davies, S. (1959). *The mentally retarded in society.* New York: Columbia University Press.

Davis, B. (1987). Disability and grief. *Social Casework, 68,* 352–357.

Davis, D., & Schultz, C. (1998). Grief, parenting, and schizophrenia. *Social Science & Medicine, 46*(3), 369–379.

Davison, K., Pennebaker, J., & Dickerson, S. (2000). Who talks? The social psychology of illness support groups. *American Psychologist, 55*(2), 205–217.

Day, M. (1998). Coming home. In R. Catalano (Ed.), *When autism strikes: Families cope with childhood disintegrative disorder.* New York: Plenum Press.

Deutsch, H. (1937). Absence of grief. *Psychoanalytic Quarterly, 6,* 12–22.

Doka, K., & Aber, R. (1989). Psychosocial loss and grief. In K. Doka (Ed.), *Disenfranchised grief: Recognizing hidden sorrow* (pp. 187–198). Lexington, MA: Lexington Books.

Dubas, J., & Peterson, A. (1996). Geographical distance from parents and adjustment during adolescence and young adulthood. *New Directions for Child Development, 71,* 3–19.

Dunn, B. (1993). Growing up with a psychotic mother: A retrospective study. *American Journal of Orthopsychiatry, 63*(2), 177–189.

Dunst, C., Trivette, C., & Cross, A. (1986). Mediating influences of social support: Personal, family, and child outcomes. *American Journal of Mental Deficiency, 90,* 403–417.

Duvall, E. (1977). *Marriage and family development* (5th ed.). Philadelphia: Lippincott.

Dweck, C., & Wortman, C. (1980). Achievement, test anxiety and learned helplessness: Adaptive and maladaptive cognitions. In H. Krohne & L. Laux (Eds.), *Achievement, stress and anxiety.* Washington, DC: Hemisphere.

Dyson, L. (1993). Response to the presence of a child with disabilities: Parental stress and family functioning over time. *American Journal on Mental Retardation, 98,* 207–218.

Eakes, G., Burke, M., & Hainsworth, M. (1998). Middle-range theory of chronic sorrow. *Journal of Nursing Scholarship, 30*(2), 179–184.

Eliot, C. (Ed.). (1938). *American historical documents.* New York: Collier.

Engel, G. (1961). Is grief a disease? A challenge for medical research. *Psychosomatic Medicine, 23,* 18–22.

Erickson, M., & Rossi, E. (1979). *Hypnotherapy: An exploratory casebook.* New York: Irvington Publishers.

Erikson, E. (1968). *Identity: Youth and crisis.* New York: Norton.

Eriksson, P., Perfilieva, E., Bjork-Eriksson, T., Alborn, A., Nordberg, C., Peterson, D., & Gage, F. (1998). Neurogenesis in the adult human hippocampus. *Nature Medicine, 4,* 1313–1317.

248   Chronic Sorrow

Etzioni, A. (1964). *Modern organizations.* Englewood Cliffs, NJ: Prentice Hall.

Exline, J., Dorrity, K., & Wortman, C. (1996). Coping with bereavement: A research review for clinicians. *In Session: Psychotherapy in Practice, 2*(4), 3–19.

Fairthorne, J. (1998). Diary of David. In R. Catalano (Ed.), *When autism strikes: Families cope with childhood disintegrative disorder.* New York: Plenum Press.

Featherstone, H. (1980). *A difference in the family.* New York: Penguin Books.

Federal Bureau of Investigation (FBI). (1998, 22 November). *Crime in the United States, Uniform Crime Reports, 1997, 62,* Washington, DC: U.S. Department of Justice.

Felton, B. (2000). Facing hard choices as the disabled age. *The New York Times* (January 9), Section 3, 1, 8–9.

Ferris, S., & Ferris, S. (1998). Laura's story. In R. Catalano (Ed.), *When autism strikes: Families cope with childhood disintegrative disorder.* New York: Plenum Press.

Field, N., Nichols, C., Holen, A., & Horowitz, M. (1999). The relation of continuing attachment to adjustment in conjugal bereavement. *Journal of Consulting and Clinical Psychology, 67*(2), 212–218.

Figley, C. (1983). Catastrophies: An overview of family reactions. In C. Figley & H. McCubbin (Eds.), *Stress and the family: Vol.2. Coping with catastrophe* (pp. 3–20). New York: Brunner/Mazel.

Figley, C. (1989). *Helping traumatized families.* San Francisco: Jossey-Bass Publishers.

Frankl, V. (1962). *Man's search for meaning: An introduction to logotherapy.* Boston: Beacon Press.

Frankl, V. (1986). *The doctor and the soul: From psychotherapy to logotherapy.* New York: Vintage Books.

Fraser, M. (Ed.). (1997). *Risk and resilience in childhood: An ecological perspective.* Washington, DC: NASW Press.

Freeston, B. (1971). An enquiry upon the effect of a spina bifida child upon family life. *Developmental Medicine and Child Neurology, 13,* 456–461.

Freud, S. (1917). Mourning and melancholia. In *Standard Edition Vol. XIV.* London: Hogarth Press.

Friedlander, S. (1997). *Nazi Germany and the Jews, Volume 1.* New York: HarperCollins.

Garland, C. (1993). Beyond chronic sorrow: A new understanding of family adaptation. In A. Turnbull, J. Patterson, S. Behr, D. Murphy, J. Marquis, & M. Blue-Banning (Eds.), *Cognitive coping, families, and disability* (pp. 67–80). Baltimore, MD: Paul H. Brookes Publishing Co.

Gath, A., & Gumley, D. (1986). Family background of children with Down's syndrome and of children with a similar degree of mental retardation. *British Journal of Psychiatry, 149,* 161–171.

Gaylin, W., & Person, E. (1988). *Passionate attachments.* New York: Free Press.

Gerbode, F. (1989). *Beyond psychology: An introduction to metapsychology.* Palo Alto, CA: IRM Press.

Gerdtz, J. (1993). Introduction: Historical summary. In M. McGarrity, *A guide to mental retardation.* New York: Crossroad.

Gill, B. (1997). *Changed by a child: Companion notes for parents of a child with a disability.* New York: Doubleday.

Glidden, L., & Floyd, F. (1997). Disaggregating parental depression and family stress in assessing families of children with developmental disabilities: A multisample analysis. *American Journal on Mental Retardation, 102*(3), 250–266.

Gliedman, J., & Roth, W. (1980). *The unexpected minority—Handicapped children in America.* New York: Harcourt Brace Jovanovich.

Glover, H. (1992). Emotional numbing: A possible endorphin-mediated phenomenon associated with post-traumatic stress disorders and other allied psychopathologic states. *Journal of Traumatic Stress, 5*(4), 643–675.

Goddard, H. (1912). *The Kallikak family: A study in the heredity of feeblemindedness*. New York: Macmillan.

Goddard, H. (1917a). Mental levels of a group of immigrants. *Psychological Bulletin, 14* (Feb), 68–69.

Goddard, H. (1917b). Mental tests and the immigrant. *Journal of Delinquency, 2* (Sept.), 243–79.

Goffman, E. (1963). *Stigma: Notes on the management of a spoiled identity*. Englewood Cliffs, NJ: Prentice-Hall.

Goldberg, R. (1992). Special feature: Simon Olshansky, 1913–1991; Obituary. *The Journal of Rehabilitation, 58*, 2, 1–6.

Goldfarb, L., Brotherson, M., Summers, J., & Turnbull, A. (1986). *Meeting the challenge of disability or chronic illness: A family guide*. Baltimore, MD: Paul H. Brookes Publishing Co.

Goldhagen, D. (1996). *Hitler's willing executioners: Ordinary Germans and the holocaust*. New York: Alfred A. Knopf, Inc.

Goldstein, C. (1998). Looking for answers. In R. Catalano (Ed.), *When autism strikes*. New York: Plenum Press.

Golfus, B. (1994). *When Billy broke his head . . . and other tales of wonder* (Videotape). Boston: Fanlight Productions.

Goode, W. (1963). *World revolution and family patterns*. New York: Free Press.

Gorer, G. (1965). *Death, grief and mourning in contemporary Britain*. London: Cresset Press.

Gould, E., Beylin, A., Tanapat, P., Reeves, A., & Shors, T. (1999). Learning enhances adult neurogenesis in the hippocampal formation. *Nature Neuroscience, 2*, 260–265.

Gould, R. (1972). The phases of adult life: A study in developmental psychology. *American Journal of Psychiatry, 129*, 33–43.

Greenblatt, M. (1978). The grieving spouse. *American Journal of Psychiatry, 135*(1), 43–47.

Haederle, M. (1997). Essays tell weight of disability. *The Dallas Morning News*. (June 15), 45–47.

Haig, R. (1990). *The anatomy of grief: Biopsychosocial and therapeutic perspectives*. Springfield, IL: Charles C. Thomas.

Hainsworth, M. (1994). Living with multiple sclerosis: The experience of chronic sorrow. *Journal of Neuroscience Nursing, 26*(4), 237–240.

Hainsworth, M., Busch, P., Eakes, G., & Burke, M. (1995). Chronic sorrow in women with chronically mentally disabled husbands. *Journal of the American Psychiatric Nurses Association, 1*(4), 120–124.

Harrington, M. (1963). *The other America*. New York: Macmillan.

Harry, J. (1976). Evolving sources of happiness for men over the life cycle: A structural analysis. *Journal of Marriage and the Family, 2*, 289–296.

Hays, J., Gelso, C., Van Wagoner, S., & Diemer, R. (1991). Managing countertransference: What the experts think. *Psychological Reports, 69*, 138–148.

Herbert, T., & Cohen, S. (1993). Stress and immunity in humans: A meta-analytic review. *Psychosomatic Medicine, 55*, 364.

Herman, J. (1992). *Trauma and recovery*. New York: Basic Books.

Hewson, D. (1997). Coping with loss of ability: "Good grief" or episodic stress responses? *Social Science Medicine, 44*(8), 1129–1139.

Hiroto, D. (1974). Locus of control and learned helplessness. *Journal of Experimental Psychology, 102*, 187.

Hiroto, D., & Seligman, M. (1974). Generality of learned helplessness in man. *Journal of Personality and Social Psychology, 31*, 311.

Hobdell, E. (1993). The relationship between chronic sorrow and accuracy of perception of cognitive development in parents of children with neural tube defect. (Doctoral dissertation, University of Pennsylvania.)

Hobfoll, S. (1989). Conservation of resources: A new attempt at conceptualizing stress. *American Psychologist, 44,* 513–524.

Horowitz, M. (1976). *Stress response syndromes.* New York: Aronson.

Horowitz, M. (1985). Disasters and psychological response to stress. *Psychiatric Annals, 15,* 161–167.

Horowitz, A., & Shindelman, L. (1983). Reciprocity and affection: Past influences on current caregiving. *Journal of Gerontological Social Work, 5,* 5–20.

House, J., Landis, K., & Umberson, D. (1988). Social relationships and health. *Science, 241,* 540.

Ingalls, R. (1978). *Mental retardation: The changing outlook.* New York: John Wiley & Sons.

Irwin, M., Daniels, S., Risch, C., Bloom, E., & Weiner, H. (1988). Plasma cortisol and natural killer cell activity during bereavement. *Biological Psychiatry, 24,* 173–178.

Jacobs, B., van Praag, H., & Gage, F. (2000). Depression and the birth and death of brain cells. *American Scientist, 88,* 340–345.

Jahoda, M. (1959). *Current concepts of positive mental health.* New York: Basic Books.

Johnson, E. (1990). *The deadly emotions: The role of anger, hostility and aggression in health and emotional well-being.* New York: Praeger.

Johnston, L. (1978). Mourning in parents of the handicapped and its relation to certain parenting behaviors (Doctoral dissertation, George Peabody College for Teachers, 1977). *Dissertation Abstracts International, 39,* 384B.

Josselson, R. (1987). *Finding herself: Pathways to identity development in women.* San Francisco: Jossey-Bass.

Josselson, R. (1992). *The space between us: Exploring the dimensions of human relationships.* San Francisco: Jossey-Bass.

Kalish, R. (1968). Life and death: Dividing the indivisible. *Social Science and Medicine, 2,* 249–259.

Kalish, R. (1985). *Death, grief, and caring relationships* (2d ed.). Pacific Grove, CA: Brooks Cole.

Kanner, L., & Lesser, L. (1958). *Early infantile autism. The pediatric clinics of North America.* Philadelphia: W. B. Saunders.

Kanner, L. (1964). *A history of the care and study of the mentally retarded.* Springfield, IL: Thomas.

Kelly, G. (1955). *The psychology of personal constructs, Vols. 1 & 2.* New York: Norton.

Kennedy-Moore, E., & Watson, J. (1999). *Expressing emotion: Myths, realities, and therapeutic strategies.* New York: Guilford Press.

Kernberg, O. (1980). Boundaries and structures in love relations. In O. Kernberg (Ed.), *Internal world and external reality.* New York: Aronson.

Kerlin, I. (1858). *The mind unveiled; or, A brief history of twenty-two imbecile children.* Philadelphia: U. Hunt and Son.

Kiecolt-Glaser, J., & Glaser, R. (1991). Stress and immune function in humans. In R. Ader, D. Felten, & N. Cohen (Eds.), *Psychoneuroimmunology* (2d ed.). San Diego: Academic Press.

Kiecolt-Glaser, J., Garner, W., Speicher, C., Penn, G., & Glaser, R. (1984). Psychosocial modifiers of immunocompentence in medical students. *Psychosomatic Medicine, 46,* 7.

Keniston, K. (1971). *Youth and dissent: The rise of a new opposition.* New York: Harcourt Brace Jovanovich.

Kiely, M. (1987). The prevalence of mental retardation. *Epidemiology Reviews, 9,* 194–218.

Kirshbaum, H. (1991). Disability and humiliation. *Journal of Primary Prevention, 12*(2), 169–181.

Klass, D., Silverman, P., & Nickman, S. (Eds.). (1996). *Continuing bonds: New understandings of grief.* Washington, DC: Taylor & Francis.

Klein, S. (1972). Brother to sister, sister to brother. *Exceptional Parent* (June/July; Aug./Sept.; Oct./Nov.).

Klinger, E. (1977). *Meaning and void: Inner experience and the incentives in people's lives.* Minneapolis: University of Minnesota Press.

Kobasa, S. (1979). Stressful life events, personality and health: An inquiry into hardiness. *Journal of Personality and Social Psychology, 37,* 1–11.

Kocsis, J. (1991). Is lifelong depression a personality or mood disorder? *The Harvard Mental Health Letter, 8*(2), 8.

Kohut, H. (1980). Reflections. In A. Goldberg (Ed.), *Advances in self psychology.* New York: International Universities Press.

Kohut, H. (1983). Selected problems of self-psychological theory. In J. Lichtenberg & S. Kaplan (Eds.), *Reflections on self psychology.* Hillsdale, NJ: The Analytic Press.

Konstantareas, M., & Homatidis, S. (1989). Stress and differential parental involvement in families of autistic and learning disabled children. In E. Hibbs (Ed.), *Children and families: Studies in prevention and intervention.* Madison, CT: International Universities Press.

Krafft, S., & Krafft, L. (1998). Chronic sorrow: Parents' lived experience. *Holistic Nursing Practice, 13(1),* 59–67.

Krause, M., & Seltzer, M. (1993). Current well-being and future plans of older caregiving mothers. *Irish Journal of Psychology, 14*(1), 48–63.

Kübler-Ross, E. (1969). *On death and dying.* New York: Macmillan.

Lagaipa, S. (1990). Suffer the little children: The ancient practice of infanticide as a modern moral dilemma. *Issues in Comprehensive Pediatric Nursing, 13,* 241–251.

Lane, C., & Hobfoll, S. (1992). How loss affects anger and alienates potential supporters. *Journal of Consulting and Clinical Psychology, 60*(6), 935–942.

Langer, W. (1974). Infanticide: A historical survey. *History of Childhood Quarterly, 1,* 353–366.

Lazarus, R., & Folkman, S. (1984). *Stress, appraisal and coping.* New York: Springer.

Lazzari, A. (1983). Parent versus professional perception of mothers' adjustment to their multihandicapped offspring. (Doctoral thesis, Virginia Polytechnic Institute and State University).

Lee, R., & Martin, J. (1991). *Psychotherapy after Kohut.* Hillsdale, NJ: Analytic Press.

Lehman, D., Davis, C., DeLongis, A., Wortman, C., Bluck, S., Mandel, D., & Ellard, J. (1993). Positive and negative life changes following bereavement and their relations to adjustment. *Journal of Social and Clinical Psychology, 12,* 90–112.

Levav, I., Friedlander, Y., Kark, J., & Peritz, E. (1988). An epidemiological study of mortality among bereaved parents. *New England Journal of Medicine, 319,* 457.

Levinson, D. (1978). *The seasons of a man's life.* New York: Ballantine.

Levy, S., & O'Rourke, M. (1997). Technological assistance. In M. Batshaw (Ed.), *Children with disabilities* (4th edition). Baltimore, MD: Paul H. Brookes Publishing Co.

Lindemann, E. (1944). Symptomatology and management of acute grief. *American Journal of Psychiatry, 101,* 141–148.

Lindgren, C. (1996). Chronic sorrow in persons with Parkinson's and their spouses. *Scholarly Inquiry for Nursing Practice. 10*(4), 351–366.

Lindgren, C., Burke, M., Hainsworth, M., & Eakes, G. (1992). Chronic sorrow: A lifespan concept. *Scholarly Inquiry for Nursing Practice, 6,* 27–40.

Lippman, T. (1995). *Understanding Islam: An introduction to the Muslim world.* New York: Meridian.

Liptzin, B., Grob, M., & Eisen, S. (1988). Family burden of demented and depressed elderly psychiatric in-patients. *The Gerontologist, 28,* 397–401.

Litz, B. (1992). Emotional numbing in combat-related post-traumatic stress disorder: A critical review and reformulation. *Clinical Psychology Review, 12,* 417–432.

Lowes, L., & Lyne, P. (2000). Chronic sorrow in parents of children with newly diagnosed diabetes: A review of the literature and discussion of the implications for nursing practice. *Journal of Advanced Nursing, 32*(1), 41–48.

Macarov, D. (1978). *The design of social welfare.* New York: Holt, Rinehart & Winston.

MacGregor, P. (1994). Grief: The unrecognized parental response to mental illness in a child. *Social Work, 39*(2), 160–166.

Mairs, N. (1986). *Plaintext.* Tucson, AZ: The University of Arizona Press.

Mairs, N. (1989). *Remembering the bone house.* New York: Harper & Row.

Mairs, N. (1993). *Ordinary time: Cycles in marriage, faith, and renewal.* Boston: Beacon Press.

Mallow, G., & Bechtel, G. (1999). Chronic sorrow: The experience of parents with children who are developmentally disabled. *Journal of Psychosocial Nursing, 37*(7), 31–35.

Marcus, L. (1977). Patterns of coping in families of psychotic children. *American Journal of Orthopsychiatry, 36,* 388–395.

Marsh, D. (1992). *Families and mental retardation: New directions in professional practice.* New York: Praeger Publishers.

Marsh, J. (Ed.). (1994). *From the heart: On being the mother of a child with special needs.* Bethesda, MD: Woodbine House.

Martin, T., & Doka, K. (1996). Masculine grief. In K. Doka (Ed.), *Living with grief after sudden loss.* Bristol, PA: Taylor & Francis.

Martin, T., & Doka, K. (1998). Revisiting masculine grief. In K. Doka & J. Davidson (Eds.), *Living with grief: Who we are and how we grieve* (pp. 133–142). Philadelphia: Brunner/ Mazel.

Massie, R., & Massie, S. (1975). *Journey.* New York: Knopf.

Mays, S. (1993). Infanticide in Roman Britain. *Antiquity, 67*(257), 883–888.

McCubbin, H., & Figley, C. (1983a). *Stress and the family: Vol. 1. Coping with normative transitions.* New York: Brunner/Mazel.

McCubbin, H., & Figley, C. (1983b). Bridging normative and catastrophic family stress. In H. McCubbin & C. Figley (Eds.), *Stress and the family: Vol. 1. Coping with normative transitions* (pp. 218–228). New York: Brunner/Mazel.

McCubbin, H., Hunter, E., & Dahl, B. (1975). Residuals of war: Families of prisoners of war and servicemen missing in action. *Journal of Social Sciences, 31*(4), 95–109.

McCullough, M. (1981). Parent and sibling definition of situation regarding transgenerational shift in care of a handicapped child (Doctoral dissertation, University of Minnesota).

McHugh, M. (1999). *Special siblings: Growing up with someone with a disability.* New York: Hyperion.

McMillen, J. (1999). Better for it: How people benefit from adversity. *Social Work, 44*(5), 455–467.

Millen, L., & Roll, S. (1985). Solomon's mothers: A special case of pathological bereavement. *American Journal of Orthopsychiatry, 55,* 3, 411–418.

Miller, S. (1980). Why having control reduces stress: If I can stop the roller-coaster, I don't want to get off. In J. Garber & M. Seligman (Eds.), *Human helplessness: Theory and applications.* Orlando, FL: Academic Press.

Miller, S. (1990). *Family pictures.* New York: HarperCollins.

Miller, T., Lestina, D., & Spicer, R. (1996). Highway and crash costs in the U.S. by victim age, restraint use, and blood alcohol level. Association for the Advancement of Automotive Medicine, 40th Annual Proceedings.

Monat, A., & Lazarus, R. (1991). Stress and coping: Some current issues and controversies. In A. Monat & R. Lazarus (Eds.), *Stress and coping: An anthology* (3d ed., pp. 1–15). New York: Columbia University Press.

Mullins, J. (1987). Authentic voices from parents of exceptional children. *Family Relations, 38,* 30–33.

Murphy, M. (1982). The family with a handicapped child: A review of the literature. *Journal of Developmental and Behavioral Pediatrics, 3*(2), 73–82.

Natanson, M. (1970). *The journeying self.* Reading, MA: Addison-Wesley.

Neugeboren, J. (1997). *Imagining Robert: My brother, madness, and survival.* New York: William Morrow & Company, Inc.

New York Times News Service (1999). CEO, wife accused of abandoning disabled son. *The Dallas Morning News* (December 29).

Newman, R. (1995). Coping. In J. Marsh (Ed.), *From the heart: On being the mother of a child with special needs.* Bethesda, MD: Woodbine House.

Nichols, B. (1998) Mentally disabled man reportedly lured, slain. *The Dallas Morning News* (August 29).

Nichols, P. (1967). *Joe Egg.* New York: Grove Press.

Nirje, B. (1969). The normalization principle and its human management implications. In R. Kugel & W. Wolfensberger (Eds.), *Changing patterns of residential services for the mentally retarded.* Washington, DC: President's Committee on Mental Retardation.

Norcross, J., Alford, B., & DeMichele, J. (1992). The future of psychotherapy: Delphi data and concluding observations. *Psychotherapy, 29*(1), 150–158.

Noyes, R., & Kletti, R. (1976). Depersonalization in the face of life-threatening danger: A description. *Psychiatry, 39,* 19–27.

Nye, F. (Ed.). (1976). *Role structure and analysis of the family.* Vol. 24. Beverly Hills, CA: Sage Publications.

O'Connor, T., Allen, J., Bell, K., & Hauser, S. (1996). Adolescent-parent relationships and leaving home in young adulthood. *New Directions in Child Development, 71,* 39–52.

Oh, K. (1993). A study of variables affecting the level of maternal adjustment to the child with mental retardation. (Doctoral dissertation. Southern Illinois University at Carbondale).

Olshansky, S. (1962). Chronic sorrow: A response to having a mentally defective child. *Social Casework, 43,* 4, 190–193.

Olshansky, S. (1966). Parent responses to a mentally defective child. *Mental Retardation, 4,* 4, 21–23.

Olshansky, S. (1970). Chronic sorrow: A response to having a mentally defective child. In R. Nolen (Ed.), *Counseling parents of the mentally retarded.* Springfield, IL: Charles C. Thomas.

Park, C. (1982). *The seige: The first eight years of an autistic child.* Boston: Little, Brown.

Parkes, C. (1975). What becomes of redundant world models? A contribution to the study of the adaptation to change. *British Journal of Medical Psychology, 48,* 131–137.

Parkes, C. (1980). *Bereavement.* London: Penguin.

Pearlman, L., & Saakvitne, K. (1995). *Trauma and the therapist.* New York: Norton.

Pesut, D. (2000). Tap nurses' talents. In Special report: The opportunity century. *The Futurist* (January/February)

Peterson, C. (2000). The future of optimism. *American Psychologist, 55*(1), 44–55.

Phillips, M. (1991). Chronic sorrow in mothers of chronically ill and disabled children. *Issues in Comprehensive Pediatric Nursing, 14*(2), 111–120.

Pieper, E. (1976). *Sticks and stones: The story of loving a child.* Syracuse, NY: Human Policy Press.

Pincus, L. (1976). *Death and the family.* London: Faber.

Pollock, G. (1981). Aging or aged: Development or pathology. In S. Greenspan & G. Pollock (Eds.), *The course of life, Vol. 3: Adulthood and the aging process.* Washington, DC: Government Printing Office. DHHS Pub. No. (ADM) 81–1000.

Powers, I. (1974). The National League of Families and the development of family services. In H. McCubbin, B. Dahl, E. Hunter, & P. Metres (Eds.), *Families of prisoners of war and servicemen missing in action.* Washington, DC: Government Printing Office.

Price-Bonham, S., & Addison, S. (1978). Families and mentally retarded children: Emphasis on the father. *The Family Coordinator, 27,* 221–230.

Quayhagen, M., & Quayhagen, M. (1988). Alzheimer's stress: Coping with the caregiving role. *The Gerontologist, 28,* 391–396.

Rando, T. (1988). *Grieving: How to go on living when someone you love dies.* Lexington, MA: Lexington.

Rando, T. (1993). *Treatment of complicated mourning.* Champaign, IL: Research Press.

Raphael, B. (1984). *The anatomy of bereavement.* London: Hutchinson.

Reeve, C. (1998). *Still me.* New York: Random House.

Rife, J. (1994). *Injured mind, shattered dreams.* Cambridge, MA: Brookline Books.

Rivara, J., Jaffe, K., Fay, G., Polissar, N., Martin, K., Shurtleff, H., & Liao, S. (1993). Family functioning and injury severity as predictors of child functioning one year following traumatic brain injury. *Archives of Physical Medicine and Rehabilitation, 74*(10), 1047–1055.

Robarge, J. (1989). Perceptions of caretakers of children having Duchenne muscular dystrophy. (Master's thesis, Medical College of Ohio at Toledo.)

Rolland, J. (1987). Family illness paradigms: Evolution and significance. *Family Systems Medicine, 5,* 482–503.

Rolland, J. (1989). Chronic illness and the family life cycle. In B. Carter & M. McGoldrick (Eds.), *The changing family life cycle: A framework for family therapy, second edition.* New York: Allyn and Bacon.

Roos, P., & Albers, R. (1965). Performance of retardates and normals on a measure of temporal orientation. *American Journal of Mental Deficiency, 69,* 835–838.

Roos, P. (1977). Parents of mentally retarded people. *International Journal of Mental Health, 6*(1), 96–119.

Roos, S. (1996). Literary look. *MADDvocate, 9,* 1, 24.

Rosen, D. (1974). President's address: Observations of an era of transition. *Mental Retardation, 12,* 61–63.

Roskies, E. (1972). *Abnormality and normality: The mothering of thalidomide children.* Ithaca, NY: Cornell University Press.

Rubin, S. (1984). Mourning as distinct from melancholia: The resolution of bereavement. *British Journal of Medical Psychology, 57,* 339–345.

Russell, L., Grant, A., Joseph, S., & Fee, R. (1993). *Planning for the future: Providing a meaningful life for a child with a disability after your death.* Evanston, IL: American Publishing Co.

Sapolsky, R. (1998). *Why zebras don't get ulcers: An updated guide to stress, stress-related diseases, and coping.* New York: W. H. Freeman and Company.

Scanzoni, J. (1977). *The black family in modern society: Patterns of stability and security.* Chicago: University of Chicago Press.

Scanzoni, L., & Scanzoni, J. (1981). *Men, women and change.* New York: McGraw-Hill.

Schilling, R., Schinke, S., & Kirkham, M. (1985). Coping with a handicapped child: Differences between mothers and fathers. *Social Science and Medicine, 21,* 857–863.

Scheerenberger, R. (1982). Treatment from ancient times to the present. In P. Cegelka & H. Prehm, *Mental retardation: From categories to people.* Columbus, OH: Charles E. Merrell Publishing Company.

Scheerenberger, R. (1983). *A history of mental retardation.* Baltimore, MD: Paul H. Brookes Publishing Co.

Schoech, D., & Arangio, T. (1979). Computers in the human services. *Social Work, 24,* 96–102.

Schulz, R., & Williamson, G. (1991). A 2-year longitudinal study of depression among Alzheimer's caregivers. *Psychology and Aging, 6,* 569–578.

Schulze, C. (1998). The river Jordan. In R. Catalano (Ed.), *When autism strikes: Families cope with childhood disintegrative disorder.* New York: Plenum Press.

Searl, S. (1978). Stages of parent reaction. *Exceptional Parent, 8,* 27–29.

Secunda, V. (1997). *When madness comes home.* New York: Hyperion.

Seligman, M. (1975). *Helplessness: On depression, development and death.* San Francisco: W. H. Freeman.

Shapiro, F. (1995). *Eye movement desensitization and reprocessing: Basic principles, protocols, and procedures.* New York: The Guilford Press.

Shea, C. (1986). Coping with arthritis: A descriptive study of adaptation to chronic illness. (Doctoral Dissertation, Rutgers University, State University of New Jersey.)

Siedick, K. (1984). *Or you can let him go.* New York: Delacorte.

Siegman, A. (1994). Cardiovascular consequences of expressing and repressing anger. In A. Siegman, & T. Smith (Eds.), *Anger, hostility, and the heart.* Hillsdale, NJ: Erlbaum.

Sigmon, J. (1999). Victimization of individuals with disabilities. *National Victim Assistance Academy Curriculum.* Washington, DC: U.S. Department of Justice.

Silver, R., & Wortman, C. (1980). Coping with undesirable life events. In J. Garber & M. Seligman (Eds.), *Human helplessness:Theory and applications.* New York: Academic Press.

Simon, P. (1993). Statements on introduced bills and joint resolutions. *Congressional Record. Daily Ed.,* 10 Mar., S2610–2676.

Skeels, H. (1966). Adult status of children with contrasting early life experiences: A follow-up study. *Monographs of the Society for Research in Child Development, 31* (Ser. #105).

Skodak, M., & Skeels, H. (1949). A final follow-up study of one hundred adopted children. *Journal of Genetic Psychology, 75,* 85–125.

Sleek, S. (1993). Effects of stress remain after family member dies. *APA Monitor, 24*(11), 23.

Smith, A., & Borgers, S. (1988). Parental grief response to perinatal death. *Omega: Journal of Death and Dying, 19,* 203.

Sobsey, D. (1994). *Violence and abuse in the lives of people with disabilities: The end of silent acceptance?.* Baltimore, MD: Paul H. Brookes Publishing Co.

Solomon, M. (1973). A developmental conceptual premise for family therapy. *Family Process, 12,* 179–188.

Spitzer, S. (1975). Toward a Marxian theory of deviance. *Social Problems, 22,* 638–651.

Spolyar, L. (1973). The dynamics of grief of wives and family members of military personnel missing in action. *Medical Service Digest, 34,* 20–24.

Stark, E., & Flitcraft, A. (1988). Personal power and institutional victimization: Treating the dual trauma of woman battering. In F. Ochberg (Ed.), *Post-traumatic therapy and victims of violence* New York: Brunner/Mazel.

Steiner, C. (1975). *Scripts people live: Transactional analysis of life scripts.* New York: Bantam Books.

Stern, D. (1985). *The interpersonal world of the infant.* New York: Basic Books.

Stoneman, Z., & Berman, P. (1993). *The effects of mental retardation, disability, and illness on sibling relationships.* Baltimore, MD: Paul H. Brookes.

Strong, M. (1989). *Mainstay.* New York: Penguin.

Sudnow, D. (1967). *Passing on: The social organization of dying.* Englewood Cliffs, NJ: Prentice-Hall.

Sumnar, W. (1906). *Folkways.* New York: Ginn.

Tedeschi, R., & Calhoun, L. (1995). *Trauma and transformation: Growing in the aftermath of suffering.* Thousand Oaks, CA: Sage Publications.

Tedeschi, R., & Calhoun, L. (1996). The post-traumatic growth inventory: Measuring the positive legacy of trauma. *Journal of Traumatic Stress, 9,* 455–471.

Tew, B., Laurence, K., Payne, H., & Rawnsley, K. (1977). Marital stability following the birth of a child with spina bifida. *British Journal of Psychiatry, 131,* 79–82.

Torrey, E. (1988). *Surviving schizophrenia: A family manual* (rev. ed.). New York: Harper & Row.

Trent, J. (1995). *Inventing the feeble mind: A history of mental retardation in the United States.* Los Angeles: University of California Press.

Tunali, B., & Power, T. (1992). Creating satisfaction: A psychological perspective on stress and coping in families of handicapped children. *Journal of Child Psychology and Psychiatry, 34*(6), 945–957.

Turnbull, A., & Turnbull, H. (Eds.). (1978). *Parents speak out: Views from the other side of the two-way mirror.* Columbus, OH: Charles E. Merrill.

Turnbull, A., & Turnbull, H. (1990). *Families, professionals, and exceptionality: A special partnership* (2nd ed.). Columbus, OH: Charles E. Merrill.

Tyiska, C. (1998). Working with victims with disabilities. *Office for Victims of Crime Bulletin,* 8–12. Washington, DC: U.S. Department of Justice, Office for Victims of Crime.

Tyor, P., & Bell, L. (1984). *Caring for the retarded in America: A history.* Westport, CT: Greenwood Press.

Uchino, B., Kiecolt-Glaser, J., & Cacioppo, J. (1994). Construals of preillness relationship quality predict cardiovascular response in family caregivers of Alzheimer's disease victims. *Psychology and Aging, 9*(1), 113–120.

Ulman, R., & Brothers, D. (1988). *The shattered self.* Hillsdale, NJ: The Analytic Press.

U.S. Bureau of the Census. (1994). *Americans with disabilities 1991–92.* Washington, DC: Author.

Vaillant, G. (2000). Adaptive mental mechanisms: Their role in a positive psychology. *American Psychologist, 55*(1), 89–98.

Van Wagoner, S., Gelso, C., Hayes, J., & Diemer, R. (1991). Countertransference and the reputedly excellent therapist. *Psychotherapy: Theory, Research and Practice, 28,* 411–421.

Viorst, J. (1987). *Necessary losses.* New York: Ballantine.

Volkan, V. (1970). Typical findings in pathological grief. *Psychiatric Quarterly, 44,* 231–250.

Volkan, V. (1975). Re-grief therapy. In B. Schoenberg et al. (Eds.), *Bereavement: Its psychosocial aspects.* New York: Columbia University Press.

Volkan, V. (1983). Complicated mourning and pathological mourning. In S. Akhtar (Ed.), *New psychiatric syndromes, DSM III and beyond.* New York: Aronson.

Wallace, M. (1987). *The silent twins.* New York: Ballantine.

Warda, M. (1992). The family and chronic sorrow: Role theory. *Journal of Pediatric Nursing, 7*(3), 205–209.

Waxweiler, R., Thurman, D., Sniezek, J., Sosin, D., & O'Neil, J. (1995). Monitoring the impact of traumatic brain injury: A review and update. *Journal of Neurotrauma, 12,* 4.

Weiss, R. (1974). *Loneliness: The experience of emotional and social isolation.* Cambridge, MA: MIT Press.

Werner, E., & Smith, R. (1992). *Overcoming the odds.* Ithaca, NY: Cornell University Press.

Westergren, G. (1990). Time. Experiences, perspectives and coping strategies. (Published doctoral thesis). Stockholm: Almquist & Wiksell International.

Wikler, L., Wasow, M., & Hatfield, E. (1981). Chronic sorrow revisited: Parent vs. professional depiction of the adjustment of parents of mentally retarded children. *American Journal of Orthopsychiatry, 51,* 63–70.

Wikler, L., Wasow, M., & Hatfield, E. (1983, July/August). Seeking strengths in families of developmentally disabled children. *Social Work,* 313–315.

Wikler, L. (1983). Chronic stresses of families of mentally retarded children. In L. Wikler & M. Keenan (Eds.), *Developmental disabilities: No longer a private tragedy* (pp. 102–110). Silver Spring, MD: National Association of Social Workers and Washington, DC: American Association on Mental Deficiency.

Wikler, L. (1986). Family stress theory and research on families of children with mental retardation. In J. Gallagher & P. Vietze (Eds.), *Families of handicapped persons: Research, programs, and policy issues* (pp. 167–195). Baltimore, MD: Paul H. Brookes Publishing Co.

Williams, J., & Koocher, G. (1998). Addressing loss of control in chronic illness: Theory and practice. *Psychotherapy, 35,* 325–335.

Williamson, G., & Schulz, R. (1990). Relationship orientation, quality of prior relationship, and distress among caregivers of Alzheimer's patients. *Psychology and Aging, 5,* 502–509.

Wolfelt, A. (1998). Companioning vs. treating: Beyond the medical model of bereavement, Part 1–3. *Forum Newsletter of Association of Death Education and Counseling, 24,* 4–6.

Wolff, S., Narayan, S., & Moyes, B. (1988). Personality characteristics of parents of autistic children: A controlled study. *Journal of Child Psychology and Psychiatry, 29,* 143–153.

Wortman, C., & Brehm, J. (1975). Responses to uncontrollable outcomes: An integration of reactance theory and the learned helplessness model. In L. Berkowitz (Ed.), *Advances in experimental social psychology* (Vol. 8). New York: Academic Press.

Wynne, L., & Singer, M. (1963). Thought disorders and family relations of schizophrenics: II. A classification of forms of thinking. *Archives of General Psychiatry, 9,* 199–206.

Yalom, I. (1980). *Existential psychotherapy.* New York: Basic Books.

Young, M., Nosek, M., Howland, C., Changpong, G., & Rintala, D. (1997). Prevalence of abuse of women with physical disabilities. *Archives of Physical Medicine and Rehabilitation, 78* (December).

INDEX

Aber, R., 57
Adams, J., 108
Addison, S., 52
Adoption Quest, 154
Aesthetic beauty in sorrow, 100–101
Affect modulation, 190–195
    attenuation of, 98, 101
Albers, R., 228
Alborn, A., 169
Alford, B., 234, 235–236
Allen, J., 105
Aloneness and chronic sorrow, 137–140
Alzheimer's, 108, 157
American Association on Mental
    Deficiency, 18
American Psychiatric Association, 41
American Psychologist, 224
Americans with Disabilities Act, 81
Americans with Disabilities (U.S. Bureau of
    Census), 40
Andreasen, N., 68
Anger and chronic sorrow, 165–168,
    193–194
Anisman, H., 169
APA Monitor, The, 156
Arangio, T., 235
Arc, the, 15, 18–19, 40
Aristotle, 4
Arnett, Jeffery, 104–106
Asperger's syndrome, 33
Association for Death Education and
    Counseling (ADEC), 231
Associations for Retarded Citizens—U.S.,
    143
Attenuation of affect, 98–101
Autism, 33, 41, 59, 69–70, 71, 94, 95, 108,
    116, 124, 150–151, 174, 201, 217
Avicenna, 5

Bandler, R., 198
Bandura, A., 157, 166
Barnes, Clive, 84
Bartak, L., 217
Bateson, G., 74
Batshaw, M., 40
Bauby, Jean-Dominique, 78–80, 96
Baynton, Douglas, 232
Bechtel, G., 41, 51
Beebe, B., 53
Bell, K., 105
Bell, L., 15, 20
Bernard, J., 52
Berne, E., 34, 161, 166, 183
Beylin, A., 169
Binet-Simon IQ test, 10, 11
Bipolar affective disorder, 40
Birth defects/handicaps, historical
    overview of, 4–21
Bjork-Eriksson, T., 169
Blatt, Burton, 16
Bleuler, M., 159–160
Blindness, 108
Bloom, L., 43
Bluck, S., 157
Bluebond-Langner, M., 220
Bohannon, J., 51
Borgers, S., 51
Born on the Fourth of July, 82, 134
Bowlby, J., 30, 43, 218
Bradley, Donald, 107
Brady, Jim, 50
Brady, Sarah, 50
Brain injuries, 70, 81
Brandt, Karl, 13
Brehm, J., 66
Briere, J., 195
Brink, J., 114

Brock, D., 236
Brothers, D., 161
Brotherson, M., 114
Brown, Carrie, 86–87
Brown, Patricia Leigh, 231–232
Buchanan, A., 236
Buck, Pearl, 71–72, 134
Burke, M., 24, 45, 190, 216, 227
Burke/NCRCS Chronic Sorrow
    Questionnaire, 227
Burleigh, M., 12–13
"Burned out," 32
Busch, P., 24

Cacioppo, J., 157
Calhoun, L., 157
Callahan, John, 92, 182
Callahan, R., 198
Calvin, John, 6
Caplan, G., 43
Carson, Rachel, 230
Carter, B., 103, 104, 107
Catalano, Madeline, 115–116
Catalano, Robert, 72–73
Catholic church/nations (historic),
    5–6
Centers for Disease Control and
    Prevention, 41
Changed by a Child (Gill), 138
Changpong, G., 89–90
Childhood disintegrative disorder
    (CDD), 28–29, 72–73, 108,
    116–117
Children of mentally ill parents, 73–74
Child Who Never Grew, The (Buck), 134
Chisholm, L., 105
Chomicki, S., 27
Christianity denouncing infanticide, 5
Christmas in Purgatory (1966), 16
Chronic mental illness and chronic
    sorrow, 24, 145
Chronic sorrow:
    characteristics of loss, 43
    chronic mental illness, 24
    clinical significance of recognition,
        35–39
    comparisons and distinctions, 26–35
    continuing presence of source of loss
        or object of loss, 44–45
    depathologizing of grief, 232–234
    description of, 1

development of concept, 23–26
distinguishing from major depression
    and dysthymic disorder, 32
doctor shopping, 209
element of chronicity, 33, 73
extent of, 40–42
flashbacks and triggers, 31, 96–98
goals and interventions, 37–38, 186–
    210
grief terminology and nomenclature,
    26–27
initial, continuing, and recurring grief
    responses, 44
level of functioning, 30, 32
living with, 69–101
marker bereft, 96, 151
models for grief and mourning, 42–43
as paradigm shift, 21–22
parents of mentally retarded, 1–3
pathological bereavement, 25
prevalence of, 236–239
prevalent beliefs and taboos, 222
professional education, 230–232
proposed definition, 26
proposed model of, 42–46
psychotherapy trends, 234–236
servicemen missing in action (MIAs),
    25–26, 222
severity of distress, 32
trends, 229–239
triggers, 31, 96–98
unexplained disappearances, 25
"wired in" details, 31
See also fantasy, role in
See also "other-loss"
See also "self-loss"
Cleveland, D., 124
Codependency, 45–46
Cohen, B., 100
Cohen, S., 156
Cohler, B., 52
Coleman, S., 121
Collins, M., 23, 27
Complicated mourning, 30–31
Complicating factors:
    anger, 165–168
    depression, 168–173
    disordered intimacy and attachment,
        164–165
    guilt, 159–161
    identity, 161–162
    immune competence, 155–156

loss spirals, 173–175
stress, 154–159
symbiotic enmeshment, 162–163
Conservation of Resources (COR) stress
model, 166–167
Continuing bonds/continuing attach-
ment, 233
Cook, J., 52
Copeland, Libby, 127–128
Cox, A., 217
Coyne, J., 166
Critical stress points and chronic sorrow,
87–89
Cross, A., 51, 156
Crossman, P., 183
Crypto widower/widow, 59
Cummings, N., 236
Cummings, S., 52, 156
Cusitar, L., 89
Cystic fibrosis, 108, 237

Dahl, B., 25–26
Daly, B., 134
Damrosch, S., 52, 156
Daniels, N., 236
Daniels, S., 43
Davies, S., 11
Davis, B., 34
Davis, C., 157
Davis, D., 24, 51
Davison, K., 235
Day, M., 73
Definition of chronic sorrow, 26
DeLongis, A., 157
DeMichele, J., 234, 235–236
Depleted caregivers, 124–129
Depression and chronic sorrow, 32, 40,
148, 168–173, 209, 217
Deutsch, H., 30
Diabetes, 108
*Diagnostic and Statistical Manual of Mental
Disorders* (*DSM-IV*), 41
Dickerson, S., 235
Diemer, R., 185–186
Disabilities:
disability studies, 231–232
risk of victimization, 89–90
Disillusionment and chronic sorrow,
135–137
Disordered intimacy and attachment and
chronic sorrow, 164–165

Diving Bell and the Butterfly, The (Bauby),
78–80
Dix, Dorothea, 8
Doka, K., 51, 57
Don't Worry, He Won't Get Far on Foot
(Callahan), 92
Dorrity, K., 178, 199, 209, 213
Down syndrome, 70, 110–111, 148–150,
237
Dubas, J., 105
Dunn, B., 73–74, 160
Dunst, C., 51, 156
Duvall, E., 103
Dweck, C., 66
Dyson, L., 112
Dysthymic disorder and chronic sorrow,
32

Eakes, G., 24, 45
Eisen, S., 59
Elephant Man, The, 82
Eliot, C., 6
Ellard, J., 157
Emotional numbing, 99–100
Engel, G., 42
Epilepsy, 108
Erickson, M., 188, 204
Ericksson, P., 169
Erikson, E., 105
Etzioni, A., 235
Existential issues:
aloneness, 137–140
disillusionment, 135–137
inequity, 143–145
insignificance, 145–147
intimacy, 138
mortality, 151–152
past temporal orientation, 147–151
professional sensitivity, 134–135
religious beliefs/supreme being, 138–
139
vulnerability, 140–143
Existential losses, 113
Exline, J., 178, 199, 209, 213
Extent of chronic sorrow, 40–42
External losses, 113

Fairthorne, J., 73
Families, loss, and chronic sorrow:
course of chronic diseases, 109

Families, loss, and chronic sorrow (*Cont.*):
 depleted caregivers, 124–129
 differentness of the family, 111–112
 existential losses, 113
 external losses, 113
 family coping and adaptation, 113–118
 family life cycle, 103–106
 family stress and loss, 107–113
 incapacitation of chronic illness, 110
 internal losses, 113
 loss of family privacy, 116
 marital and social relationships, 112–
  113
 onset of conditions, acute and gradual,
  108
 onset of mental illness of family
  member, 113
 outcome of disease condition, 109–110
 siblings, 118–124, 125
Family Pictures (1990), 82–84
Fantasy, role in chronic sorrow, 27–29,
 32
 religious beliefs/supreme being, 138–
  139
 relinquishment of fantasies invalidated
  by the loss, 199–203
 role at stress points, 88
Fatalistic philosophy, 139
Featherstone, H., 112, 114, 117–118,
 119–120, 141, 168, 208
Federal Bureau of Investigation (FBI),
 89
Fee, R., 128
Felton, B., 126–127
Fernald, Walter, 8
Fernald State School, 8
Ferris, Laura, 116–117
Ferris, Stephen, 116–117
Ferris, Sue, 116–117
Field, N., 233
Figley, C., 107–108, 181–182, 195, 196,
 198
Financial resources, 77
Flashbacks and triggers, 31, 96–98
Flitcraft, A., 199
Flowers for Algernon, 82
Floyd, F., 227
Folkman, S., 154
Frankl, V., 157
Fraser, M., 157
Freeston, B., 164
Freud, S., 43

Friedlander, S., 12, 13
Friedlander, Y., 156
*From the Heart: On Being the Mother of a
 Child with Special Needs* (Marsh), 33
Futurist, The, 235

GAF Scale, 227
Gage, F., 169
Galen, Count, 13
"Gallows" humor, 94–95
Garland, C., 117
Garner, W., 156
Gath, A., 51, 156
Gaylin, W., 43
Gelso, C., 185–186
Gender differences, 50–55
Genetic "tailoring" of babies, 236–237
Gerbode, F., 198
Gerdtz, J., 4, 5
Germany, post World War I beliefs
  about birth defects and mental
  retardation, 12–14
Gill, B., 30, 110–111, 114, 138, 210
Glaser, R., 156
Glidden, L., 227
Gliedman, J., 220
Glover, H., 99, 100
Goals and interventions for chronic
  sorrow, 37–38, 186–210
Goddard, Henry, 10–11
God or fate, beliefs in, 138–139
Goffman, E., 55, 132, 161
Goldberg, R., 3, 21
Goldfarb, L., 114
Goldhagen, D., 13
Goldstein, C., 150–151
Golfus, Billy, 81
Goode, W., 103
Gorer, G., 30
Gould, E., 169
Gould, R., 104
Grant, A., 128
Grant-Hall, R., 195
Greenblatt, M., 218
Grief:
 depathologizing of, 232–234
 models for, 42–43
 normal responses, 233, 234
 process of grieving, 29
Grinder, J., 198
Grob, M., 59

Guilt and chronic sorrow, 74, 159–161
Gumley, D., 51, 156

Haederle, M., 75–76
Haig, R., 43, 51
Hainsworth, M., 24, 45
Haley, J., 74
Harrington, M., 230
Harry, J., 104
Harvard Mental Health Letter, 217
Hatfield, E., 23, 27, 164
Hauser, S., 105
Hays, J., 185–186
Health problems and chronic sorrow, 70
Heller's syndrome, 72–73
Herbert, T., 156
Herman, J., 99, 184, 198, 199
Hewson, D., 154
Hiroto, D., 169
Historical overview of mental retardation
    Aktion T-4 euthanasia program, 13,
        14
    American Asylum for the Deaf and
        Dumb, 6
    ancient periods, 4–5
    Christianity and infanticide, 5
    Christmas in Purgatory (1966), 16
    custodial/subtrainable cases, 9
    deinstitutionalization, 18, 229
    development of intelligence tests, 10
    early institutional programs, 8–9
    Ellis Island, 11
    eugenics movement, 11
    Europe and the New World, 6–9
    first mental hospitals, 5
    The Great Depression, 12, 16
    Greek culture, 4
    the Inquisition, 5
    Islamic culture and mental retarda-
        tion, 5
    managed care and cost containment,
        21
    medieval times through the Renais-
        sance, 5–6
    moron, introduction of term, 10
    normalization, 17–18
    perceived threat of childbearing-age
        females, 9, 11
    Pompeii archaeological evidence, 4
    post World War I Germany and Adolf
        Hitler, 12–14
    post World War II changes in United
        States, 14–15, 16
    prejudicial attitudes, 6, 9, 10–11, 12,
        19
    Roman culture, 4–5
    segregation and sterilization of, 10–11,
        12, 18
    "social junk," 16
    in the twentieth century, 9–21
    use/misuse of IQ tests, 11–12
    witch-hunts and persecution, 5
Hitler, Adolf, on birth defects, mental
    retardation, and mental illness, 12–
    14
HIV/AIDS, 24, 42, 109, 110, 157, 222,
    238
Hobdell, E., 24, 51
Hobfoll, S., 166–167
Hoffer, M., 114
Hoffschmidt, B., 52
Holen, A., 233
Holocaust survivors, 100
Homatidis, S., 52
Horowitz, A., 156
Horowitz, M., 99, 100, 233
House, J., 156
Howe, Samuel, 7–8
Howland, C., 89–90
Human Genome Project, 236
Humor and chronic sorrow, 115–116,
    211
Hunter, E., 25–26
Hurrelmann, K., 105
Hutchison, Roy, 107

Identity and chronic sorrow, 161–162
Imagining Robert (Neugeboren), 27–28
Incapacitation of chronic illness, 110
Inequity and chronic sorrow, 143–145
Infanticide, historical use of, 4–5
Ingalls, R., 7
Insignificance and chronic sorrow, 145–
    147
Institution for Deaf Mutes (Paris), 7
Internal losses, 113
Internet use and support, 235
Interpreting the loss:
    crypto widower/widow, 59
    gender differences, 50–55
    "no choice rule," 63
    pseudo widower/widow, 59

Interpreting the loss (*Cont.*):
  psychological or social death, 57, 58
  real loss and loss of fantasies, 63–68
  self-loss and other-loss, 55–63
  subjectivity of the loss, 47–50
  suicide risk, 62–63, 67
Intimacy and chronic sorrow, 138
Invasion of the Body Snatchers, The, 57, 58
IQ tests, use/misuse of, 11–12
Irwin, M., 43
Islam, 5, 139
Itard, Jean, 7

Jackson, D., 74
Jacobs, B., 169
Jahoda, M., 225
Jewish culture, 5
Joe Egg (1967), 84–86, 95
Johnson, E., 166
Johnston, L., 51
Joseph, S., 128
Joseph P. Kennedy, Jr., Foundation, 17
Josselson, R., 50, 63, 106, 161, 164
Journal of Rehabilitation, The, 3

Kalish, R., 43, 57
Kallikak family study, 10
Kanner, L., 8, 217
Kaplan, Fred, 16
Kark, J., 156
Kelly, G., 43
Kendrick, Asher, 33–34
Kendrick, Martie, 33–34
Kendrick, Zachary, 33
Keniston, K., 105
Kennedy, John F., 17
Kernberg, O., 164
Kerrigan, Nancy, 47–48
Kiecolt-Glaser, J., 156, 157
Kiely, M., 40
King, Martin Luther, Jr., 230
Kirkham, M., 53
Kirshbaum, Hal, 77–78
Klass, D., 233
Klein, S., 119–120
Kletti, R., 100
Klinger, E., 66
Kobasa, S., 157
Kocsis, J., 217
Kohut, H., 161

Konstantareas, M., 52
Koocher, G., 66
Kovacs, Ron, 134
Krafft, L., 88, 231
Krafft, S., 88, 231
Krause, M., 126
Kübler-Ross, E., 43

Lagaipa, S., 4
Lamb in Love (Brown), 86–87
Landis, K., 156
Lane, C., 166–167
Langer, W., 4
Laub, D., 195
Laurence, K., 164
Lazarus, R., 115, 154
Lazzari, A., 88
Lee, R., 22
Lehman, D., 157
Lesser, L., 217
Lestina, D., 42
Levav, I., 156
Level of functioning with chronic
    sorrow, 30, 32
Levinson, D., 105
Levy, S., 237
Lindemann, E., 30, 42, 108, 218
Lindgren, C., 24, 45
Lippman, T., 139
Liptzin, B., 59
Litz, B., 99
Living with chronic sorrow:
    abuse and neglect, 73–74
    attenuation of affect, 98–101
    children of mentally ill parents, 73–74
    critical stress points, 87–89
    fictionalized works, 82–87
    grievances about mental health
        services, 74
    guilt and loyalty, 74
    humor/"gallows" humor, 94–95
    isolation, 74
    life markers, 96
    "numb response," 99–100
    personal accounts, 69–81
    rewards and self-discovery, 100–101
    social supports, 74–75
    triggers, 31, 96–98
    unintentional intrusiveness, 93–94
    Us/Them dichotomy, 81
    victimization anxiety, 89–92

Locke, John, 6, 7
"Locked-in syndrome," 78
Longmore, Paul, 232
Lorenzo's Oil, 82
Loss of privacy, 116
Loss spirals and chronic sorrow, 173–175
Lovaas behavioral program, 116
Lowes, L., 231
Luther, Martin, on mental retardation, 6
Lyne, P., 231

Macarov, D., 229–230
MacGregor, P., 113, 201
Maimonides, 5
Mairs, Nancy, 35, 55–56, 75, 133
Mallow, G., 41, 51
Managed care systems, 225–226, 230, 234
Mandel, D., 157
Mann, Horace, 8
Marcus, L., 164
Marker bereft, 96, 151
Marsh, D., 114, 115, 158, 179
Marsh, J., 33, 36, 114
Martin, J., 22
Martin, T., 51
Massachusetts School for Idiotic and Feeble Minded Youth, 8
Massachusetts School for the Feeble-Minded, 8
Massie, R., 71
Massie, S., 71
Mays, S., 4
McCubbin, H., 25–26, 107–108
McCullough, M., 125–126
McGoldrick, M., 103, 104, 107
McHugh, Mary, 119, 120–124, 126
McMillen, J., 157
Mein Kampf, 12
Mentally retarded, 70, 108
  historical overview, 4–21
  parents and chronic sorrow, 1–3, 87
  population of, 40
Millen, L., 25, 217
Miller, N., 124
Miller, S., 204
Miller, Sue, 82–84
Miller, T., 42
Model of chronic sorrow, 42–46
Models for grief and mourning, 42–43
Monat, A., 115

Moron, introduction of term, 10
Mortality and chronic sorrow, 151–152
Mothers Against Drunk Driving (MADD), 65–66
Moyes, B., 217
Mullins, J., 69–71
Multiple sclerosis (MS), 24, 35, 42, 55, 75–77, 108, 142, 148–150, 237
Murphy, M., 220
Muscular dystrophy, 24, 42, 88, 237
Musso, Louis, victimization of, 90–91
My Left Foot, 82

Narayan, S., 217
Natanson, M., 43
National Association for Retarded Children, 15
National Association for Retarded Citizens, 15
National Association of Parents and Friends of Retarded Children, 15
National Center on Child Abuse and Neglect (NCCAN), 89
National Institute of Neurological Disorders and Stroke, 42
National Multiple Sclerosis Society, 42
National Parkinson Foundation, 42
National Rehabilitation Information Center, 89
National Victim Assistance Academy, 89
"Necessary losses," 34, 136
Neugeboren, J., 27–28, 134
Neural tube defects, 24
Neuromuscular problems, 70
Newman, R., 142
Nichols, B., 90
Nichols, C., 233
Nichols, P., 84–86
Nickman, S., 233
Nirje, B., 17–18
Norcross, J., 234, 235–236
Nordberg, C., 169
Normalization, 17–18
Norris, A., 68
Nosek, M., 89–90
Noyes, R., 100
"Numb response," 99–100
Nursing Consortium for Research on Chronic Sorrow (NCRCS), 23, 216, 231
Nye, F., 118

Obsessive-compulsive disorder, 40
O'Connor, T., 105
Office for Victims of Crime, 89
Oh, K., 27
Olshansky, S., 1, 3, 16, 21–22, 23, 45,
    64–65, 216
O'Neil, J., 41
Organic brain disorders, 58
Organic personality disorder, 40
O'Rourke, M., 237
Other America, The (Harrington), 230
"Other-loss," 26, 31, 33, 76
    critical stress points, 88–89
    interpreting the loss, 55–63
    preventing maladaptive coping styles,
        208
    relinquishing fantasies, 201
    rewards and self-discovery, 100–101
    well spouses, 76–77, 133

Paraplegia, 134
Parental grief:
    giving up child for adoption, 24–25
    mentally retarded children, 1–3
    periodic resurgence of pain and grief, 1
    placement/institutionalization of
        mentally retarded children, 2
Parent-to-Parent program, 18–19
Park, C., 71, 134
Parkes, C., 43
Parkinson's disease, 24, 42, 108, 237
"Passing," 3
Passion Fish, 82
Pathological bereavement, 25, 217
Payne, H., 164
Pearlman, L., 195, 213
Penn, G., 156
Pennebaker, J., 235
Perfilieva, E., 169
Peritz, E., 156
Perkins Institution for the Blind, 7
Perry, L., 52, 156
Person, E., 43
Personal accounts of chronic sorrow, 69–
    81
Personality death, 160
Pervasive developmental disorder (PDD),
    33, 41
Pesut, D., 234–235
Peterson, A., 105
Peterson, C., 224–225

Peterson, D., 169
Phillips, M., 24
Pickett, S., 52
Pieper, E., 71
Pincus, L., 43
Plaintext (Mairs), 55–56
*Planning for the Future: Providing a
    Meaningful Life for a Child with a
    Disability after Your Death* (Russell,
    Grant, Joseph, and Fee), 128
Plato, on birth defects and mental
    retardation, 4
Pollock, G., 34–35
Positive mental health, 225
Post-traumatic stress disorder (PTSD),
    symptoms of, 30, 31, 154–155, 209
Power, T., 107
Powers, I., 26
Price-Bonham, S., 52
Professionals/professional community:
    enforcing family responsibility, 239
    experience and training with mental
        retardation, 2–3
    professional education, 230–232
    view of parents of mentally retarded
        children, 2
Professional support and treatment:
    adaptive emotional behavior, 192
    affect modulation, 190–195
    anger dyscontrol, 193–194
    basic assumptions, 180–183
    client impression of control, 195
    desirable attributes of professional and
        therapist, 183–186
    diagnostic assessment and interpreta-
        tion, 186–190
    embracing what is, 203
    eye movement desensitization and
        reprocessing (EMDR), 198
    hazards and pitfalls, 210–213
    hypnotherapy techniques, 198
    imagery, 212
    preventing maladaptive coping styles,
        207–210
    quick fixes, 212
    reexamination and update of belief
        systems, 203–207
    reframes, 211–212
    relinquishment of fantasies invalidated
        by the loss, 199–203
    restoration of self-efficacy and control,
        198–199

"special" or "chosen" messages, 213
structured writing, 192–193
structure in therapy, 183
suggested goals and objectives, 186–
    210
supplemented companioning model,
    178–179
thought field therapy (TFT), 198
three P's of therapy, 183–185
trauma resolution, 195–198
traumatic incident reduction (TIR),
    198
Proposed definition of chronic sorrow,
    26
Protestant church/nations (historic), 5–6
Pseudo widower/widow, 59

Quadriplegia, 78–80, 92
Quayhagen, M., 58

Rando, T., 30, 51, 135
Raphael, B., 30
Rawnsley, K., 164
Real loss and loss of fantasies, 63–68
Recognition of chronic sorrow, 35–39
Reddy, M., 134
Reeve, Christopher, 50, 61–62, 80,
    157–158
Reeve, Dana, 50, 62, 80
Reeves, A., 169
Religious beliefs/supreme being, 138–
    139
Remembering the Bone House (Mairs), 35,
    75
Research, implications and directions for:
    accessibility of treatment and support,
        226
    Burke's Chronic Sorrow Question-
        naire, 227
    dependent variables, 227–228
    Global Assessment of Functioning
        Scale, 227
    independent variables, 218–226
    Mother-Child Picture Test (MCPT),
        227
    nature of the loss, 221–223
    Nursing Consortium for Research
        on Chronic Sorrow (NCRCS), 216
    personality tests, 227
    person variables, 218–221

Questionnaire on Resources and Stress
    data, 227
reinterpretation of existing studies,
    216–218
Roos Time Reference Inventory, 228
Severity of Psychosocial Stressors
    scale, 227–228
support groups/social organizations,
    226
treatment effectiveness, 223–226
Rewards and self-discovery with chronic
    sorrow, 100–101
Rife, J., 28, 114, 133
Rintala, D., 89–90
Risch, C., 43
Rivera, Geraldo, 16
Robarge, J., 24, 88
Robinson, Amy, victimization of, 91–92
Roll, S., 25, 217
Rolland, J., 66–67, 108–110
Roos, P., 134, 143, 228
Roos, S., 128
Rosen, D., 18
Roskies, E., 53
Rossi, E., 188, 204
Roth, W., 220
Rubin, S., 43
Russell, L., 128
Rutter, M., 217

Saakvitne, K., 213
Sanger, Margaret, 230
Sapolsky, R., 155, 168–169
Scheerenberger, R., 4, 5, 6, 9, 11, 12
Schilling, R., 53
Schinke, S., 53
Schizophrenia, 24, 40, 41, 58, 70
Schoech, D., 235
Schultz, C., 24, 51
Schulz, R., 156, 157
Schulze, Craig, 28–29
Searl, S., 37
Secunda, V., 138, 158–159, 160
Seguin, Edouard, 7
Self-help groups, 235
"Self-loss," 26, 31, 33
    critical stress points, 88–89
    humiliation with disability, 77–78
    insignificance, 146
    interpreting the loss, 55–63
    loss spirals, 174

"Self-loss" (*Cont.*):
negative responses or ostracism,
139–140
rewards and self-discovery, 100–101
victimization anxiety, 90
Seligman, M., 169, 204
Seltzer, M., 126
Selye's General Adaptation Syndrome,
166
Servicemen missing in action (MIAs),
25–26, 222
Shapiro, B., 40
Shapiro, F., 198
Shea, C., 223
Shindelman, L., 156
Shors, T., 169
Shriver, Eunice Kennedy, 17
Siblings of disabled, 118–124, 125
Siedick, K., 70
Siegman, A., 191
Sigmon, Jane, 89
Silver, R., 157
Silverman, P., 233
Simon, P., 215
Singer, M., 74
Skeels, H., 15
Skodak, M., 15
Sleek, S., 156
Smith, A., 51
Smith, R., 157
Sniezek, J., 41
Sobsey, D., 89
Solomon, M., 103
Sosin, D., 41
Speech and language disorders, 70
Speicher, C., 156
Spicer, R., 42
Spina bifida, 70
Spinal cord injuries, 80, 92, 237
Spitzer, S., 16
Spock, Benjamin, 230
Spolyar, L., 26
SPS Scale, 227–228
Stark, E., 199
Steiner, C., 161
Stern, D., 53
Stigma (Goffman), 55, 132
Still Me (Reeve), 62
Stone, Oliver, 134
Stress and chronic sorrow, 154–159
Strokes, 237
Strong, M., 76–77, 133, 142

Subjectivity of the loss, 47–50
Sudnow, D., 57
Suicide and chronic sorrow, 62–63, 67
Summers, J., 114
Sumnar, W., 4
Supplemental Security Income (SSI), 127
Support groups/social organizations, 226,
235
Symbiotic enmeshment and chronic
sorrow, 162–163
Syracuse School for Mental Defectives, 8

Tanapat, P., 169
Teacher, Teacher, 82
Tedeschi, R., 157
Temporal orientation and chronic
sorrow, 147–151
Tew, B., 164
Thurman, D., 41
Torrey, E., 41
Tourette syndrome, 33
Traumatic brain injury, 28, 41
Traumatic spinal cord injury, 42
Trent, J., 10, 16
Triggers and flashbacks, 31, 96–98
Trivette, C., 51, 156
Tunali, B., 107
Turnbull, A., 114, 134, 180
Turnbull, H., 134, 180
Tyiska, C., 89
Tyor, P., 15

Uchino, B., 157
Ulman, R., 161
Umberson, D., 156
Unexplained disappearances of loved
one, 25
Unintentional intrusiveness, 93–94
United Cerebral Palsy Association
(UCPA), 41–42
United States Bureau of Census, 40
United States Department of Justice, 89

Vaillant, G., 225
van Praag, H., 169
Van Wagoner, S., 185–186
Victimization anxiety, 89–92
Vincent de Paul, 6
Vineland Training School, 10

Viorst, Judith, 34, 51, 136
Volkan, V., 30, 31, 43, 218
Vulnerability and chronic sorrow,
    140–143

Wallace, M., 163
Warda, M., 118
Wasow, M., 23, 27, 164
Waxweiler, R., 41
Weakland, J., 74
Weiner, H., 43
Weiss, R., 43
Well spouses, 76–77, 133
Werner, E., 157
Westergren, G., 228
When Autism Strikes (Catalano), 72–73,
    150–151
When Billy Broke His Head (1994), 81
Wikler, D., 236

Wikler, L., 23, 27, 87, 110, 164
Wilbur, Hervey, 8
Wild boy study by Itard, 7
Williams, J., 66
Williamson, G., 156, 157
Willowbrook (New York), 16
Wolfelt, A., 178, 198
Wolff, S., 217
World War I, enlistment of men with
    mental deficiencies, 12
Wortman, C., 66, 157, 178, 199, 209,
    213
Wynne, L., 74

Yalom, I., 43, 140
Young, M., 89–90

Zacharko, R., 169